YEATS AND AFTERWORDS

Edited by

MARJORIE HOWES *and* **JOSEPH VALENTE**

University of Notre Dame Press

Notre Dame, Indiana

Manufactured in the United States of America

Library of Congress Cataloging-in-Publication Data

Yeats and afterwords / edited by Marjorie Howes and Joseph Valente.
pages   cm
Includes bibliographical references and index.
ISBN 978-0-268-01120-8 (paperback) — ISBN 0-268-01120-6 (paper)
1. Yeats, W. B. (William Butler), 1865–1939—Criticism and interpretation.
I. Howes, Marjorie Elizabeth, editor.   II. Valente, Joseph, editor.
PR5907.Y37   2014
821'.8—dc23
2014022371

CONTENTS

ACKNOWLEDGMENTS

We would like to thank the two anonymous readers for their insightful comments, and Stephen Little of the University of Notre Dame Press for his guidance, professionalism, and patience. We are grateful to the *Irish University Review* for permission to reprint Ronald Schuchard's essay, originally published in *Irish University Review* 34:2 (2004): 291–314.

YEATS AND AFTERWORDS

Introduction

MARJORIE HOWES AND JOSEPH VALENTE

The objective of this volume is to articulate W. B. Yeats's powerful, multilayered sense of cultural belatedness as part of his complex literary method. We wish to explore how Yeats's deliberate positioning of himself at various historical endpoints—of Romanticism, of the Irish colonial experience, of the Ascendancy, of civilization itself—came to fuel an innovative, distinctively modernist poetics of iteration by which the experience of finality and irrevocability might be registered. While the crafting of such a poetics remained a constant throughout Yeats's career, the particular shape that it took varied over time. By tracking these vicissitudes, our volume affords new ways of thinking about the overarching trajectory of Yeats's poetic engagements.

The extraordinary hold of the past upon the present has long been a staple of Irish historical and literary scholarship; Ireland itself could be said to bear a certain belatedness.[1] And the Irish Literary Revival obviously sought to create a vibrant future for Ireland by resuscitating the past. Yeats's famous retrospective on himself and his revivalist circle as "the last romantics," in "Coole and Ballylee, 1931," has rightly been taken to invoke not just the chivalric tradition of courtly love, established in the Middle Ages, but also the British poetic tradition of the late eighteenth and early nineteenth century. To appreciate the full import of his remark, however, it helps to consider the discursive cable linking these two fields of reference: the medieval revivalism of the latter literary movement. This medieval revivalism was responsible for its name and certain of its signature documents, such as Shelley's *The Cenci,* Scott's *Lay of the Last Minstrel,* or Keats's "La Belle Dame Sans Merci." It was also responsible for what were arguably its founding gestures (one Anglo and one Celtic): the anachronistic impostures of Thomas Chatterton (the Rowley file) and James MacPherson (the Ossian sagas). But the broad based cultural renaissance for which Yeats was a symbol, spokesman, and literary architect took up the Irish past not as a nostalgic lost origin, but as a reality that persisted, in suppressed or marginalized forms, in the ongoing Irish present and could, accordingly, provide a renovated cultural foundation on which to build the Irish future. As befits those engaged in a decolonizing enterprise, the revivalists tended to cherish the indigenous potential rather than the antiquity of "hidden Ireland,"[2] the contemporary urgency rather than the lostness of the objects they sought to recover. It is therefore at once curious and telling that, while the apparently backward glance of his own literary movement remained forward looking, Yeats eventually came to identify his literary circle with a re-"visionary company" who were of (and looked to) a bygone era. Whereas the Irish Revival instanced a kind of reverse vanguardism, its leader did not so much suffer as embrace a doubly reinforced belatedness in their name.

Understood in literary-historical context, then, Yeats's description of the main revivalists in "Coole and Ballylee, 1931" suggests that although his conscious investment in the movement had doubtless gone to its revolutionary cultural nationalism, his deeper unconscious investment may well have been in its mainly formal aspect of rememoration and retrieval. In other words, the revivalist project answered more to the temporal logic of his imagination than to the content of his political beliefs. One way of thinking about Yeats's distinctive contribution to the Irish Literary Revival is as an attempt, in a subtle variation on his philosophical model, Nietzsche, to shape a memory, a history, of the here and now, less to view the present as an inexorable thrust into the future than to view the future as the deferred action, a Freudian *Nachträglichkeit*, of the past. Such a reading of the evidence would help to explain why Yeats's verse retained its revivalist temper long after he had abandoned the populist, armchair Fenianism that animated his early revivalist labors. Indeed, it even helps to explain the greater plangency and profundity of the later, conservative poetry, where the objects of recovery and homage (the Big House, aristocratic ceremony, the cultural mandarinate of Gregory, Synge, Lane, et al., the Ascendancy at large) possessed no sustained, dynamic future, no vital prospects, to disturb the sense of fatal belatedness that was, still more than Maud Gonne, Yeats's true muse.

Finally, it also helps to explain the resurgence of a formalist interest in and approach to Yeats's poetry after the decades-long dominance of an Irish Studies approach modeled on the New Historicism. As espoused in Nicholas Grene's *Yeats's Poetic Codes*, in Helen Vendler's magisterial *Our Secret Discipline*, or in Michael Woods's synoptic *Yeats and Violence*, this new formalist school not only prioritizes the contours of the poetic text—its prosody, internal structure, generic affiliations—over its political objectives and ideological import, but in so doing, it also privileges the contours of poetic memory—how verse records the loss and the recovery of a past simultaneously—over the unspoken motives this practice might serve.[3] The notion of Yeats's "afterwords" aims to extend this formal line of analysis—without forfeiting the abundant insights historicism has to offer—by elucidating the poetic device whereby history comes to occupy the text, not just as a set of substantive concerns, pressures, or determinants, but as a registration of the dynamics of time, that retroactive looping in which the possibility of creation and the inevitability of loss pass into one another.[4]

With this in mind, Yeats's revivalism, in the sense intended here, comprises a dialectical logic of temporality that Yeats elaborated, varied, and refined throughout his life, rather than a cultural project animating a specific period of his career. The problem to which this logic responded, a similarly evolving and permutating sense of belatedness, is typically understood as backward looking, oriented toward a past made weighty by its irrevocability. But belatedness more properly figures an intricate nexus of temporal vectors and demands a correspondingly flexible literary method. Belatedness is first of all a mode of be-ing in the world, of present experience, and if that experience finds its defining conditions in bygone eras, faded orders, or missed opportunities as impossible to reclaim as to forget, the meaning and the value of that experience resides in a future to be shaped by those very impossibilities. When Hegel wrote in *The Phenomenology of Mind* that the owl of Minerva flies at dusk, he pegged dialectical wisdom— so strenuously pursued by Yeats—as a correlative of belatedness, and he conversely held belatedness—so acutely suffered by Yeats—to imply a dialectical phenomenology, one in which the several modalities of lived time would be inextricably conjoined in their opposition to one another.

Taking this *discordia concours* as its nucleus, Yeats is able to explore the dialectics of time across diverse registers and in different directions in his philosophical, dramatic, and poetic writings. The vast historical cycles of the System, for example, careered according to the interlocking movements of the antinomous gyres, and, as a result, every one of Yeats's famous lunar phases is, in a sense, out of phase as well. That is, each phase only has its distinctive consistency in carrying forward from some anterior stage of development the seeds of its own coming obsolescence. Owing to this interplay of temporal self-identity and self-difference that the gyres enact, any given historical moment or conjuncture admits of multiple temporal logics for Yeats to conjure with, elaborate upon, and translate into varying modes (or "Moods") of poetic address. Counterpoint was fundamental to Yeats's method and his vision: he explicitly stages its workings as a confrontation of personae in the great dialogue poems ("Ego Dominus Tuus," "Michael Robartes and the Dancer," "A Dialogue of Self and Soul"), as a meticulous calibration of personal and cultural self-assessment in the Big House poems ("The Tower," "Meditations in Time of Civil War," "In Memory of Eva Gore-Booth and Con Markiewicz"), and as a delicate syncopation of sexual desire in the love poems of *The Wind Among the Reeds*. We are here proposing that this same contrapuntal method, the rhetorical correlate of Yeats's inveterately dialectical way of thinking, functions implicitly to structure the temporal consciousness and the related sense of historical engagement expressed in Yeats's verse.

Yeats's prophetic mode, for example, in which he explores what Michael Wood calls "that instant *just before* the event,"[5] inevitably conceives "the coming times" not just in relation to an unalterable past that has produced them, but as themselves a pastness, a lostness, located in an emergent future: an event or set of events that already bears, in the advent of its appearance, a cast that cannot be changed, only witnessed. The prophecy of a poem like "The Second Coming" is just such a witnessing, neither predictive nor providential, but a dwelling in revelation, the continued futurity of which renders it uncertain but no less fated, a site of combined anxiety and conviction. Another poem in the prophetic mode, "Sailing to Byzantium,"[6] looks ahead to a transcendent consummation ("once out of nature") that has in a sense already arrived ("I have sailed the seas and come / To the holy city of Byzantium") because it takes its character *entirely* from what it is not, that "no country for old men" which paradoxically exists in a *present anterior* to Yeats's completed odyssey—an "artifice of eternity" indeed. "The Magi" (*VP*, 318) too prophesies one of those imminent apocalyptic scenarios, though neither in the manner of prediction nor of testimony but rather one of anticipation, a desire that envisions a predestined yet unprecedented future as a replication, a paradoxical memory ("once more"), of a still unprocessed past.

Other poetic engagements with the future in Yeats's work eschew prophecy and center instead on the sheer unknowability of what will follow, a crucial aspect of any future *qua* future. Yeats's penchant for ending poems with questions, particularly abstruse metaphysical questions ("The Cold Heaven") or questions of fundamental life values ("What Then?"), refuses closure in the present and points to some later moment of potential knowledge while at the same time suggesting that this moment cannot, by definition, come to pass. In either case, the question is posed by a ghost (the speaker's, Plato's), indicating that the solution may be lodged, mnemonically, in the bygone life to come. The afterlife, that most indefinite of futures, turns into a sign of belatedness.

The belatedness that besets Yeats's meditations on the past comes in similarly varied and complex forms. Many poems struggle with loss, remorse, and disillusionment, both personal and political, but the tenor of that struggle and its emotional yield changes with the temporal logics that Yeats puts into play. Both "To A Shade" and "Nineteen Hundred and Nineteen," for example, enact belated recognitions of harsh truths but speak to distinct temporal configurations that give Yeats's sense of belatedness a radically different turn in each. In "To A Shade" (*VP,* 292–93) contemporary Ireland remains tethered to and therefore untaught by its recent past, specifically the rise of a Philistine middle class. But if it is too late for the poet and his stalking horse, Parnell, to change Ireland in the now, if reforming the present entails having already reformed the past, there nevertheless remains hope for the future ("The time . . . has not come"). Yeats's sense of belatedness in "To A Shade" is epistemological, a matter of cultural *mis*recognition, and so while profound (he is again left speaking to ghosts), it is also potentially redeemable (the recognition produced by the poem itself may lead, in time, to the ghost's return). In "Nineteen Hundred and Nineteen" (*VP,* 428–33) contemporary Europe, in the form of a Yeatsian "we," has been violently dissevered from its recent past ("seven years ago") and violently disabused of the illusions of that time. But it finds the recognition itself to be utterly unavailing, or worse, an awareness of an earlier poisoning that is itself poisonous. Yeats's sense of belatedness on this occasion is ontological: it is evidently long past time to refashion our very being, and any recognition of this reality, to Yeats's mind, partakes in tone, form, and affect of the reality itself. In "To A Shade" the past holds the present hostage, leaving the future isolated as the locus of a residual utopian hope. In "Nineteen Hundred and Nineteen" the dystopian present discredits every truth the past proclaimed, retroactively toppling the foundations for any future development.

The dialectics of time in other Yeats poems reach a more affirmative posture of retrospection; the speaker experiences regret, loss, and even bitterness, but achieves acceptance, at least temporarily, of what is and has been. These poems tend to have a more inward focus or intimate point of reference, broaching possible distinctions to be charted, over the course of Yeats's oeuvre, between personal and collective temporalities. In "A Dialogue of Self and Soul" (*VP*, 477–79) the aging Yeatsian speaker, his past now all but coextensive with his fate, casts out the "remorse" attendant on each by turning them into an imaginary future he wills for himself. A classic instance of Nietzschean *amor fati*, Yeats's "afterword" here becomes his new life: "I am content to live it all again / And yet again." In a slightly different vein, "No Second Troy" apprehends the past as a classical-contemporary palimpsest, at once layered and disjointed, that brought forth Maud Gonne as she positively had to be, while "post-figuring" some lost potential destiny for her.

Yeats further complicates the temporal dialectics his poems take up by subjecting his poetic text to its own play of retroaction and renewal, a "revivalism" of its own. An inveterate reviser of his own work, Yeats constantly provided "afterwords" to previously finished poems in the form of new versions. As a believer in belief who could never let go of skepticism, he routinely countered his apparently certain or categorical statements with the afterwords of qualifications. It is precisely the act of qualification, the afterword, rather than the assertion of certainty, that we find central to his poetics. Indeed, one of Yeats's most distinctive and innovative poetic strategies altogether blurs the line between word and afterword by setting up a pattern of iteration, an echo chamber, wherein the new poems of his middle and late periods comprise a tissue of citations and allusions to his earlier works. At a certain point in his career, Yeats's poetic enterprise *begins to move forward and backward simultaneously*, into a future constituted by its recursive critique of his former attitudes, assumptions, and assertions and by its ongoing indebtedness to his previous rhetorical experiments and constructions. Owing to this self-citational strategy, the signature principle of intertextuality that Yeats brought to his books of verse—wherein each poem resonates, meaningfully and in detail, across an entire series—can be traced through his entire corpus.

If Yeats may be conceived as a kind of poetic angel of history, facing insistently backwards as he is borne ceaselessly into the future, his status derives as much from the imaginative mode as the cultural sites of his engagements. As a result, the retroversive dynamic described here unfolds not only in the themes of his poems but also in the very tissue of his language. Yeats may also then be conceived, with a slight shift of emphasis, as an angel of poetic history. Just as his imagination dwelt on the "woman lost" (*VP*, 413), on the afterimages of vanished beauty and vanquished glory, so Yeats's words are always afterwords in which past valences, prior usages, defunct contexts, from both Yeats's own oeuvre and the wider poetic tradition, re-sound and re-circulate. On the level of the poetic line, Yeats's words achieve their richest effects as afterwords. Michael Wood identifies two such effects, which he calls the "follow-on effect" and the "rear-view effect": "The first . . . makes you feel that afterthoughts are always preparing some sort of ambush; the second retroactively alters the meaning of the sentence."[7] And Yeats's dazzling array of verb tenses, and the complex temporalities they create, still awaits a full exploration.

This volume proceeds in three stages, involving past-pastness, present-pastness, and future-pastness. The first, entitled "The Last Romantics," examines how Yeats consistently reiterates classic motifs and verbal formulations from his literary forebears in order to express the circumscribed cultural options with which he struggles. The essays in this section often see Yeats as positioning himself after sources and precursors that are surprising or have been relatively neglected by scholars. Renée Fox examines the early Yeats's engagement with the kind of afterlife offered by that important Victorian cultural institution, the museum. She argues that, in contrast to the dominant tradition in English poetry that associated museums with imperialism and transhistorical, deadened aesthetic forms, Yeats forged a revivalist ideology of cultural reanimation through collection and preservation, one that was equally applicable to museums and literature, and that was optimistic, enabling, and forward-looking. Joseph Valente finds that Yeats did not abandon aestheticism and decadence in order to turn to Irish revivalism; rather, he shows that Yeats structured his revivalism through aestheticist ideology. Aestheticism, in other words, has its afterword, not its antithesis, in the Irish Literary Revival.

Yeats's relationship with various individual precursors and traditions ranging from Romantic poetry to eighteenth-century Ireland to Nietzsche has been ably examined by a number of prominent scholars.[8] "Influence" is an inadequate term for Yeats's deliberate, even violent inventions of the traditions he claimed to inherit, mine, and extend.[9] In keeping with this insight, James Murphy's essay on Yeats and Carleton shows Yeats creating a Carleton who embodied the artless authenticity of the Irish peasant. Murphy argues that it was this appropriative gesture, rather than the accuracy of his portrayal of Carleton, that made Yeats a true follower of his predecessor: Carleton himself was prone to strong misprisons of other writers for his own ends. Elizabeth Cullingford's analysis of Yeats's use of mythological and folkloric materials highlights how selective and specific Yeats's engagement with the Chuchulain sagas was. Over and over again, Yeats chose the theme of fathers who kill their sons rather than any of the many other aspects of his sources. Cullingford concludes that, ironically, Yeats was, in the end, more attached to the tragic foreclosure of future possibility embodied in that theme than he was to the potential of a revitalized Irish culture.

The second section, entitled "Yeats and Afterwords," looks at how Yeats subjects his own past sentiments and insights to critical negation, crafting his own afterwords in various ways. Margaret Mills Harper analyzes Yeats's revisions of *A Vision,* arguing that the 1937 version is very different from the 1925 edition, more so than previous scholars have noted, and that these differences provide insight into how Yeats's writing in the 1930s in general reworks the poetic and political stances of the 1920s. Gregory Castle focuses less on specific revisions and more on the *principle* of error and revision as central to Yeats's revivalism. Castle argues that this revivalism was devoted to the future rather than to the past, and that Yeats's apparent backward glances and afterwords are actually productive corrections of earlier errors that bear him into the future while at the same time revealing themselves, too, to be misrecognitions. Guinn Batten explores the dialectical nature of Yeats's thinking about language itself in the context of political violence and the urge to establish new human communities.

Yeats's imagining of various endpoints inevitably involved that most inevitable of endpoints, death. Few poets have written as frequently, or as movingly, about aging and death as Yeats. Works like

Jahan Ramazani's *Yeats and the Poetry of Death* have established death as a central muse for Yeats.[10] In this volume, Marjorie Howes traces representations of graves and burial in the late Yeats to uncover two conflicting impulses provoked by that muse. In one, Yeats asserts his will to manage his passing and his legacy, to determine what kinds of afterwords he will leave behind. But, Howes argues, the late Yeats relinquishes that project and embraces a more disturbing, less controlled version of death and memorialization as a more fitting endpoint to his literary endeavors.

Finally, a third section, entitled "Yeats's Aftertimes," explores how, thanks to the stature Yeats achieved through its invention, his style of belatedness itself comes to be reiterated as the future of other writers. Yeats is a towering figure in literary history, hard to follow and harder to avoid, and later writers often found themselves producing words that were, in some sense, his afterwords. In his comparison of the late Eliot and the late Yeats, Jed Esty argues that the poets stage contrasting ways of confronting individual mortality and civilizational crisis. While Eliot sought the end of personal and national history in the transcendent shapes of national revival and divine order, Yeats abandons his earlier myth-making and submits to the empty succession of time. In this, Esty argues, Yeats looks ahead to the existential anxieties of later writers such as Auden, Beckett, Camus, and Sartre. Seán Kennedy traces part of Beckett's complex response to the later Yeats, arguing that Beckett's unpublished story "Echo's Bones" conducts a critique of Yeats's preoccupation with authoritarian politics, aristocratic reproduction and genealogies, and the declining fortunes of the Anglo-Irish. Here, too, the temporality of the afterword is complex; Kennedy suggests that "Echo's Bones" responds proleptically to imaginative and political tendencies that Yeats would display most strongly in *Purgatory*, which was written after Beckett's story. Vicki Mahaffey's essay explores the affinity of Yeats's later poetry and the short fiction of his Anglo-Irish compatriot, Elizabeth Bowen. For Mahaffey, Yeats's express awareness of the incommensurability of loss and mortality in their objective and subjective dimensions, as adamantine facts and fluid modes of experience, finds a responsive elaboration in Bowen's wartime experiments with layered and recursive narrative temporality, which, for its part, supplies something of a foreword to the magical realism of much postwar, postcolonial literature.

Ronald Schuchard's essay finds that Yeats's legacy for four contemporary Irish poets lies in his struggle to negotiate between the claims of transcendent art and those of historical entanglement, a struggle that left profound marks on their poetry, whether they resisted Yeats, embraced him, or did both. Yeats's aftertimes are, of course, still unfolding, as new generations of writers confront the powers and dangers offered by his example. His modes of belatedness continue to provoke other writers into similarly belated stances.

Much excellent previous Yeats scholarship has explored aspects of his belatedness: Yeats's relation to precursors, his revivalism, his grappling with death, and all the contributors to this volume are profoundly indebted to such work. What we hope distinguishes this volume from previous work is that it illuminates belatedness, not as a period in Yeats's career (like the Irish Literary Revival) or a theme (like death), but as a central, underlying logic that structures his poetics from beginning to end. Indeed, this logic stretches further, extending to writers, current and future, who craft their words in belated response to Yeats's own afterwords.

NOTES

1. See, for example, Una Frawley, ed., *Memory Ireland*, vol. 1, *History and Modernity* (Syracuse: Syracuse University Press, 2011); Ian McBride, ed., *History and Memory in Modern Ireland* (Cambridge: Cambridge University Press, 2001); and Kevin Whelan, "Between Filiation and Affiliation: The Politics of Postcolonial Memory," in *Ireland and Postcolonial Theory*, ed. Claire Carroll and Patricia King (Notre Dame, IN: University of Notre Dame Press, 2003).

2. The phrase refers to Robert Scally's *The End of Hidden Ireland* (New York: Oxford University Press, 1996), which uncovers the previously unknown lives of Irish peasants on the eve of the famine.

3. Nicholas Grene, *Yeats's Poetic Codes* (New York: Oxford University Press, 2008); Helen Vendler, *Our Secret Discipline: Yeats and Lyric Form* (Cambridge, MA: Harvard University Press, 2007); Michael Wood, *Yeats and Violence* (Oxford: Oxford University Press, 2010). See also Vereen M.

Bell, *Yeats and the Logic of Formalism* (Columbia: University of Missouri Press, 2006).

4. The long, distinguished tradition of historicist scholarship on Yeats has been exemplified, in fact, by some of the contributors to this volume, including Marjorie Howes, Elizabeth Cullingford, and Ron Schuchard. See Marjorie Howes, *Yeats's Nations: Gender, Class, and Irishness* (Cambridge: Cambridge University Press, 1996); Elizabeth Cullingford, *Gender and History in Yeats's Love Poetry* (Cambridge: Cambridge University Press, 1993); Ron Schuchard, *The Last Minstrels: Yeats and the Revival of the Bardic Arts* (Oxford: Oxford University Press, 2008).

5. Wood, *Yeats and Violence*, 70.

6. *The Variorum Edition of the Poems of W. B. Yeats*, ed. Peter Allt and Russell K. Alspach (New York: Macmillan, 1957), 407–8. Hereafter cited parenthetically as *VP*.

7. Wood, *Yeats and Violence*, 122.

8. On the Romantics, the defining work has been that of George Bornstein. On the Irish eighteenth century, see Donald Torchiana, *W. B. Yeats and Georgian Ireland* (Washington DC: Catholic University of America Press, 1992). On Yeats and Nietzsche, see Frances Nesbitt Oppel, *Mask and Tragedy: Yeats and Nietzsche* (Charlottesville: University of Virginia Press, 1987).

9. For an excellent recent examination of Yeats as a strong (mis)reader of nineteenth-century Irish literary traditions, see R. F. Foster, *Words Alone: Yeats and His Inheritances* (London: Oxford University Press, 2011).

10. Jahan Ramazani, *Yeats and the Poetry of Death: Elegy, Self-Elegy, and the Sublime* (New Haven: Yale University Press, 1990).

Part I

THE LAST ROMANTICS

CHAPTER 1

The Revivalist Museum
Yeats and the Reanimation of History

RENÉE FOX

Throughout the nineteenth century, the British Museum haunted the imaginations of English poets, provoking meditations on the relationship between aesthetics, mortality, and history, as well as the relationship between their own art and its unstable participation in an inevitably political history. The collections in the Museum provided poets like Dante Gabriel Rossetti, John Keats, and Thomas Hardy with objects upon which to consider how divorcing—or failing to divorce—the aesthetic from the historical altered the ethical and structural integrity of art. For these poets, the British Museum, in seeking to collect and make into British art the historical relics of other cultures, becomes an imaginative site of both cultural death and colonial reanimation. The artifacts of ancient cultures (the Elgin Marbles, for instance) that comprise the subjects of much nineteenth-century museum poetry are remnants whose resuscitated life in English poetry catalyzes the poets' anxiety about the inherently imperial, and thus destructive, nature of their own art. As an English institution dating back to 1753, the British Museum was for these poets a fundamental and inescapable symbol of material history and the politically flawed transformation of history into art.

William Butler Yeats, who began his poetic career in the 1880s, had a different, less Gothic sense of the relationship between collecting, history, and art than did the English poets around him. Although he lived in London surrounded by—and much enamored with—its museums, he did not share the museum-inspired imperial guilt of his English counterparts, nor did he have an equivalent Irish institution to occupy a similar position in his early poetry. What is now the Irish National Museum, once the Dublin Museum of Science and Art, only broke ground in 1885, and Yeats began writing at a moment in Irish history when the structure, contents, political purpose, and social function of a national collection were all hotly under debate. While Yeats spent his later decades mired in frustrated controversies about Dublin's museums and art collections,[1] the Victorian Yeats had faith in the political, aesthetic, and historical efficacy of the national collection as a site for the synthesis of a national sense of self.

With plans for an institutional museum of ancient artifacts still nascent and unformed in Dublin, Yeats's early works, particularly his anthologies of Irish fairy tales and his long poem "The Wanderings of Oisin," create textual museums out of historical fragments, stories, and poetic forms. Born just as Victorian England was feeling flush with an influx of new museums in the wake of the Great Exhibition of 1851—between 1850 and 1882 the number of museums in Britain expanded from fewer than 60 to more than 250—Yeats emerged onto the literary scene three decades later amidst a waning Victorian sense that national identity could be developed and displayed in public collections of the past. Yet Yeats's early work retrenches the mid-century Victorian optimism about the political and aesthetic power of the historical collection, reimagining the alienating act of collecting as a process of national revitalization.[2] In doing so, Yeats writes against the notion, increasingly prevalent in the late nineteenth century, that the museum was a space of death rather than a space of life.

As Theodor Adorno writes at the beginning of his essay "Valéry Proust Museum," "Museum and mausoleum are connected by more than phonetic association. Museums are like the family sepulchers of works of art. They testify to the neutralization of culture."[3] Adorno's essay offers two different understandings of how this neutralization of culture relates to mortality. Reading Paul Valéry's discomfort with museums in "The Problem with Museums" and Marcel Proust's meditations on the afterlife of art in *À la Recherche du Temps Perdu*, Adorno argues that an understanding of the museum as a space of death emerges from Valéry's sense of art as a "pure thing" that loses its "expressive realization"—is put to death—when it becomes part of the chaotic cultural jumble of a museum.[4] Proust, in contrast, according to Adorno, sees works of art as "from the outset something more than their specific aesthetic qualities . . . they are part of the life of the person who observes them."[5] Whereas Valéry, as he writes in "The Problem of Museums," thinks that the "juxtaposition of dead visions" in the museum "has something insane about it," for Proust, "only the death of the work of art in the museum [can] bring it back to life," for only when art is "severed from the living order in which it functioned" will its "true spontaneity" be released.[6] To Valéry, the very fact of seeing artworks out of context sounds their death knell, but to Proust, the presence of viewers allows objects to live again, to have an ongoing, active place in an ever-changing culture.

Yeats would seem to share this Proustian ecstasy at the revivifying power of decontextualization, yet for Yeats, the museum is less a place of historical dismemberment than a space in which the multiplicity of world history swirls together in synergistic recombination. Like Walter Pater, in whose vampirically reborn Mona Lisa the experiences of humanity are collected and regenerated, Yeats accorded the museum a reanimating power, a power to give the dead a new, exciting, and culturally weighty life rather than a denigrated or monstrous one. Yeats's late nineteenth-century museum is not Adorno's space of neutralized culture, or Valéry's insane juxtaposition of dead visions, or Proust's elated severing of art from function; rather, Yeats imagined the museum as a model for the culturally revivifying power of poetry, for the ways in which fragments of history could be resuscitated—and re-historicized—by the modern aesthetic imagination. Although his later poems that deal explicitly with national collections excoriate what he sees as their institutionalization of mortality, in the last decades of the nineteenth century Yeats's efforts at literary collecting demonstrate an idealistic captivation with the poetic and political potential of collecting the past in order to bring a national future to life.

NECROMANCY IN THE BRITISH MUSEUM

In "The Burden of Nineveh," one of the most famous "museum poems" of the nineteenth century, Dante Gabriel Rossetti sees England's own future ruin in the statue of a "wingéd beast" being brought into a room in the British Museum:

> For as that Bull-god once did stand
> And watched the burial-clouds of sand,
> Till these at last without a hand
> Rose o'er his eyes, another land,
>   And blinded him with destiny: —
> So may he stand again; till now,
> In ships of unknown sail and prow,
> Some tribe of the Australian plough
> Bear him afar,—a relic now
>   Of London, not of Nineveh![7]
>   (171–80)

The British Museum, full of relics of past empires, inspires a fantasy of a future in which England, too, is just a collection of relics to be carted away. Rossetti imagines the British Museum not only as a tomb of mixed ancient cultures—"dead Greece" and "the corpse of Nineveh" stand side by side—but also as a kind of slaughterhouse. The ancient statue, itself a mythical hybrid of man, bull, and winged lion, becomes a "dead disbowelled mystery," a "mummy of a buried faith / Stark from the charnel" (15–17): not just a monument brought to its final resting place but a jumbled body disgorged and left amidst a jumble of other bodies. This strange dead creature occasions Rossetti's imaginative re-creation of ancient Nineveh, but his regeneration of the ancient world never escapes the mortality from which it emerges. "From their dead Past thou liv'st alone," Rossetti writes of the sculpture, torn from its vanished dead culture (48), and his wonder at its shadow, cast alike by the sun of Nineveh and the sun of London, suggests not a revelatory persistence or a rebirth of the past, but rather the persistence of cultural doom and destruction.[8]

"The Burden of Nineveh" presents two possible paths for the ancient objects collected in the British Museum: they can either be the relics of history, providing an access point for modern eyes to regenerate the past; or they can be transhistorical works of art, maintained in an eternal present tense by their aesthetic value. The poem ultimately falls on the side of the latter, the side of aestheticism, rather than on the side of historical transmission. To see the museum piece as a cultural relic rather than as an instance of beauty would be ultimately to imagine its destruction and cultural appropriation, its subjective revivification by imperial imaginations and its attendant loss of meaning. By setting his poem in the British Museum, the imperial collection par excellence, Rossetti allows his own artistic effort to become a participant in the power struggle between aesthetics and political subjugation inherent in the collecting practices of the British Empire. The British Museum forces a choice between the aesthetic and the historical, between a beautiful death and an imperial re-animation.

In re-creating a world of Nineveh within its own poetic strictures, the poem reenacts the violent appropriation by which the statue came to be enclosed within the walls of the Museum. Rossetti deliberately "wakes" the poem from this imperial dream—". . . Here woke my thought" (151)—when he ceases to imagine Nineveh and begins instead to project the same fate for England. Borrowing the iambic tetrameter of much of Tennyson's "In Memoriam," "The Burden of Nineveh" is ultimately a poem of mourning, not for the lost culture of which only a sculpture remains, but for the art of England, proleptically buried and misunderstood by excavators.[9] Rossetti imagines the archaeologically ransacked colonies of the empire exacting their revenge as "some tribe of the Australian plough" (178) plunders the sculpture as a relic of English culture, or as some future archaeologist,

> ... finding in this desert place
> This form, shall hold us for some race
> That walked not in Christ's lowly ways,
> But bowed its pride and vowed its praise
>   Unto the God of Nineveh.
>   (186–90)

The pathos of this anticipatory destruction of England, however—an empire whose fall the Museum predicts in its collection of relics from other fallen empires—lies not in the demise of England itself but rather in the resultant indecipherability of its relics: the inability of art to retain its historical, spiritual, and aesthetic sensibility across time.

Imaginative reanimation becomes a cycle of imperial violence, and in this act of self-reflection the poem recognizes itself as its own imperial museum, collecting, decontextualizing, and recontextualizing the statue beyond any kind of historical recognition. By the poem's end, the sculpture comes to represent a series of interpretive errors, and Rossetti's final description of the piece focuses on its stasis, its blindness, its incurable weight:

> Those heavy wings spread high
> So sure of flight, which do not fly;
> That set gaze never on the sky;
>   Those scriptured flanks it cannot see;
> Its crown, a brow-contracting load;
> Its planted feet which trust the sod: ...
> (So grew the image as I trod:)
> O Nineveh, was this thy God—
>   Thine also, mighty Nineveh?
>   (192–200)

Yet this description also expresses a rapture in the image of a sculpture that is not *meant* to fly, or see, or read—a sculpture, in other words, that has no purpose beyond its own aesthetic presence. Rossetti, like those future archaeologists of England, does not know what the statue represented for Nineveh, but this final stanza transforms the sculpture from a site of cultural representation to a pure aesthetic object, divorced from meaning, time, and space. Art, rather than history, becomes the poem's final presiding deity, and the question that ends the poem—"O Nineveh, was this thy God— / Thine also, mighty Nineveh?"—creates an aesthetic continuum between ancient Nineveh and modern Britain that tries to compensate for the absence of any kind of historical or cultural continuum. The poem's final stanza, which ultimately celebrates the statue's inability to do anything but stand and be looked at—"Those heavy wings spread high / So sure of flight, which do not fly; / That set gaze never on the sky" (192–94)— has a profoundly political implication: rather than perpetuating the aggression of colonial necromancy, Rossetti chooses instead to allow Nineveh to be killed into art. Choosing the aesthetic becomes an attempt to create a literary space beyond the reach of politics and historical necessity.

The young W. B. Yeats, wandering through the British Museum nearly thirty years after his much-admired predecessor wrote "The Burden of Nineveh," also found in the ancient statues there an occasion to probe the relationship between cultural displacement, aesthetic power, and historical revivification. Yet unlike Rossetti, for whom the aestheticism of the museum could offer nothing but death, Yeats found in the aesthetic conundrum of the museum the possibility for new life—and for new *Irish* life, in particular. The Victorian Yeats was fascinated with national museums and with the ways in which old artifacts collected in new places acquired, as he called it, a certain kind of "joyous energy."[10] This essay will argue that Yeats translated this excitement about the second life of museum objects into a theory of Irish cultural revivalism predicated on a full process of excavating, displacing, and refashioning old Irish legends into modern poetry. My argument has two aims: first, to show how Yeats's critically overlooked early work, "The Wanderings of Oisin," is instrumental in forming his theories of aesthetic revivalism; and second, to think about Yeats as an important bridge between Victorian studies and Irish studies, a writer whose particularly Irish idiom emerged as an engagement with Victorian literary and cultural phenomena, despite his professed hostility to Victorian ideals. It is well-trodden critical ground to suggest that Yeats derived much of his aesthetic theory from Victorian critics like Walter Pater and Matthew Arnold, even if he would deny it.[11] My point is to suggest that Victorian culture itself—Victorian institutions like the museum—offered the same fertile ground to Yeats that it did to poets like Rossetti, although the poetry that grew out of it became part of a different national dialogue.

Yeats spent the late 1880s both collecting Irish folklore for an anthology called *Fairy and Folk Tales of the Irish Peasantry* and working on a long narrative poem called "The Wanderings of Oisin." The poem, about a man going to and returning from fairyland, offers a metareflection on Yeats's own trips back and forth to Sligo collecting tales of Irish fairies. The poem also becomes, in Yeats's later recollections of its composition, an experimental attempt to discover in literary revivalism the same "joyous energy" that he found in British Museum objects. "Oisin" allegorizes the act of folklore collecting as an immersion in the land of the dead, and the process of shaping that folklore into modern poetry as the far-more-important return. Its obsession with the return from states of suspended animation, particularly apparent in its third book, which will be the focus of the second section of this essay, expresses Yeats's radical realization that retrospection and revival can never be synonymous—that cultural revival does not derive from the simple excavation of old stories but rather from a heroic act of aesthetic transformation that can reanimate those legends into bodies of modern poetry.

In May 1887, lately removed from Dublin to London, the twenty-four-year-old Yeats wrote to his friend Katharine Tynan that he had finally found a spot in London to begin work on a series of essays on Irish literature that he had been commissioned to write: the South Kensington Museum, which he grouchily described as "a very pleasant place, the air blowing through the open windows from the chestnut trees, the most tolerable spot London has yet revealed to me."[12] Throughout his first few months of feeling, as he wrote, "like a Robinson Crusoe in this dreadful London," both the South Kensington Museum and the British Museum were Yeats's work spots of choice for the essays, poems, and stories that connected him to the world of Irish literature. He fell into black moods whenever the rain meant he "lost [a] day" at the Museum.[13] During these first months, the city's museums offered a space of animated salvation from the dreary London streets where Yeats imagined "the souls of the lost are compelled to walk . . . perpetually."[14] It was during these months of 1887 and 1888 that Yeats began to write "The Wanderings of Oisin," the title poem of his first published poetry collection. During these months as well, he began the first of several anthologies of Irish writing he would compile over the next five years: a collection of Irish fairy and folk tales that emerged from visits to his native Sligo, in the West of Ireland, and from his attendant sense that Ireland was losing touch with its native past.

As Yeats worked on these texts in London, he was beginning to believe that his collection and publication of Irish legends would be able to coalesce a particular class of the Irish national public that, as he wrote in the introduction to one of his anthologies, had "been through the mould of Trinity College or of English Universities" and had little knowledge of their own Irish heritage.[15] At the same moment, across the Irish Sea, Dublin itself was working to institutionalize the same desire, in the form of a newly established Irish national museum. The Science and Art Museum Act of 1877 authorized the construction of a new public museum in Dublin to house the Irish antiquities previously privately held by the Royal Irish Academy. Yet it also placed that museum under the control of the London Department of Science and Art, which administered museums like the South Kensington Museum in London, of which Yeats was so fond. While *Irish* officials imagined the museum as an "important national institution" and a repository of the treasures of the Irish past, the Department of Science and Art saw the museum as "part of a system developed for the mutual benefit of all members of the Union"— like the South Kensington Museum, expressly intended as a tool to educate the public in the industrial arts, not in their national history.[16]

Even more important than the debates about what, precisely, should comprise the collections in the new museum, was an ongoing concern about *who* the museum's intended audience really should be, and how Ireland's antiquities could be retained and displayed for nationalist purposes while under an English administration. When the museum finally opened in 1890, its Irish antiquities collection was relegated to a far-from-prominent position on the museum's first floor—the bulk of its space, exhibitions, and lectures was devoted instead to the industrial arts of other nations, which, as one report on antique lace said, although "mostly foreign," was intended to be "highly suggestive to the lace workers of Ireland."[17] Rather than cultivating and expanding the national antiquities collection that would provide the Irish public with a material connection to its own history, the early Dublin Museum of Science and Industry became a small reproduction of the South Kensington Museum. It was devoted to providing foreign and imperial examples that could, in theory, improve the industrial production of its Irish audience. In 1892, the Irish nationalist journalist and MP William O'Brien lamented that the Royal Irish Academy had given up to the "South Kensington cabinet of curiosities, the inestimable relics of Celtic antiquity bequeathed to them by the pious patriotism of generations of Hudsons, Hardimans, and Wildes."[18] What had begun as a wish to make Ireland's treasures more publicly available, and to allow these antiquities to be an educational locus of nationalism and patriotism, had become instead an exercise in "the imperializing of Ireland."[19]

If Irish history could be institutionally relegated to the margins by a museum right in the heart of the Irish metropolis—and Irish antiquarians like William Wilde had been lamenting this very possibility since at least the 1840s[20]—then it was up to Irish writers like Yeats, who himself felt marginalized in that other, bigger British metropolis, to imagine an Irish past that could flourish right in the heart of Victorian modernity, an Irish past that could move fluidly *between* margin and metropole, between Sligo and London, between landscape and museum. Sligo and the idea of the museum were, in fact, strangely entwined for Yeats. In his 1922 autobiography, thoughts of Sligo become a frame for Yeats's recollections of the time he spent in the British Museum in the late 1880s, and for the joy that he imagined in the presence of some of the sculptures there:

> The statues of Mausolus and Artemesia [*sic*] at the British Museum, private, half-animal, half-divine figures, all unlike the Grecian athletes and Egyptian kings in their near neighbourhood, that stand in the middle of the crowd's applause, or sit above it measuring out unpersuadable justice, became to me, now or later, images of an unpremeditated joyous energy, that neither I nor any man, racked by doubt and inquiry, can achieve; and that yet, if once achieved, might seem to men and women of Connemara or of Galway their very soul.[21]

These statues, taken from the Ottoman Empire by a British archaeologist in the 1850s, had decorated the pinnacle of the famous mausoleum at Halicarnassus. They are funerary monuments, literally part of a mausoleum, and yet displaced into a museum. Yeats imagines them as ideal representations of "joyous energy" rather than as the bearers of death that Keats and Hardy, for instance, imagined the Elgin Marbles to be.

In the brief ekphrasis of this passage, Yeats reflects not only on the museum statues themselves but also on his relationship to a whole tradition of nineteenth-century museum poetry that has come before him: Shelley's "Ozymandias," Keats's "On Seeing the Elgin Marbles," Dante Gabriel Rossetti's "The Burden of Nineveh," and some now lesser known but then very popular poems by writers like Laurence Binyon and Sir Edwin Arnold.[22] By focusing his attention on the mausoleum statues rather than on these other Egyptian and Greek antiquities that had already gotten so much play in English poetry, Yeats presents an alternative narrative of the Museum's relationship to its antiquities than the dire one poets like Rossetti had already put forward. The subtext of this passage suggests that a poet's alternative focal point in the museum will generate poetry with a far more optimistic narrative of the intersection between the museum collection and poetic genesis. Rather than experiencing the lively displaced funerary statues as uncanny reminders of mortality, Yeats identifies a kind of life force in Mausolus and Artemisia. More specifically, however, and more strangely, Yeats recognizes a distinctively *Irish* life force in them—the ideal energy these statues embody, could it be somehow bottled, "might seem to men and women of Connemara or of Galway their very soul." Yeats finds in the British Museum neither the materialization of imperial violence—like Rossetti does—nor art reduced to a hollow corpse, but instead the clear evidence of an ancient and great culture experiencing an energized second life, one only *enhanced* by its presence in a modern British Museum.

These statues become to Yeats superlative figures for the revival of the Irish west—Connemara and Galway, the Celtic heart of Ireland—figures embodying not only the true soul of the Irish but also the capacity to represent that soul in a way, "if once achieved," that could render it recognizable to itself. In other words, these statues, displaced and on display in a wholly new context, are models of how the spirit of a culture might be even more available and recognizable in new forms than in old ones—models for the reanimation of the Irish past via formal recontextualization. It is telling that this recollection of a foray into the British Museum, which comes in the midst of a paragraph in Yeats's autobiography about the need to root modern poetry in a specific national landscape, does not appear wrongly placed to Yeats, although it would seem both digressive and paradoxical to praise *Persian* antiquities in an *English* museum collection in the midst of arguing for the importance of embedding art in its native ground. Yeats, however, imagines that he is himself similarly displaced; and in imagining himself displaced in a way similar to the statues, he also implicitly imagines that he is particularly suited to represent native Irish energy. The paragraph about the statues begins: "Though I went to Sligo every summer, I was compelled to live out of Ireland the greater part of every year, and was but keeping my mind upon what I knew must be the subject-matter of my poetry."[23] By beginning this way, the paragraph entwines the plight of dislocation with the necessity of Irish subject matter. Yeats argues here for the concrete nationalizing of art, yet at the same time makes the relationship between art and its native soil one based on imaginative cultural memory rather than one based on actual presence. Art and artists need not *be* in their native land, as long as their work remembers and expresses the energy of that land. And perhaps—perhaps—that energy will be best expressed in nonnative contexts or through non-

native forms. The associative process of Yeats's logic provides the stat-
ues standing in the British Museum with the symbolic resonance of
this kind of cultural memory: no longer in their native mausoleum but
emerging in a British context full of "unpremeditated joyous energy,"
the statues become models for the rebirth of antiquity, and the British
Museum itself—like poetry—the aesthetic vehicle for this new, ener-
getic life.

Yeats returns several pages later in his autobiography to the same
meditation on the relationship between poetry and native landscape
that introduces this British Museum passage, but here he instead
introduces his musing on the composition of "The Wanderings of
Oisin": "Might I not, with health and good luck to aid me, create
some new *Prometheus Unbound*; Patrick or Columbkil, Oisin or Fion,
in Prometheus' stead; and instead of Caucasus, Cro-Patric or Ben
Bulben? Have not all races had their first unity from a mythology, that
marries them to rock and hill?"[24] Again, Yeats gestures towards the
importance of native soil. But, again, as with the Persian statues find-
ing a joyous energy in the British Museum, Yeats imagines the old
Irish lands and legends finding a new life in *British* Romantic poetic
form, Shelley's *Prometheus Unbound*. George Bornstein has suggested
that in conceiving "The Wanderings of Oisin" as a kind of *Prometheus
Unbound*, Yeats imagined that the poem could "rais[e] nationalistic
feeling above party cabals and materialistic goals" by reimagining the
heroic Irish past in a context of "Shelleyan beautiful idealisms of
moral excellence."[25] But even more than this, Yeats fantasized that
recasting an Irish story in a British poetic form would be the best way
to bring the tales of ancient Ireland out of the peasant West and into
the purview of the Irish intelligentsia—the best way to make the Irish
spirit recognizable to the often Anglo-educated Irish people.

Irish poetry was already a kind of bardic museum, an oral space in
which the past was collected and preserved, but Yeats envisioned a
poetics that could be simultaneously museographic, pedagogical, and
political: "We had in Ireland imaginative stories," he continues in his
autobiography, "which the uneducated classes knew and even sang,
and might we not make those stories current among the educated
classes . . . and at last, it might be, so deepen the political passion of

the nation[?]"²⁶ In recontextualizing the legend of the Fenian hero Oisin in his poem, Yeats imagined uniting the educated Irish with the peasant mythology of the Irish landscape, while simultaneously extracting that mythology *from* the landscape into a new poetic form that could annex it to a political desire. And, as with the statues full of "joyous energy" in the British Museum, the imaginative result of this social and political recontextualization would be the reanimation of these ancient Celtic tales, tales which, displayed in new forms, "might move of themselves and with some powerful, even turbulent life."²⁷ In spite of beginning both of these passages of his autobiography with the necessity of the Irish landscape, and tied as he feels to that landscape, Yeats nonetheless accords the mystic power of cultural reanimation not to the magic of mythical native soil, but rather to a nearly museological act of cultural appropriation: if the British Museum can bring a mausoleum to life, then what might the forms of British poetry be able to do for Irish legend?²⁸

"THE WANDERINGS OF OISIN" AND THE NECESSITY OF RETURN

In asking this question, I do not mean to suggest that Yeats found a definitive answer in "The Wanderings of Oisin," only that this question was percolating both as he wrote it and when he reflected on writing it thirty years later (in the passages from *The Trembling of the Veil* discussed above). "Oisin," in fact, experiments with everything from ballad form and Shelleyan pentameter to the long, Anglo-Saxon verse form of Beowulf, but Yeats was never happy with the result—he revised the 1889 version significantly for its 1892 reprint, disappointed, as he wrote, that "only shadows have got themselves onto paper."²⁹ "The Wanderings of Oisin" both revels in and also carefully brackets off the mythic Irish landscape of fairies and folktales. It pushes us to consider the formal mechanisms of Celtic Revivalism: the ways in which Yeats was beginning to theorize the balance between a full immersion in Celticism and the need for a modern poetic form that could bring Celtic myth into the land of the living. As a parable of Yeats's own project of collecting Celtic stories, "The Wanderings of Oisin" proposes a system of Irish literature in which the Celtic past becomes the inspiration for, but never the endpoint of, the creation of a national identity.

This three-book, 915-line poem tells the story of the Fenian hero Oisin and the immortal Niamh, who falls in love with him and convinces him to come with her to her home in Tir-na-nOg, "the Country of Youth" in some legends, the land of the dead in others. Oisin spends three hundred ageless years with Niamh, and in this poem, although not in the most often-told versions of the story, he follows her to three different islands (the Island of Dancing, the Island of Victory, and the Island of Forgetfulness), on each one temporarily surrendering to its hypnotic charms before shaking himself awake and begging to move on (both to a new island and a new verse form). After three islands, Oisin gets homesick and begs Niamh to let him go back to Ireland, even if only for twelve hours. But when he arrives he discovers that, though he remains young, his clan has passed away and Ireland has been converted to Christianity and changed beyond recognition. Disappointed and longing to return to Niamh, he begins his journey "home," but his saddle breaks and he falls to the earth. The horse vanishes, and he instantly becomes a crippled old man, wanting nothing more than to die.

Yeats's poem tells the story as a dialogue between Oisin and St. Patrick soon after Oisin's return, and acknowledges an eighteenth-century narrative poem by Michael Comyn called "Lay of Oisin on the Land of Youth" as a primary source. Yet Yeats also acknowledges that while he used Comyn's poem and "suggestions from various ballad Dialogues of Oisin and Patrick, published by the Ossianic Society," most of the poem is "wholly [his] own, having no further root in tradition than the Irish peasant's notion of Tir-na-nOg (the Country of the Young) is made up of three phantom islands."[30] "The Wanderings of Oisin" is thus not a poem about the things, or stories, it collects—this is the dominion of the folklore collections—but rather about how material remnants can be interpreted and reconstituted as national history. That Yeats presents this reconstitution as a poem about a man coming back from the land of fairy to rediscover his poetic voice suggests, however, that he envisions this process as both

a return *from* history and a return *to* history, a return *from* the pri-
mordial land of myth and *to* the world of the historical imagination,
or, in other words, as an act of revival that escapes the past but always
requires its lingering traces to remain.[31]

In his introduction to *Fairy and Folk Tales of the Irish Peasantry*,
his 1888 anthology of Irish folklore, Yeats imagines the land of fairy
as simultaneously atemporal and steeped in historical sensibility:

> These folk tales are full of simplicity and musical occurrences, for
> they are the literature of a class for whom every incident in the old
> rut of birth, love, pain, and death has cropped up unchanged for
> centuries: who have steeped everything in the heart: to whom
> everything is a symbol. They have the spade over which man has
> learnt from the beginning. The people of the cities have the ma-
> chine, which is prose and a *parvenu*.[32]

Fairy is timeless, yet ancient, and separated from "the cities" not only
by a different sense of history but also by different language forma-
tions. The "symbolic," musical, and heartfelt realm of the peasants is
the realm of poetry (and Yeats's interest in symbolism is extant here),
while the material world of the cities can only speak in prose. When
Yeats himself begins to craft his own version of the Irish fairy tale of
Tir-na-nOg in "The Wanderings of Oisin," however, the land of fairy
becomes precisely the opposite of this realm: he conceives a place,
instead, where impossible temporality, a kind of frozen animation,
disrupts all attempts at making poetry. Exile to the land of fairy be-
comes exile to the land of the dead, and is simultaneously a crisis of
historical positioning and a crisis of poetic genesis.

The poem uses a language of intense temporal confusion to insist
that these two crises are implicitly intertwined. Much like the story of
Odysseus, to which "The Wanderings of Oisin" has been compared,[33]
Yeats's long poem begins in a state of "afterwards"; in fact, it begins in
several states of "afterwards," a condition that Yeats chose to particu-
larly emphasize in his 1892 revision of the poem.[34] We see the poem's

"post-ness" first in the retrospective narration of Oisin, now "bent, and bald, and blind," and in the post-pagan Ireland of St. Patrick, where once-worshipped fairies have become "demon thing[s]" amidst the "burial-mounds" of Oisin's Fenian friends. Even Niamh, an Immortal from Tir-na-nOg, in the poem's opening stanzas comes under the weight of its melancholic post-ness. At least, in Oisin's recollection of her, she comes aesthetically to embody an end rather than a beginning, her lips not just "like a sunset" but like a "stormy sunset on doomed ships," and a fiery color "gloom[ing]" rather than blooming in her hair (21–23). These phrases stand in explicit contrast to Niamh's own picture of Tir-na-nOg as a land from which "the blushes of first love never have flown" (85): a land of eternal dawn, not of preserved twilight. By beginning "after," the poem immediately pitches its own composition in opposition to the world of fairy it describes, "far / Beyond the tumbling of this tide": a country outside of time, a country that *has* no after (48). On one hand, it seems perfectly obvious to say that Oisin's story happens afterwards: as the only mortal to have gone to Tir-na-nOg and returned, his legend is more about the return *from* than the journey *to,* the end of a three-hundred-year absence rather than its beginning. And yet, to suggest that the poem posits its essential condition as one that requires the world of fairy to have been experienced and lost is also to suggest that this timeless, apolitical realm of legend can be a space of inspiration but not a space of poetry.

This poetic suppression emerges most profoundly in book 3 of the poem, on the Island of Forgetfulness, where giant, monstrous creatures live in a blissful state of thoughtless slumber. In this book Yeats has retreated from contemporary verse forms and writes in a version of the long, caesuraed lines of Anglo-Saxon poetry, suggesting that modern poetry and immersion in this land of deathly sleep are incompatible. When Oisin first arrives on the island, he attempts to wake its "huge white" sleepers in order to hear their stories, certain that whatever forgotten stories they have just need to be recollected:

Snatching the horn of Niam, I blew forth a lingering note;
Came sound from those monstrous sleepers, a sound like a stirring
    of flies.

He, shaking the folds of his lips and heaving the pillar of his
   throat,
Watched me with mournful wonder out of the wells of his eyes.

I cried, "Thou art surely a warrior, forgetting his famous line,
And even the names of his fathers, and even the works of his
   hands?
A good name is goodly to hear of, and a good name surely is
   thine.
Worthy's thy questioner, Oisin, he from the Fenian lands."[35]

Oisin's "long lingering note" interrupts the silent coma of the mon-
strous sleepers, but his call to bardic camaraderie and memory earns
only a wordless response from the sleeper: "His lips moved slowly in
answer, no answer out of them came." Instead, only a sound, "soft" but
"piercing," that washes away bardic memory "like a sea-covered stone"
and lulls Oisin into the same silent sleep that his horn's note briefly
disrupted. Stories and names and histories are lost on the Island of
Forgetfulness, irretrievable through language, and Oisin's failed ap-
peals to memory and poetry mark his essential difference from the
inhabitants of this island. And though he is lulled to sleep with the
huge white creatures, "a century . . . forgot," still "the ancient sadness
of man" rises in him, and he wakes, begging to return to the world of
the living:

I cried, "O Niam! O white one! if only a twelve-houred day,
I must gaze on the beard of Fin, and move where the old men and
   young
In the Fenians' dwellings of wattle lean on the chessboards and
   play,
Ah, sweet to me now were even bald Conan's slanderous tongue!"
                                                        (O, 43)

Oisin again breaks the forgetful silence of the sleepers, articulating
the most plaintive part of his desire to leave the island as a wish to
hear the language of his own people, even in slanderous version: to re-
turn from the exile of fairy to the world of words.

Seamus Deane has claimed in his book *Strange Country* that the exilic position of the human in the fairy world "is one of the most effective" poetic positions, for he "remains within Ireland as part of its true and permanent history and yet in exile from all that in Ireland is part of its transient and yet actual existence."[36] However, in positing these islands of Tir-na-nOg not only as places to which Oisin has been exiled (or has exiled himself), but also as places *from* which poetic language exiles him, Yeats suggests instead that the human in the world of fairy cannot occupy any kind of poetic position at all. He can witness, he can immerse himself, and he can remember, but he cannot create: in short, he can be a collector but not, in the moment of immersion, an artist. Deane proposes that Yeats uses the trope of the child/woman/man gone with the *sidhe* in order to create a space for poetry that was bound to Ireland's Celtic identity but divorced from the "greasy till" banality of modern Ireland that we see in a poem like "September 1913." But in contrast to these claims that the mythical realm of fairy is the realm of a particularly symbolic, particularly authentic, particularly Yeatsian Irish poetry, exile to Tir-na-nOg in "The Wanderings of Oisin" has more muddled implications for the relationship between poetry, memory, and nationality that Deane (and Yeats, too, in the introduction to his folklore anthology) packages so neatly. The poem suggests instead that while poetry can synthesize the materials of immersion, be they fairy stories or literary traditions, in order to create a national mythology, it can only do so afterward—the mythology can *only* be an afterword. Oisin describes his years of forgetful sleep as an impossible stasis: "So lived I and lived not, so wrought I and wrought not, with creatures of dreams," he says, stuck in this moment between life and death, between creation and absence, caught in the land of fairy but unable to generate anything out of it (*O*, 42). The poet here is mired in a "dream" tradition from which he, in order to remain a bardic poet, has no choice but to wake.

"The Wanderings of Oisin," like Tennyson's "The Lotos-Eaters," to which the poem bears important similarities,[37] locates the creation of national heritage at home, in the world of battles, toil, death, and memory, rather than in the fairyland of forgetfulness and eternity. Yet while Tennyson's English mariners end "The Lotos-Eaters" by dismissing the importance of bardic tradition and insisting that they "will not wander more,"[38] Yeats's Irish Oisin wakes and follows the "keen[ing]" of "Remembrance" back to the homeland from which he can tell his story (O, 152). This call of poetry—for what phrase could more perfectly describe Yeats's sense of Irish poetry than the "keening of Remembrance"?—brings Oisin back from the land of the dead, in part because he believes so wholeheartedly in the power of his own poetry to wake the dead. Upon his return to Ireland, Oisin, little more than a singing corpse walking on the graves of his dead friends, insists to St. Patrick that he can "go to the Fenians, / O cleric, to chant / The war-songs that roused them of old; they will rise" (O, 51). He imagines that his poetry will reanimate the friends and the history so many years gone. Yet only belatedly does he recognize that *he* is the dead that poetry, or the desire for poetry, has brought back to life. The historical imagination, for this Yeats poem, *does* reside in "greasy till" Ireland, in national, bardic language—in the return from the land of forgetting and the land of the dead.

There are many ways to read Oisin's return to Ireland and to poetry: as a dismissal of the Celtic periphery as a locus of national identity; as the literal and literary revival of Fenian history ("they will rise ... [i]nnumerable, singing, exultant" [O, 51]); as a recognition that cultural identity emerges out of the ragged remains of history rather than in a Tennysonian distance from it; as a voice of resistance to the mundane forces of colonization embodied by St. Patrick; as a melancholy understanding that poetry lives in the aftermath of irretrievable loss; or as some combination of all of these. The ambiguous entwining of melancholy and transformative potential seems to be Yeats's point, for poetry, in Yeats's oeuvre, can never and should never provide an unequivocal theory of how literature should relate to its historical rags and bones. Once home, Oisin can "dwell in the house of the Fenians, be they in flames or at feast": he can both tell his tale and imagine his reentrance into history, whether that history be something to celebrate or something to lament. However, he has been gone too long, and his return to life is also a return to death: "I rose, and walked on the earth, / A creeping old man" (O, 50), he tells us. The state of "afterwards" that makes poetry possible proves to be a profoundly isolating condition: "Ah me! to be old without succour, a show unto children, a stain, / Without laughter, a coughing, alone with remembrance and fear," the last section of the poem begins, suggesting that, in this liminal moment between fairy tale and history, even poetry can be a state of exile (O, 52).

The character Oisin stands as Yeats's youthful warning—perhaps a forgotten warning—against the immersive lure of Celticism. In his letters from the late 1880s Yeats may describe London as a land of the dead, but he describes Sligo that way even more forcefully: "Going for a walk is a continual meeting with ghosts. For Sligo for me has no flesh and blood attractions—only memories."[39] Fifty years later, however, it is neither London nor Sligo but a museum—once the sort of place where Yeats would have found a life force—that Yeats imagines as the land of the dead. In "The Municipal Gallery Revisited," Yeats stands among the portraits of dead friends and recalls with melancholy his youthful belief that "All that we did, all that we said or sang / Must come from contact with the soil, from that / Contact everything Antaeus-like grew strong."[40] Now, the museum and the possibility of native poetry stand at odds with one another, and rather than offering a space of productive formal revival, the museum and poetry together offer a bureaucratically aestheticized version of Ireland:[41] "'This is not,' I say, / 'The dead Ireland of my youth, but an Ireland / The poets have imagined, terrible and gay.'" If the Irish Municipal Gallery represents not the reanimation of dead Ireland but rather an imaginary Ireland disconnected from its spirit, it also embodies precisely Dante Gabriel Rossetti's Victorian sense of a politically deadening museum that the younger Yeats resisted so strongly. In reading "The Wanderings of Oisin" as a version of the Victorian museum poem—one that valorizes rather than decries the aesthetically transformative power of collecting old things in new places—we can see in a later poem like "The Municipal Gallery Revisited" Yeats returning to his Victorian roots and finding them bent, and bald, and blind.

NOTES

1. I refer here to the controversy surrounding Hugh Lane's gift of French impressionist paintings to the City of Dublin, as well as to the difficulty in establishing a permanent museum to house Lane's collections. I discuss these issues at greater length below.

2. In her recent book, *Museum Trouble: Edwardian Fiction and the Emergence of Modernism* (Charlottesville: University of Virginia Press, 2012), Ruth Hoberman makes a related argument about the museological aesthetic of Yeats's later poetry, arguing that he envisions Byzantium as a kind of museum and that his Byzantium poems "dramatize the creative process as an intersection of museal with nonmuseal world: art objects suffused with their own deracination, separated from the world of the living, endlessly absorb and transform images drawn from the world" (175). While Hoberman focuses on how the early twentieth-century museum influences Yeats's modernist aesthetic, however, she does not address the ways that Yeats's earlier poetry sees the nineteenth-century museum as a model for a specifically Irish national aesthetic.

3. Theodor W. Adorno, "Valéry Proust Museum," in *Prisms*, trans. Samuel Weber and Sherry Weber (London: Neville Spearman Limited, 1967), 175.

4. Ibid., 181, 182.

5. Ibid., 181.

6. Paul Valéry, "The Problem of Museums," in *Degas Manet Morisot*, trans. David Paul (Princeton: Princeton University Press, 1989), 203; Adorno, "Valéry Proust Museum," 182.

7. Dante Gabriel Rossetti, "The Burden of Nineveh." All quotations are taken from the version printed in Frances O'Gorman, ed., *Victorian Poetry: An Annotated Anthology* (London: Blackwell Publishing, 2004), and cited by line number in the text.

8. Barbara Black points out that in the 1856 version of this stanza the Egyptian mummy is called a "pilgrim" rather than an "alien," and argues that this change indicates Rossetti's "increasingly more accurate understanding of the irreverent and hostile undertaking of museum acquisition" (Barbara Black, *On Exhibit: Victorians and Their Museums* [Charlottesville: University Press of Virginia, 2000], 144). I would add that the word "alien" suggests at least as much, if not more, about the *unheimlich* nature of the museum display as it does about the acquisition process—this stanza reflects the disconcerting experience both of cultural mishmash and of the presence of this oriental mishmash in the domestic space of the London museum.

9. In this, the poem shares much with Shelley's "Ozymandias," although by bringing the statue into the British Museum rather than leaving it in the desert it makes an even more insistently proleptic comparison between the ruin of Nineveh and the ruin of England.

10. W. B. Yeats, *The Trembling of the Veil* (London: T. Werner Laurie, 1922), 38.

11. See George Watson's discussion of Yeats and Victorian philosophical sensibility in "Yeats, Victorianism, and the 1890s," in *The Cam-*

bridge Companion to W. B. Yeats, ed. Marjorie Howes and John Kelly, 36–58 (Cambridge: Cambridge University Press, 2006).

12. *The Letters of W. B. Yeats,* ed. Allan Wade (New York: Macmillan, 1955), 39.

13. Ibid., 59, 78.

14. Ibid., 81–82.

15. *A Book of Irish Verse, Selected from Modern Writers,* with an introduction and notes by W. B. Yeats (London: Methuen, 1895), xxvi.

16. Elizabeth Crooke, *Politics, Archaeology, and the Creation of a National Museum of Ireland* (Dublin: Irish Academic Press, 2000), 114.

17. Ibid., 124.

18. Ibid., 123 (quoted from *Gaelic Journal,* July 1892, 164).

19. Ibid., 109.

20. In his 1849 *The Beauties of the Boyne,* William Wilde, father of the famous Oscar and eventual compiler of the first catalogue to accompany the Royal Irish Academy's collection, bemoans the Irish National Education Board's willingness to teach their students about every other country, "but [to] never once allude, in their system of education, to the national history of the people they are employed to teach." That "the ordinarily educated—and above all, that the learned of any country—should be unacquainted with the materials of our Irish history, is a lamentable fact," he writes, insisting that in writing this book that describes the landscape, history, and archaeological remains of the most famous river in Ireland, one of his main objects has been "to popularize [the great mass of Irish historic manuscripts]—to render my countrymen familiar with facts and names of Irish history" (William Wilde, *The Beauties of the Boyne, and its Tributary, the Blackwater,* 2nd ed. [Dublin: James McGlashan, 1850], vi-vii).

21. Yeats, *The Trembling of the Veil,* 38–39.

22. See, for instance, Binyon's 1908 poem "In the British Museum" and Arnold's 1853 "To the Statue of Eumousia in the British Museum." Yeats was an admirer of Binyon, in particular, whom he asked to succeed Hugh Lane as the director of the Irish National Gallery after Lane's death in 1915.

23. Yeats, *The Trembling of the Veil,* 38.

24. Ibid., 79.

25. George Bornstein, *Yeats and Shelley* (Chicago: University of Chicago Press, 1970), 24. See 23–27 for a discussion of Yeats's "The Wanderings of Oisin" as an attempt to rewrite Shelley's *Prometheus Bound* on Irish soil, and the ways in which Yeats's poem revised the themes of magic and immortal love from several of Shelley's other poems.

26. Yeats, *The Trembling of the Veil,* 79.

27. Ibid.

28. Yeats reverses this question in "The Celtic Element in Literature" (1897), asking instead what Celtic legend might be able to do for British poetry: "I will put this differently and say that literature dwindles to a mere chronicle of circumstance, or passionless phantasies, and passionless meditations, unless it is constantly flooded with the passions and beliefs of ancient times, and that of all the fountains of the passions and beliefs of ancient times in Europe, . . . [the Celtic] has again and again brought the 'vivifying spirit' 'of excess' into the arts of Europe. . . . 'The Celtic movement,' as I understand it, is principally the opening of this fountain [of Gaelic legend], and none can measure of how great importance it may be to coming times, for every new fountain of legends is a new intoxication for the imagination of the world" (*The Complete Works of W.B. Yeats*, vol. 4, *Early Essays*, ed. Richard J. Finneran and George Bornstein [New York: Simon and Schuster, 2007], 136–37).

29. *The Letters of W. B. Yeats*, 87.

30. Ibid., 132.

31. "The Wanderings of Oisin" is of particular interest in this regard, for while it carries the classic elements of Irish revivalism—the retelling of Irish myth, the romanticization of nationalism, the hero who is lost and then returns—it also has its hero return not as a reborn youth but as a decrepit old man. The classic image of Irish revivalism, Yeats's and Lady Gregory's Cathleen ni Houlihan, who begins as an old woman but is transformed into a beautiful Irish maiden as soon as she has found men who will go out and fight for Ireland, has its counterpart in Oisin, who spends most of the poem as a young man but becomes old and broken as soon as he sets foot on Irish soil. Joep Leerssen uses the image of Cathleen to exemplify the impulse of revivalism in Irish national discourse: "A nationalistic recourse to the unspoilt freshness of Ireland could signal an escape out of the seemingly inevitable process of decay, decrepitude, and cultural entropy. The most expressive encapsulation of this mood was the notion of a *revival*, or rebirth: youth rising from the ashes, a bright future rising from a crumbling past" (Joep Leerssen, *Remembrance and Imagination: Patterns in the Historical and Literary Representation of Ireland in the Nineteenth Century* [Notre Dame, IN: University of Notre Dame Press, 1997], 194–95). "The Wanderings of Oisin" exemplifies a different kind of revivalism, one that revives not the past itself but the past as a source of artistic inspiration.

32. W. B. Yeats, ed., *Fairy and Folk Tales of the Irish Peasantry* (New York: Simon and Schuster, 1998), 5.

33. See in particular Martin McKinsey, "Counter-Homericism in Yeats's 'The Wanderings of Oisin,'" in *W.B. Yeats and Postcolonialism*, ed. Deborah Fleming, 235–51 (West Cornwall, CT: Locust Press, 2001).

34. Unless otherwise stated, the quotes from "The Wanderings of Oisin" come from Yeats's original 1889 version rather from his 1892 revision, which has become the standard anthologized version. The quotes in this paragraph, however, are from the revised version, and book and line numbers are taken from *The Collected Poems of W.B. Yeats,* ed. Richard J. Finnerman (New York: Simon and Schuster, 1996). I quote from Yeats's revision here because the later version offers a more concrete blending of the personal and national melancholy than the first version of the poem suggests.

35. W. B. Yeats, *The Wanderings of Oisin and Other Poems* (London: Paul Trench, 1889), 39. Hereafter cited parenthetically as *O.*

36. Seamus Deane, *Strange Country: Modernity and the Nation* (New York: Clarendon Press, 1997), 113.

37. The tradition of Yeats's Island of Forgetting in book 3 is twofold, for it is as much Tennyson's 1832 island of "The Lotos-Eaters" as it is a locale of Irish folklore. Oisin's linguistic displacement from the island, which echoes both his physical displacement from the battle-torn Ireland of his youth and his spiritual displacement from St. Patrick's Christian Ireland upon his return, represents the impossible lyrical position of a poet mired in multiple traditions. This compound dislocation certainly expresses the fraught condition of Yeats's own Anglo-Irish identity, which pushed him into a complex dilemma of simultaneous identification with and distance from both the Sligo peasantry and the London/Dublin literary aristocracy. The process of folklore collecting, which required an immersion into an Irish landscape that was both Yeats's home and very much not his home, was in many senses an expression of just this kind of national dislocation. Equally significant, however, the third book of "Oisin" functions in a similarly complex relationship to English poetic tradition, paying homage to Victorian British obsessions with classicism, Homericism more particularly, and even Tennyson himself as Poet Laureate, at the same time that it virulently contravenes the ahistorical somnolence with which Tennyson ends his famous poem. Yeats embraces the English canon while simultaneously refuting it by writing an alternative ending, a historical ending, an Irish ending, to Tennyson's English story. As much as "Oisin" is about an immersion into and return from Irish folklore, so too is it a poem about the return from English poetry and the reconstruction of its remnants into an Irish national tradition.

38. The lotos-eaters' island is "a land / In which it seemed always afternoon," a land "where all things seem'd always the same" (3–4, 24). The "seem'd always" in these lines suggests the island as a place, like Yeats's island, without history or memory, a constant present tense that serves as an escape from the ongoing formation of cultural heritage in the mariners' "Fatherland" (39). This "Fatherland," the mariners' distant Ithaca, has become a place where "the minstrel sings / Before them of the ten years' war in Troy, /

And our great deeds, as half-forgotten things," a realm to which they could only return "like ghosts," killed into national memory (120–24). When the mariners insist on remaining on the island in the poem's final stanza, they reject the bardic songs that transform their actions into tradition, even disavowing their fundamental identities, their essential place in the *"race* of men" (165, emphasis mine):

> We have had enough of action, and of motion we,
> Roll'd to starboard, roll'd to larboard, when the surge was seething free,
> Where the wallowing monster spouted his foam fountains in the sea.
> Let us swear an oath, and keep it with an equal mind,
> In the hollow Lotos-land to live and lie reclined
> On the hills like Gods together, careless of mankind.
> . . . .
> Surely, surely, slumber is more sweet than toil, the shore
> Than labour in the deep mid-ocean, wind and wave and oar;
> Oh rest ye, brother mariners, we will not wander more.
>
> (150–73)

("The Lotos-Eaters," in *Tennyson's Poetry: A Norton Critical Edition*, ed. Robert W. Hills, Jr. [New York: W. W. Norton, 1999]).

39. *The Letters of W. B. Yeats*, 54–55.

40. W. B. Yeats, *The Variorum Edition of the Poems of W. B. Yeats*, ed. Peter Allt and Russell K. Alspach (New York: Macmillan, 1957), 601–4.

41. Yeats was, indeed, outraged over the bureaucratic waffling surrounding the establishment of a permanent location for Hugh Lane's Municipal Gallery (it did not open in its permanent space in Parnell Square until 1933). As Yeats wrote in 1915, shortly before Lane died on the *Lusitania,*

> The difference between Dublin *talkers* and any real workers is that the *talkers* value anything which they call a principle more than any possible achievement. All achievements are won by compromise and these men, wherever they find themselves, expel from their own minds—by their minds' rigidity—the flowing and existing world.
>
> The Sinn Fein party in order to affirm the abstract principle that an Irish building should have an Irish architect supported Dr. Murphy in defeating Hugh Lane's municipal gallery project.
>
> He offered £70,000 worth of pictures, and a man believed by many to be the greatest of living architects—but they preferred their abstract principle. It was nothing to them that we have no Irish architect whom anybody suspects of remarkable talent. They preferred their mouthful of east wind. (*The Letters of W. B. Yeats*, 591–92)

The gallery continued to be a space of contestation over the next several decades, as Dublin and London fought over the bequest of a collection of Lane's French paintings. Lady Gregory—Lane's aunt—worked tirelessly to have these paintings returned to Dublin, and Yeats wrote impassionedly in defense of Dublin's claim. Not until 1959 was an agreement to share the paintings finally reached. That is to say, when Yeats wrote about the gallery in the 1930s, it was, to him, still very much an emblem of bureaucratic malfeasance and frustration.

CHAPTER 2

The Death of Cuchulain's Only Son

ELIZABETH CULLINGFORD

Yeats was a founding member of what Terry Eagleton has termed Ireland's "archaic avant-garde":[1] a romantic decolonizing movement that based its claim to a new and independent national future on the glories of Irish antiquity.[2] "It is precisely the remote past, uncontaminated by recent time, which can provide the most stirring image of the future," writes Eagleton.[3] For romantic nationalists like Yeats and Lady Gregory, Ireland's cultural and historical difference was an essential foundation on which to build a case for political autonomy. Both of them explored and reframed the Irish saga materials in order to prove that ancient Ireland was the equal of intellectually prestigious ancient Greece, so-called cradle of Western Civilization, and to replace the inferiority complex generated by centuries of colonial rule with a healthy dose of cultural pride.[4] Paradoxically, however, in choosing from and adapting the Irish heroic tales Yeats focused primarily on the story of a father who kills his only son, an ancient mythic narrative that symbolically forecloses all generative, future-oriented possibilities.[5] My essay will show how Yeats's fascination with this particular incident accords with his philosophical and aesthetic credo, "we begin to live when we have conceived life as tragedy,"[6] and argue that his sense of cultural belatedness, his attraction to end times and lost causes, outweighed his imaginative investment in the future.[7]

Cuchulain,[8] the central figure in Yeats's revival of Irish antiquity, is best known as the gallant seventeen-year-old hero of the most famous episode in the Ulster Cycle, the *Táin Bó Cúailnge*, in which he single-handedly defends Ulster against the invading army of Queen Maeve, holding the line until the men of the North can awake from their lethargy and dispatch the marauders back to Connacht. Yet Cuchulain as Yeats reinvents him in poetry and drama is never a handsome and successful teenage warrior. Except in the comic play *The Green Helmet* (a version of *Bricriu's Feast*), he is represented as a middle-aged hero who, from his first appearance in 1892 to his last in 1939, is shadowed and defined by a single tragic act. In Yeats's early poem "The Death of Cuchulain," Cuchulain unwittingly kills his only son Connla, and, grief-stricken, dies fighting the waves. It is characteristic of Yeats's pessimism that he introduces his mythical hero on the day of his death and the extinction of his bloodline. This tragic event is central to all Yeats's Cuchulain plays, which eschew the better-known and more conventionally heroic martial narrative of the *Táin*. Cuchulain's fatal conflict with the warrior princess Aoife, which will lead to the death of their only child, is set up and prophesied in *At the Hawk's Well* (1916). His killing of Connla is the central action of *On Baile's Strand* (1903). *The Only Jealousy of Emer* (1919) and *Fighting the Waves* (1929) represent the aftermath of his struggle with the sea, from which his wife Emer rescues him. In *The Death of Cuchulain* (1939) the aged Aoife returns to kill her former lover, but she is distracted by their regretful discussion of Connla's death, a poignant conversation with no analog in any of Yeats's sources.

Yeats first encountered Cuchulain in Standish O'Grady's *History of Ireland: The Heroic Period*, which he read as a teenager,[9] and he subsequently claimed that O'Grady "founded modern Irish literature."[10] Despite his conservative and Unionist politics O'Grady helped to augment national pride: he praised the Irish Heroic Age even above the Greeks. In 1900 Alfred Nutt, the prominent Celtic scholar and publisher for whom Yeats had undertaken numerous copying jobs in his penurious youth, published a pamphlet entitled *Cuchulainn, the Irish Achilles,* in which he drew parallels between "Greeks of the Homeric period, say, 1200–900 B. C. [and] Irish Celts of the heroic period."[11] Although he makes no claims about literary influence, Nutt sees the *Táin* as "the Iliad of the Western Gael."[12] In focusing on the story of Cuchulain, Yeats sought to elevate the status of what Nutt claimed was "the most ancient *vernacular* literature of modern Europe."[13] Despite the chaotic transmission history and corrupted state of the surviving Celtic tales, antiquity in itself conferred a cultural prestige that, in turn, helped to justify Ireland's claim to political independence. Though his country lacked a Homer, Yeats argued that its legends, many of which had not yet been translated or published when he began to write, were fragments of "the buried Odyssey of Ireland."[14] He hoped that Lady Gregory's synoptic retelling would raise them from the dead, and he therefore praised her *Cuchulain of Muirthemne* (1902) somewhat over-lavishly: "The most beautiful book that has come out of our country in my time. One thinks of Homer," mocks Joyce's Buck Mulligan.[15] Although Yeats did not in fact compare Lady Gregory to Homer, he did desire a coherent pre-Christian origin myth that would rival that of the Greeks, the founders of Western Civilization, and render irrelevant contemporary sectarian divisions between Anglo-Irish Protestants and native Catholics. As early as "To the Rose upon the Rood of Time" (1892), Cuchulain is established as a representative of "*the ancient ways*" that the poet claims are superior to British imperial modernity.[16] In Yeats's eclectic and comprehensive politics of culture, ancient myths and modern poems could produce a distinctively Irish identity: "Irish singers, who are genuinely Irish in thought, subject and style, must, whether they will or no, nourish the forces that make for the political liberties of Ireland."[17]

Yeats later claimed that "O'Grady started us off by re-creating Cuchullain in the image of Achilles" (*VPl,* 572). But if Cuchulain is a Homeric epic hero, an Irish Achilles, his killing of Connla and subsequent fight with the sea provides an analog for Yeats's Nietzschean concept of tragedy: a valiant but doomed struggle against impossible odds. In the little-known late poem "Alternative Song for the Severed Head" (1934), Yeats designates "Cuchulain that fought night long with the foam" as one of his "tragic characters" (*VPl*, 549). Despite Yeats's fervent cultural nationalism, the tragic mode does not on the face of it offer much practical assistance to a colonized people hoping to throw off the imperial yoke. Yet Padraig Pearse, who saw the road to victory as leading inevitably through the valley of defeat, took Cuchulain as his role model, mainly because of his reckless courage and his willingness to die young in pursuit of honor. Few critics have noted, however, that Pearse's Cuchulain is very different from Yeats's Cuchulain: he is either a brave and beautiful prepubescent boy, a creation of Pearse's undeniably homoerotic imagination, or he is the sacrificial Christ-figure later memorialized by Oliver Shepherd's statue in the General Post Office.[18] Son-killing is not on his agenda. In Yeats's Irish version of Greek drama, on the other hand, Cuchulain's anguish is the result of his *hamartia*, which Aristotle defines not as a fatal flaw but as a tragic error. For Yeats, the association between Cuchulain and his tragic error becomes habitual: the hero is almost always accompanied by some linguistic variant of the formula "Cuchulain killing his son and fighting the sea."[19] For example, in "To The Rose upon the Rood of Time" (*VP*, 100–101) his descriptive tag is not "Cuchulain battling with ferocious Maeve," nor "Cuchulain battling with his dearest friend" (two factually and metrically possible alternatives) but "*Cuchulain battling with the bitter tide.*" Like King Canute, whose inability to command the sea has become iconic, Yeats's Cuchulain is indelibly associated with human failure to master the implacable forces of nature.

When Yeats looks back on his early poetic and dramatic themes in "The Circus Animals' Desertion" (1938), Cuchulain's fight with "the ungovernable sea" is approvingly described as a "heart-myster[y]," and is thus lexically related to the source of all poetic creation, "the foul rag-and-bone shop of the heart." (In contrast, Yeats's other "circus animals," Oisin and the Countess Cathleen, are quite dismissively treated.) Thinking of the father killing his son, Yeats offers a quasi-Aristotelian definition of the essence of tragic drama: "Character isolated by a deed / To engross the present and dominate memory"

(*VP,* 629–30). Yeats fuses the "character," Cuchulain, with his isolating "deed," the killing of Connla. It is ironic, then, that Yeats revives this ancient warrior only to deny that the Homeric Ireland he represents has a viable future. For Yeats, tragedy subsumes epic: the heroic code with its emphasis on war and violence as the constitutive elements of masculinity is seen to produce stultifying and inhumane consequences. War normally entails the premature death of sons rather than the appropriate or timely death of fathers. If Cuchulain is the Irish Achilles, who like his Greek counterpart deliberately chooses a brief life but a glorious one,[20] we should remember that Achilles in Hades rejects the heroic code, saying that he would rather be a living peasant than a dead hero.[21]

Yeats's obsession with the tragic motif of the father who destroys his only child is related to a larger mythical and literary matrix in which the struggle between the generations does not necessarily end in the defeat of youth. Greek cosmogony was founded on the father-son conflict, but on Olympus the outcome suggests that the younger generation will inevitably replace the old. Time, rather than war, is the enemy of the patriarch; as the seasons turn, winter must give way to spring. Jealous Uranos, first ruler of the Greek universe, imprisoned all his children in Tartarus; but the youngest, Cronos, assisted by his mother Gaia, eventually castrated and killed his father. Informed by an oracle that he would be supplanted in his turn,[22] Cronos took the more extreme precaution of eating his children as soon as they were born. But once more a mother chose her son over her husband: Cronos's wife Rhea saved her youngest, Zeus, who dethroned the patriarch. This repetitive infanticidal paradigm, in which the older man is always the aggressor but always defeated, reflects less the son's desires than the father's anxieties: his fear of age and impotence, his suspicion that his wife prefers his son to him, and his wish to stave off the encroachments of time.

Yeats's version of *Oedipus Rex* was successfully staged at the Abbey Theatre in 1926, but he had been wanting to produce the play in Dublin since 1903, partly as a political provocation: it had been banned in England by the censor, whose writ did not run in Ireland.[23] Through Freud's overwhelmingly influential reading of Sophocles, the myth of Oedipus has become familiar to twentieth- and twenty-first-century readers as the story of a man who unwittingly kills his father and marries his mother, thus doing what every young man supposedly desires to do.[24] Reading Laius as a human version of Uranos and Cronos, however, we can understand the myth differently: as the story of a father who, resisting the prediction that he must eventually yield power to his son, attempts to pervert the course of nature. Oedipus's parents are never told that he will marry his mother; the Oracle simply informs Laius "that he was doomed to die by the hand of his own child" (*VPl*, 828). When he exposes the baby, Laius is concerned with his own survival, not with the prevention of incest. Read without the Freudian screen, *Oedipus Rex* begins with the attempted parental sacrifice of an only son.[25]

Not until the adult Oedipus consults the Oracle about his identity is part two of the double curse revealed: "I should live in incest with my mother, and beget a brood that men would shudder to look upon" (*VPl*, 831). To avoid this curse he flees his adoptive family and runs straight into his fate, encountering at the place where three roads cross an ill-mannered elderly man. Both refuse to yield the right of way; but Laius strikes the first blow, and Oedipus unwittingly kills the father who had earlier tried to kill him. In terms of plot plausibility this paradigmatic encounter depends on ignorance and long separation, but its deep structure encodes a conflict of masculinities in which nature decrees that the son's power must inevitably eclipse the father's.

The motif of father-son combat extends far beyond ancient Ireland and Homeric Greece, and was a subject of debate among the earliest students of the new discipline of anthropology. In 1902 Alfred Nutt published a monograph by the Harvard professor Murray Anthony Potter: *Sohrab and Rustem: The Epic Theme of a Combat between Father and Son; A Study of Its Genesis and Use in Literature and Popular Tradition*. Citing examples from Europe, Asia, New Zealand, Polynesia, and America, Potter argues that the theme does not derive from a single source, but has emerged independently in many different times and cultures:

> The skeleton of the tale is as follows: A man departs from home, in war service, in search of adventure or for purposes of trade, leaving behind him a wife and a son, perhaps unborn, or already quite a lad.

He is absent for years. The boy grows up, and for some reason or other seeks his father, or the latter may finally return. In either case, the two meet and, through lack of recognition, fight.[26]

Potter claims that this motif "appears in its oldest form in the Indian Mahabharata, in the Greek story of Ulysses and Telegonus, in the Irish Cuchulainn Saga, in the Persian Shah Nameh, in the German Hildebrandslied, in the Russian Ilya ballads, and elsewhere."[27] According to him, the Sohrab and Rustem story from Ferdowsi's tenth-century Persian epic, the *Shahnameh,* contains the archetypal essentials of the story. Although Potter demonstrates that the father-son combat may have a happy ending if the recognition comes in time, most of his major examples end tragically, with the death of the son (an exception is Telegonus, the son of Circe, who kills his father Ulysses and marries Penelope). In the third part of *Henry VI* Shakespeare combines both tragic outcomes in an allegorical scene that emblematizes the horror of civil war, bringing on stage a son who has killed his father and a father who has killed his only son. Schematic though the parallels may be, this scene deploys patterned repetition to striking poetic and dramatic effect, especially when the father realizes his fatal mistake: "But let me see: is this our foeman's face? / Ah, no, no, no, it is mine only son!" As in most of these stories, the father who has unthinkingly adhered to the masculine imperatives of war ends by renouncing violence, but his renunciation comes too late:

> These arms of mine shall be thy winding-sheet;
> My heart, sweet boy, shall be thy sepulchre,
> For from my heart thine image ne'er shall go;
> My sighing breast shall be thy funeral bell;
> And so obsequious will thy father be,
> Even for the loss of thee, having no more,
> As Priam was for all his valiant sons.
> I'll bear thee hence; and let them fight that will,
> For I have murdered where I should not kill.[28]

Potter's anthropological reading of his numerous texts (he argues that the story has its basis in the primitive customs of societies that are transitioning from matriarchy to patriarchy)[29] is less convincing than the sheer number of his examples, the widely separated cultures from which they come, and the fact that in the majority of them the son who is killed is the only child of either his father or his mother. The only child has always attracted considerable imaginative and cultural attention, perhaps because of the aesthetic and affective power of what is unique. A single child satisfies the narrative desire for isolated heroes, tragic victims, and strongly marked personalities, and there is no one to dilute the extremes of joy and grief he generates, in birth as in death. Shakespeare gives his most moving lament to the father who has killed his only son, and not to the son who has killed his father.

Potter does not comment on this aspect of his evidence, perhaps because the structure of the trope as he defines it (the father leaves a pregnant wife or a very young son) will almost always entail just one offspring. Nor does Potter discuss the Bible, in which the parallel stories of Isaac and Jesus also present the near-death or death of the only son at the hands of his father but lack the element of misrecognition that he deems so essential. Yet these two closely related examples of child sacrifice bring the Judeo-Christian religious tradition into partial alignment with Potter's Indian, Asian, Australasian, and Native American legends about the combat between the generations. In Genesis Isaac's position as the sole inheritor of the Jewish "nation" inspires one of the most disturbing narratives of the Old Testament. God decides to test Abraham's obedience by ordering him to kill the legitimate son for whom he had waited so long: "And he said, Take now thy son, thine only son Isaac, whom thou lovest, and get thee into the land of Moriah; and offer him there for a burnt offering."[30] Abraham does not question or complain, and Isaac functions simply as a unique and precious object, most appropriate for a sacrifice. Countless painters were fascinated by the charged moment when Abraham lifts the knife and the angel intervenes: "And he said, Lay not thine hand upon the lad, neither do thou any thing unto him: for now I know that thou fearest God, seeing thou hast not withheld thy son, thine only son from me."[31] Most modern readers shudder both at God's idea of the ultimate ethical test and at Abraham's willingness to pass it; moreover, feminists wonder why Sarah never got a vote.[32] For some readers, the emotional power of the narrative depends on the fact that, for Sarah, the longed-for child of her old age is irreplaceable.

The story of Isaac exemplifies the conflict between the father's patriarchal desire to establish his lineage or found a nation, and his unconscious jealousy of the young male who will inevitably supersede him.[33] While his Old Testament prototype is saved in the nick of time, Jesus, the New Testament Isaac, dies in agony on the cross. His father's act is represented not as a barbaric ritual sacrifice but as a generous redemptive offering: "For God so loved the world, that he gave his only begotten Son, that whosoever believeth in him should not perish, but have everlasting life."[34] God, omniscient as well as omnipotent, offers the resurrection of his only son as a pledge of immortality, and cannot be imagined as grieving for a death that was always intended to be temporary. Jesus's human mother is left to bear the burden of bereavement and grief: her swoon at the foot of the cross is a common motif in sculpture and painting. Roman Catholics who are invested in the perpetual virginity of Mary reject the Protestant doctrine that Jesus had brothers and sisters as an error of Biblical translation, and pre-Reformation Christian artists accepted the "only" story, not necessarily on theological grounds, but because it is so aesthetically and affectively powerful. The pietà, Mary cradling the dead body of her only child, evokes unalloyed Christian maternal pathos, intensified by the knowledge that the bereaved woman has no other children.

Fathers who slay their only sons in hand-to-hand combat constitute a reverse-Oedipus subset of the mythical contest between the generations. In the cosmological or vegetation myth, terms that were coming into use at the turn of the century, after the publication of Sir James Frazer's The Golden Bough (1890), we might interpret this motif as the symbolic defeat of spring by winter: something that is never supposed to happen. On a human level the story is profoundly unnatural; children should bury their parents, not the other way around, and such extreme reversals increase narrative interest and poignancy. Yeats was familiar with (and critical of) Matthew Arnold's 1853 poem "Sohrab and Rustum," which retells the episode from Ferdowsi's epic, the Shahnameh, which Murray Potter identifies as the perfect exemplar of the motif. It seems almost too obvious to point out that Arnold's conflicts with his famously overbearing father, Thomas Arnold of Rugby, may have intensified his interest in Ferdowsi, or that Yeats's intense and troubled relationship with John B. Yeats may have led him to rework the mythical paradigm offered by the *Shahnameh* and the story of Cuchulain.[35]

Arnold is quite faithful to Ferdowsi's story. In "Sohrab and Rustum" the charismatic Persian warrior Rustum impregnates a foreign princess, gives her a token to pass on to their child, and disappears from her life. Rejecting the heroic code of masculinity, and fearing that Rustum may return to transform his child into a warrior like himself, she writes to him that the baby is a "puny girl."[36] In fact Sohrab is a beautiful, brave, and talented boy, who soon sets out in quest of his father. When they meet in single combat Rustum is fighting incognito and does not know that he has a son. Sohrab intuitively pleads for his friendship, but the boy's superior skill in battle and gracious sparing of his life enrages the older man, who suddenly roars out, "Rustum." Sohrab lets down his guard, and is run through by his adversary's spear: killed, if you like, by the name of the father. The phallic imagery attached to Rustum is unmistakable (he is described as "Sole, like some single tower"[37]) and his abuse of Sohrab is derogatively gendered: "'Girl! nimble with thy feet, not with thy hands! / Curl'd minion, dancer, coiner of sweet words!'"[38] As Sohrab lies dying, Rustum, still ignorant that he has killed his only son, is nevertheless moved to pity: he

> saw that youth,
> Of age and looks to be his own dear son,
> Piteous and lovely, lying on the sand,
> Like some rich hyacinth, which by the scythe
> Of an unskilful gardener has been cut,
> Mowing the garden grass-plots near its bed,
> And lies, a fragrant tower of purple bloom,
> On the mown, dying grass—so Sohrab lay,
> Lovely in death, upon the common sand.[39]

Arnold's epic simile exploits the natural pathos of wilting flowers, but additionally develops the homoerotic implications of Rustum's previous insult, "minion," by alluding to the passion of Apollo for the androgynous boy Hyacinth, whom he killed by mistake and regenerated in the "purple bloom." Despite his valor, Sohrab's youthful grace and beauty are coded as effeminacy. Yeats disparaged the style of Arnold's poem: he called it "a classical imitation and not an organic thing, not the flow of flesh under the impulse of passionate thought."[40] Nevertheless, this moment of sexualized pathos, as Sohrab's "fragrant tower of purple bloom" is toppled, and his father's mature masculinity triumphs, suggests both that Arnold could manage the classical epic simile better than Yeats allows, and that Yeats's stated objections to "Sohrab and Rustum" may be cloaking an unacknowledged personal investment in the theme of the overbearing father figure and the feminized son. After the tragic *anagnorisis* the wounded boy has to prevent his distraught father from killing himself; and when Sohrab is at the point of death, Rustum explicitly curses the heroic code and the "life of blood" that has led him to destroy his only child. Like Achilles, he sees fame for the empty thing it is, and would prefer the humdrum existence of "a common man" to the military glory he has hitherto enjoyed:

> What should I do with slaying any more?
> For would that all whom I have ever slain
> Might be once more alive; my bitterest foes
> And they who were called champions in their time,
> And through whose death I won that fame I have—
> And I were nothing but a common man,
> A poor, mean soldier, and without renown,
> So thou mightest live too, my Son, my Son![41]

The heroic code of "blood and battles" has been the foundation of Rustum's masculine identity. Now his recognition that masculinity itself has entailed the loss of his child causes the precipitous collapse of his phallic similes:

As those black granite pillars, once high-reared
By Jemshid in Persepolis, to bear
His house, now 'mid their broken flights of steps
Lie prone, enormous, down the mountain side—
So in the sand lay Rustum by his son.[42]

For all his scorn of classical imitation Yeats clearly had "Sohrab and Rustum" and the question of masculinity at the forefront of his mind when he wrote "The Death of Cuchulain" in 1892 and *On Baile's Strand* in 1903.

"The Death of Cuchulain" first appeared in Parnell's weekly paper, *United Ireland*. During 1891–92, Yeats published sixteen articles in this venue, as well as two poems, one of which was his elegy for Parnell, "Mourn—and then Onward," which appeared on October 10, 1891 (*VP*, 737–38). "The Death of Cuchulain" appeared on June 11, 1892, on the same page as an advertisement for a booklet containing the "Words of the Dead Chief."[43] Yeats famously thought that the fall of Parnell had created a political vacuum, and began "to bid for that forsaken leadership"[44] through his literary-political activities, including strategic appearances in Parnell's old publication.[45] "The Death of Cuchulain" advertises Yeats's Celtic Revivalist wares as blatantly as the adjacent column advertises Pure Coffee and Clerical Hats. Yeats's proprietary brand is a vision of Ireland derived from the heroic sagas, mediated through the prose of Standish James O'Grady, the poetry of Sir Samuel Ferguson, and the folklore collections of the American scholar Jeremiah Curtin. His vision is crafted to bear out his claim that "there is no nationality without literature, no literature without nationality."[46] Despite Yeats's recognition of the cost exacted by the male heroic code, "The Death of Cuchulain" represents a more masculine aspect of the Celticization project than the fairy poems he later excluded from his canon.[47] Even then he must have suspected that the little people were unlikely to move his culture away from the "buffoonery and easy sentiment"[48] that he deplored in the Stage Irish version of the national character. Fairies and "easy sentiment" go only too well together. In reworking the saga material Yeats was challenging Arnold's characterization of the Celt as feminine, unreliable, and

"Sentimental,—*always ready to react against the despotism of fact.*"[49] Reviewing Sir Samuel Ferguson's poetry he claimed that

> In these poems and the legends they contain lies the refutation of the calumnies of England and those amongst us who are false to their country. We are often told that we are men of infirm will and lavish lips, planning one thing and doing another, seeking this to-day and that tomorrow. But a widely different story do these legends tell. The mind of the Celt loves to linger on images of persistance [*sic*]; implacable hate, implacable love, on Conor and Dierdre, and Setanta [Cuchulain] watching by the door of Cullan. . . . [Celtic legend appeals to] those young men clustered here and there throughout our land, whom the emotion of Patriotism has lifted into that world of selfless passion in which heroic deeds are possible and heroic poetry credible.[50]

The courage and persistence of the young Setanta, who got his name, Cuchulain, the Hound of Cullan, when he volunteered himself as a substitute for the giant watchdog he had killed, offers a potent model to young men who have decided to oppose English rule. Yet it is a model not of military effectiveness or success, but of intensity sustained in the face of defeat. "This faithfulness to things tragic and bitter, to thoughts that wear one's life out and scatter one's joy, the Celt has above all others. Those who have it, alone are worthy of great causes. Those who have it not, have in them some vein of hopeless levity, the harlequins of the earth."[51] No Stage Irish buffoons need apply. Connecting aesthetics, politics, and poetry, Yeats insists that, "All the great poems of the world have their foundations fixed in agony."[52] In constructing his own aesthetics of agony, Yeats can imagine nothing more "tragic and bitter" than the sacrifice of an only son at his father's hand. As Sohrab says to Rustum, "Fierce man, bethink thee, for an only son! / What will that grief, what will that vengeance be?"[53]

The placement of "The Death of Cuchulain" in *United Ireland* brings Parnell into imaginative alignment with Cuchulain. This ostensibly counterintuitive juxtaposition of the fallen Anglo-Irish politician with the doomed Celtic hero was no mere accident of publication. Yeats told Joseph Holloway in 1905 that "he had Charles Stewart Parnell in his mind when he wrote *On Baile's Strand*. 'People who do aught for Ireland,' he said, 'ever and always have to fight with the waves in the end.'"[54] Presumably he was thinking not primarily of the father-son combat but of dull King Conchubar's attempt to tame the sexually wayward hero by making him swear allegiance to the bourgeois domestic hearthstone rather than to the wild witches of the air or to his former mistress, the warrior queen Aoife. Yeats's political moral is that if Conchubar had left Cuchulain to his own sexual devices, and permitted him to welcome his son, and if the Irish Party had not rejected Parnell because of his affair with Mrs. O'Shea, both ancient and modern Ireland would have been better served.

Yeats's association of Parnell with Cuchulain was not a passing *aperçu;* it persisted over time. He reemphasized the connection in the introduction to his 1929 Cuchulain play, *Fighting the Waves,* by quoting a stanza from his own poem, "Parnell's Funeral" (*VPl,* 568). Parnell, a solitary, tragic, and sacrificial figure, is contrasted with "the Great Comedian" (*VP,* 541) Daniel O'Connell, and other unsatisfactory Irish politicians from all sides of the political spectrum: Eamon de Valera, W. T. Cosgrave, and the Blueshirt Eoin O'Duffy:

> Their school a crowd, his master solitude;
> Through Jonathan Swift's dark grove he passed, and there
> Plucked bitter wisdom that enriched his blood.
>
> (*VP,* 543)

Parnell's "bitter wisdom" connects lexically with Cuchulain's "bitter tide" and the "tragic and bitter" mode of Yeats's early Celticism. "Bitter wisdom" involves a clear-eyed acceptance of the worst, including the betrayal of the solitary hero by his own sexually timid and conventional people.

When Yeats composed "The Death of Cuchulain" in 1892 he had not yet met Lady Gregory, and she had not yet published her version of the Ulster Cycle, *Cuchulain of Muirthemne* (1902). Although

Standish O'Grady recounts most of the Cuchulain stories, he deliberately omits the killing of Connla, because it conflicts with his idea that the hero died too early to have a son with whom he could plausibly have fought: "The greatest of the Irish heroes died young, yet there is extant a celebrated tale in which he is represented as contending in single combat with his own son."[55] In O'Grady's *History of Ireland: The Heroic Period*, Cuchulain has two small children, Conla and Finscota, who are both still alive at the time of his death on the plain at Muirthemne. Neither Yeats nor Gregory was able to access the marvelous free-standing bardic tale *Aided Óenfhir Aífe* (*The Death of Aoife's Only Son*), which dates from the ninth or tenth century[56] and was transcribed at the end of the fourteenth century in the *Yellow Book of Lecan*, because Kuno Meyer's translation of this story did not appear in the journal *Ériu* until 1904. (In *Aided Óenfhir Aífe* Connla is indeed only seven, but nevertheless trounces several Red Branch heroes, and would have beaten his father but for Cuchulain's magic spear, the *gae bolga*). So Yeats derived "The Death of Cuchulain" from a folk rather than a saga source: "My poem is founded on a West of Ireland legend given by Curtin in 'Myths and Folklore of Ireland,'" he wrote in a footnote.[57]

In Jeremiah Curtin's "Cucúlin," Conlán is Cuchulain's only son by his abandoned mistress, the Virago of Alba (Alba is Scotland, the homeland of Queen Aoife, and though Curtin never gives the Virago a proper name, she is certainly a version of Aoife). She is furious to learn that Cuchulain has married, and in her jealous rage sends Conlán to find him, putting him under oath "not to yield to any man . . . nor tell your name to any man till you fight him out."[58] She is condemning her son to almost certain death, since she knows that only Cuchulain is similarly bound. The role of the woman in the son-slaying triangle varies considerably (in "Sohrab and Rustum" it is minimal), but in Curtin the mother is the villain of the piece:

> Conlán knew by the description his mother had given that Cucúlin was his father, but Cucúlin did not know his son. Every time Conlán aimed his spear he threw it so as to strike the ground in front of Cucúlin's toe, but Cucúlin aimed straight at him.

They were at one another three days and three nights. The son always sparing the father, the father never sparing the son.[59]

As in "Sohrab and Rustum," the prowess of the son is equal or superior to the prowess of the father. In the natural cycle of life, a strong young man will eventually prevail, but both Sohrab and Conlán are reluctant to press their advantage. However, like Sohrab, Conlán is momentarily distracted and lets down his guard:

Cucúlin's spear went through his head that minute, and he fell. "I die of that blow from my father," said he.
"Are you my son?" said Cucúlin.
"I am," said Conlán.
Cucúlin took his sword and cut the head off him sooner than leave him in the punishment and pain he was in. . . .
"Go now," said Conan, "and bind him to go down to Bale strand and give seven days' fighting against the waves of the sea, rather than kill us all."[60]

Conan's assessment of the intensity of a father's agony is correct: Cucúlin has destroyed his sole genetic link to the future, and his homicidal rage threatens the whole community. Only the bitter tide can withstand his passion.[61]

When he went to Bale strand Cucúlin found a great white stone. He grasped his sword in his right hand and cried out: "If I had the head of the woman who sent her son into peril of death at my hand, I'd split it as I split this stone," and he made four quarters of the stone. Then he strove with the waves seven days and nights till he fell from hunger and weakness, and the waves went over him.[62]

Curtin's Cucúlin blames the Virago of Alba, who has sacrificed their only son in order to revenge herself on a man she has not seen for eighteen years.

Yet, in his first version of "The Death of Cuchulain" Yeats transfers the Virago's sexual jealousy and reckless gamble with her child's

life to Emer, Cuchulain's deserted wife. This substitution of charac-
ters, which occurs in no other version of the story, ancient or modern,
has caused critics a minor interpretative headache. A. N. Jeffares sug-
gests that the name Emer is simply a mistake: he assumes that Yeats
must have meant Aoife, Cuchulain's warrior mistress from Scotland.[63]
Certainly Aoife is the mother of Connla in *On Baile's Strand* and in all
Yeats's later references to the story. But in 1892 Yeats already knew
from Standish O'Grady that Cuchulain's wife was called Emer. More-
over, since "The Death of Cuchulain" appeared in Yeats's best-selling
volume *Poems* (1895), which was reprinted fifteen times during his
lifetime, this inveterate reviser had ample opportunity to correct the
mistake, if mistake it was. Why did he use and always retain Emer,
even after he had written subsequent works that contradicted the
names he had used in his early poem?

First, the poem's plot structure would not have permitted the met-
rically possible substitution of one disyllabic name for another. Cuchu-
lain is coming home from the wars, not paying a belated return visit
to his mistress. Second, the replacement of a cast-off lover by a jealous
wife allows Yeats to pursue a Greek analogy. As we have seen, Yeats
continually promoted the Irish legends as equal to the Greek, credit-
ing this insight to O'Grady, who, "his mind full of Homer, retold the
story of Cuchulain that he might bring back an heroic ideal" (*VPl*,
567). But Yeats also knew that the fragmentary and contradictory
state of the surviving versions was problematic: "Instead of the well-
made poems we might have had, there remains but a wild anarchy of
legends. . . . [A]nd here and there some great hero like Cuchullin,
some epic needing only deliberate craft to be scarce less than Homer."[64]
Using his own "deliberate craft" he worked on the problem in mini-
ature, rhetorically transforming Curtin's folk version of the Cuchulain
story into a classical scenario that is closer to Greek tragedy than to
heroic epic. "When Lady Gregory wrote her 'Folk History Plays' and
I my plays in verse, we thought them like Greek plays," he claims, and
the same may be said of this early poem (*VP*, 572). His use of Emer
instead of Aoife or Curtin's Virago, and his insertion of a new young
mistress into the story, allows him to construct a subtle allusion to
Aeschylus's family drama *Agamemnon,* itself a work haunted by the
father's sacrifice of his daughter Iphigenia.[65]

Like Agamemnon, Cuchulain has been away at war for many years, and Yeats's poem opens, as does Aeschylus's play, with the words of a lookout who has been posted on the sea-cliffs to warn of his master's return. The faithful swineherd interrupts Cuchulain's wife Emer at her domestic activity, "dyeing cloth with subtle care." In his 1925 revision, Yeats changed this line to the more forcefully alliterative, rhythmic, and lexically strange "raddling raiment in her dun." Concomitantly, "stretching out her arms, red with the dye" becomes "raising arms all raddled with the dye." Emer's punishment of the swineherd for bringing the unwelcome news of Cuchulain's new mistress is direct, personal, and colorful—instead of delegating his beating to her servants she "smote with raddled fist" (*VP*, 105–6). Raddle is the red ochre smeared on the underbelly of a ram so that the shepherd can see which of the ewes have been tupped; in its agricultural context it has strongly sexual connotations. It also suggests the "raddled" face of an old or careworn woman, which hints at the age differential between Emer, mother of a teenage son, and Cuchulain's new young mistress. Another meaning of raddle is "to weave," and a raddle is the part of the loom that keeps the warp threads separate.[66] Although it is unlikely that Emer is literally both dying and weaving the same cloth, "raddle" connects lexically with the weaver's word "web," used twice to describe her fabric: "Emer cast the web upon the floor," and the terrified swineherd subsequently falls "upon the web-heaped floor" (*VP*, 105–6). The word "raddle" is thus doing a lot of associative work, and its penumbra of meanings suggests that, in revising the poem, Yeats was concerned to strengthen his allusion to Aeschylus.

Most obviously the "raddle" foreshadows the blood that will be spilt as a result of the swineherd's news, and Emer's raddled arms mark her as the origin of that bloodshed. In the *Agamemnon*, when Clytemnestra reenters the scene after murdering both her husband and his young mistress Cassandra, her forehead is smeared with their blood. More subtly, Emer's raddled "web" evokes both the ill-omened red carpet upon which Clytemnestra persuades Agamemnon to tread as he enters the palace and the deadly net in which she entangles him after he does so. The allusion is far from exact (Clytemnestra uses her lover, not her son, to help her get revenge) because Yeats crosses the

Agamemnon with *Oedipus Rex,* the classical locus of the fight between a father and a son who do not recognize each other. Yeats alludes to the situation of the *Oresteia* to add classical weight and order to his retelling of Irish myth, to strengthen his political claims for his own native culture, and to distinguish it from that of England: "Greek literature was founded on a folk belief differing but little from that of Ireland; . . . Roman, like English literature, was founded upon the written word" (*VPl,* 573). But whereas the *Oresteia* concludes with the ending of the curse on the House of Atreus and Athena's establishment of civil law rather than blood vendetta, the story of Cuchulain and Connla cannot be made into a hopeful or rational model for a future Irish polity.[67] In mood and outcome it is ultimately closer to the pessimism of *Oedipus Rex* than to the positive conclusion of the *Oresteia.*

Emer sends her only son out to kill her husband without hesitation or regret. The boy is impatient with life on the farm and eager to prove himself in battle, and Emer thinks he is invincible, possessing "the heaviest arm under the sky," though he reminds her, ironically, that his father Cuchulain is still alive. After a little verbal sparring about the relative strength and merits of her son and husband, Emer has the last word, and the boy yields to her direction: "I only ask what way my journey lies, / For He who made you bitter made you wise." So Yeats's recurrent epithet "bitter" belongs initially to Emer, who hatches a plot that will force the two men in her life to destroy each other. She binds her son to

> tell alone your name and house to him
> Whose blade compels and bid them send you one
> Who has a like vow.
>
> (*VP,* 108) (1892)

She knows that only Cuchulain is similarly bound. The *geis,* or bond of honor, one of the most striking and puzzling aspects of the Irish heroic code, frequently leads to disaster. Philip O'Leary explains the social structures within which these strange taboos must be understood:

Early Irish literature depicts a heroic warrior society for which honor was a virtually absolute value, providing a universally accepted and shared standard of ideals and behavior and serving as a profound emotional force for social cohesion. Definition and interpretation of this standard was traditional, external and public, directed and imposed by society, with shame and disgrace the major sanctions and acknowledged honour and posthumous glory the ultimate rewards. These rewards had, moreover, to be earned and maintained through almost ceaseless aggressive competition.[68]

O'Leary does not say so, but this code, which strongly resembles the Greek culture of honor and shame, is the distilled essence of martial masculinity. The *gessi* that bind both Cuchulain and Connla (never to step aside for anyone on the road, never to give their names except at sword point, and never to refuse single combat) absolutely ensure that they will be involved in "ceaseless aggressive competition." Not yielding the right of way, of course, undid Laius and Oedipus. Joan Radner points out, however, that "time and again in the Ulster tales warriors find themselves unable to function without violating sacred bonds," and adduces Cuchulain's slaying of his son and his foster brother Ferdia as the disastrous consequences of his *gessi*.[69] For her, the whole Ulster Cycle presents "a picture of society moving to dysfunction and self-destruction."[70] Radner ascribes the representation of the Ulstermen as "heroic but doomed" to their enemies, the O'Neills, who were the ones that wrote down the stories.[71] But we hardly need her ingenious theory to explain why this epic construction of masculinity is doomed: its destruction is guaranteed by its self-consuming foundational codes.

When Connla reaches the Red Branch camp, Ulster's warriors are feasting Cuchulain's return, and the High King Conchubar is singing his praises. The mistress he has brought back from the war is completely starstruck: his

> young sweetheart . . .
> Stared on the mournful wonder of his eyes,
> Even as Spring upon the ancient skies.
>
> (*VP*, 108)

Yeats's Cuchulain, in defiance of the better-known legends, is represented as well past middle age, and he has forgotten the passionate and devious nature of the wife who has been waiting so long for his return. He walks into her trap (her net, or perhaps her "web") when he asks the identity of the young man who has been hunting and singing near the camp, and summons him out of the forest into battle. Ironically, the young man reminds him of her: "Your head a while seemed like a woman's head / That I loved once" (*VP*, 110).

In contrast with the long fight in "Sohrab and Rustum," in which Sohrab is potentially the victor, with *Aided Óenfhir Aífe*, in which Cuchulain's seven-year-old son can only be defeated by a magic weapon, and with Yeats's immediate source, Jeremiah Curtin, in which the son is always "sparing the father," the outcome of this brief skirmish is never in doubt: the father is the greater warrior. Yeats knows that as the only son of the solar god Lugh and a mortal woman, Cuchulain is half divine. Connla is only a quarter divine, and therefore cannot match his father's supernatural "war-rage": "And through that new blade's guard the old blade broke" (*VP*, 110). So the young man must reveal his identity as he gives up his life. Here Yeats did make a significant mistake in nomenclature: in 1892 he called Cucuhlain's son "Finmole," and when he revised the poem in 1925, he heightened the psychodrama (though not the accuracy) by calling the son after his father in a rhetorically striking chiasmus: "Cuchulain I, mighty Cuchulain's son" (*VP*, 110). In killing his namesake, Cuchulain has symbolically killed himself. A parent who loses one of several children does not cease to be a parent: his identity as a father remains intact. A parent who loses an only child also loses a foundational dimension of his identity.

After recognizing each other, Arnold's Sohrab and Rustum have a long and emotional conversation, but in Yeats's sparer aesthetics of agony, Cuchulain never tells his son who he is, so there is no reconciliation, no Celtic sentiment, no Arnoldian pastoral turn after the tragic tale is done. Cuchulain simply puts the young man out of his misery and falls into a catatonic trance, which gives Conchubar and the druids time to get organized. In the spirit of kill or be killed, they send him against the only adversary he cannot match, the sea:

In three days' time he stood up with a moan,
And he went down to the long sands alone,
For four days warred he with the bitter tide,
And the waves flowed above him and he died.

(VP, 111) (1892)

When Yeats published "The Death of Cuchulain" in his 1892 volume, *The Countess Kathleen and Various Legends and Lyrics*, the frontispiece was a woodcut of Cuchulain fighting the waves. This visual cue gives the poem star billing and draws our attention to the "heroic" aspect of the volume. Yeats was initially certain that death is the only possible end of this contest. Without his only son Cuchulain now has no future, literal, genetic, or symbolic.

Ten years later, however, Lady Gregory collated oral tradition, Keating's *History of Ireland*, Charlotte Brooke's *Reliques*, and Curtin's folk story to create *Cuchulain of Muirthemne* (1902), a book that Yeats called "the best that has come out of Ireland in my time."[72] Gregory's version of the story, like Standish O'Grady's, directly contradicts the end of Yeats's poem: "Then he fought with the waves three days and three nights, till he fell from hunger and weakness, so that some men said he got his death there. But it was not there he got his death, but on the plain of Muirthemne."[73] Yeats let the original ending of "The Death of Cuchulain" stand until 1925, when he retroactively brought his conclusion into line both with Gregory's version and with his own 1919 play, *The Only Jealousy of Emer*, a sequel to *On Baile's Strand* in which Emer heroically renounces Cuchulain's love in order to bring him back from death by drowning. He changed the poem's title from "The Death of Cuchulain" to "Cuchulain's Fight with the Sea," and left the outcome open:

Cuchulain stirred,
Stared on the horses of the sea, and heard
The cars of battle and his own name cried;
And fought with the invulnerable tide.

(VP, 111)

The end of the 1903 version of *On Baile's Strand* is similarly open: "There, he is down! He is up again! He is going out into the deep water," cries the Fool (*VPl*, 524). In the 1906 and all subsequent printings of the play the Fool repeats four times that "the waves have mastered him," but Cuchulain is not pronounced dead (*VPl*, 524–25).

Yeats chose *On Baile's Strand* as the opening production of the Abbey Theatre in December 1904. It was paired, significantly, with a revival of *Kathleen ni Houlihan,* another play in which a son is sacrificed, although the hero Michael offers his life to a female avatar of his country, while his father would prefer him to remain safely at home. One play directly urges the young men in the audience to die for Ireland; the other re-creates a heroic past through which a national community worthy of their sacrifice might be forged. In *On Baile's Strand,* Yeats developed his protagonist's character more fully, seeking as always to intensify the tragic aesthetics of agony. His earlier Cuchulain is the victim of Emer's plot and his own blind adherence to the heroic code; his brief intimation of the resemblance between Emer and the young man is Yeats's only concession to pathos. Cuchulain's agony is unexpressed, and must be inferred from his three days of silence and stillness. But in the play, as in classical Greek tragedy, Cuchulain's *hamartia* is more obviously connected to his own character:

> I have also to make the refusal of the sons affection tragic by suggesting in Cuchullains character a shadow of something a little proud, barren & restless as if out of shere strength of heart or from accident he had put affection away. . . . He is a little hard, & leaves the people about him a little repelled—perhaps this young mans affection is what he had most need of. Without this thought the play had not any deep tragedy.[74]

Yeats was approaching forty when he wrote the play, and his roller-coaster relationship with Maud Gonne had left him without any prospect of a family of his own. First she insisted that they undertake a platonic spiritual marriage, then in 1903 she tried a real marriage with John MacBride, and when this speedily broke up she demanded Yeats's constant help and attention during her extremely sticky divorce. Yeats began *On Baile's Strand* in 1901, published the first version at the Cuala Press in 1903, revised it for the Abbey opening in December 1904, and published a very different version in *Poems, 1899–1905* in 1906. The development of the play therefore counterpointed a particularly stressful time in his affective life, in which the problems of Maud Gonne's marriage and children, both legitimate (Sean MacBride) and out-of-wedlock (Iseult Gonne) were at the forefront of his attention. Later he wrote frankly about the genetic rather than the emotional cost of his relationship with Gonne:

> *Pardon that for a barren passion's sake,*
> *Although I have come close on forty-nine,*
> *I have no child, I have nothing but a book,*
> *Nothing but that to prove your blood and mine.*
> (*VP*, 270)

The word "barren" connects his earlier description of Cuchulain with his later description of himself, and in the 1903 version of *On Baile's Strand* he meditates on the paradoxical relationship between desire and barrenness.

Haunted by his brief, violent relationship with the warrior queen Aoife (an avatar for Gonne), Cuchulain sees sexual passion as antithetical to procreation:

> I think that a fierce woman's better, a woman
> That breaks away when you have thought her won.
> For I'd be fed and hungry at one time.
> I think that all deep passion is but a kiss
> In the mid battle, and a difficult peace
> 'Twixt oil and water, candles and dark night.
> (*VPl*, 478)

Yet he is uncharacteristically wistful about the power of children to create permanence in marriage and restrain a wandering heart:

Cuchullain: [To one of the young Kings beside him.]
　　　　　　　　　One is content awhile
With a soft warm woman who folds up our lives
In silky network. Then, one knows not why,
But one's away after a flinty heart.
The Young King: How long can the net keep us?
Cuchullain:　　　　　　　　All our lives
If there are children, and a dozen moons
If there are none, because a growing child
Has so much need of watching it can make
A passion that's as changeable as the sea
Change till it holds the wide earth to its heart.
At least I have heard a father say it, but I
Being childless do not know it.
　　　　　　　　　　　　　　(*VPl*, 486, 488)

Shortly after this unusual exchange about fatherhood, as Conchubar tries to interest him in architectural drawings, Cuchulain is distractedly "looking in his shield" and "imagining a woman that I loved" (*VPl*, 494, 496). These words prepare the entry of the Young Man, who has come over the sea in a boat with a woman's face on its prow, and is carrying "*a shield with a woman's head painted on it*" (*VPl*, 498). Under the sign of Amazonic femininity Connla announces himself as a member of Aoife's army come to challenge Cuchulain. The rhyming shields suggest a phantasmal "only son" triangle: two men linked by the image of a woman, mistress to the first and mother to the second. In the 1903 version of the play there is no possibility of misreading this image, because the Blind Man has already given the Fool a full synopsis of the backstory, including character and motive. The Young Man is Cuchulain's only son by Aoife, "and now she hates him because he went away, and has sent the son to kill the father. . . . And she never told him who his father was, that he might do it" (*VPl*, 466). In the 1906 version the Blind Man knows who the young man's father is but, Tiresias-like, won't tell the Fool; as in *Oedipus Rex*, however, the audience is never deceived.

Yeats omitted this touching discussion of children, fatherhood, and fidelity in the extensively revised 1906 version of the play, replacing it with a harsher eugenic argument about authority and inheritance. Although in the early years of the century Yeats's interest in eugenics was not as passionate or as strident as it would later become, the unnatural temporal logic of a story in which the son is weaker than his father fits the popular eugenic narrative of racial degeneration that was becoming so widespread at the turn of the century. Because Conchubar wants to leave "a strong and settled country to my children" (*VPl*, 479), and Cuchulain's unfixed and reckless existence, "like a bird's flight from tree to tree" (*VPl*, 493), makes those (weakling) children nervous, he demands that Cuchulain take an oath of allegiance, declare his fidelity to home and hearth, and renounce the life of the hawk who sails upon the wind. When the Blind Man parodies the High King's demand, he uses Cuchulain's failure to reproduce as evidence that he lacks masculine authority: "Take the oath, Cuchulain. . . . What are your riches compared with mine? And what sons have you to pay your debts and to put a stone over you when you die? Take the oath, I tell you" (*VPl*, 463, 465). Cuchulain initially resists this bourgeois prospect, but even his young followers want him to comply because, as he sarcastically points out, marriage and children have made them conservative and "biddable" (*VPl*, 483). Marriage hardly seems to have affected Cuchulain himself, who never mentions his barren and absent wife Emer. Instead, he insults Conchubar's offspring as degenerates who exemplify the regression towards the mean:

> I do not like your children—they have no pith,
> No marrow in their bones, and will lie soft
> Where you and I lie hard.
>
>   (*VPl*, 481)

He thinks that they should "Re-mortar their inheritance, as we have, / And put more muscle on" (*VPl*, 507). Conchubar does not contest this disparaging estimate of his heirs, but turns the argument another way:

> You rail at them
> Because you have no children of your own.
>
> *(VPl*, 481,483)

Cuchulain responds to this thrust by escalating his "proud" and "re-pellent" rhetoric:[75] he asserts that he is glad he has no son because he too would be a degenerate, a botched replica of himself, a "pallid ghost or mockery of a man" (*VPl*, 483), "one that marred me in the copying" (*VPl*, 485). But Conchubar insists that Cuchulain's "hard-ness" (these adjectives come from Yeats's own analysis of Cuchulain, quoted above) is merely a defensive screen:

> I know you to the bone,
> I have heard you cry, aye, in your very sleep,
> 'I have no son', and with such bitterness
> That I have gone upon my knees and prayed
> That it might be amended.
>
> *(VPl*, 483)

This emphasis on Cuchulain's "bitter" longing for a child intensifies the dramatic irony, since the audience knows or guesses that he does have a son, who has already arrived in Ireland to challenge him. Iro-nies accumulate when he claims that he

> would leave
> My house and name to none that would not face
> Even myself in battle.
>
> *(VPl*, 485)

He defiantly celebrates Ireland's enemy Aoife, the antithesis of do-mesticity and bourgeois motherhood, whom Conchubar denigrates as a "fierce woman of the camp." Aoife alone, Cuchulain somewhat belatedly declares, was eugenically sound: "No other had all beauty, queen or lover, / Or was so fitted to give birth to kings." Conchubar, who has observed Cuchulain in unguarded moments, remembers that after a few drinks he used to say that "you'd sooner that fierce woman of the camp / Bore you a son" than any other queen (*VPl*, 487). So

Yeats takes care to establish that the Young Man who will shortly make his dramatic entry is as near to perfection as any son Cuchulain could have desired, and the child he will destroy is the only child whom he could certainly have loved. Eugenic theories about botched copies, although they may provide convenient rationalizations for a man who has no children, offer a false consolation.

In the oath to which Cuchulain reluctantly subscribes at the behest of Conchubar, the witches who represent "the will of woman at its wildest," the Shape Changers whom "none can kiss and thrive," are driven out and replaced by allegiance to domesticity, to "the threshold and the hearthstone" (*VPl*, 495). Aoife, the "fierce woman of the camp," is replaced by Conchubar, who creates a homosocial bond between himself and Cuchulain: "We are one being, as these flames are one," he asserts. When Cuchulain swears to "be obedient in all things / To Conchubar, and to uphold his children" (*VPl*, 499), he might be a bride swearing to love, honor, and obey her husband.

This male bond is cemented just as the Young Man, the androgynous reincarnation of Aoife, makes his appearance to test it. Cuchulain trembles on the brink of recognition, noting the boy's resemblance to his mother, admiring his courage—"He has got her fierceness, / And nobody is as fierce as those pale women" (*VPl*, 505)—and offering him friendship instead of combat. He thus threatens to violate all of his *gessi* at once. The Young Man reciprocates his instinctive affection, concerned only that his mother will think him a coward if he does not fight. Aoife, the Amazonic woman, subscribes to the masculine culture of honor and shame, which she has passed on to her son. But, in an unwittingly dynastic gesture, Cuchulain threatens to break this code when he spontaneously offers his unknown son the cloak of his grandfather, the god Lugh:

> My father gave me this.
> He came to try me, rising up at dawn
> Out of the cold dark of the rich sea.
> He challenged me to battle, but before
> My sword had touched his sword, told me his name,
> Gave me this cloak, and vanished.
>
> (*VPl*, 508)

Lugh saluted Cuchulain's willingness to fight in accordance with his *geis* but did not pursue the combat because, as a god, he would necessarily have killed his only son. Cuchulain also understands that "if I had a son /And fought with him, I should be deadly to him" (*VPl*, 511). In passing on his father's gift, Cuchulain is on the brink of validating his son's masculinity and establishing his dynasty without violence: to confirm their affection he will refuse the challenge, break the *geis*, and abandon the heroic code. Most significantly of all, he will permit Aiofe to think that he, and not his son, is a superstitious coward: "tell her that I heard a raven croak / On the north side of the house, and was afraid" (*VPl*, 508). This surrender of his masculine honor is so uncharacteristic, and so antithetical to the culture of shame that obtains throughout the Ulster Cycle, that Conchubar assumes Cuchulain has been possessed by the female Shape Changers. Piling on the dramatic irony, however, Cuchulain insists that the androgynous Young Man has simply reawakened an old love: "His head is like a woman's head / I had a fancy for."[76] For a brief utopian moment (the phrase is Jill Dolan's),[77] the gender breakdown of Ulster's foremost hero promises to establish Cuchulain and his only son in a noncompetitive, non-Oedipal friendship, united against the world. "Boy, I would meet them all in arms / If I'd a son like you," says Cuchulain, and the Young Man reciprocates, "We'll stand by one another from this out" (*VPl*, 510). Patriarchy is momentarily threatened by partnership as the hard, proud, barren, and repellant Cuchulain finds his arrogant theories about eugenic degeneration refuted by the presence of a worthy successor. Perhaps, to repeat Yeats's words, "this young mans affection is what he had most need of. Without this thought the play had not any deep tragedy."

The jealous Conchubar, however, understands the threat to male homosocial authority, and to the construction of heroic masculinity premised on the *geis*, that is posed by their refusal to fight: "I will not have this friendship. / Cuchulain is *my man*, and I forbid it" (*VPl*, 511; italics mine). In defense of the Young Man Cuchulain lays hands on the High King, a serious breach of protocol that leads Conchubar to cry out, "Witchcraft" (*VPl*, 512). This fatal accusation implies that

Cuchulain, who has previously consorted with the Shape Changers, is now possessed by the anarchic spirit of femininity, and it finally succeeds in turning the father against his thoroughly bewildered son. Cuchulain obeys his *geis*, resumes the abandoned challenge, and picks up the narrative thread of the male myth, which had briefly threatened to turn out differently. Apparently the heroic code of "blood and battles," the culture of shame, is stronger than individual affection or a father's need for a beloved son and heir. Of course, in Yeats's version, Cuchulain does not realize that the Young Man is his child. In the starker ancient text, *Aided Óenfhir Aífe* (which Yeats and Gregory originally did not know and later may have chosen to ignore), both Cuchulain and his wife Emer are aware of Connla's identity, but over Emer's passionate objections Cuchulain kills his only son deliberately, for the honor of Ulster.

Yeats's dramatic irony, necessarily absent from *Aided Óenfhir Aífe*, is only made possible by the ignorance of Cuchulain and all the other characters except the Blind Man. Three women attendants misinterpret the omens:

> *First Woman:*   I have seen Cuchulain's roof-tree
> Leap into fire, and the walls split and blacken.
> *Second Woman:* Cuchulain has gone out to die
>
> . . . .
>
> Who could have thought that one so great as he
> Should meet his end at this unnoted sword!
>
> (*VPl*, 514)

The second woman incorrectly interprets the burning roof-tree to mean that the Young Man will win the fight; she does not understand that by killing the young challenger Cuchulain will destroy not his literal but his dynastic "house"—his sole lineal descendant. Cuchulain has indeed gone out to die because he will destroy his only son. When he returns, wiping his child's blood off his sword, a series of Oedipus-like questions and answers with the reluctant Blind Man and the garrulous Fool gradually reveals the dead boy's identity:

Fool: It is Cuchulain who is trembling. It is Cuchulain who is shaking the bench.

Blind Man: It is his own son he has slain.

(*VPl*, 522)

Cuchulain as the man who deliberately kills his seven-year-old only son for the honor of Ulster belongs to ancient heroic myth, in which the *geis* matters much more than the individual blood line or human affection; Cuchulain as the man who *almost doesn't* kill his only son belongs to modern tragedy, in which the obligations of heroic masculinity and humane paternity are recognized as competing but equally important codes. Yeats heightens the situational irony and the agony of loss by giving Cuchulain time, however brief, to love his unknown child and appreciate his worthiness. He increases the intensity by bringing the pair within a hair's breadth of recognition: the arm ring that Cuchulain twice requests from the boy in exchange for his cloak must be the identifying token that, in most versions of the story, Cuchulain left with Aoife. When the boy finally offers the ring, Cuchulain is preoccupied with the cloak and does not look at it. We might say that an accident of timing robs him of his only child, but his sudden change of heart when Conchubar cries "Witchcraft" implies a degree of personal responsibility. At that moment he has a choice between his paternal instinct and the homosocial culture of masculine honor, and he makes a tragic error. Cuchulain certainly blames the High King for the disaster, but in *On Baile's Strand* Yeats omits the druidic spell that, in the Curtin source and in his earlier poem, deflects the distraught father from Conchubar and turns him towards the sea. Spontaneously running to meet the "bitter tide," Cuchulain accepts his own responsibility and courts his own demise.

There are other models of the only child more subtle than this one, but none more painful. With the death of the child comes the symbolic death of the parent, whose affective investment in the future is cancelled. If the father himself kills his son, the trauma is doubled: in Yeats's aesthetics of agony no higher intensity is possible. As he kept vigil at Coole Park with the dying Lady Gregory,[78] who had lost her only son Robert in the Great War, he reflected that she was now the "last inheritor." Without a male heir to keep it going, Coole would soon be sold and dismantled. In "Coole Park and Ballylee, 1931," Yeats used stately *ottava rima* to elegize not only his now-childless old friend, but their joint ambition for a Greek-inflected Irish literature, derived from the oral tradition ("the book of the people"), that would emulate the achievement of Homer:

> We were the last romantics—chose for theme
> Traditional sanctity and loveliness;
> Whatever's written in what poets name
> The book of the people; whatever most can bless
> The mind of man or elevate a rhyme;
> But all is changed, that high horse riderless,
> Though mounted in that saddle Homer rode
> Where the swan drifts upon a darkening flood.
>
> (*VP*, 491–92)

Pegasus, the Greek symbol of poetic inspiration, lacks a guiding hand, Homer is gone, and, like the contemporary Irish nation, the solitary swan drifts helplessly on the "filthy modern tide" ("The Statues"). Pearse may have "summoned Cuchulain to his side"[79] in the Post Office, but the statue that commemorates that event recalls the dead Christ rather than the works of Phidias. In the modern Irish Free State, which by the 1930s was notorious for a repressive Catholic culture that endorsed both literary censorship and sexual prudery, neither Homer, Cuchulain, nor Lady Gregory will have an appropriate Irish heir. The unspeakable loss represented by the death of an only child stands as a synecdoche for what Yeats considered the larger cultural failure of post-Independence Ireland.

NOTES

I am grateful to my writing group, Margot Backus, Helen Burke, Susan Harris, Sarah McKibben, Paige Reynolds, and Mary Trotter, for extremely thorough critiques of an earlier draft of this essay; also to Charlotte Nunes, my exemplary research assistant. And thanks as usual to Alan Friedman, who has endured several versions of this work.

1. Terry Eagleton, *Heathcliff and the Great Hunger: Studies in Irish Culture* (London: Verso, 1995), 273–319.

2. Yeats began in the 1880s by collecting and publishing the fairy beliefs of what he called "the peasantry." In the 1890s, however, several collections of myths and hero tales, including Jeremiah Curtin's *Myths and Folklore of Ireland* (first published in 1890), made newly available in English a wealth of previously untranslated bardic literature. Mary Helen Thuente has documented Yeats's subsequent shift from folklore to mythology in *W. B. Yeats and Irish Folklore* (Dublin: Gill and Macmillan, 1980), 230–38.

3. Eagleton, *Heathcliff and the Great Hunger,* 281.

4. The Greek analogy was politically as well as aesthetically functional because of the longstanding mythological identification of England, the colonial oppressor, with the Trojans who founded the Roman Empire, and with Aeneas's grandson Brutus, who went on to establish London as Troynovant. For a more extended discussion of this analogy, see Elizabeth Cullingford, "British Romans and Irish Carthaginians: Anticolonial Metaphor in Heaney, Friel, and McGuinness," *PMLA* 111 (1996): 222–39.

5. I first suggested this line of argument in Elizabeth Cullingford, *Ireland's Others: Gender and Ethnicity in Irish Literature and Popular Culture* (Cork: Cork University Press, 2001), 231. Gerardine Meaney has developed it further in "The Sons of Cuchulainn: Violence, the Family, and the Irish Canon," *Eire/Ireland* 41 (2006): 242–50.

6. W. B. Yeats, *Autobiographies* (London: Macmillan, 1966), 189. For Yeats and Nietzsche's tragic vision, see Maeve Good, *W. B. Yeats and the Creation of a Tragic Universe* (Macmillan: London, 1987), 75–80.

7. Using a very different methodology from my own, Nicholas Miller has explored some of these questions in *Modernism, Ireland, and the Erotics of Memory* (Cambridge: Cambridge University Press, 2002). See his chapter "Fighting the Waves: Yeats, Cuchulain, and the Lethal Histories of 'Romantic Ireland,'" 127–52.

8. There are many spelling options for both Cuchulain and his son Connla. Except where I am quoting someone else, I will use these two.

9. "O'Grady was the first, and we read him in our teens" (Yeats, *Autobiographies,* 221).

10. W. B. Yeats, *The Variorum Edition of the Plays of W. B. Yeats,* ed. Russell K. Alspach (New York: Macmillan, 1969), 567. Hereafter cited parenthetically as *VPl.*

11. Alfred Nutt, *Cuchulainn, the Irish Achilles* (London: David Nutt, 1900), 35.

12. Ibid., 51.

13. Ibid., 3.

14. *Uncollected Prose by W. B. Yeats,* vol. 1, ed. John P. Frayne (New York: Columbia University Press, 1970), 92 (hereafter cited as *Uncollected Prose*).

15. James Joyce, *Ulysses*, ed. Hans Walter Gabler (New York: Vintage Books, 1986), 178.

16. On Yeats, romantic nationalism, and modernity, see Elizabeth Cullingford, *Yeats, Ireland and Fascism* (New York: New York University Press, 1981), 1–15. For a more recent and extended version of the argument, see Michael Valdez Moses, "The Rebirth of Tragedy: Yeats, Nietzsche, the Irish National Theatre and the Anti-Modern Cult of Cuchulain," *Modernism/ Modernity* 11 (2004): 562: "Yeats saw his efforts to assist in the rebirth of ancient tragedy as an essential part of a militant cultural and political program to free modern Ireland from imperial British rule. Yeats's literary midwifery aimed to establish a free and independent Irish nation that would offer a counterweight to the forces of (English or British imperial) modernity. Though nationalism itself might be said to be a distinctively modern ideology, Yeats hoped to cultivate an independent Irish nation on nominally premodern or non-modern grounds."

17. *Uncollected Prose*, 1:100n.

18. In Cullingford, *Yeats, Ireland and Fascism*, I briefly discussed the roles played by both Cuchulain and Christ in Yeats's political and literary relationship with Pearse (85–101). In "The Boys of St. Enda's: The Rhetoric of Redemption in Padraig Pearse's Social and Aesthetic Theaters," chap. 5 of *Ireland's National Theaters: Political Performance and the Origins of the Irish Dramatic Movement* (Syracuse: Syracuse University Press, 2001), 137–66, Mary Trotter has definitively addressed this subject; for Cuchulain, see especially 147–54. In "Excess of Love: Padraig Pearse and the Erotics of Sacrifice," chap. 3 of *Gender and Modern Irish Drama* (Bloomington: Indiana University Press, 2002), 123–66, Susan Cannon Harris directly tackles the question of Pearse's homosexuality; see especially 143–50. See also Miller, *Modernism, Ireland, and the Erotics of Memory*, 129–30.

19. W. B. Yeats, *The Variorum Edition of the Poems of W. B. Yeats*, ed. Peter Allt and Russell K. Alspach (New York: Macmillan, 1957), 843. Hereafter cited parenthetically as *VP*.

20. In book 9 of the *Iliad*, Achilles reports his mother's prophecy that if he stays to fight in Troy his life will be short but his glory everlasting; if he goes home, his life will be long but inglorious (Homer, *The Iliad*, trans. Robert Fagles [Harmondsworth: Penguin, 1990], 265). In the *Táin*, the boy Cuchulain overhears the druid Cathbad say "any stripling who on that day should for the first time assume arms and armor, the name of such an one forever would surpass those of all Ireland's youth's besides. His life, however, must be fleeting, short." Cuchulain immediately persuades Conchubar to let him take arms (Tom Peete Cross and Clark Harris Slover, eds., *Ancient Irish Tales* [Totowa, NJ: Barnes and Noble Books, 1969], 142–43).

21. "I'd rather slave on earth for another man— / some dirt poor tenant farmer who scrapes to keep alive— / than rule down here over all

the breathless dead" (Homer, *The Odyssey,* trans. Robert Fagles [Harmonds-worth: Penguin, 1996], 265).

22. Oracle given to Cronos: "You shall be knocked from power by a son" (Ovid, *Fasti,* ed. and trans. A. J. Boyle and R. D. Woodard [London: Penguin, 2000], 88).

23. *The Collected Letters of W. B. Yeats,* vol. 3, *1901–1904,* ed. John Kelly and Ronald Schuchard (Oxford: Clarendon Press, 1994), 329. See also 3:691n.

24. "It is the fate of all of us, perhaps, to direct our first sexual impulse towards our mother and our first hatred and our first murderous wish against our father" (Sigmund Freud, *The Interpretation of Dreams,* ed. and trans. James Strachey [New York: Basic Books, 1955], 262).

25. On child sacrifice in Anglo-Irish literature, see Margot Backus, *The Gothic Family Romance: Heterosexuality, Child Sacrifice, and the Anglo-Irish Colonial Order* (Durham: Duke University Press, 1999).

26. Murray Anthony Potter, *Sohrab and Rustem: The Epic Theme of a Combat between Father and Son; A Study of Its Genesis and Use in Literature and Popular Tradition* (London: David Nutt, 1902), 1.

27. Ibid., 3.

28. William Shakespeare, *3 Henry VI,* Act 2, Scene 5.

29. Like many early anthropologists Potter is a follower of Bachofen and espouses his now-discredited theories of matriarchy.

30. Gen. 22:2 (Authorized King James Version) (hereafter cited as AV).

31. Gen. 22:12 (AV).

32. See Carol Delaney, *Abraham on Trial: The Social Legacy of Biblical Myth* (Princeton: Princeton University Press, 1998).

33. For such a reading, see Leon Shaskolsky Sheleff, "Beyond the Oedipus Complex: A Perspective on the Myth and Reality of Generational Conflict," *Theory and Society* 3 (1976): 1–44.

34. John 3:16 (AV).

35. In the introduction to her early compilation, *The Cuchullin Saga in Irish Literature* (London: David Nutt, 1898), Eleanor Hull also points out the Sohrab and Rustem parallel (xxxi–xxxii).

36. Matthew Arnold, "Sohrab and Rustum," in *The Poetical Works of Matthew Arnold,* ed. C. B. Tinker and H. F. Lowry (New York: Oxford University Press, 1957), 79.

37. Ibid., 71.

38. Ibid., 74.

39. Ibid., 80.

40. W. B. Yeats, "Art and Ideas," in *Essays and Introductions* (London: Macmillan, 1969), 354. See also "The Poetry of Sir Samuel Ferguson—II," in *Uncollected Prose,* 92.

41. Arnold, "Sohrab and Rustum," 85.

42. Ibid., 86.

43. My thanks are due to the library at Boston College, which supplied me with an image of the page.

44. W. B. Yeats, *Memoirs,* ed. Denis Donoghue (London: Macmillan, 1972), 60.

45. He sometimes wrote for conservative papers too, but there is nothing in his early journalism like this concentrated set of submissions to one paper.

46. "The Publication of Irish Books," in *Uncollected Prose,* 224.

47. For a definitive discussion of Yeats's attempts to distance himself from the perceived femininity of "Celticism," see Marjorie Howes, *Yeats's Nations: Gender, Class, and Irishness* (Cambridge: Cambridge University Press, 1996), 16–43.

48. W. B. Yeats and Lady Gregory, "Manifesto for the Irish Literary Theatre," in Lady Gregory, *Our Irish Theatre* (Gerrards Cross: Colin Smythe, 1972), 20.

49. Matthew Arnold, "On the Study of Celtic Literature," in *The Complete Prose Works of Matthew Arnold,* ed. R. H. Super (Ann Arbor: University of Michigan Press, 1962), 344.

50. "The Poetry of Sir Samuel Ferguson—II," in *Uncollected Prose,* 104.

51. "The Poetry of Sir Samuel Ferguson—I," in *Uncollected Prose,* 87.

52. "Clarence Mangan (1803–1849)," in *Uncollected Prose,* 118.

53. Arnold, "Sohrab and Rustum," 78.

54. Joseph Holloway, *A Selection from His Unpublished Journal "Impressions of a Dublin Playgoer,"* ed. Robert Hogan and Michael J. O'Neill (Carbondale: Southern Illinois University Press, 1967), 58.

55. Standish James O'Grady, *History of Ireland: The Heroic Period* (London: Sampson Low, Searle, Marston, & Rivington, 1878), x.

56. Joanne Findon, *A Woman's Words: Emer and Female Speech in the Ulster Cycle* (Toronto: University of Toronto Press, 1997), 144–45.

57. In the same footnote Yeats also observed correctly, "The bardic tale of the death of Cuchullin is very different" (*VP,* 799). "The bardic tale" to which Yeats refers is not *The Death of Aoife's Only Son* but Cuchulain's last battle on the plain of Muirthemne, which he found in O'Grady and Ferguson, and later adapted in the play *The Death of Cuchulain.*

58. Jeremiah Curtin, *Myths and Folk-Lore of Ireland* (Boston: Little, Brown, and Company, 1911), 324. Curtin's tale of the death of Conlán is a brief postscript to a long story about Cucúlin's wooing and winning his wife, whom Curtin calls Gil an Og.

59. Ibid., 325.

60. Ibid., 325–26.

61. In the bardic version of the story, *The Death of Aoife's Only Son,* the motif of fighting the waves is absent: Cuchulain is warned by his wife Emer that the boy is his own child, but the honor of Ulster demands that he engage in the combat nevertheless. When he has mortally wounded his son he bitterly offers him to the other Red Branch warriors: "Here is my son for you, Men of Ulster," but does not attack either them or the waves. In recognition that this is also a story of maternal loss, all the cows of Ireland are separated from their calves for three days (Cross and Slover, *Ancient Irish Tales,* 172–75). Curtin's folktale is the only version that contains the image of the lone man in contest with the sea.

62. Curtin, *Myths and Folk-Lore of Ireland,* 326.

63. A. Norman Jeffares, *A New Commentary on the Poems of W. B. Yeats* (London: Macmillan, 1984), 26.

64. "Bardic Ireland," in *Uncollected Prose,* 165–66.

65. The mythical backstory of the *Oresteia* begins with the ritual sacrifice of a child: Tantalus, the founder of the house of Atreus, killed his own son Pelops and cooked him as a feast for the gods. Continuing the culinary project, Pelops's son Atreus murdered two of his brother Thyestes's sons, and served them to him in a stew. In the play itself, Clytemnestra's lover Aegisthus, one of Thyestes's surviving sons, helps to kill Agamemnon in revenge for his murdered elder brothers; with the same blow Clytemnestra avenges her daughter Iphigenia, sacrificed to Artemis by Agamemnon in return for a fair wind to Troy. Aeschylus's chorus evokes another gruesome gastronomic event when it compares the cries of Cassandra to the lament of the nightingale for her nephew Itys, who was killed by his mother Procne and served *en casserole* to his father Tereus.

66. *Oxford English Dictionary,* s.v. "raddle" (online version accessed June 15, 2011).

67. Many years later, in "Leda and the Swan," he returned more directly to the apocalyptic image of "Agamemnon dead" (*VP,* 441).

68. Philip O'Leary, "Honour-Bound: The Social Context of Early Irish Heroic *Geis,*" *Celtica* 20 (1988): 93. I am grateful to Sarah McKibben for her generous help with the old Irish materials of this paper.

69. Joan Radner, "Fury Destroys the World: Historical Strategy in Ireland's Ulster Epic," *Mankind Quarterly* 23 (1982): 48.

70. Ibid., 47.

71. Ibid., 46–47.

72. W. B. Yeats, "Preface," in Lady Gregory, *Cuchulain of Muirthemne* (Buckinghamshire: Colin Smythe, 1984), 11.

73. Lady Gregory, *Cuchulain of Muirthemne,* 241.

74. *The Collected Letters of W. B. Yeats,* 3:527.

75. For a discussion of the poetic consequences of Yeats's interest in eugenics, see Elizabeth Cullingford, *Gender and History in Yeats's Love Poetry*

(Cambridge: Cambridge University Press, 1993), 279–87. For *On Baile's Strand* specifically, see Paul Scott Stanfield, *Yeats and Politics in the 1930s* (Basingstoke: Macmillan, 1988), 145–49, and Donald J. Childs, *Modernism and Eugenics: Woolf, Eliot, Yeats, and the Culture of Degeneration* (Cambridge: Cambridge University Press, 2001), 186–89.

76. *VPl*, 508; for a brilliant analysis of gender in this play, to which I am much indebted, see Harris, *Gender and Modern Irish Drama*, 79–89.

77. Jill Dolan, *Utopia in Performance: Finding Hope at the Theatre* (Ann Arbor: University of Michigan Press, 2005), 5.

78. See R. F. Foster, "Yeats and the Death of Lady Gregory," *Irish University Review* 34 (2004): 109–21.

79. *VP*, 611. Yeats's late play *Purgatory*, which on its first production in 1938 shared a double-bill with *On Baile's Strand* (Christopher Murray, *Twentieth Century Irish Drama: Mirror Up to Nation* [Syracuse: Syracuse University Press, 2000], 32), repeats the killing of an only son by his father in a violently grotesque, actively anti-Romantic key. If *On Baile's Strand* evokes a Shakespearian empathy for the unwittingly filicidal parent, *Purgatory* replaces it with an alienating modernist aesthetics of revulsion. Yeats's horrible Old Man, son of an aristocratic lady and a drunken groom, has previously murdered his father; now, in a stylized, absurdist act of negative eugenics, he deliberately puts an end to his own hybrid and therefore polluted blood line: "My father and my son on the same jack-knife!" (*VPl*, 1048). Parodying its dramatic partner and forerunner *On Baile's Strand*, *Purgatory* presents the murder of an only child as a solution to the problem of Anglo-Irish degeneracy.

CHAPTER 3

The Dark Arts of the Critic
Yeats and William Carleton

JAMES H. MURPHY

Throughout his career W. B. Yeats operated on many different fronts, in varying combinations, at the same time: poet, dramatist, cultural activist, theatre director, critic, commentator, and even politician. In the early part of his career, the late 1880s to the mid 1890s, he was intent on establishing his standing as a man of letters in his own right and in becoming recognized as a leader in that still inchoate movement both in London and later in Dublin for the revival of Irish literature, particularly Irish literature in English. His own creative work would lead him to success in poetry and later on in drama. In this early period, however, both as a critic and a writer, a good deal of his interest was in fiction, which, in terms of the entire arc of his career, would in retrospect appear an anomaly. Much of his energy went into criticism of fiction, particularly of nineteenth-century Irish fiction, and into the compiling of anthologies, of fairy and folktales, and of

the work of established Irish fiction writers and poets.[1] He collabo-
rated on *Poems and Ballads of Young Ireland* (1888) and co-edited *The
Works of William Blake* (1893), whom he viewed as a sort of honorary
Celt. His interest in fairy and folklore led him to compile *Fairy and
Folk Tales of the Irish Peasantry* (1888) and *Irish Fairy Tales* (1892),
while *Stories from Carleton* (1889) and *Representative Irish Tales* (1891)
attested to his interest in nineteenth-century Irish fiction, and *A Book
of Irish Verse Selected from Modern Writers* (1895) in poetry.

In all of this Yeats was certainly positioning himself at a variety of
apparent literary endpoints in order to launch both himself and the
Irish literary movement into an as yet undetermined future. Perhaps
it might be better to refer to them as putative, or even constructed,
endpoints, designed to meet present needs. Yeats was ultimately more
concerned with teleology than any authentic etiology. He faced sev-
eral specific issues that blurred the distinction between personal career
advancement and the forwarding of the new Irish literary movement.
During these years Yeats struggled with various models of Irishness
on which a national literature might be based. The one closest to hand
was Celticism.[2] Discourse concerning this notion was of course domi-
nated by Matthew Arnold's ideas of the feminine Celt as the comple-
ment to the masculine Saxon. Yeats was drawn to ideas of Celtic
passion and excess but tried to refashion the Celt as masculine rather
than feminine by refocusing the notion through the prism of his own
vision of the heroic and primitive Irish peasant as fundamental to
thoughts on Irishness. The ennobling poverty of the Irish peasant
thus replaced the femininity of the Celt as a necessary condition for a
national literary ideal and one that conveniently validated the still
existing socioeconomic order of Anglo-Irish dominance—though,
paradoxically, a position of peasant economic dependence can itself
be gendered as feminine, no matter how rugged one's exterior. In spite
of this Yeats would later identify a modicum of economic prosperity
with an enervating feminization of proper masculine energies. Thus
in *Cathleen ni Houlihan* (1902), a play written with Lady Gregory, a
young man is summoned to stern nationalist self-sacrifice by an alle-
gorical figure of Ireland, from a situation in which he is being admired
for the style of his wedding clothes.

Then there were the perceived obstacles to literary advancement presented by the existing literary establishment. In a way rather conveniently, these were embodied for Yeats during these years in his conflicts with two individuals, Edward Dowden, professor of English at Trinity College, Dublin, and Sir Charles Gavan Duffy, who had returned from his antipodean exile to assume leadership of the literary revival, or rather, to reassume leadership of the agenda of the Young Ireland movement of the 1840s of which he had been such a prominent part. For Yeats, Duffy was a real obstacle in his attempts to gain control over the Irish revival. Duffy came, perhaps unfairly, to represent a philistine utilitarian nationalism that Yeats claimed was inimical to the emphasis on imagination needed for the literary revival. Yeats had to work hard at setting up the less combative Dowden as an opponent and representative of nonnationalist literary cosmopolitanism.

Finally, there was the problem of language and literature. Yeats was not proposing a new Irish literature in Gaelic but in English. If this was something new, then it had to be seen to be different, and, indeed, better, than the existing large body of Irish writing in English. As a literary critic Yeats set himself the task largely to disparage that literature while locating and praising individual writers from the past that seemed to him to embody those literary values that might form the basis for future revival. In poetry he did locate a group of poets who at least illustrated individual elements of the new literature Yeats was hoping for: Thomas Davis with his aspirations as a national poet; James Clarence Mangan as a writer whose suffering gave him authenticity; William Allingham with his emphasis on place; and Samuel Ferguson with his Celtic note.[3] About the only contemporary prose writer whom Yeats lauded was Standish O'Grady, "The only person who while belonging to the head class has the central fire of the old people is O'Grady. Everything he does is a new creation, a new miracle."[4]

As Yeats's remarks on O'Grady illustrate, what was required was not simply a new literary style, but a style that was authentically expressive of the lives of the peasantry, hence the importance for Yeats during these years of William Carleton (1794–1869), the so-called peasant novelist, who had made such an impact in Ireland and England during the second quarter of the nineteenth century. Carleton had grown up in a Catholic peasant community in Ulster and come to Dublin where he wrote stories for evangelical Protestant magazines before publishing acclaimed collections of short stories in the 1830s, a series of important novels in the 1840s, and a less highly thought of collection of novels in the 1850s and 1860s. The figure of Carleton thus brought together many of the strands that were preoccupying Yeats during these years. Through his criticism and anthologizing, Yeats constructed Carleton personally as an embodiment of the masculine Irish peasant and his writings as the exemplar of the resultant, authentic, though spontaneous, Irish style. Ironically, few of the characters in Carleton's work can be said to embody a rugged masculinity; many are grotesques. It would seem rather that, in setting forth Carleton as the masculine Irish peasant, Yeats was imaging a Carleton endowed with masculinity by the very bleakness of the settings in his novels. Carleton's masculinity was thus a deductive conclusion from Yeats's reading of his work.

According to Yeats, Carleton had "no conscious art at all," and lived "a half-blind, groping sort of life, drinking and borrowing,"[5] in a construction that was to echo through Yeats's later writing career down to the battering blind men of "A Dialogue of Self and Soul." Carleton thus became a weapon against Duffy, Dowden, and the majority of contemporary Irish writers, and a fillip to Yeats's own authority. Ironically, Carleton was far from the unspoiled peasant of Yeats's imagination. Recent criticism has portrayed him as a recycler of English literary conventions rather than as an authentic peasant voice, and he was himself a canny manipulator of critical discourse in a manner that Yeats might have found familiar and laudable, had he known about it.

Yeats's trouble with Duffy centered around the proposed "Library of Ireland," which Yeats hoped would be published by Fisher Unwin. The institutional context for the proposal was the Irish Literary Society in London, which was established in December 1891 with the participation of Duffy, having grown out of the Southwark Irish Literary Club, and which had its first meeting in May 1892. For Duffy the project was a taking up of the work of the Young Ireland movement of nearly fifty years before; for Yeats it was to be something new. With the help of T. W. Rolleston, Duffy gained control over the project, though it was a pyrrhic victory, as the resulting series of volumes was not a success. In an intriguing footnote to the proceedings Yeats recalled that at one stage Duffy produced "an unpublished novel by William Carleton, into the middle of which he had dropped a hot coal, so that nothing remained but the borders of every page."[6] Though Carleton had briefly allied himself with Young Ireland, he was in Yeats's mind very much a separate force, and in Yeats's recollection of this incident there is a hint of a belief in the destructive effects of Young Ireland and of Duffy in particular on creativity.

By this time Yeats had already written of Carleton at length, most notably in the introductions to *Stories from Carleton* (1889) and *Representative Irish Tales* (1891), in which Carleton also featured. In the former, Yeats had written of Carleton as "a great Irish historian. The history of a nation is not in parliaments and battle-fields, but in what the people say to each other on fair-days and high days, and in how they farm, and quarrel, and go on pilgrimage. These things has Carleton recorded."[7] Carleton was not only a social historian; his work spoke of a peasant suffering that arose from closeness to a bleak nature. His novels had "a kind of clay-cold melancholy." Reading them was like "looking out at the wild, torn storm-clouds that lie in heaps at sundown along the western seas of Ireland; all nature, and not merely man's nature, seems to pour out for me its inbred fatalism."[8]

Yeats privately anticipated that many of the objections to the book would be on the grounds of Carleton's anti-Catholicism. The lines of his defense of Carleton were already apparent in a letter written to the influential Jesuit and editor of the *Irish Monthly*, Matthew Russell, in mid 1889. Yeats wrote that Carleton's "heart always remained Catholic, it seems to me."[9] In an anonymously published piece of October 1889 Yeats repeated the point and claimed that Carleton had written his most important novels "after his heart at any rate had returned to Catholicism."[10] Turning to one of Carleton's novels, Yeats asserted in a now familiar vein that "through all its mournfulness there runs a kind of unhuman fatalism that makes one think of barren moors at moonlight and leaden sunsets over sea."[11] He ended by claiming that "The great thing about Carleton was that he always remained a peasant, hating and loving with his class."[12]

The expected blow came in a review in the *Nation* on December 28, 1889, which called Carleton "envenomed" and a "renegade" and deserving of "the Literary Pillory." Yeats replied in a letter written on January 3, 1890, and published in the paper on January 11, pleading that Catholics could afford to be generous over Carleton. The people "will not forget this one great peasant writer of their country" who remained "full of all their passion, all their feelings," though many of Carleton's best works were by then out of print.[13] As Roy Foster has pointed out, Yeats's immersion in Carleton at this point influenced his use of dialogue and depiction of the peasantry in his ballads. More notably, perhaps, the controversy surrounding the book marked the first of many struggles with Irish public opinion.[14]

With the introduction to *Representative Irish Tales*, a collection of fictional extracts from nineteenth-century authors, only one of whom was still alive, Yeats had the opportunity to assess Carleton in the context of the work of other writers. The reason why the writers were from earlier generations was because, as he told Russell, "all these writers had a square built power no later Irishman or Irish woman has approached." Carleton, together with Banim, came at the top of the list as they saw "the brutal with the tender, the coarse with the refined," though Gerald Griffin and Charles Kickham were also good. Yeats was here trying to locate a distinctive Irish writing quality, as he went on to say that the Irish stories of his own day "sail the sea of common English fiction. . . . The Irish manner has gone out of them though." As Yeats characterizes this latter fiction as being intent on pleasantness, it is clear once more that he is locating the Irish style in a "fiery shorthand," in the grittiness of masculine peasant experience.[15]

In his introduction to the collection itself, Yeats, in part adopting an established critical note whose origins we shall explore later, was scathing in his views on some of Carleton's contemporaries, themselves included in the collection. There were two voices, "the accent of the gentry, and the less polished accent of the peasantry and those near them; a division roughly into the voice of those who lived lightly and gayly, and those who took man and his fortunes with much seriousness and even at times mournfully. The one has found its most typical embodiment in the tales and novels of [T. Crofton] Croker, [Samuel] Lover, and [Charles] Lever, and the other in the ruder but deeper work of Carleton, Kickham, and the two Banims." Again, there was a link between literary quality and social origins, the one being the expression of the other. "There is perhaps no other country in the world the style and nature of whose writers have been so completely governed by their birth and social standing."[16] No matter how hard they try, writers from a privileged background cannot write authentically of the peasantry. This line of thought is here pushed to such an extreme that Carleton is praised for having "no conscious art at all" and the achievements of his writing are put down to his supposedly "living a half-blind, groping sort of life, drinking and borrowing."[17] Yeats, however, did feel obliged to account for the generally accepted falling off in Carleton's work in the latter part of his career. This was, he argued, for one or more of a number of reasons: because Carleton had said all he had to say about the peasantry, because the audience for the work had diminished in the aftermath of the failure of the 1848 rebellion, or because of a wish "to please the more numerous and less intelligent of the class he had sprung from."[18]

Yeats's scorn was reserved for Lever and Lover. Their social class "has been almost entirely an evil."[19] "They had found the serious passions and convictions of the true peasant troublesome and longed for a servant who would make them laugh, a tenant who would always appear merry in his checkered rags."[20] The true peasant, on the other hand, was always awkward and troublesome. Returning to a favored telluric metaphor Yeats concluded that in their writing "I miss the deep earth song of the peasant's laughter."[21] Writing elsewhere around the same time Yeats presented Lever and Lover in a manner reminiscent of his attitude to the life of bourgeois Victorians in general and cosmopolitan littérateurs, such as Edward Dowden, in particular. "Lever and Lover, kept apart by opinion from the body of the nation, wrote ever with one eye on London. They never wrote for the people, and neither have they ever, therefore, in prose or verse, written faithfully of the people."[22]

Yeats's conflicts with Dowden clustered in the mid 1890s and took place within the context of a particular fashion for issuing lists of the supposedly best books that had been developing in Ireland during the 1880s. These lists were implicitly exercises in the prospective as well as the retrospective, both in canon formation and in pointing the way forward, as particular authors saw it, for the growing Irish literary movement. An early example from the *Freeman's Journal* of 1886 by R. Barry O'Brien, the historian of the liberal-nationalist alliance, was later published as a pamphlet. Tellingly, O'Brien wrote anonymously under the name "Historicus." In arguments not unlike those later deployed by Yeats, O'Brien wrote that the Irish fiction of the early nineteenth century was an historical source and that its worth depended to a degree on the closeness of the authors, certainly in terms of understanding and feeling, to the peasantry. "The insight of Irish character and society which Miss Edgeworth and her fellow workers in the regions of fiction give us must be regarded as a valuable aid to the acquisition of knowledge about Ireland or the Irish. . . . That she understood or felt the character of the Irish peasantry as thoroughly as did Griffin, Banim and above all Carleton may be doubted, but she certainly felt and understood it to a very great extent."[23] The Banims, Griffin, and Carleton, though, were certainly the most reliable authorities on Irish character, according to O'Brien. By the mid 1890s the Jesuit *New Ireland Review* was publishing its own list of best Irish books, in which three novels by Carleton figured in the first of three classes of fiction.[24] The trend was taken up in the anthologizing projects of the time, which included *The Cabinet of Irish Literature* (1879–80, 1902) and the ten-volume *Irish Literature* (1904).

Yeats himself entered the lists in early 1895, apparently picking a fight with Dowden and stoking up controversy, possibly as a means of drawing attention to his forthcoming *A Book of Irish Verse*.[25] In comments made after a public lecture early in January 1895 and reported in the newspapers, Dowden appeared to criticize the poetry not only of Samuel Ferguson, the subject of the lecture, but of Thomas Davis and James Clarence Mangan.[26] The incident caused quite a correspondence in the newspapers over the next few weeks. In a letter to Katharine Tynan written the same day as the newspaper report, Yeats seemed to agree with Dowden over poetry at any rate. "My own idea is that our verse is better than the old but that our prose—except in essays like bits of Hydes [*sic*] Love Songs—is far behind Carleton & Lover & Croker at their best." He went on to write of different authors being in different classes, in anticipation of a categorizing attempt of this own, and to regret that modern writers like Jane Barlow and Emily Lawless did not have "the central fire of the old people."[27] In spite of these apparent views on Irish verse, Yeats chose to take issue with Dowden in a number of letters published in the papers in the following weeks. His most substantial was published in the *Daily Express* on January 26. It was a scathing attack on Dowden's alleged lethargy concerning the promotion of Irish literature, which Yeats contrasts with the vigor of the movement of which he thought himself a leader:

> Professor Dowden has been for years our representative critic, and during that time he has done little for the reputation of Ferguson, whom he admires, and nothing for the reputation of these others, whom Ferguson admired. Our "movement," on the other hand, has only existed three or four years, and during that time it has denounced rhetoric with more passionate vehemence than he has ever done. It has exposed sentimentality and flaccid technique with more effect than has been possible to his imperfect knowledge of Irish literature, but, at the same time, it has persuaded Irish men and women to read what is excellent in past and present Irish literature, and it has added to that literature books of folk-lore, books of history, books of fiction, and books of verse, which, whatever their faults, are yet the expression of the same dominant mood, the same creative impulse which inspired Ferguson and the poets I have named.[28] Nor is it a self-conscious endeavour to make a literature, but the spontaneous expression of an impulse which has been gathering power for decades and which makes itself heard in the lull of our political tumults.[29]

All this led to the publication in the *Daily Express* on February 27 of Yeats's list of the thirty best Irish books. "During our recent controversy with Professor Dowden certain of my neighbours here in the West of Ireland[30] asked me what Irish books they should read." Yeats wrote that he had excluded books with "strong political feeling" and "included only books of imagination or books that seemed to me necessary to the understanding of the imagination of Ireland."[31] The first thirteen books on the list were "novels and romances," followed by nine in the category of "folk lore and bardic tales," three history books, and five books of poetry. The novels and romances were ranked in order, and works by Carleton ranked third, fourth, and fifth, after Edgeworth's *Castle Rackrent* and a story by Ferguson, presumably there to make a point after the recent controversy. It would have been hard to dislodge *Castle Rackrent* from the top of a list of the best Irish novels, so Carleton's position was a very prominent one, and Yeats went on to praise Carleton's *Fardorougha the Miser* in particular by commenting that "I do not think modern fiction has any more strange, passionate and melancholy creation than the old miser Fardarougha [*sic*]," though he also praised Banim's *The Nowlans* at the same time. Yeats's praise here for Carleton was strong and, indeed, surprising, given Carleton's then rather reduced reputation. Yeats was to use this paradox to develop a theory concerning Irish literature throughout various publications in 1895 that would put him in a position to be prescriptive concerning current trends in Irish literature. The sort of canon formation that the drawing up of lists of best books implied could thus be turned into an implement for the shaping of a future Irish literature. In this letter Yeats accounts for the paradox of novels of such high quality, or at least of such potentially high quality, as those of Carleton not being recognized as great literature as follows:

> These books can only have been prevented from taking their place as great literature because the literary tradition of Ireland was, when Carleton and Banim wrote, so undeveloped that a novelist, no matter how great his genius, found no fit convention ready to his hands, and no exacting public to forbid him to commingle noisy melodrama with his revelations.[32]

Remarkably, and in a line of argument that partly seemed superficially to contradict some of his earlier appraisals of Carleton, Yeats was here admitting that in some ways the novels of Carleton and the Banims were flawed works. They were written without the support structure of a sophisticated Irish literary tradition and readership. Whereas before Yeats had argued that Carleton was important because being himself a peasant he had captured something essential about Irish peasant experience that needed to be relished and celebrated, he was now arguing that Carleton, for all his flaws, was essential because he was the best Ireland, with its undeveloped literary tradition, had to offer. "England can afford to forget these books, but we cannot, for with all their imperfections they contain the most memorable records yet made of Irish habits and passions."[33] The controversy continued, with Dowden issuing his own list of best books, and several commentators worrying over whether political books should be included or not. At one point Dowden wrote, rather perceptively, that "Mr Yeats tilts at windmills."[34] Yeats was privately quite pleased with the controversy, telling John O'Leary that "it seems to me an excellent opportunity for getting a little information about Irish books into the heads of Dublin Unionists."[35] Dowden, however, did not really respond to the more sophisticated elements in Yeats's case, and when he rather cannily argued for Celtic, race, and Catholic criteria for Irish literature Yeats had to agree, perhaps fearing that not to do so would increase suspicions of him in various quarters. "Are not 'Fardarougha [*sic*] the Miser', 'The Nolans [*sic*]', and 'Castle Rackrent' informed with the inspiration of our 'racial tradition'?"[36] This letter has sometimes been seen as ironic, given Yeats's later identification with the eighteenth-century Ascendancy tradition, because in it Yeats appears to be critical of Dowden's inclusion in his list of works by Ussher, Swift, and Berkeley. In fact the criticism of them is really of Dowden's Celtic, race, and Catholic criteria and is thus a form of questioning of Dowden's sincerity concerning them.

Yeats returned to the more interesting arguments he had been incubating concerning Irish literature that same year in a series of four articles on "Irish National Literature" that included a list of best books and that appeared in the *Bookman,* then the leading British literary review.[37] Carleton figured prominently in the list of best books in part four, together with Yeats's own *A Book of Irish Verse,* though Yeats lamented the futility of such lists, given the lack of availability of some of the books on the list, itself a testament to low standards of taste among the reading public:

Carleton's great novel, *Fardorougha,* has but now gone to its second edition, and his scarce less impressive *Black Prophet* is still out of print, while his formless and unjust *Valentine McClutchy* and his feeble *Willy Reilly* have gone to numberless editions; for this zealous public loves vehement assertion better than quiet beauty and partisan caricature better than a revelation of reality and peace.[38]

Though peace was not a usual quality for Yeats to attribute to the work of Carleton, he went on to repeat the point he had made during the Dowden debate concerning the deleterious effects of the lack of a proper Irish literary tradition and receptive audience. The latter had "persuaded some of our best writers to immense stupidities, as when it set Carleton writing stories now against intemperance, now against landlords, and it has created out of itself, besides, some few of genius, a multitude of bad writers who fare better than the best."[39]

The first article, however, entitled "From Callanan to Carleton," was perhaps more important. Yeats began by announcing that he was only going to deal with Irish writers "who have written under Irish influence and of Irish subjects." When a country "has carried to maturity its literary tradition, its writers, no matter what they write of, carry its influence about with them."[40] Thus Carlyle was always a Scots writer, even when his subject was German kings. Ireland, Yeats argued, did not have a mature literary tradition. To reach prominence Irish writers, like Thomas Moore, had had to borrow English modes of writing. Yet there were other Irish writers who drew on either of the two available Irish traditions, the Gaelic and the peasant. The latter was that of "the customs of the poor, their wakes, their hedge-schools, their factions, their weddings, their habits of thought and feeling, and this could best be described in prose." This was the tradition of Edgeworth, the Banims, and, above all, of Carleton:

Only Carleton, born and bred a peasant, was able to give us a vast multitude of grotesque, pathetic, humorous persons, misers, pig-drivers, drunkards, schoolmasters, labourers, priests, madmen, and to fill them all with an abounding vitality. He was but half articulate, half emerged from Mother Earth, like one of Milton's lions, but his wild Celtic melancholy gives to whole pages of *Fardarougha* [*sic*] and of *The Black Prophet* an almost spiritual grandeur. The forms of life he described, like those described with so ebullient a merriment by his contemporary Lever, passed away with the great famine, but the substance which filled those forms is the substance of Irish life, and will flow into new forms which will resemble them as one wave of the sea resembles another. In future times men will recognise that he was at his best a true historian, the peasant Chaucer of a new tradition, and that at his worse he fell into melodrama, more from imperfect criticism than imperfect inspiration. In his time only a little of Irish history, Irish folk-lore, Irish poetry had been got into the English tongue; he had to dig the marble for his statue out of the mountain side with his own hands, and the statue shows not seldom the clumsy chiseling of the quarryman.[41]

In praising Carleton as Ireland's true historian Yeats was of course also denigrating Duffy and Young Ireland, as Roy Foster has suggested.[42] Most of the elements of Yeats's most sophisticated view and use of Carleton were here. Carleton is a peasant and without literary art. His work, both in terms of history and imaginative energy, is the authentic expression both of the Celtic and masculine peasant traditions. These are the traditions that need to be the criteria for a renewed Irish literature in Yeats's enervated present and for the establishment of an Irish literary tradition, the deleterious effects of the absence of which can also be seen in the crudities and deficiencies of Carleton's work. So powerful was Yeats's construction of Carleton as "the first significant native Irish writer of fiction in English" that this view of Carleton has persisted largely unchallenged down to the present.[43]

Carleton's disinterest in nationalism and his consequent nonportrayal of peasant leadership also suited Yeats, as Emer Nolan has noted, as it empowered the Anglo-Irish, here in the person of Yeats himself, with a continuing role in cultural leadership.[44] In several ways then Yeats's Carleton gave Yeats a prescriptive authority that he was not slow to use. In the second article in the series one of his victims was famously the novelist Emily Lawless, a poor choice in retrospect given her subsequent positive reputation.[45] Lawless was of course a novelist of peasant life, and Yeats, in spite of partial praise, is severe in his criticism, drawing on notions of authentic and defective tradition. "Despite her manifest sincerity and her agile intellect," she was "in imperfect sympathy with the Celtic nature." Her almost Leveresque "conception of Irish character as something charming, irresponsible, poetic, dreamy, untrustworthy, voluble, and rather despicable" had blighted her imagination and came "between her and any clear understanding of Irish tradition."[46] She thus had no real understanding of either the Celtic or peasant-experience criteria for authentic Irish literature.

With all of this Yeats was almost finished with Carleton. When he reviewed D. J. O'Donoghue's edition (and completion) of Carleton's autobiography in 1896, Yeats, largely ignoring the book itself, moved further still towards his refined version of Carleton, no longer just or even an exemplar of good Irish writing from the past, but a resource for Yeats's prescriptions concerning good Irish writing in the present. Carleton was "not an artist" but "the creator of a new imaginative world, the demiurge of a new tradition."[47] His work demonstrates how the "Gaelic race lives between two worlds, the world of its poverty, and a world of wild memories and of melancholy, beautiful imaginations."[48] O'Donoghue had his own ideas about the offense Carleton had given to the differing religious sides at various times during his career. Because he was short of money "he was forced to rely upon one party or the other and consequently wrote for either or both. He might, perhaps, have done this in a less fierce and partisan manner, but it was next to impossible for him to write moderately or calmly. His vigorous personality is in all he wrote."[49] But by then Carleton had served his purpose for Yeats. In 1898 his father was doing illustrations for a republished version of *The Black Prophet*,[50] and Yeats himself was courting Dowden as a guarantor of the Irish Literary Theatre.[51] By 1904 Yeats wrote in a copy of *Stories from Carleton* presented to John Quinn, "I had thought no end of Carleton in those days & would still I dare say if I had not forgotten him."[52] Nonetheless, Yeats's version of Carleton left its mark. Writing of Carleton in *The Cabinet of Irish Literature* (1902), Katharine Tynan commented that "the Irishman always witty, good humoured and blundering was almost annihilated by the stern realism of Carleton, who painted him as he too often is—sad, brooding and amid unhappy surroundings."[53]

As for Carleton himself,[54] he had been in agreement with the view Yeats was to take that he was an historian of the Irish people:

> I have become the historian of their habits and manners, their feelings, their prejudices, their superstitions, and their crimes; if I have attempted to delineate their moral, religious, and physical state, it was because I saw no other person willing to undertake a task which surely must be looked upon as an important one.[55]

Others had come to the same conclusion: even in the early part of Carleton's career it was widely accepted that he had insight into peasant life. H. R. Montgomery, who despised fiction of all kinds as trivial, nonetheless thought Carleton's stories of great importance. "They are powerful sketches of a portion of our population, whose very virtues had been long traduced and distorted into vices—written with the fidelity and discrimination of a moral historian, and in the spirit of a philanthropist and patriot."[56] But modern critics have not agreed. Helen O'Connell has recently argued that "Carleton's writing emanates from the written conventions of improvement discourse and does not provide an authentic representation of pre-Famine oral culture."[57] In this view Yeats's judgments concerning peasant and Gaelic authenticity both fall. "Carleton does not celebrate or preserve Irish-language oral culture in his stories and novels. Instead, his writing shows the extent to which that culture was already mediated by a range of discourses and conventions which effectively prevented any kind of authentic representation in writing."[58]

Nor did Carleton live his life in peasant authenticity. Indeed, for most of the time he lived a rather bourgeois existence in Dublin. Nor did he live a life of professional literary naiveté, as Yeats liked to imagine. He, like Yeats, used his personal authority, a considerable one in the case of the "peasant novelist," in his role as literary critic to excoriate his enemies. Multiple ironies exist, therefore, in Yeats's valorizing of Carleton as a guarantor of authenticity. Indeed, Yeats and Carleton had a lot in common as literary critics. Each was intent on manipulating the literary consensus in the way that best suited his own literary and professional agendas.

Carleton's principal target as a critic was Lever,[59] whom he unmercifully attacked in the pages of the *Nation* on two occasions in late September and early October 1843.[60] Ostensibly, the criticism was on cultural grounds and in terms of a literary patriotism. Lever "offers disgusting and debasing caricatures of Irish life, and feeling, as characteristic of our country."[61] But Carleton could not hide a less creditable element of professional jealousy of Lever, the popular and wealthy novelist and editor of the *Dublin University Magazine*. Lever "devotes his whole life and soul . . . to the unscrupulous acquisition of popularity." His work is "a libel upon his country—or an insult upon his people." He "is literally selling us for pounds, shillings, and pence, and, not unlike a common informer, is receiving good pay from England for bearing false evidence against his country." And, in a criticism that Yeats would take up, Carleton accused Lever of having no authentic knowledge of the peasantry. As a result Lever was forced, "from ignorance of their characters and virtues, to fall back upon the vile old travesties which are to be found, in the dramatic malice of our enemies."[62] In fact Lever had considerable knowledge of the peasantry, though he could not claim to be a peasant himself. He had worked as a doctor in County Clare during the cholera epidemic of 1832. Carleton by contrast had been cosseted in Dublin for decades. As one of Lever's biographers observed, "this article was written by Carleton, who lived in a glass house, but was not afraid to hurl stones at his brother novelist."[63] Nonetheless, Carleton's attacks did enormous damage to Lever, encouraging others to attack him and precipitating Lever's permanent departure from Ireland for the continent where he wrote his numerous, unpopular later novels, with their frequent threnodic note of exile.

The condemning contrast between the supposedly telluric Carleton and writers from privileged backgrounds who wrote about the peasantry in terms of humorous stereotypes was not confined to Yeats, but it, too, turns out to be a consequence of literary politics rather than cultural authenticity. The point is well put by Bayle Bernard, a biographer of Samuel Lover,[64] whose reputation for indulging in inane stereotypes, if anything, fared slightly worse than that of Lever:

> [Lover] saw them [the peasants] always as he saw them first, only on the sunny side of their nature, in all its gaiety, its tenderness, its humour, and simplicity. . . . Had it been his fate, *like some other writers* [emphasis added], to pass his days amongst the peasantry, and witness the wants and oppressions which have so often stirred their passions and overcast their history, he would doubtless have felt bound to show that these generous and affectionate but still fiery and impulsive beings had a tragic side to their character which was just as essential to its truth.[65]

The reference to other writers is obviously to one writer in particular, Carleton. The implication is that the somber, or melancholy to use Yeats's word, side of peasant experience was Carleton's province. Writers such as Lover and Lever may have written as they did, therefore, in part out of a reluctance to trespass on the territory of Carleton, the peasant novelist, perhaps out of fear of comparison with or attack by Carleton. All of this may also have given Lover's defenders pause. Lover's work is quite complex in its political and satirical dimension. But all Bernard lamely says of it is that his novels "had a purpose under their merriment, which bestows on them some dignity." This was "not to advocate the rights or paint the sufferings of the peasant," but "to renovate his character and to divest him of the vice and coarseness which had been so repugnant to English sympathy."[66]

The difference between Yeats and Carleton as critics during the periods we have been examining is that Yeats was an as yet unrecognized writer using criticism to build up his own reputation and influence within the literary movement of the 1890s. Carleton was an already acclaimed writer who used criticism to neutralize his potential rivals. Each used arguments concerning authenticity of representation that implicitly evoked notions of tradition. Carleton presented himself as the authentic historian of the Irish peasantry whereas modern criticism currently sees him rather harshly as the recycler of the tropes borrowed from English genres. Yeats's version of Carleton was inno-

cent of stylistic artifice or literary politics. He was the authentic mas-
culine and Celtic peasant, whose work, in its strengths, illustrated the
qualities that a revived Irish writing in Yeats's time required, and, in
its weaknesses, warned of the need for a guiding literary tradition,
which Yeats's prescriptive criticism would supply. In each case,
Carleton and Yeats were perhaps not so much the inheritors of tradi-
tions, happening to find themselves at their respective literary end-
points, so much as the deliberate inventors of traditions that they
hoped would be of use to them in the present and for the future.

NOTES

1. R. F. Foster, *W. B. Yeats: A Life*, vol. 1, *The Apprentice Mage* (Oxford:
Oxford University Press, 1997), 97–98.
2. Marjorie Howes, *Yeats's Nations: Gender, Class, and Irishness* (Cam-
bridge: Cambridge University Press, 1996), 16–43.
3. Terence Brown, *W. B. Yeats: A Critical Biography* (Dublin: Gill and
Macmillan, 1999), 65.
4. *The Collected Letters of W. B. Yeats*, vol. 1, *1865–1895*, ed. John Kelly
(Oxford: Clarendon, 1986), 425.
5. W. B. Yeats, *Representative Irish Tales* (Gerrards Cross: Colin
Smythe, 1979), 28.
6. W. B. Yeats, *Autobiographies* (London: Macmillan, 1955), 224;
quoted in Foster, *The Apprentice Mage*, 121.
7. W. B. Yeats, introduction to *Stories from Carleton*, in Yeats, *Represen-
tative Irish Tales*, 363.
8. Ibid., 363–64.
9. *Collected Letters of W. B. Yeats*, 1:174.
10. [W. B. Yeats], "William Carleton" [Review of *Stories from Carleton*
and *The Red-Haired Man's Wife*, *The Scots Observer*, October 19, 1889], in
W. B. Yeats, *Early Articles and Reviews*, ed. John P. Frayne and Madeleine
Marchaterre (New York: Scribner, 2004), 90.
11. Ibid., 91.
12. Ibid., 92.
13. *Collected Letters of W. B. Yeats*, 1:206–7.
14. Foster, *The Apprentice Mage*, 97–98.
15. *Collected Letters of W. B. Yeats*, 1:199.
16. Yeats, *Representative Irish Tales*, 25.
17. Ibid., 28.

18. Ibid., 29.

19. Ibid., 25.

20. Ibid., 26.

21. Ibid., 27.

22. "Popular Ballad Poetry of Ireland" [*The Leisure Hour,* November 1889], in Yeats, *Early Articles and Reviews,* 108.

23. Historicus [R. B. O'Brien], *The Best Hundred Irish Books Introductory and Closing Essays by Historicus and Letters from the Archbishop of Cashel . . .* (Dublin, 1886; reprinted from the *Freeman's Journal* [1886]), 9.

24. "The Best of Irish Books," *New Ireland Review* 3 (April 1895): 122–32.

25. Foster, *The Apprentice Mage,* 146.

26. *Uncollected Prose of W. B. Yeats,* vol. 1, *First Reviews and Articles, 1886–1896,* ed. John P. Frayne (New York: Columbia University Press, 1970), 346–47.

27. *Collected Letters of W. B. Yeats,* 1:424.

28. In the letter Yeats had mentioned J. J. Callanan, Edward Walsh, Thomas Davis, J. C. Mangan, Michael Doheny, William Allingham, and Aubrey de Vere.

29. *Uncollected Prose of W. B. Yeats,* 1:548.

30. Yeats was then living in Sligo.

31. *Collected Letters of W. B. Yeats,* 1:440.

32. Ibid., 1:442.

33. Ibid., 1:442.

34. *Uncollected Prose of W. B. Yeats,* 1:351.

35. *Collected Letters of W. B. Yeats,* 1:446.

36. *Uncollected Prose of W. B. Yeats,* 1:352.

37. The series of articles are reprinted in Yeats, *Early Articles and Reviews.* Page numbers refer to its location in the collected volume, while the month refers to the issue of the 1895 *Bookman* in which it originally appeared: "Irish National Literature, I: From Callanan to Carleton," (July), 263–67; "Irish National Literature, II: Contemporary Prose Writers—Mr O'Grady, Miss Lawless, Miss Barlow, Miss Hopper, and the Folk-Lorists," (August), 270–76; "Irish National Literature, III: Contemporary Irish Poet—Dr Hyde, Mr Rolleston, Mrs Hinkson, Miss Nora Hopper, AE, Mr Aubrey de Vere, Mr Todhunter, and Mr Lionel Johnson," (September), 280–87; "Irish National Literature, IV: A List of the Best Irish Books," (October), 288–92.

38. Yeats, "Irish National Literature, IV," 288.

39. Ibid., 289.

40. Yeats, "Irish National Literature, I," 264.

41. Ibid., 267.

42. Foster, *The Apprentice Mage*, 147.

43. Emer Nolan, *Catholic Emancipations: Irish Fiction from Thomas Moore to James Joyce* (Syracuse: Syracuse University Press, 2007), 97.

44. Ibid., 100.

45. James H. Murphy, *Irish Novelists and the Victorian Age* (Oxford: Oxford University Press, 2011), 157–59, 178–81, 211–13.

46. Yeats, "Irish National Literature, II," 272–73.

47. W. B. Yeats, "William Carleton" (review of D. J. O'Donoghue, ed., *The Life of William Carleton*, 2 vols. [London: Downey, 1896] in the *Bookman* [March 1896]), in Yeats, *Early Articles and Reviews*, 298.

48. Ibid., 300.

49. *The Life of William Carleton: Being His Autobiography and Letters; And an Account of His Life and Writings, from the Point at which the Autobiography Breaks Off*, by David J. O'Donoghue, 2 vols. (London: Downey, 1896), 2:57.

50. *The Collected Letters of W. B. Yeats*, vol. 2, *1896–1900*, ed. Warwick Gould, John Kelly, and Deirdre Toomey (Oxford: Clarendon, 1997), 122–23.

51. Ibid., 2:428.

52. Yeats, *Early Articles and Reviews*, 89.

53. Charles A. Read and Katharine Tynan Hinkson, eds., *The Cabinet of Irish Literature*, 3 vols. (London: Gresham, 1902), 3:310.

54. Murphy, *Irish Novelists*, 45–65.

55. *The Life of William Carleton*, 2:361.

56. [H. R. Montgomery,] *An Essay towards Investigating the Causes that have Retarded the Progress of Literature in Ireland* (Belfast: Phillips, 1840), 71.

57. Helen O'Connell, *Ireland and the Fiction of Improvement* (Oxford: Oxford University Press, 2006), 18.

58. Ibid., 126.

59. Murphy, *Irish Novelists*, 71–91.

60. Ibid., 63–65.

61. William Carleton, "John Banim," *Nation*, September 23, 1843, 794–95, at 794.

62. William Carleton, "The 'Dublin University Magazine' and Mr Lever," *Nation*, October 7, 1843, 826–27, at 826.

63. Edmund Downey, *Charles Lever: His Life and His Letters*, 2 vols. (Edinburgh: Blackwood, 1906), 1:184.

64. Murphy, *Irish Novelists*, 65–69.

65. Bayle Bernard, *The Life of Samuel Lover, R.H.A., Artistic, Literary, and Musical, with Selections from his Unpublished Papers and Correspondence*, 2 vols. (London: Henry S. King, 1874), 1:14.

66. Ibid., 1:201.

CHAPTER 4

Nation for Art's Sake
Aestheticist Afterwords in Yeats's Irish Revival

JOSEPH VALENTE

For understandable reasons, scholars in Irish Studies have been disinclined to credit aestheticism and its counterpart, decadence, with significant generative impact upon the Irish Literary Revival, despite the fact that the moving spirit and chief architect of that Revival, W.B. Yeats—the man who founded its major institutions, furnished the bulk of its poetic, dramatic, and critical material, recruited much of its talent, and proved its most effective international promoter—concurrently apprenticed himself to and affiliated himself with leading aestheticist and decadent figures, including Hallam, Pater, Wilde, Villiers de l'Isle Adam, Verlaine, Johnson, Dowson, and Symons. The contradictions that obtain between the official agendas or received profiles of the two movements, "seem [to leave] little possibility," as Stephen Regan has observed, "of any collaboration between these distinctive tendencies."[1] But inasmuch as Yeats was almost instinctively dialectical in his every intellectual proceeding, we must develop a critical framework that accounts for how those very contradictions could animate, rather than forestall, his incorporation of aestheticism into, *as the very form of,* his revivalism.[2] More specifically, in order to see more clearly the importance of aestheticism to Yeats's brand of revivalism, it is necessary to cultivate a double historical vision, to look past the official agenda and profiles while continuing to pay them due regard, to discern (a) how the received profile of aestheticism factored into Yeats's appropriation of its philosophical perspective and representational strategies and (b) how that appropriation in turn helped to redefine or redirect the agenda of Yeats's revivalism, to mold it, in effect, as an "afterword" of aestheticism.

By the time the Irish Literary Revival had begun, aestheticism had already come to stand for a hermetic vision of the arts, most famously articulated in Pater's "Conclusion" to *Studies in the History of the Renaissance* and extended in Wilde's *Intentions*. Both men assigned aesthetic expression the role of enhancing, multiplying, and intensifying the fugitive moments of sensuous impression as they register upon the "narrow chamber of the individual mind."[3] In keeping with this introspective and even introversive orientation, aestheticism assumed a radically anti-instrumentalist posture, dedicated to establishing art as a truly autonomous domain, pared of any external purpose: social, political, moral, or scientific. Swinburne offered an explicit statement of the program, subsequently to be identified with Pater's later use of the shibboleth "art for art's sake" in his "Conclusion":

> Handmaid of religion, exponent of duty, servant of fact, pioneer of morality [art] cannot in any way become; she would be none of these things though you were to bray her in a mortar. All the battering in the world will never hammer her into fitness for such an office as that. It is at her peril, if she tries to do good.[4]

Oscar Wilde looked to expand this closed, self-regarding dynamic from the artwork and the experience thereof to the tradition writ large: "Art never expresses anything but itself. This is the principle of my new aesthetics. It has an independent life, and develops precisely along its own lines."[5]

Aestheticism, then, can be, has been, seen to bring a radically individualistic and a strongly autotelic conception of the aesthetic function into mutually reinforcing alignment. As an avowed specimen of cultural nationalism, the Irish Literary Revival was held to navigate an opposed course, to synchronize a collectivist model of aesthetic inspiration with a strongly instrumentalist notion of aesthetic functionality. Native forms of literary expression were to be enlisted directly in the service of national, which is to say, political objectives, typically cast as moral imperatives. Hovering somewhere between authorial design and audience expectation, this dual mandate of the Revival finds a perfect encapsulation in the event of Yeats's 1893 lecture, "Nationality and Literature," which aimed to relaunch the literary movement in the wake of Douglas Hyde's recent and celebrated Gaelic League address, "The Necessity of De-Anglicizing Ireland."[6] At the culmination of a history of literary *form*, curiously modeled on Pater's program of the arts in "Winkelman," Yeats heralds a "new epoch" of organic Irish writing, drawn exclusively from "the unexhausted *material* lying within our national character, about us in our scenery and in the clearly marked outlines of our life, and in the multitude of our legends" (*NL*, 273, emphasis added). Ignoring Yeats's cultural survey of both past and future, the chief respondent, Rev. J. F. Hogan, congratulated the speaker on an entirely implicit, if not imaginary, political message: "When Hungary was making a struggle for National independence, similar to that which [we] were making in Ireland, they had three literary men who did more, perhaps, for their country than any three generals who led the army to battle (applause)" (*NL*, 275). His response bears out the anxiety Yeats anticipated in the appropriately titled "Hopes and Fears for Irish Literature," published one year earlier: that the aestheticist virtue of "devotion to form" and the Irish interest in the "art of living," which Yeats wished to synthesize in a "wonderful new literature," might prove in their popular culture mediation to be perpetually dislodging or preempting one another.[7] With this problem of reception in mind, it comes as little surprise that Yeats's own deepening commitment to revivalism from this point forward has been seen as countering and ultimately overriding the aestheticist adherences which informed the initial stages of his poetic career.[8] The Irish Literary Revival was bound, almost by definition, to work from premises and toward ends that the aesthetic movement had the reputation of rejecting.

But of course any reasonably complete picture of aestheticism at the fin-de-siècle admits of nuance, ambiguity, internal variance, and conflict elided in its received or popular image, and perhaps no one could boast greater familiarity with the shades of disparity between the one and the other than Yeats himself, who not only made a point of reading, studying, and reviewing the works of Pater, Wilde, Symons, Johnson, Dowson, and Verlaine, but counted them, variously, as influences, mentors, colleagues, or friends. More importantly, for our purposes, Yeats possessed a sufficiently acute awareness of and sensitivity to the dialectics of aestheticism to recognize how far its internal dissonance complemented his own emerging dissent from the reigning ideology of Irish revivalism.

Yeats could not but have been struck by those salient occasions on which leading exponents of the precept art for art's sake crafted supplementary arguments allowing or ascribing a moral, political, religious, and therefore social or collectivist dimension to the aesthetic function. Take Swinburne's essay "Victor Hugo," which seeks, among other things, to reckon with the political impetus of *L'Annee Terrible:*

> The one primary requisite of art is artistic worth—art for art's sake first. . . . [F]rom him that has not this one indispensable quality of the artist, shall be taken away even that which he has. [But] we refuse to admit the art of the highest kind may not ally itself with moral or religious passion, with the ethics or politics of a nation or age.[9]

Witness the "Conclusion" to Pater's "Essay on Style," which introduces a decisive content-based element to aesthetic judgment:

> The distinction between great art and good art depending immediately, as regards literature at all events, not on its form. . . . It is on the quality of the matter it informs or controls, its variety, its alliance to great ends, or the depth of the note of revolt, or the largeness of hope in it, that the greatness of literary art depends. . . . Given the [formal] condition I have tried to explain as constituting

good art . . . if it be devoted further to the increase of men's happiness, to the redemption of the oppressed, or the enlargement of our sympathies with each other, or to such presentiment of new or old truth . . . as may enable or fortify us . . . it will also be great art.[10]

Finally, consider the argument of Wilde's *The Soul of Man under Socialism*. Art equates with individualism, but individualism, far from being an atomized condition, operates as a powerful social lever: "Art is Individualism and Individualism is a disturbing and disintegrating force. Therein lies its immense value. For what it seeks to disturb is monotony of type, slavery of custom, tyranny of habit, and the reduction of man to the level of machine."[11]

An attempt could be made to square these propositions with the logic of art for art's sake by drawing a distinction between the purity of the aesthetic aim and the variousness of the achieveable effect. For a dialectical thinker like Yeats, however, these assertions have their greatest significance in exemplifying what Jacques Lacan called "the logic of the exception."[12] In their deviation from the guiding principle of aestheticism, they harbor the hidden or underlying truth of the principle that the signature modes of aestheticist attachment and disaffiliation—from the projection of a subject "ringed round by a thick wall of personality" (*R*, 157) to the divorce of art from politics and morality, to the decadent insouciance toward life itself—were all, in fact, critical versions of their opposites: concern, involvement, affiliation, and engagement, not the absence of Pater's "enthusiasm of humanity" but a negative translation thereof (*R*, 159). As Adorno has written, defending aestheticism from a Marxist perspective, "art becomes social by its opposition to society, and it occupies this position only as autonomous art."[13] That is to say, while the aestheticist program might be construed as declining to enter the social dialogue of its historical moment, it in fact entered that dialogue precisely and in some sense more radically by rejecting or reformulating the terms on which it was conducted, substituting, for example, the argument *to* concrete forms for the argument *from* abstract norms.

We can trace this strategy as unfolding across three levels. At the primary level, the aestheticist refusal to regard the artwork as the bearer of a specified content or message amounts in part to a refusal to sanction certain socially mandated values that content was expected to enforce. Thus, a theory of hyperborean aesthetic detachment or transcendence, as exemplified by Wilde's notorious proclamation, "all art is perfectly useless,"[14] could and often did serve a practice of trenchant social critique, as evident in Wilde's famously insouciant comedies, *The Importance of Being Earnest* and *Lady Windermere's Fan*. At a secondary level, the move can amount to a refusal to sanction the very project of inculcating *particular* social norms or imposing socially mandated values upon individuals as the price of aesthetic experience—in sum a refusal to mobilize aesthetic expression as a vehicle of cultural engineering.[15] Here again, the disavowal of a social agenda evinces a social purpose. At a tertiary level, in contesting the conscription of art objects to extrinsic social designs, aestheticism not only insists upon the distinctive integrity of the aesthetic function, it repudiates a more comprehensively instrumental logic endemic to society itself, the systemic canalizing of individual passions and affects, the marshalling of individual efforts and energies, to larger purposes or ulterior ends. That is to say, the anti-instrumentalism of the aestheticist program not only looked to save the arts from being appropriated to the powers of social normalization and middle-class hegemony, not only looked to defend the arts as a spiritual refuge from these same powers, but looked to mobilize art as an emblem, even an agency, of resistance to the pervasive reduction of the particularity of human experience.[16]

At this meta-level, where the critical engagement of aestheticism has its most generalized application, it also has, paradoxically, its most specific historical purchase. The attempt to raise the ideal of beauty beyond the reach and the taint of the pragmatic and the profitable went beyond boycotting the pieties of the dominant metropolitan culture of bourgeois materialism (the cultural equivalent of a general strike) to assailing, under the rubric of philistinism, the utilitarian ideology that was its keynote. It was on this score that aestheticism and the Irish Literary Revival found common cause, with Yeats as their middleman, shuttling between the London Rhymers and Dublin's National Literary Society.

Instead of rejecting Matthew Arnold's notorious stereotype of the melancholy, emotionally incontinent, fatally impractical, imaginatively gifted, spiritually animated Celt as a condescending colonial blend of fetishism and abjection, early Irish revivalists sought to embrace and transvalue this depiction, emphasizing its more favorable elements in order to project an honorable image of native Irish ethnicity. Yeats's strategy for accomplishing this task of resignification was precisely to map the discourse of Celticism onto the discourse of aestheticism. In his essay "The Celtic Element in Literature," Yeats sees still abroad in the Irish countryside an aboriginal "Celtic culture, the bearer of a unique, racially imprinted spirituality," whose "fountain of legends" answers perfectly the "religious" appetite for a "sacred book" among contemporary aestheticist poets.[17] Quoted at the outset of the essay, Arnold's well-known racial slight, "The Celt's react[ion] against the despotism of fact," finds its echo at the essay's conclusion, in Yeats's approval of aestheticism's "reaction against materialism of the nineteenth century" (*EI*, 187). By this framing device, Yeats resignifies the Arnoldian Celt as a natural (or native) born aesthete and the aesthete as a modern, cosmopolitan stepchild of the Celt.

The transvaluation of the Celt on the part of the early revivalists inevitably involved a certain accommodation of the radical othering Arnold's stereotype comprised. The new "Celtic movement," to use Yeats's designation, may have served up a more palatably dignified portrayal of the "mere" or "native" Irish, but it remains one that has a homogenizing effect—what Memmi called colonial "massification"—spiced with a hint of exoticism.[18] One obvious reason for this compromise formation was that even as the early revivalists identified themselves with the Irish people-nation, their struggles, their forms of life, and their political aspirations, they continued to regard their aboriginal brethren with a settler's gaze. Gregory, Hyde, Russell, Synge, and Yeats were all Anglo-Protestants, whose literary and dramatic conceptions of Ireland arose in large measure out of their own ethnographic field work (Gregory's Kiltartan series, Synge's *The Aran Islands*, Yeats's *Fairy and Folk Tales of the Irish Peasantry*), which bore a predictably colonial impress.[19] Given the trickiness of the revivalists' position, which a flood of criticism from middle-class (i.e., Catholic)

Ireland would subsequently confirm, Yeats's decision to ennoble the Arnoldian caricature of Irishness by filiating the Celt with aestheticism, an English-identified discourse in Ireland, could only call attention to Yeats's own outsider status—an ethno-sectarian difference compounded by London residence that tended to undermine his credibility as a nationalist, cultural or otherwise. The drawback to this Celticist gambit seems too glaring for Yeats, an able enough literary politician, to have simply overlooked. That he persisted in this line, accordingly, suggests an underlying identification with the aestheticist movement that compromised his allegiance to the Irish Revival, even as that latter allegiance appeared—but *only* appeared—to displace it. Still more surprisingly, I would argue, Yeats sustained this identification not just in spite but, in some sense, *because* of the alienating implications it bore for his revivalist profile.

Yeats's identification with aestheticism was profoundly, one might even say, hyper-dialectical, a dialectical identification with the dialectical form of aestheticism itself. This complexity results in large part from the fact that Yeats's receptivity to certain themes, concepts, and motifs of aestheticism grew in part from his sense of affinity with the *social* contours of aestheticism that we have been discussing. I will endeavor to explain this multitier dialectic on a step-by-step basis.

Yeats's primary point of identification with aestheticism was its outward or received image code, specifically its code of spiritual detachment and independence (the will to "isolate himself" that James Joyce, as a young aesthete, deemed the "radical principle of artistic economy")[20] designed to ensure the faithfulness of the artist to his vision (Wilde's "self-culture"), of the work to properly aesthetic criteria (Swinburne's "art for art's sake"), and of the critic, as Pater says, to his own impressions (*R*, xii–xiii). For Yeats, this ideal preserved the attraction of an impossible desire, so fully did it run counter to his own social instincts. As Roy Foster has observed, Yeats was an organizational man, someone who regularly assembled, joined, and presided over groups (the Irish Literary Society, the National Literary Society, the Golden Dawn, the Rhymers Club, the National Literary Theatre or Abbey, the United Arts Club), even as he likened the frustrations and distractions of public life to "drag[ging] road metal."[21]

Yeats thus begins by identifying with aestheticist subjectivity at the point of greatest difference from his own make-up.

Among the numerous conceptual jewels that Yeats mined from the aestheticist landscape, including Pater's elaboration of "mood" and "Unity of Self," the most important was the logic of the Wildean mask, which proved uncannily germane to Yeats's own mode of identification with this entire school of thought. In "The Decay of Lying," Wilde holds our individuating characteristics, everything that gives us our distinct identities, to repose entirely in our masks, our artifacts of "self-culture," rather than in our given being (*CW*, 914). In "The Critic as Artist," he poses the mask as the gateway to authentic expression, to the inner reality of the subject: "Man is least himself when he talks in his own person; give him a mask and he will tell you the truth" (*CW*, 984). In "The Truth of Masks," finally, Wilde averred that the concept of the mask holds the key to "realizing Hegel's system of contraries," the dialectic, for it crystallizes the principle of truth-in-contradiction (*CW*, 1017). Yeats adapted Wilde's philosophy to construe the mask as both "double . . . and anti-self . . . most like me . . . and most unlike" (*VP*, 371), a supplement of identity that at one level *contradicts* the self, being "an emotional antithesis to all that comes out of their internal nature," and so "the opposite of all I am in daily life."[22] But in so doing, the mask also gives shape to what the self is not, what, in other words, the self is most missing, most lacks, most desires, and hence what alone "rouses the will to full intensity" (*A*, 167). (Hence Yeats's most precise definition of the mask: "an image evocative of a state of mind which is of all states not impossible the most difficult to man, race or nation" [*A*, 167].) Insofar as "the will" is another name for the ego or the self in its most basic form, the mask proves to be, *via negativa*, the innermost truth of selfhood; it is, in Lacanian terms, that which is "in you more than you"—precisely, and here is the dialectical turn, insofar as it is *not* in you at all.

Yeats could readily see in his relationship to the aestheticist tradition the operation of this dynamic principle that he had derived from the tradition. Aestheticism, or rather the cachet of aestheticism, its outward expression, constitutes a version of the mask for Yeats; the spirit of detachment, noninvolvement, resolutely individual self-culture was a desideratum emotionally antithetical to his own "inner nature" and so most difficult, though not yet impossible, to compass. What makes this quest sublimely difficult is that, as an embodiment of anti-self, the mask cannot simply replace the "inner nature" of the self and become the primary state of mind or being. It "rouses the will to full intensity" only insofar as it is realized in the very performance and expression of the "daily life" that it *continues to contradict,* that is, as a part of the ongoing operation of a "system of contraries."

Reference to its "outward expression" reminds us that aestheticism too was subject to the "system of contraries," and Yeats's secondary, deeper, and less conscious vector of identification with the movement shifts from taking aestheticism as his mask to taking aestheticism as a model of how the mask as such might be realized. To elaborate upon Adorno's insight above: aestheticism *becomes* social, realizes its desideratum of engagement, by its cultivation of "autonomous art," its withdrawal from the social dialogue. In Yeats's terms, it realizes the anti-self in and through its enactment of the self, fulfills by contradicting its "nature." Yeats completes his identification with aestheticism by mirroring this process, by reflecting or doubling it *in reverse order:* he realizes his mask of spiritual and artistic distinction, separateness, even isolation in and through institutional commitment and sociopolitical engagement. More than any other group to which he belonged, popular or esoteric, literary, spiritualist, or political, the Irish Literary Revival afforded him renewable opportunities to execute this dialectic, which is one reason his affiliation with the movement proved to be as long and deep as it was contentious and controversial.

Yeats's articulation of his role as architect and spokesman of the Irish Literary Revival grew increasingly double-voiced as his position at the center of its dominant institution, the Abbey Theatre, consolidated. In essays such as "Art and Ideas," "What Is Popular Poetry?" "The Autumn of the Body," and even "The Celtic Element in Literature," Yeats interleaved his self-presentation as a representative of authentically Irish cultural difference with claims of authority predicated upon his *distance* from the people-nation: his aestheticist immersion in classical and Renaissance traditions of art, philosophy, and manners; his fellowship with the contemporary post-Romantic avant-garde in Europe and Britain; his ties to London and Big House society; and so forth. Certain of the early revivalists, such as Douglas Hyde, downplayed or elided the Anglo-Protestant roots that separated them from their projected constituency and a correlatively nativist vision of Irishness. Not so Yeats. Feeling that such a vision threatened his claims to be a national yet irrevocably Anglo-Irish poet, Yeats regularly remarked aspects of his background or experience that distinguished him from his audience, but did so, and this is crucial, as part of a generalized discourse of Irish belonging and community. That is to say, Yeats set himself *apart* in and through his *participation* in the Irish Literary Revival, which functioned within a "system of contraries" to afford him an organizational web as an individuating backdrop and to nurture, amid all the managerial bother, what Yeats called an "outlawed solitude."[23]

Once we grasp Yeats's leadership of the Revival as simultaneously a leavetaking, the conventional narrative of a career starkly divided between early and late, Irish and Anglo-Irish, populist and elitist modulates in some measure. The ideological "break," typically placed at or around the *Playboy* controversy,[24] appears less decisive and the whole takes on a more continuous, evolutionary cast. Instead of contrasting the populist cultural revolutionary with the mandarin reactionary, we can witness the sense of estrangement and the promotion of self-culture characteristic of Yeats's post–Free State defense of Anglo-Irish privilege to be anticipated, however gently, in the tendency of his fin-de-siècle and pre-war rhetoric to strike a separate peace for himself within the communitarian movement he fronted. Indeed, the supposed shift from Yeats "for the people" to Yeats "contra the mob" has often been attributed, not least by Yeats himself, to the influence of that "strong enchanter," Nietzsche, whom he read seriously in 1903.[25] But the critical writings of Wilde, bolstered by the public hysteria surrounding his persecution, had already nudged Yeats to strike a hyperborean pose toward mass opinion, even as he continued to headline a presumptively "mass" movement. It is not surprising, therefore, that Yeats envisaged his eventual adoption of an aristocratic ethos in aestheticist terms, that is, the cultivation of individual style as the mask of personality (*A*, 341), even borrowing his epitome thereof, "cold and passionate," from the end of Pater's essay "Winkelman"

(*R*, 154). The flip side of this more evolutionary dialectic is that the historical circumstances in Ireland that seemed just to disillusion Yeats, utterly—from Sinn Fein's riotous denunciation of Synge and the Abbey to the institution of a mass Catholic theocracy in 1922— must also be seen as serving to realize his long-harbored inner mask, the perpetual joiner's desire for an "outlawed solitude," and so to bring Yeats more to himself (in every sense). If so, we might have the beginnings of an answer to an old and troubling riddle: why did Yeats's poetry get so much better as his politics got so much worse?

Yeats's identification with the dialectical form of aestheticism, but in reverse order, required him to craft a Janus-faced approach toward the movement to complement the ambidexterity of his revivalism. Yeats's vacillating adherences in this area have not passed unnoticed, but they have not, in my view, been fully comprehended. I think George Watson furnishes one of the more elegant and precise formulations of the critical consensus when he writes that Yeats's "early work dances an elaborate gavotte between patriotism and aestheticism" in which, Watson continues, patriotism or at least cultural nationalism, ultimately prevails: "the people win the battle for his allegiance."[26] The problem with this conclusion is that it takes up aestheticism and revivalism as opposed terms, between which some decision must be made, and then reads Yeats's critical work in light of his institutional trajectory and destination (from aesthetic associations to revivalist institutions). But if we read Yeats's early criticism against his creative production of the same period, the so-called Celtic Twilight poetry, the dance steps he executes look very different and much more complicated. His Celtic Twilight verse, the volumes *The Rose* and, especially, *The Wind Among the Reeds*, bears the figurative trappings, not to mention the atmospherics, of both aestheticism and cultural nationalism, indicating that Yeats did not as yet feel them to exist in the kind of tension or opposition that would require him to decide or even to vacillate between them. This was because the two approaches took hold at different pragmatic levels of Yeats's verse, even as they shared a certain semantic grounding. The Celtic Twilight rubric itself presents Yeats's early verse as belonging to a nativist ethnic, hence *statutory*, lyrical tradition toward which Yeats, because he had no working knowledge of the native language, could only maintain a broadly symbolic, thematic, and ethnographic relationship. Aestheticism, as a *substantive* method, could operate within that statutory framework, within its symbolic and thematic registers, offering Yeats the stylistic means to infuse them with a personalizing intensity. And given that a specifically Irish revivalist *poetics* was as yet scarcely defined, those aestheticist elements of Yeats's verse could not but begin to define it *from the inside*.[27] The collective enterprise of revivalist verse, as Yeats spearheaded it anyway, was to be informed in its emergence by an individualizing impulse.

Viewed in this twi- (which is to say double) light, we can see that Yeats's early criticism charts an analogous course. There is no gavotte danced between patriotism and aestheticism; patriotism, or at least revivalism, represents the meta-perspective delineating the arena of Yeats's inquiry, and within this arena, Yeats dances a "gavotte" between conflicting assessments of what aestheticism has to offer the new Irish poets and dramatists. Rather than being embraced only to be discarded, aestheticism is, over a series of lectures and essays, held in *strict abeyance*, with Yeats moving from approval of one aspect to disapproval of another and back again. In "Hopes and Fears for Irish Literature" (1892), Yeats directly addresses the "art for art's sake" precept: "Art and poetry are becoming every day more entirely ends in themselves, and all life is made more and more but so much fuel to feed the fire" (*EA*, 185). The result is an increasing attention to craftsmanship, "devotion to form . . . and hatred of the commonplace and banal," all of which Irish literature has yet to learn and must, if it is to flourish at all (*EA*, 187). But the same autotelic principle fosters an absence of the "conviction" necessary to arouse "noble emotions," leaving behind "mere subtleties of form," which Irish literature with its "legends and history of lofty passions," may look in time to surpass (*EA*, 186, 187). In "Mr. Arthur Symons' New Book" (1894), Yeats dismisses the decadence as having "finished its great work for this epoch of the world" (*EA*, 335), a gesture consistent with his recent nomination of revivalism as the poetic mode of "the new epoch." But at the same time, he praises Symons's *Amoris Victima* for qualities uncontestably identified with decadence: "exquisite impression," a "revery of that bitter wisdom" that seems older than time, "a revolt against the manifold . . . and the external" (*EA*, 334–35). Taking up the stylistic properties of aestheticist poetry in "The Autumn of the Body" (1898), Yeats judges the "faint lights and faint colours and faint outlines and faint energies which many call the decadence" to be blanched foretokens of a new dispensation in the arts rather than a manner to be emulated (*EI*, 191). But in "The Symbolism of Poetry," just two years later, Yeats declares "we would cast out of serious poetry . . . energetic rhythms . . . and seek out those wavering, meditative, organic rhythms, which are the embodiment of the imagination" (*EI*, 163). In "Discoveries" (1906), Yeats recommends eschewing, in favor of more earthly concerns, the ascending idealism of "refined and studious men" for whom "literature becomes religion" (*EI*, 267), a reference to the so-called "religion of art" associated with aestheticism. But Yeats's writings in *Autobiographies* and *Essays and Introductions* fairly teem with idealist invocations of "the Church of the poetic tradition" (*A*, 115) with its "priesthood of forgotten faith" (*EI*, 203), "sacred book" (*EI*, 187), "garments of religion," and, most tellingly, "our ancient church where there is an altar and no pulpit," a religious figuration of the art for art's sake doctrine (*EI*, 348). Finally, in "Art and Ideas" (1913), Yeats credits the "delicacy of sensation" characteristic of "the aesthetic school" with making him a poet, while announcing he has left it behind for the "familiar names and conspicuous hills [of Ireland], that I might not be alone amid the obscure impressions of the senses" (*EI*, 349).

Each of these essays, in themselves and in their relation to Yeats's other writings holds aestheticism under a suspended judgment, which is to say in some doubt, by comparison with the revivalist enterprise. By taking this tack, Yeats maintains the distance necessary to intimate, if not declare, that the elaboration of a nationalist mythopoetics, compact of heroic legend, romance, folklore, and so on, enables a more substantial, satisfying, and consequential artistic legacy than an aesthetic program enclosed on itself, concerned neither with public debate nor public morality, but with refining the formal and stylistic artifice of the work and the perceptual, emotional, and imaginative capacities of author and audience. At the same time, under cover of this display of nationalist *bona fides*, Yeats's suspended judgment also maintains aestheticism as a philosophical and poetic resource, to be drawn upon as the occasion demands. And Yeats's willingness to do exactly that, in poetry and prose, *irrespective of the various strictures on aestheticism he pronounced,* indicates that, far from embracing aestheticism only to discard it, he held aestheticism in abeyance in theory so that he could embrace it in practice, and as a particular *kind* of practice. In this extended, intermittent deliberation between perhaps the quintessential fin-de-siècle effort at a collectivist poetics and a movement notorious for taking aesthetic individualism to the brink of solipsism, Yeats opts for the ethnonational endeavor, but he does so, paradoxically, as a means for allowing the individualist approach to set the terms for that endeavor, to determine its typifying formal and stylistic features.

We can see this clearly in *The Wind Among the Reeds* (1899), where such poems as "He Remembers Forgotten Beauty," "He Hears the Cry of the Sedge," "The Travail of Passion," "He Wishes his Beloved Were Dead," and, of course, "The Secret Rose," not only fit comfortably into any aestheticist canon of verse, they also apotheosize all of the properties of which Yeats's contemporaneous writings disapprove: super-subtleties of form, the absence of familiar landscapes, loneliness "amid obscure impressions of the senses," "faint lights and faint colours and faint outlines and faint energies," the absence of the shared "convictions" that galvanize "noble emotions," and the accoutrements of a religion of art, from liturgical imagery to an atmosphere of flowers and incense. The nominal Irishness of the volume, buttressed by a couple of poems on the Sidhe, does not distinguish its contours from a work Yeats himself would deem aestheticist, but rather allows for an aestheticist contouring of the revivalist brand. So too do Yeats's extended notes to several of these poems ("He Hears the Cry of the Sedge," "He bids his Beloved be at Peace," "The Secret Rose," "He Mourns for the Change"), which locate scene, sentiment, and action on a mythic Irish terrain infused with a languorous, medieval Christian atmosphere much affected by the aestheticist movement. Yeats perfectly encapsulates this discursive reversal in the poem "Into the Twilight" (*VP,* 147–48). The reference to "Mother Eire" in line 5 marks the "twilight" of the title the Celtic

Twilight, reminds us in fact that the poem was originally published under the title "The Celtic Twilight" (in the *National Observer*, 1893), making this, in a sense, the signature lyric of Yeats's early Revival period. Strikingly, the poem contains no familiar Irish landscapes, no folk or heroic lore, no distinctively Irish furnishings, no Irish figures, no shared reality of any sort. The speaker does not even address an audience but instead communes with his own "heart" whose decadent "outworn" condition mirrors that of his age (an "Outworn heart in a time outworn"). It is as if Yeats set about representing the aestheticist subject in Pater's "Conclusion" "ringed round" by his own personality, experiencing not the outside world—which in this instance consists of those "faint colors and faint outlines"—but, as Pater indicates, "the impressions of the individual in his isolation" (*R*, 157). Furthermore, the speaker's condition in the poem, which might deservedly be dubbed solipsistic, represents not his fate, but his *desire:* he calls for his heart to leave behind both social disputes ("the fires of a slanderous tongue") and moral questions ("nets of wrong and right"), and to flee to a remote pastoral version of the church of art ("where God stands winding his lonely horn"). The Celtic dimension of the poem neither endorses nor controverts nor substantively engages the discourse of Celticism to which it gestures: it turns the vacant landscape the speaker occupies into a revivalist stage on which his cherished solitude will be relieved, and yet thrown into relief, by seeming emblematic of a racial or national sensibility. Here again, the nominal or allegorical shadow of belonging to the tribe exists mainly to intensify the impact and enhance the significance of a deeper spiritual seclusion.

Yeats's running theatre commentary, *Samhain*, turns the *actual* revivalist stage to much the same purpose.[28] The Irish literary theatre embodied the Revival at its most community-oriented, and in that spirit Yeats announces in the 1902 issue, "Our movement is a return to the people" (*S*, 96), thereby ratifying the general expectation of a topical, socially conscious, politically engaged repertoire. Three pages before, however, he had already warned the reader, and by extension, the public of the dangers of such expectations. "In Ireland, where we have so much to prove, we are ready to forget that the creation of an emotion of beauty is the only kind of literature that justifies itself" (*S,* 93). This aestheticist note, combining the consecration of passion and beauty with a call for artistic freedom, sounds repeatedly in the series, often laying explicit claim to outright priority over the sort of considerations endemic to cultural nation-building:

> *Samhain* 1903: "It is a supreme movement in the life of a nation when it is able to turn now and again from its preoccupations, to delight in the capricious power of the artist as one delights in the movement of some wild creature." (*S,* 105)
>
> *Samhain* 1903, "The Reform of the Theatre": "If we are to do this we must learn that beauty and truth are always, justified of themselves, and that their creation is a greater service to our country than writing that compromises either in the seeming service of a cause." (*S,* 107)
>
> *Samhain* 1903, "An Irish National Theatre": "Literature is always personal, always one man's vision of the world, one man's experience." (*S,* 114)

In each of these passages, the national community that the theatre purportedly exists to serve is urged to accommodate itself to prospective dramas embodying a series of romanticist-aestheticist tenets: the work as extension of the artist's will (or caprice); the work as externalization of individual consciousness ("one man's experience"); and the work as end in itself, validated entirely on aesthetic grounds ("beauty and truth"). If we hearken back to our basic definition of a literary revival, which seemed incompatible with an aestheticist program—in other words, native forms of literary expression enlisted in the service of national objectives—we can see that Yeats looked to flip the script, to place the national aspect of the movement at the disposal of aesthetic objectives. He envisages a revivalism that is not just compatible with but contoured by aestheticism, whose "supreme moment" is a collective acquiescence in the autonomy of the singular artist.

At a couple of points later in the *Samhain* series, Yeats goes a crucial step further, baring the device as it were. In 1904, Yeats proclaims the Irish "a hard masterful race" based on "the nearness to reality of those few scattered people who have the right to call themselves the Irish race. It is only in the exceptions," he continues, "in the few minds where the flame has burnt as it were pure, that one can see the permanent character of the race" (*S*, 147). The allusion here to Pater's "hard gem-like flame," which likewise marks an ecstatic proximity to the real, frames those exceptional minds as creative, aesthetic types, if not aesthetes. And in this case, not only are the collective institutions of national culture to serve the individual exceptions, but national identity itself is, by right, vested in them. In keeping with the dialectic of the Yeatsian mask, singularity becomes the "supreme moment" of belonging, individuality the "supreme moment" of collectivity, aestheticism the "supreme moment" of cultural nationalism. By essentializing the nation in its artists—"in the long run, it is the great writers of the nation who become its image in the minds of posterity" (*S*, 192)—Yeats squares the art versus patriotism circle, giving us "the nation for art's sake."

I want to close with two works by Yeats, one a drama and one a longer poem, the former produced at the dawn of the Revival in 1894, the other penned at the bitter end of Yeats's robust identification and participation in the movement (1913). What they reveal, I believe, is the perhaps unexpected persistence of Yeats's effort to appropriate aestheticist elements to the revivalist project as a way of altering its ideological DNA.

The Land of Heart's Desire dramatizes an Irish fairy tale in a relatively straightforward fashion.[29] Unhappy with her everyday life as an Irish peasant and at odds with her shrewish mother-in-law, a new bride, a class especially vulnerable to fairy kidnapping, chooses to minister to one of the "good people," in the shape of a young girl, and allows her entrance to the cottage, resulting in her own abduction from home, family, and mortal life to become one of them. Yeats is careful to observe all manner of ritual motifs and regulations associated with fairy lore, as one would expect from the revivalist exercise the play purports to be. But there is one crucial narrative he invents or imports, a narrative with *no specific relevance to fairy legend as such*. Given the literary stir around at the time of the play's composition, the added element seems to be a complex allusion to *The Picture of*

Dorian Gray. The bride, Marie Bruin, is initially seduced into trafficking with the fairies, corrupted from the Christian life represented by the family and their resident priest, and brought to her doom—like Dorian, metaphorically poisoned—by a book. Like Dorian's book, Marie's is untitled, treated only in a summary manner and regarded as especially strange. As with Dorian's book, moreover, the outline given suggests a rejection of the productivist ideology of bourgeois materialism and any notion of rationality attendant to it. Where Dorian's book is written in the style of aestheticism—the decadents or the symbolists depending on the text—the little we know of Marie's book concerns its association with folk-aesthetics: the passion of the previous owner for it had brought "little good . . . because it filled his house with roaming bards and roaming ballad makers and the like" (*L*, 7). Like Dorian's book, Marie's poisons her by representing in its pages the course of life it induces her to follow. For Dorian, that course involved a sampling of "passions and modes of thought" that transgressed the norms of his own time; Marie likewise breaks with the norms of her social context—the housework her mother-in-law demands and, above all, the reproductive imperative her husband, priest, and father-in-law repeatedly invoke—in order to traverse an alternative universe. The latter tells her "when we are young we long to tread a way none tread before" (*L*, 13), but unlike her peers, and like Dorian, Marie actually does so. In the supposed model of Dorian's book, Huysmans's *À Rebours,* the protagonist Des Essientes describes aestheticism as a quest for an impossible ideal or beatitude, and Marie like Dorian finds her book promoting just such an ideal, the tale of Princess Arlene abandoning her royal seat for the "land of faery." Like Dorian's ideal, Marie is decidedly aesthetic: Princess Adene "is still there [in Fairyland] busied with dance" (*L*, 8), and the fairy who spirits Marie away likewise performs intricate dances to "faint music" and "invisible pipes" (*L*, 24). (Indeed, Yeats may so heavily emphasize Marie's resistance to a life of child-bearing to draw a contrast between what Wilde called the "exquisite sterile emotions" that art properly awakens and the accustomed biological fertility of agrarian life.)[30] Like Dorian, Marie's breach of social norms increasingly singles her out, separates her, from the society to which she nonetheless continues to belong, and her separation, like Dorian's, culminates in her becoming a creature of art, her body left to one side, her very being now undead, like Dorian's picture. Like Dorian, finally, she comes to internalize the criticism of her as regret for her fatal decision, but like him, she persists because the book itself and the aestheticist course it prescribes answers to her innermost desire, a desire for infinitude that Yeats everywhere identified with the aesthetic impulse. Amid the family voices bidding her remain in the here and now, the fairy-child declares, irrefutably, "I keep you in the name of your own heart," and Marie concedes, "I always loved her world" (*L*, 29, 31).

The importance of this dense web of allusion is not simply that Marie emerges as an aboriginal, allegorical avatar of aestheticism, but rather that, in being so, she emerges as a type, a Yeatsian type, of the Celtic revivalist. A native, Irish-Irish family, the Bruins stand as representatives of a peasantry that was itself widely idealized at the time as iconic of the virtuous Irish people-nation. Yet they have been thoroughly alienated from their Celtic roots—for Yeats, pagan, mystical, and folk-aesthetic—by the twin forces of devotional Catholicism and economic familialism. In this respect, they are forerunners of the Gillane family in *Cathleen Ni Houlihan*, who could not recognize the sovereignty goddess when she was sitting in their parlor. Marie's proto-aestheticist adherences, instilled by a poisonous book, install her as the Michael Gillane of this piece, the figure who sacrifices his life by committing himself to a truly native Ireland, in the form of its persona or locus geni. Cultural rather than political, Marie's embrace of the *unheimlich* stranger in the house likewise leads to an encounter with the authentic spirit(s) of Ireland, "white-armed Nuala and Aengus of the birds, and Feacra of the hurtling foam, and Finvarra and their Land of Heart's Desire" (*L*, 28). More than that, Marie follows the path charted by another legendary Irish figure of Yeats's reimagining, the ancient king Fergus, who in the poems "Fergus and the Druid" and "Who Goes with Fergus," composed during the same period as *The Land of Heart's Desire*, is shown to quit his tribal niche and bonds for an isolating proto-aestheticist world of "dream" and "dance." Her family's insistence on classifying the fairies (and presumably the druids) as "fiends," in accordance with a Christian cosmology, resonates by contrast as an ingrained abhorrence of what were the original, precolonial Irish cultural dominants, the very thing the

Revival proposed to summon forth. Given their representative stand-
ing, the attitude of the Bruins leaves the impression that while the
Revival may proceed on behalf and in the name of the national com-
munity, it is to be undertaken by individualistic adventurers willing to
defy the normative pressures of that same community in order to
uncover the realm of imagination that was Ireland's primal estate,
here denominated as "the land of heart's desire." Under the Celticist
dispensation, founded upon the transvaluation of Arnold's racial
caricature, the Irish Literary Revival conceived itself to be driven by
Irish exceptionalism, a spiritualized ethnic counterweight to British
vulgarity and philistinism. But in this play, Yeats shows that Celtic
counterweight to linger on in/as an aestheticist sensibility *exceptional
among the Irish themselves* and, by reason of that very singularity, able
to claim exclusive "right" to authentic Irishness, troped in the play as
a communion with the Gaelic spirit-world.

By 1913, when Yeats published the volume *Responsibilities,* the
exception he was, and the exception he took, to the dominant nation-
alist movements in Ireland had made themselves felt, and on that
account Yeats alternately saw himself as having resigned (see "Sep-
tember 1913," "Paudeen," "A Coat") or having been driven out (see
"To a Friend," "To a Shade," "Notoriety"). Yeats seized the occasion to
reconsider and recalibrate his position vis-à-vis the interplay of po-
litical and cultural decolonization in Ireland. Tellingly, the first titled
poem of the volume, "The Grey Rock" (*VP,* 270–76), initiates the
deliberations by staging an encounter of Yeats's aestheticist appren-
ticeship with the Rhymers ("*poets with whom I learned my trade*") and
his more recent revivalist practice ("an old story I've re-made," a god-
dess's tale of love, loss, and grievance). Yeats begins by assuring his
now deceased "Companions of the Cheshire Cheese" that though
they have little cognizance of the Irish mythic frame from which the
tale derives, "*the moral's yours because it's mine.*" In this way, Yeats indi-
cates he has carried forward his Rhymer pedigree as a shaping influ-
ence over the core meaning of his revivalist work, controverting the
conventional narrative, adduced previously, that interest in cultural
nationalism came to displace his earlier aestheticist attachments. To
the contrary, Yeats interrupts his recitation between the framing nar-
rative and the goddess's story to pronounce the Rhymers worthy,

in death, to behold the glorious spectacle of the ancient Irish gods, because, in life, they *"kept the Muses sterner laws,"* never compromising their art for ulterior ends, such as *"a heavier purse"* or *"loud service to a cause."* The Rhymers, in short, personify the volume's overarching theme of "responsibilities" by their steadfast fidelity to the art for art's sake ethic.

The goddess Aoife's ensuing tale issues in a desperate call for vengeance upon her dead lover, whom she feels has betrayed her. At the battle of Clontarf, out of a sense of solidarity with his endangered prince and duty to his nation, he removed the magical pin or brooch she had given him to protect him from mortal harm for hundreds of years. Now with this gesture, he might be seen to have acted heroically, to have taken responsibility for his actions in the field of political conflict, as the Rhymers had in the field of poetic expression. (Not coincidentally, they too *"had to face their ends when young."*) To be sure, Yeats had celebrated similar acts of self-immolation for Ireland, most notably in the aforementioned *Cathleen Ni Houlihan,* which had in the intervening decade spawned numerous imitations. So it must be accounted the poem's decisive twist that Yeats sees his own responsibility as lying on the side of the goddess, not the soldier, for which attitude, symbolically speaking, he has suffered the opprobrium of the nationalist community. I quote the final verse:

> *I have kept my faith, though faith was tried,*
> To that rock-born, rock-wandering foot;
> And the world's altered since you died,
>   And I am in no good repute.
>   With the loud host before the sea,
>   That thick sword strokes were better meant
>   Than lover's music—let that be,
> *So that the wandering foot's content.*

This apologia has been read as preferring love to war or amorous to political alliance. But that is to ignore the *crucial metonymies* of Yeats's allegiance to Aoife. His faithfulness does not occur on the same ground as the soldier's faithlessness, though both are exposed by their respective choices to the slings and arrows of hostility. Yeats proclaims his dedication not to the lover but to the "*lover's music,*" that is, to her art. More curiously, he swears loyalty not to the goddess but to her "*rock-born, rock-wandering foot.*" Now the "rock" featured in the poem is Slievenamon, appropriately "Mountain of Women," where the goddess decries her erstwhile favorite to her fellow immortals. But this "rock" is best known for housing the divine artisan and legendary Irish mason-god, Goban, who appears in the poem as both the craftsman of fine silver goblets and tapers and the sole brewer of the gods' sacred wine.[31] As "*rock-born*" and "*rock-wandering,*" then, the goddess comes from and carries forward a lineage of divine artifice, of which her own charmed pin and love story are specimens. It is precisely in this respect that Yeats, whose Rhymer club lineage likewise intermingles the aesthetic, the romantic, and the religious (as lines 49–64 make clear), identifies with her. Indeed, it is only on these grounds that his triangulation of the goddess's address to her fellow immortals and Yeats's address to his all-too-mortal fellows makes compelling sense. Yeats is, in effect, saying, "My revivalist practice, in not only recovering the letter but renewing the spirit of Irish legend, has advanced a sensibility and a set of commitments emblematic of you, my dear deceased Rhymers, and which the 'sword strokes' of nationalist history—often taken to begin at Clontarf—have all but diminished among my current fellows." Reflecting upon his years in the revivalist movement, Yeats finds himself set quite apart after all ("*in no good repute*"). He has realized his mask with a vengeance. But in that obscurely desired "artistic economy of isolation," that lived belief in the autonomy of art and the artist, he has also discovered with whom he still belongs. This truth, being a dialectical truth, can only be uttered belatedly: "the moral's yours because it's mine"; that is, your aestheticism has had its afterlife, its afterword, in me; it has been revived in an Irish revivalism I have made mine alone.

NOTES

1. Stephen Regan, "W. B. Yeats and Irish Cultural Politics in the 1890s," in *Cultural Politics at the Fin de Siècle,* ed. Sally Ledger and Scott McCracken (Cambridge: Cambridge University Press, 1995), 71.

2. Yeats's dialectical tendencies must be understood not as adhering to the popular notion of Hegelian dynamics, wherein contradictions are sublated in a moment of totalizing synthesis, but rather as unfolding in accordance with the Hegelian text, where the moment of synthesis serves to spotlight the irresolvability of the contradictions themselves. For this reading of Hegel, which consists more closely with the paradoxes of Wilde's aestheticism, as well as the antinomies of Yeats, see Slavoj Žižek, *The Sublime Object of Ideology* (London: Verso, 1989), 208–9.

3. Walter Pater, *Studies in the History of the Renaissance* (New York: Mentor, 1959), 157. Hereafter cited parenthetically as *R*.

4. Algernon Swinburne, *William Blake: A Critical Essay* (London: Hotten, 1868), 90.

5. Oscar Wilde, "The Decay of Lying" (*Intentions*), in *The Complete Works of Oscar Wilde* (Cambridge: Bookmart, 1990), 926. Further references to the *Complete Works* are abbreviated *CW*.

6. W. B. Yeats, "Nationality and Literature" (*United Ireland*, May 27, 1893) in *Uncollected Prose of W. B. Yeats*, vol. 1, *First Reviews and Articles, 1886–1896*, ed. Johnathan P. Frayne (New York: Columbia University Press, 1970), 266–75. Hereafter cited parenthetically as *NL*.

7. W. B. Yeats, *Early Articles and Reviews* (New York: Scribner, 2004), 185–88. Hereafter cited parenthetically as *EA*.

8. Regan, "W. B. Yeats and Irish Cultural Politics in the 1890s," 66.

9. Algernon Swinburne, "Victor Hugo: *L'Annee Terrible*," *Fortnightly Review* 12, September 1, 1872, 257.

10. Walter Pater, *Appreciations with an Essay on Style* (London: Macmillan, 1897), 37–38.

11. Oscar Wilde, *The Soul of Man under Socialism* in *CW*, 1030.

12. See Žižek, *The Sublime Object of Ideology*, 21–22.

13. Theodor Adorno, *Aesthetic Theory* (Minneapolis: University of Minnesota Press, 1997), 225.

14. Oscar Wilde, preface to *The Picture of Dorian Gray* (New York: Norton, 1988), 4.

15. Stanley Kubrick's *A Clockwork Orange* is a classic exposition of the possibilities and dangers of such cultural engineering as aestheticism repudiated.

16. The point is forcefully made in Oscar Wilde, "The Critic as Artist, Part II," in *CW*, 971–98.

17. W. B. Yeats, "The Celtic Element in Literature," in *Essays and Introductions* (New York: Collier, 1968), 186–7. Further references to *Essays and Introductions* are abbreviated *EI*.

18. Albert Memmi, *The Colonizer and the Colonized* (New York: Onion, 1965), 57.

19. For a full, anthropologically informed argument to this effect, see Gregory Castle, *Modernism and the Celtic Revival* (Cambridge: Cambridge University Press, 2001).

20. James Joyce, "The Day of the Rabblement," in *The Critical Writings of James Joyce* (New York: Viking, 1959), 69.

21. R. F. Foster, *W. B. Yeats: A Life,* vol. 1, *The Apprentice Mage, 1865–1914* (Oxford: Oxford University Press, 1997), 89. W. B. Yeats, "The Fascination of What's Difficult" in *The Variorum Edition of the Poems of W. B. Yeats,* ed. Peter Allt and Russell K. Alspach (New York: Macmillan, 1957), 260. Further references to *The Variorum Edition of the Poems* are abbreviated *VP*.

22. *The Collected Works of W. B. Yeats,* vol. 3, *Autobiographies,* ed. William H. O'Donnell and Douglas N. Archibald (New York: Scribner, 1999), 163, 218. Hereafter cited parenthetically as *A*.

23. Yeats was impressed with Augustus John's drawing of him for capturing this occulted aspect of his temperament (Foster, *The Apprentice Mage,* 371).

24. James Pethica, "Aesthetics," in *W. B. Yeats in Context,* ed. David Holdeman and Ben Levitas (Cambridge: Cambridge University Press, 2010), 208.

25. Stephen Coote, *W. B. Yeats: A Life* (London: Hodder and Stoughton, 1997), 228.

26. George Watson, "Yeats, Victorianism, and the 1890s," in *The Cambridge Companion to W. B. Yeats,* ed. Marjorie Howes and John Kelly (Cambridge: Cambridge University Press, 2006), 55. James Pethica concurs in "Aesthetics," 208.

27. Stephen Regan observes that aestheticism prepared the way for Yeats to embrace a modernist emphasis on poetic form, and I would contend that it left an analogous impress on Yeats's intermediate, revivalist poetry. Stephen Regan, "The *Fin de Siecle,* 1885–1898," in Holdeman and Levitas, *W. B. Yeats in Context,* 27.

28. The *Samhain* series is published in W. B. Yeats, *Explorations* (New York: Macmillan, 1961), 73–221. Hereafter cited parenthetically as *S*.

29. W. B. Yeats, *The Land of Heart's Desire* (London: T. Fisher Unwin, 1894). Hereafter cited parenthetically as *L*.

30. Oscar Wilde, "The Critic as Artist," in *CW,* 977.

31. A. Norman Jeffares, *A New Commentary on the Poems of W. B. Yeats* (London: Macmillan, 1984), 103.

Part II

YEATS AND AFTERWORDS

CHAPTER 5

"The Age-Long Memoried Self"
Yeats and the Promise of Coming Times

GREGORY CASTLE

Everyone has an origin, most of the time a dreamed one.
—Jonathan Littell

In memory only, reconsidered passion.
—T. S. Eliot

In the wake of the riots surrounding the première of J. M. Synge's *The Playboy of the Western World,* February 1907, W. B. Yeats wrote of the need to be "free from all the rest, sullen anger, solemn virtue, calculating anxiety, gloomy suspicion, prevaricating hope," so that we might be "reborn in gaiety."[1] He was writing in "Poetry and Tradition," a pivotal essay that spells out his revamped theory of tradition (no longer that which is grounded in the folk) and the centrality of poetry and personality to it. It echoes the tenor of Nietzsche's *The Gay Science*, in which the philosopher notes that "the one thing needful" is "to 'give style' to one's character—a great and rare art!" To give style to character is to open life itself up to alteration, correction, revision. The "great liberator" for Nietzsche is "the idea that life could be an experiment of the seeker for knowledge—and not a duty, not a calamity, not trickery."[2] This is the crux of Nietzsche's "gay science" and, I would argue, of Yeats's conception of personality as a "deliberate self-delighting happiness" that "builds up into a most personal and wilful fire." This "shaping joy" that "must be always making and mastering" is the work of the artist's hands and tongue; but his eyes lead him to the "submissive, sorrowful contemplation of the great irremediable things." The poet's transfiguring gaiety is a rectifying drive that unfolds "at the trysting-place of mortal and immortal, time and eternity."[3] Yeats consistently uses the temporality of mortality (memory, remembrance, commemoration) to illustrate the process of "shaping" oneself, "for no man has ever . . . found that trysting-place, for he could but come to the understanding of himself, to the mastery of unlocking words after long frequenting the great Masters, hardly without ancestral memory of the like."[4]

By reframing the relation between the artist and tradition in terms of a coordination of timely rectification and timeless truth, Yeats seeks to redefine the relation between memory and desire, history and futurity. The image of the "trysting-place" suggests a space in which temporalities converge, in which the "age-long memoried self"—a figure for the dialectical entwinement of eternity and mortal time—emerges at a crisis point "that joins [it] for certain moments to our trivial daily mind."[5] If Yeats revives the past it is in order to fulfill the promise of this crisis, which means that "revival" is not really about the past at all but about the *production of futurity*. What Yeatsean revivalism (indeed, what revivalism at large)[6] accomplishes is the liberation of the future from the past. This perspective requires us to regard the past as always, in some sense, *in error*, and it is this quality of being in error that permits a rectifying leap forward that prepares us for yet another leap. I am offering here a way of understanding Yeats's revivalism as a mode of critical self-reckoning in which the poet's "corrective gaze" lays bare a future that belongs to the future, not the past. His entire career bears the stamp of this futural state; his work persistently looks forward to a moment in which misprision can be revised, but it just as persistently insists that any re-vision will be, in its turn, a kind of *felix culpa,* a staging ground for yet another reckoning. Yeats's work posits a new kind of subject, akin to Nietzsche's "free spirits," those "philosophers of the future" who wish to be "something more, higher, greater and thoroughly different," something "that does not want to be misunderstood or taken for what it is not." The free spirit, even when targeting himself, longs to "blow away . . . ancient and stupid prejudice and misunderstanding."[7]

This Nietzschean vision of a rectifying future can help us read the underlying temporal dynamics of misprision, which is governed by a dialectical logic of misrecognition first theorized by G. W. F. Hegel and later developed by the psychoanalyst Jacques Lacan and the neo-Hegelian theorist Slavoj Žižek. According to Žižek, in Hegelian dialectics (specifically in the moment of synthesis that Hegel called the "negation of the negation") "what first appears as an external obstacle reveals itself to be an inherent hindrance, i.e., an outside force turns into an inner compulsion."[8] The negative character of the obstacle constitutes the moment of misrecognition, and it has a necessary role to play in the dialectical process, which Lacan understood when he theorized misrecognition (*mésconnaissance*) as fundamental to the formation of the ideal ego.[9] What has not been theorized in this line of thought is the *temporality* of misprision (of error, of misrecognition), which posits a time of recognition (which is always an opportunity for rectification) that is itself partial and erroneous, that demands further opportunities to recognize. My argument offers a new understanding of temporality that significantly alters how we read Yeats, who has for too long been understood in terms of mythic memory, of nostalgic yearning, of "celtic twilights" and legendary heroics. It offers a new way of reading not a mythologized past but a mythology of the future, one that requires our attendance on error and misrecognition, for in them we discover, as Yeats did, the promise of "the dim coming times."[10]

As early as 1897, in "The Celtic Element in Literature," Yeats warned against simplistic, essentialist, and stereotyped characterizations of the Irish, but he did not hesitate to misrecognize Ireland and the Irish past in his turn, proffering his own idealizations in order to supplant Matthew Arnold's colonialist primitivism (the Celt as "undisciplinable, anarchical, and turbulent by nature") with a more noble and desirable essence, the "ancient religion" that for him lay at the foundation of Irish society.[11] In the self-reflexive span of his career, this naïve, ethnographic idealism gives way ultimately to the testamentary bard who wishes to make the unity of his own experience (his aesthetic *Bildung*) coextensive with a unity of culture. However, critics who have looked at Yeats's career tend to leave unexamined its temporal dimension. Richard Greaves, for example, speaks of "the figure of Yeats the poet, textually constructed, existing within the work," while at the same time insisting on a "flesh-and-blood" Yeats who "guarantees a connection between the work and the life."[12] Yug Mohit Chaudhry is also interested in a "textual" Yeats, specifically as manifested in the original publication and reception of his work, which had, especially in the revivalist phase, "a contradictory and mutually antagonistic character."[13] Missing from these and other historical formulations is a consideration of a temporality that subverts easy distinctions between living authors and timeless texts and that draws out the logic of misprision in the succession of published works. Late in his life, Yeats wrote that a poet "is never the bundle of accident and incoherence that sits down to breakfast; he has been reborn as an idea, something intended, complete."[14] I believe that he had come to understand that the poet's labor was to know his own relationship to time, and that the idea of completeness could only be understood in a futural state, in a "coming time" pregnant with promise. The pathway to this future, the unfolding of a career (*Bildungsprojekt*), knits together mistakes and misrecognitions and transforms them into necessities. Put another way, "truth grabs error by the scruff of the neck in the mistake."[15]

My understanding of Yeats invites us to accommodate an aesthetic that, like the temporality it unfolds, is fundamentally rectifying. Thus the recapitulation of Arnold's Celticism, which Yeats believed was a matter of critical restatement, can be read as a rectifying moment that makes possible later, more canny instances of productive error. We see throughout his career this reuse of the "backward glance" so often associated with superficial understandings of revivalism, one that serves a rhetorical purpose in pitching the text, and the reader, toward a revival yet to come, a rectifying corrective gaze that enables the poet to regard the past not for what it *was* but for what it *will have been*. This uncanny temporality is rather like Rome as Freud described it, the "ancient public buildings and temples" surviving in the present "not by ruins of themselves but of later restorations."[16]

To show how consistently the logic of misprision enables a fresh perspective on Yeats's revivalism and his attitude toward time, I will focus on three very different phases of his work: (1) the early love poems, (2) the Cuchulain plays, and (3) the late elegiac and testamentary poems. The love poems are less about lovelorn nostalgia (despite the aura of legendary past-time they so effortlessly create) than a tactical *mis*remembering whose affective charge is marked in a recursive relay of verb tenses in which memory provokes in the present a vision of how the past produces futural states. We see a similarly "tensed" temporality in the Cuchulain plays, which articulate futurity in terms of a renown that is forever deferred, the better to savor it as a just reward. Finally, the memorializing tenor of the late poetry, in which Yeats takes on the mantel of the Anglo-Irish bard, can be read anew through the lens of misprision. What we find in the great elegies is a refinement of the corrective gaze, now cast over an entire career, and a mature understanding of the futurity of the future.

THE TIME OF LOVE AND LEGEND

In the temporality of revival, the past holds the promise of the future; it is a schooling in doubt and mortality that requires the backward glance (nostalgia) in order to come to the knowledge that will build the future because it is *of* the future. This coming-to-knowledge is the *corrective gaze* that in principle can find no horizon—not because knowledge is a form of absolute extension but because it must always account in advance for what is presently unknowable. Truth, eternal beauty, the absolute: these are all postulates or aspirations that organize errors and give them the character of destiny. This dynamic of self-overcoming, understood as a logic of misrecognition, is first strongly evident in the early love poems, which are infused with a sense of otherworldly longing for what is yet to come, which in the folkloric world is so often spatialized, set off in an enchanted "elsewhere." Elizabeth Cullingford has argued that the early love poems borrow the traditions of courtly love and that this investment in literary history is cut across by identifications with "women, fairies, primitives, lunatics, and saints," which fractures "the phallic, unified Cartesian self, foundation of the Law of the Father."[17] Over against this unified Cartesian self we find in these poems a preoccupation with a self riven by disunifying temporalities, akin to being immersed in "faery glamour,"[18] where time "drops in decay, / Like a candle burnt out" ("The Moods," *VP*, 142), but it is not absolutely annihilated. Here we might well speak of a break in time, or more radically of time's fundamental dehiscence.

Misprision in these poems frequently manifests in a kind of temporal decay, a falling away from *chronologos* into a recursive relay of tenses that acts out the poet's struggle with recognition. They open into worlds in which, for the poet and the reader, something is reckoned with, corrected, and rectified—if only to clear a space for future recognitions of error, mistake, divergence, straying.[19] In "He remembers Forgotten Beauty" (*VP*, 155–56), the poet reduplicates the temporal ambivalence of a backward glance that is not yet a corrective gaze. But the "loveliness" the poet wants, which "has long faded from the world," is not annihilated, for the addressee of the poem is idealized and internalized, transformed into an enigmatic, unknowable kernel in "a more dream-heavy land, / A more dream-heavy hour than this." He uses mystical symbols (flames, thrones, swords) that are multiplied in the spatial imbrication that stands in for the temporality of misrecognition, "flame on flame," "throne over throne"—pure elements, celestial beings, all are at best "in half sleep" where they "Brood [or *brood on*] her high lonely mysteries." Barton Friedman observes of this poem that it tells of "an absent presence, persisting only in memory."[20] But if memory is the key, it is because the time of memory allows for the hope of demystification and pure presence—that is to say, of *recognition*.

It is notable that so many of the love poems tactically redeploy the tropes of faery to express an inexpressible desire, one that lies "in the deep heart's core" ("The Lake Isle of Inisfree," *VP*, 117). They explore the mind and memory of a beloved, who is, like the faeries, the enchanted and sublime object of the lover's longing. In some cases, she stands amid tumultuous "otherworlds," able to quell even the power of the "Horses of Disaster" that "plunge in the heavy clay" and cause a fundamental disturbance in the heavens, "their hoofs heavy with tumult" ("He bids his Beloved be at Peace," *VP*, 154). In others, the beloved is knit into the hazy and rich crepuscular temporality of the fairy and legendary worlds. The beloved is often, in memory, like one who has passed; if not actually dead, she is stranded in a death-like zone either through the poet's own labyrinthine regard or through faery connivance. "For the early Yeats," writes Jahan Ramazani, "mournful love is the wellspring of poetic utterance" and it leaves its mark in the "aggressive absenting of the beloved."[21] It should be noted that this absenting and its aggression in the text is a function of the poet's increasingly willful misrecognition of his beloved in memory.

Many of the poems in *The Wind Among the Reeds* make a spectacle of the beloved's presence, paradoxically through the intricate play of tenses. In memory, in the writing that conjures the remembered object, her presentness has the ontological status of a revenant:

> *I had* a beautiful friend . . .
> *She looked* in my heart one day
> And saw your image there;
> She *has gone* weeping away.
>> ("The Lover mourns for the Loss of Love," *VP*, 152,
>> emphasis added)

After the simple declaration of a narrative past ("She looked in my heart *one day*"), the "beautiful friend" is suspended in the present perfect tense of nonspecific temporality, *having gone* "weeping away." Yeats achieves here a kind of proleptic haunting, the ceremonial return of the revenant that stands as proof against the reductive charms of dialectical closure (either as unforgettable memory or total forgetfulness). The specter of the past evades being fixed because, as Jacques Derrida writes, "haunting is historical, to be sure, but it is not *dated*, it is never docilely given a date in the chain of presents, day after day, according to the instituted order of a calendar."[22] The poet knows that there can be no closure, only "gradual Time's last gift, a written speech" ("Upon a House Shaken by the Land Agitation," *VP*, 264), which takes on here a spectral character, for it must have extension, must be transmissible into the future as a *last* gift.

These poems mark a crucial turning point in the development of Yeats's aesthetics, for in them he is able to work out the temporalities of misrecognition in a way that helps him overcome the naïve backward glance, so tempting to the revivalist, and to revitalize what is remembered, to bring it into the circuit of present consciousness, wherein the curious forward momentum of memorial narrative rushes toward what is to come. Looking back is not a nostalgic or reifying gesture, then, but a tactical and recuperative one, which performs a largely semiotic function. As we have seen, verb tenses are of particular importance in the poetry, where they mark multiple "tensed" temporalities in the expressed world (the "otherworld" of fairy and of the lover's memory), while acknowledging, by their canniness and excess, that they do not mark "real time."[23] In some cases, as in "A Woman Homer Sung" (*VP*, 254–55), from *The Green Helmet* (1910), Yeats intensifies the effects of otherworldly temporalities by using a mythic trope, Helen of Troy, that doubles as the sign of the poet's present desire. Helen is a mythological sign, borrowed from a *time long passed*, and as such stands in for the beloved (say, "Maud Gonne," yet another sign) and thereby performs the temporal and ontological ambivalence at the heart of misrecognition.

In the commingled worlds of fairy and memory, the lover seems to balance in equal measures the backward glance and the corrective gaze:

If any man drew near
When I was young,
I thought, 'He holds her dear,'
And shook with hate and fear.
But O! 'twas bitter wrong
If he could pass her by
With an indifferent eye.

(*VP*, 254–55)

The poet keeps his "hate and fear" to himself but castigates in thought any man who *may have once* remained indifferent to his beloved and judges it a "bitter wrong" that indifference should result in such a massive misrecognition of his beloved's beauty *back then*. This works upon the poet's memory and is the cause for what he writes now, which is in part a reflection on his own past ("When I was young"). For in the dream of the present, signaled definitively by the change in physical appearance ("now, being grey"), he reimagines his own poetic tributes to the "thing her body was" and misrecognizes them as prophecies that for others *had been* "shadowed in a glass." The temporal *volta*, "And now, being grey," signals the past perfect of memory, in which the poet dreams of bringing his thought to "such a pitch" that he can thrust it forward and settle it upon the future ("That coming time can say"). "The perfect," writes Émile Benveniste, "creates a living connection between the past event and the present in which its evocation takes place. It is the tense for the one who relates the facts as a witness, as a participant; it is thus also the tense that will be chosen by whoever wishes to make the reported event ring vividly in our ears and to link it to the present." But it is not appropriate for history, for such a tense, like the present, is "incompatible with the historical intention."[24] In the retr(o)action of memory, in the nesting of perfect tenses, the past is wrought to the pitch of a "heroic dream"— the poet's *present* reward for remembering well his own desire, an instance of misremembering that also limns the futural state already present in the nested past.

The costs of this misremembering are reckoned in "To a Child Dancing in the Wind" (*VP*, 312) and "Two Years Later" (*VP*, 312–13) (from *Responsibilities*, 1916). Though at first blush the works of an early period, these poems are exquisitely balanced between the eroticized imagery of faery and the complex temporal shifts that mark the middle and later periods. Yeats rehearses here the themes of "Among School Children" and "Prayer for my Daughter," the idea of the dance as impervious to time, to "wind or water's roar," and the image of youth unscarred by lost love or "fool's triumph" ("To a Child," *VP*, 312). The image of the dancing girl epitomizes youth, but Yeats challenges the image by following it with a frankly pedagogical reconsideration of the experience "two years later." Like Wordsworth in "Tintern Abbey," Yeats announces a temporal gap that structures the meaning of the poem, a meaning which is all about structuring a gap between inaugural naïve misrecognitions and subsequent actions that are themselves more canny instances of misprision. They draw out the bitter truth of the dialectics of time. As James Rolleston puts it, "the energized present moment opens onto the entirety of the past; but the resultant vision of sovereignty and intellectual coherence is in drastic tension with a sense of the present as exiled, unfree, provisional."[25] The poet sees that the "daring / Kind eyes" of his beloved "should be more learn'd," but he also understands that time has dropped a veil between them. "I could have warned you, but you are young, / So we speak a different tongue" (*VP*, 212–13). He speaks conditionally ("I could have") from the future in "a barbarous tongue," perhaps because he has placed himself beyond the pale of youth. His beloved seems to dance in a time no longer available to him, and his recognition of this fact is nearly buried by a conventional temporal difference ("I am old and you are young"). A bit later still, in "His Phoenix" (*VP*, 353–54) of 1919, he uses the same image of absolute division when he speaks of "that barbarous crowd" who will, in days to come, measure his beloved against "some young belle." His memory is not yet recognized as prospective; it suffices to have known her. As for those who misrecognize her, "let them have their day." As with *Responsibilities* as a whole, these poems oscillate between a backward glance tinged with regret and a corrective gaze that transforms regret into a creative longing for "that most lonely thing," the remembered beloved. The lover has not yet acceded to the place of the warrior, who also stakes everything on the truth of memory as the promise of coming times.

CUCHULAIN AND THE MYTHOLOGY OF THE FUTURE

At precisely the time when Yeats was exploring the temporalities of memory and desire in the love poems, he was dramatizing the Cuchulain legends in strikingly similar terms and, I would argue, was beginning to see pastness as a kind of futural state. These legends appealed to Yeats for much the same reason they appealed to Standish O'Grady, Lady Gregory, and Eleanor Hull: they offered a template for heroic responses to the world.[26] Lady Gregory's treatment of the legendary material was particularly useful for Yeats, in large because it reflected her own aristocratic heritage. In the "Dramatis Personae" section of *Autobiographies,* he confesses as much: "Looking back, *Cuchulain of Muirthemne* and *Gods and Fighting Men* at my side, I can see that they were made possible by her past; semi-feudal Roxborough, her inherited sense of caste, her knowledge of that top of the world where men and women are valued for their manhood and their charm, not for their opinions."[27] As Joseph Valente has demonstrated, the revivalist Cuchulain was in many ways a "redacted" version of the hero, less the "hypermasculine" figure we find in the legendary source material than an exemplar of ascendancy manhood, a "morally disciplined warrior" who "sublimat[es] his individual valor and rapacity to the defense of the social order." The fierce legendary Cuchulain is transformed in a "compacted dialectic" in which hypermasculinity is sublated in the formation of a chivalric hero.[28] I would like to suggest, as a codicil to Valente's argument, that Yeats's cycle of plays is well suited, by virtue of its temporal extension over a thirty-year period, to convey the pedagogical dynamics of the logic of misprision, in which fierce individualism can be tutored by the oceanic comforts of the tribe and futurity gained by the sublime error of self-sacrifice.[29]

The Cuchulain plays—*On Baile's Strand* (1904), *The Green Helmet* (1910), *At the Hawk's Well* (1917), *The Only Jealousy of Emer* (1919), and *The Death of Cuchulain* (1938)—explore the dimensions of a heroism defined as much by error, misrecognition, and ambivalence as by superior courage, strength, and fortitude. What matters is not present action but how that action is remembered: "I care not though I were to live but one day and one night, if only my fame and my deed live

after me."[30] In *On Baile's Strand*, Cuchulain, King Conchubar's cham-
pion, whom "nobody can buy or bid or bind," has become a threat to
the community; he struggles against his king's demand for fealty
but ultimately capitulates.[31] When a young man arrives, he seeks to
befriend him, but Conchubar claims that "Cuchulain is my man, and
I forbid it" (*VPl*, 511). Cuchulain's failure to recognize this stranger as
his son, who is "under bonds / To tell [his] name to no man" (*VPl*,
502), is less a function of naïveté then of a lack of vital information;
the result, however, is the same. The Blind Man and the Fool, para-
gons of misrecognition (of the canny and naïve variety, respectively),
form the comic frame that provides the necessary exposition for the
main dramatic action and urge Cuchulain toward a painful reali-
zation. An initial naïve misrecognition is supplanted by the tragic rec-
ognition urged upon him by the Blind Man ("It is his own son he
has slain," *VPl*, 522), which in turn leads him to lash out at his king.
Yeats leaves out of his play (though it is there in Gregory's *Cuchulain
of Muirthemne*) the essential detail that the druid Cathbad "put an
enchantment on him"[32] to channel his anger toward the waves, which
he fights, in a fury of misprision, for three days: "I cannot see him
now," cries the Fool, "He has killed kings and giants, but the waves
have mastered him" (*VPl*, 524). The Blind Man understands what the
Fool and Cuchulain himself do not, that in his misapprehending rage
the warrior conquers his master—"He sees King Conchubar's crown
on every one of them" (*VPl*, 524)—by means of a tactical disavowal of
the cultural requirement (the imposition of bonds, or *gessa*) that had
caused the crisis in the first place. It is a symbolic conquest, a delib-
erate misrecognition, for to recognize truly would be to suffer a deci-
sive ethical lapse into regicide, which would rob Cuchulain's heroism
of the positive dialectical charge required to propel his being and his
acts, as the lineaments of fame, into coming times.

For Yeats at mid-career, lover and hero fight the same battle with
time and learn the same lesson that future greatness (fame, love) is
rooted in error, violence, and bitterness. In *The Green Helmet*, heroism
is rooted in clownish misunderstandings and fictions; for the Red
Man, "that juggler from the sea [Manannan], that old red herring . . .
has set us all by the ears," and the men complain that their wives egg

them on: "We are to kill each other that [they] may sport with us" (*VPl*, 422–43, 444). Nothing is quite what it seems to be. When the Red Man demands a head for "the debt that's owing" (*VPl*, 451), Cuchulain steps forward to put an end to the cascading misrecognitions of his heroic capacity, but he is crowned, not beheaded. Unlike Conchubar, who demands recognition from Cuchulain, the Red Man requires *mis*recognition. Michael McAteer sees in this play a critical advance on the earlier one. "The final crowning of Cuchulain" in *The Green Helmet*, he writes, "acquires a farcical quality intended to pre-empt the charade of the ritual in *On Baile's Strand*." In effect, Yeats writes *The Green Helmet* "retrospectively as a prologue to the earlier play."[33] The temporal ordering needs to be reversed, however, for in the context of the poet's career, it makes more sense to see *The Green Helmet* as a corrective transition that prepares the spectator for the return of ritual in *At the Hawk's Well*, which marks time as mythic (legendary Ireland, medieval Japan) without "dating" it as past.

M. M. Bakhtin speaks of the "absolute conclusiveness and closedness" of epic time,[34] which is both evoked and deconstructed in Yeats's adaptation of Noh styles, well suited to the uncanny world of intersecting temporalities, where an Old Man and a Young Man (Cuchulain) seek the same source of eternity, the same freedom from time, from substance and matter, in the coming time of fame. Yeats's play captures the moment when the immortal Hawk Woman, guardian of the well, is misrecognized by the Young Man, who is thereby spurred to heroic accomplishment *in time:*

> Why do you fix those eyes of the hawk upon me?
> I am not afraid of you, bird, woman, or witch.
> Do what you will, I shall not leave this place
> Till I have grown immortal like yourself.
>
> (*VPl*, 409)

Cuchulain does not see a woman so much as a principle of ambivalence and misapprehension. The Old Man fears her—"I cannot bear her eyes, they are not of this world" (*VPl*, 409)—but Cuchulain seeks to master her. He defies the unknowable (because unrecognizable)

Hawk Woman in an untimely *agon* that pits mortal against what has no mortality, the Mórrígan, the goddess of war fury—who, in the *Táin Bó Cuailnge,* goads Cuchulain and "appears on his shoulder as a hooded crow, portending the scavenging of his corpse."[35] For now, the Young Man turns *agoniste* into allegiance: "Grey bird, you shall be perched upon my wrist, / Some were called queens and yet *have been perched* there" (*VPl,* 410, emphasis added). In the uncertain duration of the perfect tense, sustained by the First Musician ("I *have heard* water plash . . . he *has heard* the plash"), the Young Man goes after her "as if in a dream," but she "*has fled* from me and *hidden* in the rocks" (*VPl,* 410, 411, emphasis added). He cries, "The clash of arms again!" and then, in the third person of heroic assertion, announces himself to the future: "He comes! Cuchulain, son of Sualtim comes!" (*VPl,* 412). In an act of verbal self-estrangement that marries in its performative utterance an act and its pronouncement, the Young Man lays claim to eternity by heroically resisting an immortal foe (the "women of the hills") and asserting, through self-sacrifice, the personality that endures in the warrior's name. The play marks a further advance, for the hero's misprision is cannier, more self-aware, but it still entails a misrecognition of the vital future, which takes the form of immortality.

The Only Jealousy of Emer presents a quite different futurity, one held for ransom by Bricriu, a trickster figure who forces from Emer a tragic misrecognition—a "bitter reward"—as the price of saving her husband from the ghostly catatonia that has robbed him of his heroic identity. The doubleness staged in this play—the Figure of Cuchulain is a manifestation of "Bricriu of the Sidhe," "maker of discord among gods and men," while the Ghost of Cuchulain is a "senseless image" washed up by the very waves he had striven to conquer after unwittingly killing his son (*VPl,* 543, 535)—dramatizes the tragic contradiction of the hero whose fallible humanity is emboldened by the seductive proximity of immortality. In the occult terms that Yeats was just beginning to formulate at this time, the Figure and the Ghost model two spheres of being: the *antithetical* ("our inner world of desire and imagination") and the *primary* ("that objectivity of mind which . . . lays 'stress upon that which is external to the mind'").[36] In McAteer's reading, which follows the outlines provided by George

Mills Harper, the Ghost of Cuchulain is associated with the anti-thetical pole, while the Figure of Cuchulain is associated with the primary pole, though the latter was not pure objectivity as such, but "subjectivity distorted in a period dominated by objectivity," hence the discord he sows "is not in the nature of objectivity itself but in the subjection of the interior life to external, objective form."[37] Like Cuchulain, Yeats wrestles with time: he desires the pure objectivity of eternity, but his struggle with this purity generates the promise of coming times, where heroism sustains what the past has made possible.

The splitting and nullification of Cuchulain's heroic personality is both remedied and surmounted by his wife Emer's own heroic action. Though "she restores Cuchulain's vitality and heroic stature," Richard Cave notes, she can do so only by renouncing her love for him, an act that "sustains her own self-respect, but at a terrible cost emotionally."[38] The play begins with the otherworldly intonations of the First Musician, who sings of a loveliness mysteriously "dragged into being" and calls up the spectacle of "that amorous, violent man, renowned Cuchulain," who "lies dead or swooning," his wife Emer and his mistress Eithne Inguba by his side (*VPl*, 534, 536). Neither this "swooning" Ghost nor the "crouching" Figure in the shadows is the actual warrior whom she loves. Emer must recognize and trust that one of them harbors the true Cuchulain. But her bond of trust is "imagined within / The labyrinth of the mind" (*VPl*, 532, 534), and issues not only in loveliness but in the terror of misrecognition. Opposed to lifeless eternity is a futurity in which the hero's pledge is a hostage to time, for in the temporal process by which trust is experienced, Emer becomes bonded to Cuchulain and both learn the difference between a simulacrum and the real thing; and on the basis of this higher-order knowledge, they make reasoned decisions but also more cunning errors, more canny displacements and idealizations. Though its ratification is postponed, Emer's trust is not misgiven, for it is placed in what *will have been recovered* in the fullness of time.

Emer is caught up in a battle for trust in which she must figure out who the real Cuchulain is based solely on what she hears from simulacra of him. In fine, she must trust what she patently misrecognizes: "Although they have dressed him out in his grave-clothes / And stretched his limbs," she tells Eithne, "Cuchulain is not dead" (*VPl*,

535). She is thrown into the kind of radical doubt that calls for an equally radical, because absolute, trust; her jealousy, grounded in Eithne's assertion, which she knows to be true, that "he loves me best, / Being his newest love" (*VPl*, 537), must be overcome in the sacrifice she makes to the dialectics of heroism in which Cuchulain's future is regained by the utter negation of her own. The idea is to get past the ghostly "senseless image," which introduces the horrifying potential of endless simulacra, serving both to compound misrecognition and to conflate what the play seeks, by using stylized masks and movements, to keep apart. Emer calls on Eithne to kiss the image, for "the pressure of your mouth upon his mouth / May reach him where he is" (*VPl*, 541). To free her husband, guarantor of her trust, she must cut through prior error and misconception and, in the same moment, recognize and renounce him. "My husband is there," she cries, because Bricriu has "dissolved the dark / That hid him from your eyes, but not that other / That's hidden you from his" (*VPl*, 547). Husband and wife enact vividly the dialectics of recognition as described by Hegel, specifically the stage at which dialectical logic "breaks up" into extremes that "are opposed to one another, and of which one is merely recognized, while the other only recognizes."[39] As the one who only recognizes, Emer surrenders a future in which Cuchulain could claim and recognize her. Far from completing a dialectic, her sacrifice brings it to a standstill and articulates in a flash the tragedy of eternity, here figured as the utter loss of time. "I have but two joyous thoughts, two things I prize, / A hope, a memory, and now you claim that hope" (*VPl*, 545, 547). Without the future ("that hope"), memory degrades into nostalgia, cut off from the dialectical pleasures of fulfillment in time. What she fears to feel in the days ahead is the weight of a restive past that has not sprung forward as hope, as the pure positing power of human desire to find the repletion of being in coming times.

Not even Fand, seemingly as radiant and full as the moon in the fifteenth phase of complete beauty,[40] can reawaken the man that sleeps in the Ghost of Cuchulain. When she asks what beleaguers him, he can only reply, "Memories / Have pulled my head upon my knees" (*VPl*, 553). In a flurry of near recognitions, which mime the cascading quality of dialectical misprision, he finally sees her, as he had seen the Hawk Woman, for the incomplete, hybrid being that she is: "Half woman and half bird of prey" (*VPl*, 553). She offers temporal oblivion ("Time shall seem to stay his course"), and he begins to succumb to this otherworld

> Where no one speaks of broken troth,
> For all have washed out of their eyes
> Wind-blown dirt of their memories
> To improve their sight?
> (VPl, 555, 557)

The pathos of his temptation nearly overwhelms the action, until a single line from Emer—"I renounce Cuchulain's love for ever" (*VPl*, 561)—reorganizes the tableau and asserts *her* ethical authority. She saves her husband from an unheroic limbo utterly outside time, and thereby rightly recognizes the heroic champion of Ulster. But by renouncing her love for him, she refuses her own fame, her own claim on futurity, in order to guarantee his in trust. As if to compound the dialectical *frisson*, Eithne steps in and demands recognition *from and for* him: "Come to me, my beloved, it is I. / I, Eithne Inguba. Look! He is there" (*VPl*, 561). The Musicians' song concludes the play with a cruel reminder of Emer's "bitter reward," for her renunciation entails not only that she forfeit all hope but that she also forfeit all desire, the primal engine of all hope: for "He that has loved the best / May turn from a statue / His too human breast" (*VPl*, 563, 565). The logic of misrecognition is all but veiled by Emer's inconsolable grief that follows her "barbarous gift of self-sacrifice."[41]

This mythology of the future is sustained, nearly twenty years later, in *The Death of Cuchulain* (1938), which occludes even further the epic world in which Cuchulain's death would acquire an autonomous, commemorative status: "*A bare stage of any period*," the playwright laconically advises (*VPl*, 1051). The fantastic dualism of *Emer* is totally absent, for Cuchulain is "whole" again, ready to let death come for him. He is assaulted by mystifications, the work of Maeve and the Mórrígan, who sow misunderstanding and misconception by sending Eithne with a message purporting to be from Emer, urging

Cuchulain to attack Maeve "with all those Connacht ruffians at her back" (*VPl*, 1053). But Cuchulain has ceased to be the "violent man [who] forgave no treachery" (*VPl*, 1055) and appears to have reached a point of self-recognition that makes no demand of recognition from others. Eithne, recognizing for herself Cuchulain's resolve, lays claim to an even greater sacrifice than had Emer: "I shall denounce myself," she says, and surrenders to total annihilation "so that my shade can stand among the shades / And greet your shade and prove it is no traitor" (*VPl*, 1055, 1056). Her "wild words" cannot stand long against Cuchulain's declaration: "I make the truth" (*VPl*, 1056). He is put to the test by Aoife, mother of the son he had slain in *On Baile's Strand*, who comes to him when he is wounded and tethered to a pillar-stone. "Am I recognised, Cuchulain?" she asks. And while he is confused— "Where am I? Why am I here?"—he does recognize her, and with a hero's generosity he tells her, "You have the right to kill me" (*VPl*, 1057). With the same generosity he prompts the Blind Man, who is only earning his "twelve pennies," "you have a knife, but have you sharpened it?" (*VPl*, 1060). The corrective gaze that he casts upon his life is a purifying heroic act, which triggers a flash of knowledge that will echo like thunder into his future renown. His fame assured, his testaments made to the women in his life, the "great fighting-man" thinks of his "soul's first shape, a soft feathery shape," and recognizes at last the strangeness of his own being. He is beyond the time of his death, for his soul is ready, "it is about to sing" (*VPl*, 1060–61). That the play ends by idealizing Cuchulain in the contemporary idiom of nationalism, thus insuring further idealizations, does not materially affect the main point, which is that the truth arises out of misrecognition.

ELEGY AND THE "MEMORIED SELF"

The elegiac mood of *Emer* and *The Death of Cuchulain* is matched by much of the late poetry, in which the poet, groomed in heroic loss, aspires to a unity of being and culture, a grand misapprehension of his own desire to be remembered by his successors and descendants.

Rached Khalifa has pointed out that "Yeats's conception and over-valuation of 'unity' is something of a structural consistency, rather than of conjunctural contingency. It became the poet's lifelong alternative to modern social and subjective fragmentation."[42] The possibility of "structural consistency" is intriguing though not as a bulwark against modern fragmentation; what I think we see in Yeats's work (what Yeats himself began to recognize in mid-career) is the "memoried self" achieving a form of totality founded on a structural consistency of error. In the "Hodos Chameliontos" section of *The Trembling of the Veil* (1922), Yeats meditates on this canny form of misprision:

> I know that revelation is from the self, but from that age-long memoried self, that shapes the elaborate shell of the mollusc and the child in the womb, that teaches the birds to make their nest; and that genius is a crisis that joins that buried self for certain moments to our trivial daily mind. There are, indeed, personifying spirits that we had best call but Gates and Gate-keepers, because through their dramatic power they bring our souls to crisis, to Mask and Image. . . . They have but one purpose, to bring their chosen man to the greatest obstacle he may confront without despair.[43]

Yeats calls our attention to the necessity of obstacle, the "suffering of desire" in which the corrective gaze—"Gates and Gate-keepers" with their power over crisis—results in a Hegelian labor of obstacles overcome: "the *re-creation* of the man through the art." Michael Sidnell discerns in Yeats's memorializations "a richly satisfying autobiographical pattern,"[44] but this kind of discernment is possible only if we regard Yeats's career as abstracted from both corrosive nostalgia and the fertile ground of the future. Yeats's own sense of the pattern of his life is tempered and temporalized by "the suffering of desire." The masters of such suffering—Dante, Villon—are paradoxically free within an endless and terrifying reduplication of the self, for the "re-creation of the man through art, that birth of a new species of man, . . . is from terror."[45] Like Cuchulain, the poet's fame is secured by a reckless engagement with time: "Had not Dante and Villon understood that their fate wrecked what life could not rebuild, had they lacked their Vision of Evil . . . they could but have found a false beauty, or some momentary instinctive beauty, and suffered no change at all."[46]

In Yeats's late elegies, the generative state of futurity, in which suffering and change find their reward, emerges as the fateful "wrecking" of what does not belong to eternity. In one of his earliest poems about Coole Parke, "Upon a House Shaken by the Land Agitation," Yeats praised the "eagle thoughts that grow / Where wings have memory of wings, and all / That comes from the best knit to the best" (*VP*, 264). This finely knit world of remembered events is unraveled in "The Wild Swans at Coole" (*VP*, 322–23). The strange tense shifts that describe the "nineteenth autumn" in the second stanza—"has come upon me" . . . "since I first" . . . "I saw, before I had well finished" —posits a labyrinthine temporality, shattered by the swans that "scatter wheeling in great broken rings." The dialectics of memory is foreclosed as the future opens onto a mystery: "Among what rushes will they build," the poet asks, "delight[ing] men's eyes when I awake some day / To find they have flown away." Futurity is acknowledged ("wander where they will"), and while the poet worries that he will be left behind in the arid timelessness of nostalgia, he already positions himself *in time,* for he speaks from the future of the very future he fears he will miss: delight *will have filled* the eyes of men yet to come. The consolation of elegy is the promise of a time after loss and death— indeed, a promise of the future's promise, born of suffering desire: "I have looked upon these brilliant creatures / And now my heart is sore."

Most of the great elegies of *The Wild Swans at Coole* commemorate individuals (Robert Gregory, Alfred Pollexfen, Mabel Beardsley) as well as a way of life. "According to the elegy's standard fiction," writes Ramazani, "a collectivity mourns for an individual; Yeats inverts this dramatic configuration."[47] By means of this inversion, Yeats resignifies memory as a kind of collective fame in which the poet's self merges with the boundless futurity of Anglo-Irishry. "Heave no sigh, let no tear drop," Yeats writes in "The Gyres." "A greater, a more gracious time has gone" (*VP*, 564). Yet this is precisely what the "group elegies" disprove, for in them the Anglo-Irishry is portrayed as an object of *present* hope, not of nostalgic longing. David Ward summarizes a critical consensus when he argues that by 1898 Yeats had begun "to idealize certain Protestant aristocrats like the Gregorys along with their Gaelic peasants." Ward also notes that "he tended to identify any threats to the way of life he idealized at Coole Park as threats against himself."[48] "Coole Park, 1929" (*VP*, 488–89) reveals how this idealization was temporalized:

> They came like swallows and like swallows went,
> And yet a woman's powerful character
> Could keep a swallow to its first intent;
> And half a dozen in formation there,
> That seemed to whirl upon a compass-point,
> Found certainty upon the dreaming air,
> The intellectual sweetness of those lines
> That cut through time or cross it withershins.

The swallow-like occupants of the house, ephemeral beings whose song is short, gain something that the house confers (not the least because it is what they want from it), a level of aesthetic enjoyment that grants them access to the eternity of beauty (the swallow's "first intent"). But this eternity requires time both as a ground ("compass-point") and as a counter-tempo, predicated on misprision and misdirection ("withershins").[49] Time reverses back onto itself, which is a way of saying that it creates an infinite number of possible futures, each borne on (or born in) the cuts and crosses of misdirected temporality.

In a telling passage from *The Trembling of the Veil,* Yeats mentions that he does not dream of the woods of Coole, but they "are so much more knitted to my thought that when I am dead they will have, I am persuaded, my longest visit." The poet looks forward to a time when he will still visit Coole Park, when the past will be the very environment of his own spectral afterlife, even though he cannot concede that his death will be the end of the story. "When we are dead, according to my belief, we live our lives backward for a certain number of years, treading the paths that we have trodden, growing young again, and even childish again, till some attain innocence that is no longer a mere accident of nature, but the human intellect's crowning achievement."[50] *Dreaming back* moves the poet through experience back to innocence from a starting point that recognizes the precession of error, a starting point that is *yet to come*. In other words, the origin of innocence is this "crowning" act of positing it retrospectively from the standpoint of the future ("when we are dead"); the enjoyment of positing is the twin of the enjoyment of the symptom, which ruptures the surface of the present with a message from coming times. The nostalgic backward glance has now become a corrective gaze, one that informs and modifies the poet's commemorations.[51]

On the foundations of memory and history, Yeats creates, in poems like "In Memory of Major Robert Gregory" (*VP*, 323–28), recursive and ghostly temporalities, a remembered homecoming "beside a fire of turf in th' ancient tower." In using Robert Gregory to stand in for the archetypal Anglo-Irish gentleman, Yeats only gives him his due, in the poet's view of things, as he gave Edward Fitzgerald and Wolfe Tone theirs in "September 1913." His understanding of the latter two as "emblematic examples of upper-class Protestant *sprezzatura* and romance, generosity and leadership,"[52] chimes well with the treatment of Gregory; and both, I submit, are part of a rectifying pedagogical process in which these assessments will, in their turn, be reappraised. Indeed, "Major Robert Gregory," appears already to critique the very model of heroism it promotes, for Gregory also stands for something both aesthetically meditative and willfully destructive; he understands the "lovely intricacies of a house" but also consumes "the entire combustible world in one small room / As though dried straw." His future, back then, had been posited as a time of dreams, expressed in a complex nesting of tenses: "We dreamed that a great painter *had been born*" (my emphasis). Now the poet looks back upon his own backward glancing and thereby marks the difference of the corrective gaze, the "appropriate commentary on each."

Though on this occasion, loss "took all my heart for speech," the death of friends and colleagues gives rise in later poems to a "cold and passionate" testamentary desire, in which the "dream of the noble and the beggar-man" ("The Municipal Gallery Revisited," *VP*, 601) takes shape as a unity of culture, which the poet has already claimed as his own birthright and which therefore can be passed down, like "Sato's gift, a changeless sword," "from father unto son / And through the centuries" ("Meditations in Time of Civil War," *VP*, 421).[53] In a rectifying mood, the poet regards his own œuvre in this light: "as I look backward upon my own writing, I take pleasure alone in those verses where it seems to me *I have found* something hard and cold, some articulation of the Image which is the opposite of all that I am in my daily life."[54] Sidnell has offered a theory of this backward glance. Speaking of "The Tower," he writes that "Yeats developed a two-part dialectics: between his later work and his earlier work and between the primacies of the life in the poetry and of the poetry in the life."[55] Like other dialectical treatments of Yeats, this one mistakes static antinomy for dynamic dialectical progress. In Sidnell's view, the reciprocity of the present and the early poetic creations and the poetry-life synthesis amount to little more than summoning emblematic specters: Hanrahan, with his "horrible splendour of desire," "a woman won or woman lost" ("The Tower," *VP*, 411, 413). The problem with this reading is that it elides the temporality of misprision in which Yeats's late reflections on his earlier works and experience arise as opportunities for rectification and for staging yet another splendid instance. Of course, desire may feed on the past, may call "images and memories / From ruin or from ancient trees" (*VP*, 410), but its home is in coming times, where both fulfillment and inevitable renewal await. Indeed, the poet speaks precisely *in and of* the future of desire, for he "thought it all out twenty years ago" (*VP*, 411).

In part 2 of "The Tower," the poet recalls key figures from his early "Celtic Twilight" period under the aegis of Hanrahan, an "old lecher with a love on every wind," whose "deep considering mind" has "reckoned up every unforeknown, unseeing / Plunge . . . / Into the labyrinth of another's being" (*VP*, 413). The dialectic here is not between two abstractions—early and late Yeats—but between two moments, one a "reckoning," in which rectitude turns a cold eye on what has already passed, and one an "unforeknown" plunge, which is all the more symptomatic of what is to come for being "unseeing." To reckon up what one has not foreseen is to meditate on the futurity of the future, in which desire is "reckoned with" and found wanting, leaving open the possibility of yet another plunge. The "labyrinth of being" is the possibility of time, pregnant with its own promise; turning aside from it is tantamount to facing the horror of time's annulment:

> Does the imagination dwell the most
> Upon a woman won or woman lost?
> If on the lost, admit you turned aside
> From a great labyrinth out of pride,
> Cowardice, some silly over-subtle thought
> Or anything called conscience once;
> And that if memory recur, the sun's
> Under eclipse and the day blotted out.
>   (*VP*, 413–14)

Desire finally reveals itself inexorably implicated in loss and misrecognition ("pride," "cowardice," "over-subtle thought"), which threatens to cancel time. To sustain the future, memory must be transformed into hope and the promise of yet another future, yet another "horrible splendour." But if memory only "recurs," as it must in a static antithesis between early and late epochs, then time loses its generative power: the sun is eclipsed "and the day blotted out."

In "The Tower," in the late poems generally, Yeats moves closer to the Nietzschean estate of the free spirit, who lives according to "the dangerous formula 'beyond good and evil'"[56]—we might say as well beyond mere clock time and the static antitheses of then and now— and from this standpoint guards against taking himself for someone he is not. Hanrahan is not, on this view, the object of a nostalgic backward glance, but the living product of a corrective gaze. If he has "grown so fabulous" that no one can say "when he finished his dog's day" (*VP*, 412), it is because he has successfully resisted being taken for what he is not. We might say that Yeats haunts Hanrahan, not the other way around, and he does so in order to understand fully the "horrible splendour" of a self-generating futurity. Hanrahan embodies the very logic of misprision that the poet has learned to respect and the corrective gaze that makes of error and loss the staging ground of each new desire. In recalling Hanrahan, the poet acknowledges the value of error: "admit you turned aside / From a great labyrinth," he pleads, but what is this but the poet's own admission that he has mis-recognized "another's being"?[57]

Part 3 of "The Tower" (*VP*, 414–16) can now be read as a canny yet stately misrecognition of the poet's own futurity that attempts to overcome what pride had once placed before him as an obstacle. He makes his testamentary orientation to the past explicit by announcing, "It is time that I wrote my will." What he has to offer his inheritors, the "young upstanding men," is faith borne of caste pride, the faith of men "bound neither to cause nor to State," like Burke and Grattan, who are likened to "the morn," "the fabulous horn," and the "sudden shower," all of which recalls the "abounding glittering jet" in "Meditations in Time of Civil War," in which the poet asks whether the jet can remain "the symbol which / Shadows the inherited glory of the rich" (*VP*, 417–18). The poet vacillates between two extremes of the broken tradition he inherits: the rapacious though culturally rich founders of great houses who no longer coincide with the symbols of their subsequent greatness and the brilliant and socially privileged thinkers and artists who take pride in what they want. In the name of this pride, the poet has declared his faith. He rejects an atemporal abstract idealism—"I mock Plotinus's thought / And cry in Plato's teeth"—and asserts that time ("Death and life") did not exist until "man made up the whole," including "sun and moon and star, all."[58] Yet, in one of his most canny misrecognitions, he appropriates the very language he mocks when he says that "being dead, we rise, / Dream and so create / Translunar paradise" (*VP*, 415). The comic and chaotic misrecognitions in *The Green Helmet* are here rendered as dignified and orderly: the poet has "prepared [his] peace" with nearly all that has come before, "Poet's imaginings / And memories of love," which he now locates in the very cauldron of desire, the "mirror-resembling dream." The poet is one with his dreams, a desiring machine that produces the "superhuman" possibilities of yet more time to come.[59] He has found the "loophole," a passage back into time, which allows him to transform every memory into a promise, like the daws that "chatter and scream," dropping "twigs layer upon layer" to build a "wild nest" (*VP*, 415). The parataxis linking daws to the poet's "faith and pride" in the "young upstanding men" who will succeed him makes possible a more assured glimpse of futurity: gone are the "clamorous wings" of the swans at Coole, in their place "a bird's sleepy cry / Among the deepening shades." The "wreck of a body" once ruled by "testy delirium" is both quietened by this sleepy cry and renewed by the possibilities of the upstanding men "climbing the mountain side" (*VP*, 416).

The poet's career, his successors and descendants—these all become the tropes of time's promise. The language of testament and legacy come easily to the mature poet, now locked in "dull decrepitude," who will live on in what *will have been* produced. Poems like "The Tower" and "Meditations" concern the status of this legacy, specifically the violence at the origin of great "ancestral houses." The poet's chief concern is that the future is not yet at issue, for neither bitterness nor greatness will be honored by "the great-grandson of that house, / For all its bronze and marble, 's but a mouse" ("Meditations," *VP*, 418). At the heart of the testamentary poems is a bequest, which, like the heroic life, is an appeal to those who come later and carry out its terms. But "what if those things the greatest of mankind / Consider most to magnify, or to bless, / But take our greatness with our bitterness?" (*VP*, 418). Speaking of the novel, M. M. Bakhtin writes that "it is impossible to achieve greatness in one's own time. . . . Greatness always makes itself known only to descendents, for whom such a quality is always located in the past (it turns into a distanced image); it has become an object of memory and not a living object that one can see and touch."[60] In part to disavow the bitterness and violence that is essential to greatness, the poet attempts to bequeath his own past, not as "distanced image" but as part of a proper inheritance that would annihilate the distance separating the past from the futurity it produces. The poet creates "the future memory of a past,"[61] he *wakes up his descendents,* in the proleptic logic of a testamentary verse that lays claim to what has not yet come to pass.

The problematic status of the bequest fueled Yeats's deep sense of crisis in the Anglo-Irish world he embraced (and in part invented) as his own inheritance. From this perspective, social crisis is revalued as dialectical adversity, which is felt at every level: historical, national, genealogical, personal. Marjorie Howes argues that Yeats's Anglo-Irishry was always already in crisis. "What appears to be changeless, inherited continuity," she notes, in a discussion of "Meditations," "turns out to be repetition of an original crisis, a moment of founding or self-fashioning." It is a founding ambivalence "particular to a version of nationality that is splendidly vulnerable, that refuses to pose as natural and continuous, and that flaunts its origins in arbitrary acts of will, constant crises and the political degeneration of the class that embodies it."[62] David Lloyd makes a similar point that hinges on a necessary dialectical *failure*. Speaking of "Coole Park, 1929," he notes that its "achieved design is to forge a moment of foundation out of the explicit failure to produce the epic which would ensure the foundation or renewal of a tradition."[63] Again, this failure, like the "constant crises" that beset Yeats's Anglo-Irishry, is an opportunity made possible by desire, which looks forward to a time when failure *will have become* success and crisis a healing unity.

One of the "befitting emblems" ("Meditations," *VP,* 420) of this vulnerable and crisis-ridden tradition is the "great gazebo" in the subtly explosive "In Memory of Eva Gore-Booth and Con Markeiwicz" (*VP,* 475–76). The poet is "convicted" of guilt, of the crime of longing for the past, so he stands ready to destroy it: "Bid me strike a match and blow." The poet, like Emer, is tempted by a fatal misrecognition that promises to annihilate time. But the temptation is overcome in the very moment of time's desolation. "It is not that what is past casts its light on what is present, or what is present its light on what is past," writes Walter Benjamin; "rather, image is that wherein what has been comes together in a flash with the now to form a constellation. In other words: image is dialectics at a standstill. . . . Only dialectical images are genuinely historical—that is, not archaic—images."[64] The struck match is pure dialectical image, the rhetorical *imago* of an eternity riven with the desire for time. What is genuinely historical in Yeats's poem is the promise of a time to come, when one of the "two girls in silk kimonos" will "bid" the poet strike a match "till time catch." The poem is poised on this image, a masterful instance of a nostalgic trope (the gazebo) marshaled in the service of time's revival.

Yeats's mature elegies capture just this hesitation on the brink of time's annihilation, a hesitation that emblematizes a future without end. His attention to Coole Park and its denizens in these poems can persuade a careless reader that Yeats memorializes a dead past, when in fact memory is precisely what keeps that past from being autonomized and cut off from the living present. He casts a corrective gaze over his memories and works, which makes possible the kind of cunning misrecognitions that announce their own rectification in advance. The "scene[s] well set and excellent company," the dominant mood of "pride established in humility" ("Coole Park, 1929," *VP*, 489), are part of this new cunning, as is a dynastic temporality as old as the hills— "ancestral trees, / Or gardens rich in memory glorified / Marriages, alliances and families" ("Coole Park and Ballylee, 1931," *VP*, 491). The poet still idealizes, but he feels more keenly the burr of misprision, for no corrective gaze can exist without longing for the primary condition of misrecognition, and so each rectifying move redoubles the potential for new errors and mystification, new forms of temporal dehiscence. "Another emblem there!" the poet exclaims, at the "sudden thunder of the mounting swan," all too aware that it will be misunderstood, and that this very misunderstanding will have pedagogical value, for the emblem "is so lovely that it sets to right / What knowledge or its lack had set awry." All may have changed for the "last romantics," but the emblem remains, to chasten and set to right, to make "arrogantly pure" the "darkening flood" of time (*VP*, 490, 491, 492).

This mood of elegiac triumph, the knowledge "that time may bring / Approved patterns of women or of men / But not that selfsame excellence again" ("The Municipal Gallery Revisited," *VP*, 602), calls up the final fortifying and corrective testamentary poems that are designed to bequeath this "selfsame excellence." "Under Ben Bulben" draws on familiar signifiers of historical belonging to create such an offering. When the speaker counsels the "poet and sculptor" to "do the work" and "bring the soul of man to God, / Make him fill the cradles right" (*VP*, 638), he is speaking, I think, of the triumphant corrective gaze, of rectification and the "self-delight" that accompanies artistic freedom, "that touch of extravagance of irony, of surprise, which is set there after the desire for logic has been satisfied."[65] The poet passes on this will to rectify and asks of his inheritors that they "sing whatever is well made" and scorn the "base-born products of base beds" (*VP,* 639).

The social critique of "Under Ben Bulben," such as it is, while introducing new mystifications about race and caste inheritance, also casts a knowing eye on the poet's own habit of idealization. "The sort now growing up" (*VP* 639) is clearly not the "peasantry" whose praise he invites his inheritors to "sing" in the next line. The "base-born" are the unheroic, or those who have turned their backs on time's passage. This is less a return to old idealizations than a misrecognition that knows itself *as such*. In a further dialectical turn, there is a clear priority, beginning with the backward glance ("peasantry") followed by the corrective gaze ("*and then* / Hard riding country gentlemen") (*VP,* 639; emphasis added), which may be canny but is still misprision. That there is no commemoration is no surprise. "No marble, no conventional phrase," only a command to cast a rectifying gaze "On life, on death," and to trust the future to those who "pass by" (*VP,* 640).

The testamentary turn caps the career, redefines it, rewrites it, elaborates it not as nostalgic commemoration but as a new mythology of the future, when desire and satisfaction, crisis and unity coexist in a tensed temporality that announces what *will have been* in a time that redoubles every promise. Late works like *On the Boiler* and *Purgatory* provocatively enact this same dialectical struggle between the backward glance and the corrective gaze: while the former willfully misrecognizes a rising Catholic social order, the latter corrects this reactionary tendency by unveiling the horrific violence at the root of *all* social orders. In fact, the association of *Purgatory* with the Anglo-Irishry reinforces the point at the expense of the poet's own bardic aspirations, which is not often emphasized. In these strange, lacerating late works, Yeats issues his final corrections, his final attempts to rectify antinomies—heroic and "base born," transcendent and immanent, sage and soldier, Helen and the "raving slut"—that have entwined and defined him. They dramatize the possibility of a futural state grounded in interminable error and a heroic self-sacrifice that is, in *Purgatory,* blatantly misrecognized as parricide. The Old Man in that play is trapped in a timeless repetition of violence (he kills his own son, just as he had his father), which the Boy grasps in the crudest of temporal terms: "What if I killed you? You killed my grand-dad, / Because you were young and he was old. / Now I am young and you are old" (*VPl*, 1047). There is no corrective gaze cast on the horrific crime of the past; instead it is replayed with all its original terror. Neither is there any movement into the future, only the sound of "hoof-beats," that announce yet another repetition of the past, "because I am my father's son, / Because of what I did or may do" (*VPl*, 1045). This sublime Gothic vision of the backward glance is rectified in its turn by *The Death of Cuchulain*, which replaces the murderous Old Man—who knowingly killed his own son and confirmed the annihilation of all time—with a hero whose future is assured despite the tragedy of *unknowingly* doing the same. His greatness lies in coming to understand the tragic misrecognition that led him to kill his son on Baile's Strand, a greatness that stills Aoife's hand, though she stands poised to kill him, and lends to her equanimity the same saving dignity that we find in Emer's self-sacrifice.[66]

Purgatory is rectified once again in one of the last poems Yeats published, "The Circus Animals' Desertion," in which the poet recognizes, at last, that his work originates in human error and weakness, the "foul rag and bone shop of the heart." And though his "ladder's gone" now, he will lie down "where all the ladders start" (*VP*, 630) and reaffirm his commitment to the Nietzschean project of self-overcoming, which is, at once, a refusal to be "taken for what he is not" and a promise of coming times.

NOTES

1. W. B. Yeats, "Poetry and Tradition," in *The Collected Works of W. B. Yeats*, vol. 4, *Early Essays*, ed. Richard J. Finneran and George Bornstein (New York: Scribner, 2007), 184.

2. Friedrich Nietzsche, *The Gay Science*, trans. Walter Kaufmann (New York: Vintage, 1974), 232, 255.

3. Yeats, "Poetry and Tradition," 185–86.

4. Ibid., 186–87.

5. *The Collected Works of W. B. Yeats*, vol. 3, *Autobiographies*, ed. William H. O'Donnell and Douglas N. Archibald (New York: Scribner, 1999), 216.

6. For a more detailed discussion of revivalism and its critical history, see Gregory Castle "Irish Revivalism: Critical Trends and New Directions," *Literature Compass* 8.5 (2011): 327–39.

7. Friedrich Nietzsche, *Beyond Good and Evil: Prelude to a Philosophy of the Future*, trans. R. J. Hollingdale (Harmondsworth, UK: Penguin, 1973 [1886]), 53, sect. 44. All of "Part Two: The Free Spirit" is useful to my understanding of the pedagogical force of misrecognition. "And only on this now firm and granite basis of ignorance has knowledge hitherto been able to rise up, the will to knowledge on the basis of far more powerful will, the will to non-knowledge, to the uncertain to the untrue! Not as its antithesis but— as its refinement!" (39, sect. 26).

8. Slavoj Žižek, *Tarrying with the Negative: Kant, Hegel, and the Critique of Ideology* (Durham: Duke University Press, 1993), 25. The tradition that reads Yeats in dialectical or "antithetical" terms is long-standing. Important early works include Richard Whittaker's *Swan and Shadow: Yeats's Dialogue with History* (Chapel Hill: University of North Carolina Press, 1964), Phillip L. Marcus's *Yeats and the Beginning of the Irish Renaissance* (Syracuse: Syracuse University Press, 1987), and George Mills Harper, *The Making of Yeats's "A Vision": A Study of the Automatic Script*, vol. 1 (Houndsmills: Macmillan, 1987). More recently, Edward Larrissy focuses on "the interaction between Yeats's divided Anglo-Irish inheritance and his aesthetic" (*Yeats the Poet: The Measures of Difference* [New York: Harvester Wheatsheaf, 1994], 1), and Calvin Bedient traces the poet's movement between the material world of movement, chance, and accident and a transcendent unity (*The Yeats Brothers and Modernism's Love of Motion* [Notre Dame, IN: University of Notre Dame Press, 2009]). However, these critics, like Rob Doggett, who argues that Yeats's poetics are "relentlessly dialectical, continually shuttling between unity and disunity" (*Deep-Rooted Things: Empire and Nation in the Poetry and Drama of William Butler Yeats* [Notre Dame, IN: University of Notre Dame Press, 2006], 10), do not explore the temporal dynamics of antithetical or dialectical progress or the rectifying pedagogy at the heart of misprision.

9. See Jacques Lacan, "The Mirror Stage" and "Subversion of the Subject and the Dialectic of Desire," both in *Écrits: A Selection*, trans. Bruce Fink (New York: Norton, 2002), 294–95, 301.

10. W. B. Yeats, "To Ireland in the Coming Times," in *The Variorum Edition of the Poems of W. B. Yeats*, ed. Peter Allt and Russell K. Alspach (New York: Macmillan, 1957), 137–39. Further references to *The Variorum Edition of the Poems* are abbreviated *VP*. The word "promise" is rooted in part in "the classical Latin *prōmissum* 'assurance,' thing promised, prediction guaranteed as certain, assertion guaranteed as true, in post-classical Latin also assurance made by God, thing promised by God" (*OED* s.v. "promise"

n. 1). The promise of futurity is thus a certainty or guarantee of truth to come. I am suggesting that the future holds this promise in perpetuity.

11. Matthew Arnold, *On the Study of Celtic Literature,* in *The Works of Matthew Arnold,* vol. 5 (London: Macmillan, 1903), 91; Yeats, "The Celtic Element in Literature," in *Early Essays,* 128–29.

12. Richard Greaves, *Transition, Reception and Modernism in W. B. Yeats* (New York: Palgrave, 2002), 2. See Michael J. Sidnell, who regards Yeats's work in terms of the "sustained coherence" of his work and of his "poetic personality" (*Yeats's Poetry and Poetics* [New York: St. Martin's, 1996], 74; see also 97–107).

13. Yug Mohit Chaudhry, *Yeats, the Irish Literary Revival and the Politics of Print* (Cork: Cork University Press, 2001), 43.

14. W. B. Yeats, "Introduction," in *The Collected Works of W. B. Yeats,* vol. 5, *Later Essays,* ed. William H. O'Connell (New York: Macmillan, 1994), 204.

15. Jacques Lacan, Seminar 1, in *The Seminar of Jacques Lacan,* vol. 1, *Freud's Papers on Technique, 1953–1954,* ed. Jacques-Alain Miller, trans. John Forrester (Cambridge: Cambridge University Press, 1988), 265. Lacan is speaking of Freud's discovery of the dream work, which is the prototype of the logic of misrecognition (*mésconnaissance*).

16. Sigmund Freud, *Civilization and Its Discontents,* trans. James Strachey (New York: Norton, 1989), 32.

17. Elizabeth Cullingford, *Gender and History in Yeats's Love Poetry* (Cambridge: Cambridge University Press, 1993), 18. On "fairy-faith," see W. Y. Evans-Wentz, *The Fairy-Faith in Celtic Countries* (New Hyde Park, NY: University Books, 1966 [1911]). See also Barton Friedman, "Dissolving Surfaces: Yeats's *The Wind Among the Reeds* and the Challenge of Science," *Yeats* 7 (1989): 57–90, who likens the poems in *The Wind Among the Reeds* to the kind of "quest-romance" found in *Stories of Red Hanrahan.* Jahan Ramazani sees some of the early poems as "elegiac love poems" that "both lament the beloved's death and yet require it as their condition of possibility" (*Yeats and the Poetry of Death: Elegy, Self-Elegy, and the Sublime* [New Haven: Yale University Press, 1990], 18). I would add only that the temporality of this requirement (the lament following on the death) invites a negative dialectical reading. Opposed to all this is Edward Larrissy, who reads the first edition of *The Wind Among the Reeds* as "an occult tribute to Fenianism" (*Yeats the Poet,* 72).

18. Yeats, "Kidnappers," in *Mythologies* (New York: Collier-Macmillan, 1969), 73; see also "Drumcliff and Rosses," 88–94.

19. These terms give a fair approximation of the range of meanings of the prefix "mis-." Meanings such as amiss, wrong, bad, improper, perverse,

mistaken are predominant when this prefix is used. An Old English form with cognates in all the major medieval European languages (*OED* s.v. "mis-").

20. Friedman, "Dissolving Surfaces," 60–61.

21. Ramazani, *Yeats and the Poetry of Death*, 20, 18.

22. Jacques Derrida, *Specters of Marx: The State of the Debt, the Work of Mourning and the New International*, trans. Peggy Kamuf (New York: Routledge, 1994), 4. "*What is* a ghost? What is the *effectivity* or the *presence* of a specter, that is, of what seems to remain as ineffective, virtual, insubstantial as a simulacrum"—in short, as a remainder. *Hauntology* is "[r]epetiton *and* first time, but also repetition *and* last time, since the singularity of any *first time* makes of it also a *last time*. Each time it is the event itself, a first time is a last time. Altogether other. Staging for the end of history" (10).

23. See Émile Benveniste, *Problems in General Linguistics*, trans. Mary Elizabeth Meek (Coral Gables: University of Miami Press, 1971 [1956]): "Linguistic time is *self-referential*. Ultimately, human temporality with all its linguistic apparatus reveals the subjectivity inherent in the very [use] of language" (227).

24. Ibid., 210–11.

25. James Rolleston, *Narratives of Ecstasy: Romantic Temporality in Modern German Poetry* (Detroit: Wayne State University Press, 1987), 16. Rolleston argues that the "vocabulary of temporal breaks, central to Romantic thinking," together with the historicization of knowledge and experience "established the perspective of modernity" (12–13).

26. See Lady Augusta Gregory, *Cuchulain at Muirthemne* (Gerrards Cross: Colin Smythe, 1973 [1902]), Standish O'Grady, *History of Ireland*, vol. 2, *Cuculain and his Contemporaries* (London: Sampson Low, Searle, Marston and Rivington; Dublin: E. Ponsonby, 1880), and Eleanor Hull, *The Cuchullin Saga in Irish Literature* (London: David Nutt, 1898; rpt. New York: AMS Press, 1972). For an early discussion of this tradition, see Reg Skene, *The Cuchulain Plays of W. B. Yeats: A Study* (New York: Columbia University Press, 1974), 16–37; for a more recent treatment, see Joseph Valente, *The Myth of Manliness in Irish National Culture, 1880–1922* (Urbana: University of Illinois Press, 2011), 140–64.

27. Yeats, *Autobiographies*, 336.

28. Valente, *Myth of Manliness*, 142. Michael Valdez Moses describes precisely the reverse of this dialectic: of *On Baile's Strand* he writes that its "ultimate triumph . . . depends on the paradoxical fact that Cuchulain epitomizes a heroic conception of the Irish national character by tragically resisting the political and cultural norms of the High King of Ireland and his court, rather than happily conforming to them" ("The Rebirth of Tragedy: Yeats, Nietzsche, the Irish National Theatre, and the Anti-Modern Cult

of Cuchulain," *Modernism/Modernity* 11.3 [September 2004]: 570). On "Cuchulainoid theatre," see Valente, *Myth of Manliness*, 169–86.

29. See Skene on Yeats's intention to write "a coherent and unified play cycle" (*Cuchulain Plays*, ix–x).

30. Cuchulain's motto, according to Padraic Pearse, quoted in "The Murder Machine," in Padraic Pearse, *A Significant Irish Educationalist: The Educational Writings of P. H. Pearse*, ed. Séamas Ó Buachalla (Dublin: Mercier Press, 1980), 381.

31. *The Variorum Edition of the Plays of W. B. Yeats*, ed. Russell K. Alspach (New York: Macmillan, 1969), 479. Hereafter cited parenthetically as *VPl*.

32. Gregory, *Cuchulain*, 241.

33. Michael McAteer, *Yeats and European Drama* (Cambridge: Cambridge University Press, 2010), 83–84.

34. M. M. Bakhtin, *The Dialogic Imagination*, trans. Caryl Emerson and Michael Holquist (Austin: University of Texas Press, 1981), 16.

35. James MacKillop, *Dictionary of Celtic Mythology* (Oxford: Oxford University Press, 1998), 297.

36. Yeats, *A Vision* (New York: Collier, 1966; orig. pub. 1937), 73. Yeats quotes from "Murray's Dictionary."

37. McAteer, *Yeats and European Drama*, 102. See Harper, *The Making of Yeats's "A Vision,"* 82.

38. Richard Cave, "Commentaries and Notes," in *Selected Plays of W. B. Yeats*, ed. Richard Allen Cave (Harmondsworth: Penguin, 1997), 333.

39. G. W. F. Hegel, *The Phenomenology of Mind*, trans. J. B. Baillie (New York: Harper Torchbooks, 1967), 231.

40. Yeats, *A Vision*, 135–37.

41. Yeats, "Poetry and Tradition," 182.

42. Rached Khalifa, "W. B. Yeats: Theorizing the Irish Nation," in *W. B. Yeats and Postcolonialism*, ed. Deborah Fleming (West Cornwall, CT: Locust Hill Press, 2001), 284.

43. Yeats, *Autobiographies*, 216–17.

44. Sidnell, *Yeats's Poetry and Poetics*, 74.

45. Yeats, *Autobiographies*, 217.

46. Ibid.

47. Ramazani, *Yeats and the Poetry of Death*, 32. On the "group elegy," see 32–38, 43–51.

48. David Ward, "Yeats's Conflicts with His Audience, 1897–1917," *English Literary History* 49 (1982), 151. See Yeats, *Memoirs*, transcribed and ed. Denis Donoghue (London: Macmillan, 1972), 271. See Chaudhry, *Yeats, the Irish Literary Revival*, 14–27, for a discussion of Yeats's attitudes around the time of *Responsibilities* toward the Anglo-Irish and the rising Catholic middle class, the "conquered caste" as Conor Cruise O'Brien put it (qtd. in Chaudhry, 17).

49. "Withershins" can mean "moving in an anticlockwise direction, contrary to the apparent course of the sun"; sinister, unlucky, ill-fated, relating to the occult; also in a direction opposite to the usual; the wrong way; to stand on end (*OED* s.v. "withershins," adv. 1, 2). From Old High German *widar* "against" and *sinnen* "to travel, go," related to *sind* "journey" (*Webster's Third New International Dictionary*, s.v. "widdershin," adv.).

50. Yeats, *Autobiographies*, 283–84.

51. Rob Doggett describes a form of "historiographic desire" that uses "temporal markers as a means for constructing order in the present" by frustrating it, "revealing that the old, particularly nationalist and imperialist modes of ordering time must be cast aside before new histories of Ireland may be articulated" (*Deep-Rooted Things*, 75). In my understanding of temporality, such modes of time *cannot* be cast aside for they are the *necessary* starting point of any alternative to them.

52. Chaudhry, *Yeats, the Irish Literary Revival*, 23.

53. On Yeats's coupling of the nobleman and the beggar, see Deborah Fleming, *"A man who does not exist": The Irish Peasant in the Work of W. B. Yeats and J. M. Synge* (Ann Arbor: University of Michigan Press, 1995), 31, 69.

54. Yeats, *Autobiographies*, 218; my emphasis. Elsewhere Yeats writes: "It seems to me, looking backward, that we always discussed life at its most intense moment. . . . Certainly I had gone a great distance from my first poems, from all that I had copied from the folk-art of Ireland" (247–48).

55. Sidnell, *Yeats's Poetry and Poetics*, 66.

56. Nietzsche, *Beyond Good and Evil*, 54, sect. 44.

57. Vicki Mahaffey argues that "Yeats is tentatively admitting that he (and his youthful alter ego, Hanrahan) privileged his own imagination over the greater and more frightening mystery of another's reality" (*States of Desire* [New York: Oxford University Press, 1998], 136). In my view, this admission amounts to a *depriviledging* of imagination in the hope that he might recover the capacity for desire that will lead him back to this "frightening mystery."

58. In "Death," from *The Winding Stair*, Yeats speaks of a "great man in his pride," who "Casts derision upon / Supersession of breath; / He knows death to the bone— / Man has created death" (*VP*, 476).

59. "If desire produces, its product is real," write Gilles Deleuze and Félix Guattari. "If desire is productive, it can be productive only in the real world and can produce only reality. . . . Desire is a machine, and the object of desire is another machine connected to it" (*Anti-Oedipus: Capitalism and Schizophrenia*, trans. Robert Hurley, Mark Seem, and Helen R. Lane [Minneapolis: University of Minnesota Press, 1983 (1977)], 26).

60. Bakhtin, *The Dialogic Imagination*, 18.

61. Ibid., 19. "The future exists, and this future ineluctably touches upon the individual, has its roots in him" (37).

62. Marjorie Howes, *Yeats's Nations: Gender, Class, and Irishness* (Cambridge: Cambridge University Press, 1996), 126, 130.

63. David Lloyd, *Anomalous States: Irish Writing and the Post-Colonial Moment* (Dublin: Lilliput Press, 1993), 167.

64. Walter Benjamin, *The Arcades Project*, trans. Howard Eiland and Kevin McLaughlin (Cambridge, MA: Belknap Press, 1999), 463; see also 10.

65. Yeats, "Poetry and Tradition," 185–86.

66. Cave notes the mood of "cathartic peace" in the play, and that "Aoife wishes to sustain that mood rather than take a quick revenge, because it is balm to her soul tortured with remorse for the past" ("Commentaries and Notes," 386). She too has learned the lesson offered by Cuchulain's great error.

CHAPTER 6

Afterwardsness

Yeats in Love and the Imaginary of Community

GUINN BATTEN

In Yeats's most powerful poems, antagonism may coincide with but also arrive after amorousness. This idea is the focus of this chapter and is a topic that itself clearly comes after most readings of the "antithetical" Yeats. So does the observation that such antagonism in his poems most often emerges in encounters with the loss of a desired object, whether that object is aesthetic or amorous, that itself becomes the "object" of rage and desire. This relation to loss, to love's disappointment, generates in the poems images of fields of force that are, in effect, the spatial arrest of the movement of time, images that perhaps receive their most perfect form in the diagrams of *A Vision*. This essay returns to the contrasting, shifting emotions that characterize the love poems for Maud Gonne, in turn relating them to a few celebrated poems that specifically concern the violence of decolonization in early twentieth-century Ireland. It will be no surprise that Yeats transformed the conventions of courtly love, including those that haunt the figures of Sovereignty and Kathleen ni Houlihan in Irish tradition.[1] Neither will it be surprising to find once again that Yeats, in reviving and then transforming those conventions, was able himself to move, as well as to plead with his own imagined community— "Ireland"—to move, from embitteredness and the automatism of reprisal to a kind of satisfaction, as expressed in section 3 of "Nineteen Hundred and Nineteen": "I am satisfied with that, / Satisfied if a troubled mirror show it."[2] Through his ardor for Maud Gonne and later through his marriage with George Hyde-Lees, Yeats found a way of engaging with the "art" that is "romance," as the very living out of a genre of failed arrival to a desired end that is its own (as Lacan would say) "object-cause."[3] Yeats arrives at a term such as "satisfaction" without ignoring that his medium (the "medium" that is a poem, and also Yeats's spirit "mediums," including Lees) is a "mirror" that is "troubled." That arrival alone is crucial to my understanding of how Yeats's experience of being in love—in love with what Blake called the "productions of time" as well as with women—relates to Yeats's explorations of what Lacan called the "mirror": the "imaginary" dimension of language at the basis of which persists an enigma that can only be misrecognized (and therefore desired) as an "image." In the poetry of love that Yeats shows to us he is developing through the very failures his poems recount, "satisfaction" requires the speaker's recognition of a prior incompleteness of the beloved object *and* of himself because they are most intimately related in a shared but nonetheless singular "afterwardsness." Without the paradoxical (and partial) "satisfaction" that is "failure," his speakers remain anguished in their ardor, haunted by what lies beyond life, what Yeats insistently explored as the repetitions and returns of "death" in "life."

The image that nears perfection in Yeats's poetry, whether that almost realized ideal is aesthetic, erotic, divine, or political—and this essay will consider how these ideals converge in his most "Romantic" poems—is, in its loss, as likely to produce rage as remorse:

> But is there any comfort to be found?
> Man is in love and loves what vanishes,

What more is there to say? That country round
None dared admit, if such a thought were his,
Incendiary or bigot could be found
To burn that stump on the Acropolis,
Or break in bits the famous ivories.

(*VP*, 429–30)

This reaction is clearly in excess of the disappointment the reader might have expected to be engendered by the retrospective (but not really compensatory or comforting) wisdom to which Yeats often directly alludes. Having given his life to imagination, and more specifically to casting its images into words (and how many poets in English have done so as deliberately and publically?), Yeats portrays his devotion to poetry as an arduous, endless, and finally futile effort to thwart what "Adam's Curse" calls "time's waters" as they break immortal longing into "days and years." Even when mastery seems achieved, the poet in *The Tower* feels inadequate to the task: "what more is there to say?"

His words, on the one hand, will require of this poet even *more* work because they remain inadequate to the "image," the "dream" in "Adam's Curse" to "love in the old high way" (*VP*, 206) after the heart has been so often broken. Likewise in "Nineteen Hundred and Nineteen," a poem about the unromantic violence of revolutions and civil war, the dream that one could "mend / Whatever mischief seemed / To afflict mankind" (*VP*, 431) is exposed as the somnambulance of an outworn chivalry, only slightly less culpable than the "drowsy chargers" of Parliament and king. The experience of illusion performed in this poem Yeats openly relates to tragic irony: when the "winds of winter blow" and buffet the imagined community as it devolves into violent emergency, Romantic idealists "learn that we were crack-pated when we dreamed," singing the songs of spring when already "the swan has leaped into the desolate heavens":

That image can bring wildness, bring a rage
To end all things, to end
What my laborious life imagined, even

The half-imagined, the half-written page;
O but we dreamed to mend
Whatever mischief seemed
To afflict mankind, but now
That winds of winter blow
Learn that we were crack-pated when we dreamed.

(*VP,* 431)

Yet does that irony, that knowledge that *no* knowledge saves because it always arrives belatedly, in itself account for the experience of passionate regret at the vanishing of something not fully appreciated when it seemed in one's grasp? Knowledge in itself seems not to suffice because only after what is desired has been lost does something "more" appear, something in excess of the disappointment, about which the poet ineluctably seems compelled to *say* more, as if driven by a force beyond himself.

"Many ingenious lovely things are gone," Yeats opens "Nineteen Hundred and Nineteen," but of their making he can only add that to common sight they have no beginning and no logic for being, for they are "sheer miracle to the multitude" (*VP,* 428). That "miracle" is felt also by the reader of these lines, sharing Yeats's wonder at the rare conjunction of image and reality that must have shone forth through a work of artifice—even when known to have been wrought by human hands—to that multitude in past times. "Miracle" captures what Yeats describes throughout his writings either as eternity entering into time or (as later in this poem) taking flight from it. It is also for Yeats a momentary coincidence between what the mind may imagine, felt as a brief cessation of the furious *blaze* of desire that in "Vacillation" he describes as a *blessed* suspension in time. It suggests the satisfaction of a creative being who (if we recall the etymology of "miracle") "smiles" in satisfaction at a work that he or she sees is "good."

And yet, as in "Byzantium," the progression from the "good" that may seem such "miracle" can become a clamor for "more" that is destructive, and is felt as such in the violence of the imperial state no less than in the personal encounter. The desire for "more," on these public and private levels alike, suggests that "things," the objects we designate but also draw to us with words, whether ingenious or common, may never be "good" enough, no matter how skilled the smithies of the emperor. What the poet's hand has wrought, moving upon silence like the hand of Michael Angelo in "Long Legged Fly," enters (as the plastic arts of tile and metal in Yeats's Byzantium poems do not) the vicissitudes of time. Moving one after another diachronically in syntax, one poetic phrase and line after another, words because they are on the page certainly may be, and by experienced readers are *likely* to be, grasped synchronically, all at once. Yet what seems arrested in spatial form in itself evokes a wish to possess and make permanent, which we might more simply call a wish to *master* what seems "miraculous," a wish that in turn, as Yeats's poems so masterfully perform, leads not merely to disappointment (for to want "more" is never to hold back time's waters as they rise and fall) but may lead also to rage, the wish "to end all things, to end / What my laborious life imagined, even / The half-imagined, the half-written page."

That image of failure in "Nineteen Hundred and Nineteen"—just after Yeats's own perennial image, the swan, has vanished under its own volition, leaving the poet with "the half-imagined, the half-written"—is in fact a way to enter into what makes Yeats one of the last of the courtly lovers and of the last Romantics, a poet whose very encounter with the failure to turn "image" into lasting perfection leads him beyond the ethics of Romantic idealism and toward what Lacan has called an "ethics of the feminine." In the various ways that Yeats explores the mind's persistent "imagining" of a lost object (it is significant that in this poem he imagines an Athenian "ancient image made of olive wood" that commemorates an immortal woman, a goddess, associated with wisdom but also with the hunt) he confronts what Lacan has called the "enigma" of the "Real" that drives the sequencing of words by drawing them, and those who read, write, and speak them, into its force field. It is from this enigma that Tom Eyers, who calls it the Lacanian "Real" in his pathbreaking *Lacan and the Concept of the "Real,"* generates two languages, not one, that shape for the subject "reality," the sequential language we use everyday, what he calls "signifiers in relation," and another that circles, automatistically, around that enigma, which he calls "the signifier in isolation."[4] We have begun by asking why there is so often "more" to "love" in Yeats's poems than an Eros that binds individuals into sexual partnerships, families, communities, and nation states. In continuing to read "Nineteen Hundred and Nineteen" we will again ask, this time through another image of "woman," why Thanatos—as rage, aggression, the wish to destroy—may bewilder those who love when that love is itself excessive (as in "Easter 1916") and is cast into a form that contains an object that is a female who is beautiful, seductive, and threatening.

The lines from "Nineteen Hundred and Nineteen" that follow the memorable phrase "burn that stump on the Acropolis" present an object of whirling, forceful beauty that is both static and moving. Spinning at the cathectic center of a structure, this arrested image momentarily "tames" the "furious" "dragon" of political violence that has fallen into that structure. This image of female movement is more particularly an image of a female "structured" (and thereby arrested in movement) by the gaze of the reader toward its gyring vortex:

When Loie Fuller's Chinese dancers enwound
A shining web, a floating ribbon of cloth,
It seemed that a dragon of air
Had fallen among dancers, had whirled them round
Or hurried them off on its own furious path.

(*VP*, 430)

What we encounter in these lines, which follow the sheer viciousness of destructive energy in the preceding stanza, already haunts the "master-work of intellect or hand" that "seemed sheer miracle." We retrospectively relate this "shining web" to the earlier section's "drowsing chargers" and to "a little" burning powder, those public spectacles that are as much the source of power or "force" in a colonial city, "its great army but a showy thing," as their deployment in actual conflict. Similarly, as we look backward, this image ensnares "the dragon-ridden" days and "nightmare" hags that ride sleep even in civil peacetime in section 1.

The political idealists who, in peacetime, imagine in section 3 that they might "mend" the "state" by changing its form have dreams that are simply the obverse of that nightmare, and less true. The imagination, compared to a swan that leaps from that torn state in section 3's final stanza, is anticipated in the first stanza of that section: the uplifted and then folding wings of the dancer's veils (by the dance's end, in surviving photographs, they fold into a bat's wings) have become those of the swan; gazing into "a troubled mirror," the swan offers an "image of its state." But that imagined state, in these lines, depends on a tragic temporality: "Before that brief gleam of its life be gone." The speaker at the end of the section has been deprived of these images of beauty, and of beauty as a form for sovereignty—the dynamic force fields of the woman's dance and the swan's flight—that embodies, structures, and *contains* the very "wildness" of imaginary force. In short, he has been deprived of comfort and (like Lear on the heath) of the protections of sovereignty when it is embodied in such kings.[5] "The winds of winter" that blow in 1919 against those who dreamed of a peaceful transition to a mutually shared sovereignty under law are those of near, and distant, revolutions. Disillusioned, the dreamer can no longer escape into dance or the heavens, confirming retroactively the truth of section 1: "The night can sweat with terror as before / We pieced our thoughts into philosophy, / And planned to bring the world under a rule, / Who are but weasels fighting in a hole" (*VP,* 429). "Disillusionment," however, is far from the whole story Yeats tells in his poems of "afterwardsness."

"Afterwardsness," Jean Laplanche claims in "Time and the Other," as a psychoanalytic as well as a linguistic phenomenon, is a more accurate term than *différance* for what is haunting, and violent, in Freud's discussion of *Nachträglichkeit* (a discussion that is the source for Derrida's invention of that term). "Afterwardsness" as Laplanche explains it retains the image, albeit only as an enigmatic signifier, of an object that produces simultaneously erotic pleasure and bodily dissatisfaction, and as such generates the differential forces of signification, only when it has vanished from memory. The troubling, frustrating dimension of love's remainder is that it will be sought all the more ardently by the subject experiencing only belatedly (and still without resolving its enigma) the lost object's full value, seeking it in objects that produce *almost* the same, imagined (and now irrecuperable) satisfaction. As Laplanche writes, "what more suitable terrain is there for [*Nachträlichkeit,* "afterwardsness"] than that of loss: of the human being confronted with loss; to the extent that the dimension of loss is probably co-extensive with temporalization itself?"[6]

I have chosen the awkward terms of psychoanalytic discourse knowing that my reader might prefer the more felicitous and in literary study more conventional terms "belatedness" or "irony." The disappointments of poets with histories private and public in early nineteenth-century Europe have given us the more particular term *Romantic* irony, in which truth is realized only after an ideal object (which may be romantic or political, or both, for either may offer an end toward which desire is directed) has been lost. This is the only "truth" that the Romantic poet-protagonist may know, and know too late, long after (to adapt Yeats's words) his embodiment of that truth has been misrecognized, and indeed has been embodied as the very engine of signification, "misrecognition."[7] More specifically, Romantic irony is the knowledge that imagination exceeds *any* experience, given (according to the Romantic ironist) the finitude of human embodiment. Such knowledge—and irony—serves as the basis for the antinomies of reason offered by the leading philosopher of the Romantic Enlightenment. Yeats in his first version of *A Vision* refers to Kant's mathematical antinomies, describing them in relation to romantic love and the institution that may (including in a more cynical sense) "conclude" it: "[Marriage is] a symbol of that eternal instant where the antinomy is resolved. It is not the resolution itself."[8]

For Yeats the "daimonic" disrupts unity, in the romantic relationship as in every other, and its violence is that of the "automatistic," the repetition compulsion that persists in the "afterwardsness" of ironic deadlock. He describes such "automatic personality" in his 1925 *A Vision:*

> The automatic personality is never perhaps a puppet in the hand of the spirit that created it, but has always not only its own automatic life but that reflected from the man himself. . . . One notices there and elsewhere that mathematical clarity . . . the result of . . . obsession by an automatic personality. . . . Such relations may so cross

and re-cross that a community may grow clairvoyant. Lover and beloved, friend and friend, son and daughter, or an entire family . . . are brought by the dramatisation of the *Arcons* into such a crisis that the *primary* oppositions and harmonies of the world are exposed in their minds and fates.[9]

As such we might think of the daimon, a version of the undead that so fascinated Yeats, as, in Laplanche's way of thinking, what cannot be "metabolized" in loss.[10] As Yeats writes, "Until an act has been expiated the same circumstance occurs again and again. . . . And there is always a sense of being fated" (*AVA*, 192–93). What cannot be resolved, and what survives as suggestive of "death," felt bodily even as it is manifested in speech throughout one's life, is what, in the earliest stages of our lives, appears as (to quote Laplanche once again) "different and thus hostile."

That difference, Laplanche continues, manifests itself in two forms. The first is Kant's categorical imperative as a form of judging, and mastering, the self as well as the other or object (Lacan in his seventh seminar associates this also with the finite mind's yearning for infinitude or immortality). That imperative, in the tradition of psychoanalysis, may be as violent, and as intemperate, as what is more familiarly called the "id." The second is an "enigmatic signifier," which is in effect the hidden "sovereign" that mobilizes language as we think we know it. It is the surviving and residual present of the earliest and closest ties to the caregiver, ties that only after their severance are encountered as the *jouissance* of language. It is a signifier that is in fact the enduring (albeit unconscious) bridge, and even vehicle, across successive generations. For Laplanche those manifestations emerge from a primary place where "difference" (among such other differences as ethnicity, race, or class) is judged, and that will make "sexual difference"—and with it an unconscious "generalized dread of women"—a source not only of ambivalence but of "conflict" more generally, insofar as it "cannot be metabolized," that is, cannot be conciliated, resolved, sublated. Such an object may only in its vanishing be desired, but in its vanishing it has become a site of judgment and (hence) of fear, as well as a locus for romantic ideals, those that promote desire without possibility of satisfaction. Laplanche notes that Freud, in one of his earliest uses of "afterwardsness," refers in 1898 to a dream that will find its way into his own developing hermeneutics as the conflict that he will call "the drives": *The Interpretation of Dreams*. At the breast of a woman, Freud writes, "love" and "hunger" meet.[11]

Two years before the millennium that saw the publication of Freud's dream book, even as Yeats was ascending the ranks of dreamers in the Golden Dawn, 1898 was the year of the bicentenary of the 1798 Irish Rising, among the most notable of the many lost causes of Irish cultural memory to which Yeats was drawn. The year 1898 brought to Yeats, at the height of his engagement in the insurrectionary activities of Young Ireland (a decade after the 1888 publication of his edition *Poems and Ballads of Young Ireland*), the shock of discovering that the woman of his fantasies, Maud Gonne, had in an earlier relationship given birth to a child. Yet it was also the year that gave birth (through another important woman in Yeats's life, Lady Augusta Gregory, whom he had met two years earlier) to the Irish National Theatre. An attraction to "afterwardsness," in a different sense, led Yeats in this important decade in his "Romanticism" to Irish epics that he read as an enthusiast of antiquarians such as Samuel Ferguson, so much so that he was inspired to become a collector of, and to publish, folk ballads and tales from the west of Ireland. All of the above suggests how the conjunction of "love," "hunger," and also, finally, "hatred" would come to characterize Yeats's revival, and revision, of British Romanticism, including his relationships with fellow revivalists with whom he came to quarrel, and as he would characterize his own special place in "Romantic" literary historical succession.

From *The Green Helmet* through *The Tower*, Yeats's poetry concerns itself with the lag time of an individual's experience and recognition of loss (think, for example, of "The Stolen Child"). But already in *The Wind Among the Reeds*, in "The Song of Wandering Aengus" (*VP*, 149–50), where the poetry of courtly love takes the form of the Irish *aisling*, we can see how keenly Yeats already understands the temporality of loss. Yet he also already intimates that the very haunt-edness of a hunger that is older than the young speaker's self-aware-ness, a hunger for one kind of object (a trout), may revive something new and unexpected through the imagination, the fire in the head, *especially* when language, calling on images, repeats old patterns. The "glimmering girl," image of the ideal, arrives only in the pursuit (and frustration) of another, predictable, end. To reach her is to end time itself, and with it the felt lag, and lack, of "afterwardsness."[12] Yet in arriving at that insight the speaker drops the use of the retrospective past tense and, at the same time, immediately becomes "old," "old with wandering, / Through hollow lands and hilly lands," still expecting to live, through desire, "till time and times are done," when an ordi-nary fruit ("apples") will become the precious mineral "glimmering" suggests.

"Desire" is not itself separable from the threat of "death." Twenty years after writing *The Interpretation of Dreams* Freud will reach the conclusion that, with "love" and "hunger," there is another term that is the opposite of "Eros" that contributes to the "force" that generates language, and that inhabits melancholia and the trauma of loss. "Thanatos," or the death drive, expresses itself as Yeats's aforemen-tioned *automatism*, the relentless pursuit of what has not only been lost but has also become a phantom, an object of phantasy, and hence of pleasurable frustration (or *jouissance*) because it cannot be reunited to the lost form that would make it whole. "Afterwardsness" in this dimension of the repetition compulsion appears most obviously in Yeats's poems during those same two decades, particularly in those that explicitly concern frustrated longing, where what has been lost continues to tantalize and to terrorize through its appearance in "parts."

For example, "Memory" (*VP*, 350), written before the Easter Ris-ing in 1916, suggests Yeats's own previous struggles to abandon his private and impossible romance for "Ireland." Central to that romance had become for him a (once lovely) woman old (Maud) and a woman young (Iseult), as he continues to imagine what it would take to enter fully into the public institutions of marriage and of national life. "One had a lovely face, / And two or three had charm, / But charm and face were in vain / Because the mountain grass / Cannot but keep the form / Where the mountain hare has lain."[13] This brief poem makes the very absence of an object that has been ardently sought, even when it ostensibly has been forsaken, nevertheless still the source, and the end, of what keeps life going, even as it is also the obstacle to introducing into that life an important change: the possibility of loving differently, or loving a different object. Undead, the very form of "memory" offered in this poem works to situate in the place of what has vanished innocent perceptions—of a "face," of a trait ("charm")—that become, because they are situated in that locus of loss, images that are "imaginary," that become the basis for subsequent comparisons that may well lead to dissatisfaction, even as they keep alive what is gone. These fragments, or parts, of what might give partial pleasure become lethal because they seduce but fail to satisfy, not because they are incomplete (for in reality, what object or pleasure is not?) but because in tendering a momentary pleasure they also return the bereaved speaker to the vacant space, the form that holds the experience of (imagined) full plenitude as now one of profound loss. It is against that hollow, imageless, but obdurate object, that uncompromisable standard or category for a fantasized, originary "Good" that no "good" can reach, that Yeats in "Memory" offers his Freudian extension of "Romantic irony."

Memory, insofar as it produces both pleasure and suffering, does so not simply by reenacting a historical violence in the past that has been unacknowledged or repressed and hence survives crisis (what Freud explores as "trauma" in *Beyond the Pleasure Principle*), but also by repeating the process whereby something that once pleased (the "Good") has now become a source of harsh judgment—the Kantian categorical imperative of the superego to which Laplanche alludes—harsh in its judgment of others and also of ourselves. That ur "form" and space of imaginary creation, a form that (like that of the hare in "Memory") exemplifies "absence" as determinative of whatever seems present and still vital in "reality," can only be held back in, and *from,* memory as its standard for distinguishing between reality and fantasy (Freud's original way of explaining the time, and not simply the "space," of memory, as the lag between perception and image, and between image and word). Culturally, this judgment becomes the form of metaphysical, ethical, and aesthetic differentiations, or "judgment." As we will see, it haunts the idea of an ideal community that might be guided by "reason" insofar as its "judgments" are also "universal."

Lacan follows Freud in insisting that from the beginning this work of judgment is the work of "representation," and that it is one form that all speaking beings could be said (universally) to share, calling this process of signification *Vorstellungsrepräsentanz*, literally, "the representation of a representation." In this process the experience of memory is likewise an experience of representation. The experience of time in this process of judgment is a problem for Yeats and other cultural revivalists of belatedness and succession (the present must call on but it cannot fully know the past because it, the present cultural movement, is afterward, and as such is "different"). That same problem haunts the nationalism that contextualizes a cultural movement such as the Irish renaissance: such a movement imagines the "imagined community" as one whose members experience "time" in the same "space." Yeats, however, complicates what seems such a positive manifestation of hope for, and belief in, the future, for he locates a problem in the concept of "time" and the "nation" that is closely linked to the dissatisfactions of the automatism expressed in the very structure of the language of unconscious judgment as it whirls about the enigmatic signifier. Yeats figures both "nation" and "body" in terms of the daimon and the mask and in the temporal movement of the gyres. At the center of his own drive-like gyres, which we might see as analogous in their cathectic force-fields to the work of *Vorstellungsrepräsentanz*, Yeats in "The Double Vision of Michael Robartes" situates a dancer (the model for whom is Iseult Gonne) who, as ideal, is—like the speaker of "Meditations in Time of Civil War"—caught in the "cold snows of a dream." While dancing she *dreams* of dancing (and as such is an image not just of "beauty," at Phase 15, but of an endlessly reflexive *mise en abyme* that Lacan in Seminar XI calls "the gaze").[14] "She" stands in the place of a standard of judgment, a locus that precipitates the whirling, gyre-like force of the drives as they seek to repeat pleasure, as they test reality, to the point of destruction, such that the power of the "imaginary," or fantasy, performs its work (as it were) on "automatic." Without form because she is *all* "form," that place of judgment is what Yeats calls in "An Image from a Past Life" (*VP*, 389–90) a "hovering thing": "Now that no fingers bind, / That her hair streams upon the wind," a "thing" of "arrogant loveliness" from the past that still troubles love in the present. What issues from that form may carry the force, or even violence, of Kant's categorical imperative precisely because it is the locus of ethical, as of aesthetic, judgment. The simultaneous presence of a figure of judgment and an enigmatic signifier in that same locus, the locus of *loss*, Lacan in Seminar VII terms *das Ding*.

Slavoj Žižek has enhanced this term for the vacant but powerful center of *Vorstellungsrepräsentanz,* calling it the "Mother Thing," and goes so far as to suggest in *Metastases of Enjoyment* that something like culture, or civilization, is driven by a desperate wish to wake her from the (un)dead—could we also extend this description to Yeats's dancer whom we cannot tell from the dance?—a melancholic, remote female body.[15] He further elaborates *das Ding* as the source, symbol, and symptom of ethnic conflict (the "Nation Thing" and the "Neighbor-Thing," in his influential reading of, and departure from, Emmanuel Levinas), even while he denies that "she" has anything to do with the "reality" of an actual mother, except insofar as all mothers must be lost and thereby become the placeholder that is *das Ding*. What is left behind is an enigmatic signifier that is both a felt absence and something surplus or in excess of meaning—if one is to become a subject in language. With Lacan, Žižek links the emergence of *das Ding* with the Romantic Enlightenment, and Kant's own *Ding an sich*. But Žižek issues the caveat that this place of judgment, the "real" where *das Ding* is sovereign, cannot be deliberately claimed or occupied by worldly interests, indeed it cannot be spatially located or situated in time. It is a body that is not "material," and that is "bodily" only insofar as it is "imaginary" or phantasmatic.

Yeats in "Memory" offers just such an understanding of how the past survives, and forms, the present. For Yeats *das Ding* may be framed not only as the Dark Lady of courtly love (as Lacan suggests), but also that dark figure as she emerges in Irish, and arguably also in

British, Romanticism as a mother and as (sometimes simultaneously) a betrayed daughter. That for Yeats this figure may also be the daughter, Iseult, of the woman, Maud Gonne, who performed the part of Mother Ireland by following a script jointly produced by him and a central mother figure in his life, Lady Augusta Gregory, I suggest lends further credence to the argument that Yeats's Romanticism may not be separable from either the Freudian "family romance" or the courtly love tradition.[16]

In Paul de Man's sympathetic deconstruction of "Coole Park and Ballylee, 1931," he argues that Yeats rejects the "natural" (and even the "sexual") in favor of a "removal" from any position that would offer the possibility of "a reconciliation between image and reality," for Yeats's aesthetic "is founded on a curiously complex duality of substance and function" that produces "no reconciliation, not even a dialectic."[17] Yeats's is a tragic vision, de Man concludes, in which "only direct interventions of the divine have the power to shape and determine the content of things and events, and of these we have no knowledge, for they escape the causal network of the system altogether. Reality is ours, body and mind, but precisely insofar as it is inaccessible to us, it is nothing." De Man's conclusion, however, fails to capture the extent to which Yeats is himself concerned to consider the reality of a divine incarnation, and intervention, in human embodiment, and never more so than when it manifests itself in a rage that approaches *jouissance,* as when the swan "leaps" into a "desolate heaven" in "Nineteen Hundred and Nineteen." Indeed Yeats (but not de Man) makes this theological dimension also political, immanent to the state of emergency when sovereignty once again becomes embodied in a leadership that violently suspends the law and its democratic guarantees of protection from force.[18] In this poem that gives the image of the "weasel's tooth" to the *schadenfreude* that shows itself in war, Yeats also and contrarily represents *jouissance* in the image of a dancer, Loie Fuller, whose whirling, gyre-like fabric in fact, in the filming of her performance, folded itself into a (vampiric) bat's wings. In the poem it concludes with a "barbarous clangor": "All men are

dancers and their tread / Goes to the barbarous clangor of a gong"
(*VP,* 430). What links these disparate images of *jouissance* to the
whirling of the drives in judgment, and to the opposite of harmony,
"barbarous clamour"?

To begin to answer this question, let us take a further example of
embodiment and discord, but this time one that leads to fragmenta-
tion and endless returns, using a recurring image in the later years of
Yeats's writing, that of "dolphins." In "Byzantium" dolphins who bear
the souls of the dead reinforce the "bitter furies of complexity" that
ensue upon "images that yet / Fresh images beget" (*VP,* 498). In "News
for the Delphic Oracle" the "ancestral patterns" that dolphins perform
as they bear on their backs the souls of the suffering Innocents lead,
in the final stanza, to a vital, but "intolerable," music of "Pan's cavern,"
where parts—"Belly, shoulder, bum"—"Flash fishlike; nymphs and
satyrs / Copulate in the foam" (*VP,* 612).[19] Could such images, and
such music, so far from the Pythagorean harmony of the spheres, in
fact contribute to an evolving understanding for Yeats that sexual
violence is what happens when what cannot be made complementary
is forced into structure?

From his earliest writings, Yeats seems aware that sexual differ-
ence troubles the pursuit not simply of occult truth but of "truth," in-
sofar as it may lead to a demand for the whole truth.[20] Much later,
in *A Vision* (1925) he called this limit "woman as man's obstacle
and goal, when she is not a mother," linking "woman" with "terror."
Counterintuitively, however, this may well be the starting point for
seeing what is ethical in Yeats's aesthetic. In its very abstraction, its
systematicity, but also in its linking of the illimitable, and the "apoca-
lyptic," with "Woman" as "Sovereignty" (another, and early, version of
"Mother Ireland"), *A Vision* suggests a possible source of relief from
what drives the imaginary and therefore from what troubles, *as* "mir-
ror," human relations. "Woman as man's obstacle and goal, when she is
not a mother" in effect admits impediment to the relentless force, the
automatism, of an idealism that is the unreason within reason itself,
unless it acknowledges—and thereby, paradoxically, frees itself from
the anxiety produced by—its mortality through the very act of creat-
ing something new in either bodily or poetic generation. That "gen-

eration" does not *unite* lovers, but it does bring something "more," as *différance*, but also as *change*, the dimension of *time*, into a world in which otherwise those lovers are trapped in the cold snows of a dream. In Irish literature in particular the impediment or limit that is "Woman" as that which cannot be mastered or domesticated in a Jungian and complementary marriage of opposites ensures that there can be no successful realization of that central device of the Romantic national tale: the act of union that binds an English male to an Irish female through the resolution of the marriage plot in domestic harmony or, as Kant would say in one of his most important responses to the wars in Europe that were central to the experience of the Age of Enlightenment, the danger rather than the promise of "perpetual peace."

To "admit impediment," is this not a succinct resolution that is neither a sublation of, nor a reconciliation with, *das Ding*? Does it not apply equally to the fascination with an elusive Good that defines courtly love, the philosophy of the Romantic Enlightenment, and the political martyr for the higher cause for which she will not accept compromise? And how might this lead us to imagine the possibility of an act of creation, of generation, or even of systems- or nation-building that does not simply repeat the past but that does not also end in "fury"?

The automatism that may certainly drive each of these endeavors, as it does the nymphs and satyrs in "News for the Delphic Oracle," seems almost inevitably to lead to lethal ends, and will likely come to an end that falls short of complete resolution or reconciliation because each of these endeavors—courtly love, Enlightenment philosophy, and political martyrdom—seeks what can only be known (in Yeats's words) as "obstacle" *and* "goal." This necessary impediment to obtaining "the Good" defines the ethical relation between the sexes that Lacan throughout his career, but especially in Seminar XX, explores as on the one hand inescapable but also, on the other hand, impossible. That is in fact what Lacan characterizes as the "mathematical antinomy"—the coincidence of "limit" and "endlessness"—that is the "female" side of sexual difference and that makes what seems "beautiful" become "sublime."

In Seminar XX, Lacan continues to elaborate an ethics of the aesthetic that would establish "Woman" not as an image (a beautiful body, *objet a*) that may be represented but rather as a limit ("form") to what reason, seeking "Woman" as perfect and infinite "love," can know. What the arrival at that limit creates, in fact, is a "writing," Lacan concludes, that "won't stop" because it does not impose an "end" to what *might be known* about the future (history) and the sexually other. Yeats's poems, in fact, tell us this: that such an ethics may allow the lovesick poet—having arrived at words that even as "after" words have failed—at last to forsake, to release from bondage to an inhuman ideal, an image from past life, even as they release words to continue to fail to confine it. Likewise Lacan arrives at this truth by linking the sexual relationship to Kant's encounters with the two forms of the antinomies, the mathematical and the dynamical.[21] The feminine is "mathematical," and sublime, because in its inconclusiveness and its availability something "more" is possible but that is the grounds for judgment not of inadequacy but of possible, different, future outcomes.

It is in this sense that Yeats, regarding what we can and cannot know in, through, and of the "symbol" of "marriage" (*AVB*, 214), arrives at a truth of the aesthetic sublime. That is, reason, and with it the "universal," fails—and happy we should be that it does!—when the philosopher-poet exceeds the mortal limits of time in order to establish, as standards and as ends, "Reason" as "universal," that is, without "difference." The realization of that standard *as* an "end" would indeed be apocalyptic in its revelation, and impossible, because it exceeds the mortal limit, the insufficiency of world and time, to know fully something—"Woman," the "universe," "language"—that has no beginning and no end *because* each of these abstract entities exists only as what limits (rather than enables) an excessive wish to know, and through knowledge to master. "O body swayed to music," Yeats writes at the end of "Among School Children," defusing our wish to "know" and therefore to possess the lethal Irish *aisling* ("*Gile na Gile,*" "Brightness Most Bright"), "O brightening glance, / How can we know the dancer from the dance?" (*VP,* 446). Neither "sex" when it is embodied as what is other ("Woman") nor "language," for

Yeats or for Lacan, can be confined to either the thesis of the mathe-
matical antinomy—the universe has a beginning and an end in time
and space—nor its antithesis: the universe has no beginning and no
end in time and space. The wish to master, to think of as "whole"
either "universe" or "woman" leads first to frustration, and then to the
consolation of a solitary (and "male") "freedom" in the dynamical
antinomy: there is at least one heroic, and virile, male who is not sub-
ject to the determinism of "Nature." No longer captive to this fantasy
following his marriage, Yeats continues to play with this posture, as
expressed in the very image of "the tower."

The antinomies ultimately lead Yeats, however, in another direc-
tion, in his most interesting poems about "automatism," writing, and
love, and in the discoveries surrounding his marriage to George Hyde-
Lees: if woman is the "limit" of thought's mastery, then "she," like
"God" exists only as what is foreign within (but also determinative of)
reality. This confrontation with, and acknowledgement of, the inter-
nal, antinomial limit, "Woman" as impossible, unreachable imma-
nence (which particularly characterizes Yeats's turn from the form of
the masculine tower to its internal, winding stair), and "Woman" as
the limit of a language that the poet cannot master, may well be what
makes certain of Yeats's poems not only ethical but, indeed, universal.
His confrontation with what is both foreign and intimate to language,
as to the speaking subject, instructs his readers (and perhaps instructs
the poet) that to seek to surpass, and hence to subdue, that limit is, as
Yeats and his wife intimately understand, to encounter ghosts.

Yeats's self-mocking love poem, "Solomon and the Witch" (VP,
387–89), blesses the new bride, who, through her communication
with the dead, released the newlywed husband from the impotence
that was provoked by a fear that his troubled past, but particularly his
love for another woman, Iseult Gonne, would revive to cast a shadow
over the new marriage. In this way also the poem shares the central
concern of Blake's most erotic poems: while inevitably the "bride-bed
brings despair, / For each an imagined image brings / And finds a real
image there," there is comfort, and creativity, in shared sex, made
visible in what it leaves as a remainder, and as a reminder—in this
poem, "the crushed grass where we have lain." When Sheba cries,

from the same sort of place as that formed by the hare (Iseult) in "Memory," "O! Solomon! let us try again," it is the cry of a woman so inventive even in her early experience of sex, and so perceptive that what is "generative" may also be what is "undead" in language, that she is willing to believe that the procreative act is never the same, and that its outcome will inevitably be surprising. As George Hyde-Lees well understood, the place for such trial, a repetition that seeks not identity (as identical reproduction or representation) but something new, may ineluctably bring Eros into a writing that is nonetheless, like Thanatos, automatic even as it knows it seeks to revive, in forms that are new, the dead. There "language" approaches both the violence of automatism (or repetition compulsion, "let us try again") and the release into the freedom that the ghostly "controls" (the Yeatses' names for the spirits alleged to guide the medium's hand) will channel or limit.

Returning "again" in writing Seminar XX to his earlier explora-tion in Seminar VII of *das Ding* as sexual difference, Lacan enacts his conviction that any problem with the "ends" in ethics is a problem of how ethics deals with what mind cannot master because it is, like language and *knowledge,* potentially "endless." The problem of "wis-dom," for Kant or for Solomon, and for Yeats, is inevitably involved in the problem of any ethics, but particularly in a national emergency of civil war, which insists on the existence—and the realization—of a "Good" with which we were either once or could yet be united in full knowledge. Sheba, as "~~Woman,~~" her sexual presence representable only by the hollow that still holds love's heat, "the crushed grass where we have lain," is indeed a "limit," or problem, for an Enlightenment that would, like Yeats's Solomon (but also like his wife-witch, the wise Sheba), know "all" of the "other," and hold on to it unto eternity. That limit, posed by the "form" of what is sexually other and signifiable only as dichotomous or in absentia, is, in turn, inseparable from the prob-lem (posed by the dynamical antinomy) of "freedom" from or deter-mination by "Nature" or, to use again a term more resonant for a poet who believes spirit survives "life," "mortality."

Does Sheba's cry signify the success or the failure of marriage, and if it is the former, does "success" mean that the union, in knowledge and in love, is a final and an actual "fulfillment" that designates satiation of desire? Or is that marriage—which was clearly in the "real" lives of the Yeatses' collaborative on mental, spiritual, and physical levels (including the goal of reproduction) even when it was no longer an act of physical sexual union—successful precisely because both partners knew the possibilities, but also the limits, that are in fact internal to the symbolic order that is "language" (as the "Real" that shapes the "image") and to the "symbol" that is "marriage"? What Yeats calls the demiurgic *Arcon* that arrives to the poet as a kind of dream vision from the phase of perfect beauty and mind, phase 15, is indeed perhaps what Lacan calls the "Good," *das Ding*, which is also the testing ground, at the very foundation of our capacity to use and to understand symbols, of ethics and of art, as it is of language. The drives of Eros and Thanatos whirl around this strange muse, binding and unbinding (or as Yeats would say, winding and unwinding) a "mummy" truth, whose "images that yet, fresh images beget" (*VP*, 474; 498). There is no end to this process except Death itself, that final act of union with a seductive but lethal place of judgment—for *das Ding* is also "conscience," the superego, the categorical imperative. This nonetheless constitutes a vital, positive, and even viable legacy from the Romantic Enlightenment, which also gave us Romantic irony: a poetic ethics that doesn't stop writing the possibilities of new forms of human affection when union is no longer mandated. As a closing example of such generative power, we might recall that Yeats in his first draft of *A Vision*, in section 12 of "The Gates of Pluto," which this essay has repeatedly cited, found both his own most important writing and also the greatest disappointment of his expectations for *A Vision*.[22] The end he had reached in this version of *A Vision* was not what he had expected.

As I have argued throughout this essay, without such form, "emptiness," or loss, may take on its own uncanny vitality in the life of a family, community, or nation. What more does Yeats's poem, which significantly is titled not "Meditations in *a* Time of Civil War" but (turning "time" into an abstraction or category) "Meditations in *Time* of Civil War," contribute to our understanding of war, love, violence, and the creations of the imagination for a poet concerned that there is "more substance in our enmities / Than in our love" (*VP*, 425)?

As a sequence it reflects on the vicissitudes of temporal succession in three forms of afterwardsness: familial (the inheritance of blood, property, and with them unresolved conflicts from an earlier time of violent conquest); cultural (art, including its shaping of the tools of war); and, in the final stanza, in the development of the individual, from the "growing boy" to the "ageing man." "Meditations in Time of Civil War," its speaker haunted by the question of familial and cultural succession in a time of insurrection,[23] in its opening poem offers an image, "some marvellous empty sea-shell flung / Out of the obscure dark of the rich streams," a first "emblem" of a shared "adversity" that may be felt as emptiness; it emerges, however, on the pleasure grounds of excess. Is this what "shadows the inherited glory of the rich," what makes a state of emergency out of even the peace imposed by the culture of the Big Houses, and the sovereignty of the towers, erected by the Anglo-Irish garrison?[24]

"Meditations" concludes with what might be taken as a wish, from the tower-top, to master the swarm of successive perceptions, "Monstrous familiar images" that "swim to the mind's eye" (*VP*, 425–27). From this literalization of the dependence of the imaginary on the eye (what Lacan in Seminar XI elaborates as the "gaze"), Yeats proceeds to describe two "reveries" that "perturb the mind": one of a "rage-driven, rage-tormented, and rage-hungry troop, / . . . biting at arm or at face" and another of utter "stillness," "longing drowns under its own excess." Yet however different these two might seem, the second image soon becomes more frightening than the first, more exemplary of what Lacan would call "Kant avec Sade": "the eyes of aquamarine, / The quivering, half-closed eyelids, . . . / Or eyes that rage has brightened, arms that it has made lean." What finally differentiates that languid rage from that of the "indifferent multitude," what makes superior that arrested dwelling on "hate of what's to come" to the "afterwardsness" of its "pity for what's gone"? Again, it seems to be a question of the eye, its "complacency" when it is "indifferent." If this is the answer to the question of succession—"I, that after me / My bodily heirs may find, / To exalt a lonely mind, / Befitting emblems of adversity" (*VP,* 420)—then perhaps we cannot find sufficient the various consolations of community offered in this sequence: "an old neighbour's friendship," "a girl's love" (for whom the tower was chosen and "decked and altered" [*VP,* 423]), or even the speaker's lonely toil in a chamber from which "shadow forth" images of "How the daemonic rage / Imagined everything" (*VP,* 419). There is no consolation even in the sequence's shining examples of Romantic irony: the disparity between emblem (sword and moon) and the aching heart that "conceives a changeless work of art" (*VP,* 421). What survives as most vital in this poem of civil war comes, in two places, from an almost Wordsworthian Nature: "I count those feathered balls of soot / The moor-hen guides upon the stream, / To silence the envy in my thought;" "My wall is loosening; honey-bees, / Come build in the empty house of the stare" (*VP,* 424–25). We will conclude with that image of cracked masonry, in its loosened place where we glimpse not a human face but the absence of a bird who evokes what Yeats elsewhere will call "the staring fury" of the gaze, observing that here, in the poet's plea to creatures who make honey—and who hide and protect the body of the queen—sweetness and light combine in a Homeric, but also Romantic, image of immortality.

NOTES

1. Two particularly important books on Yeats in love have helped inform the conclusions I reach here, even though I depart from these sources: Elizabeth Cullingford, *Gender and History in Yeats's Love Poetry* (Cambridge: Cambridge University Press, 1993), and Marjorie Howes, *Yeats's Nations: Gender, Class, and Irishness* (Cambridge: Cambridge University Press, 1996). See also Gloria C. Kline, *The Last Courtly Lover: Yeats and the Idea of Woman* (Ann Arbor: UMI Research Press, 1983); Patrick J. Keane, *Terrible Beauty: Yeats, Joyce, Ireland, and the Myth of the Devouring Female* (Columbia: University of Missouri Press, 1988); and, for an understanding of gender, nationalism, and the legacies of Romanticism, Marc Redfield, *The Politics of Aesthetics: Nationalism, Gender, and Romanticism* (Stanford: Stanford University Press, 2003).

2. *The Variorum Edition of the Poems of W. B. Yeats,* ed. Peter Allt and Russell K. Alspach (New York: Macmillan, 1957), 430. Hereafter cited parenthetically as *VP.*

3. Margaret Mills Harper's important work on Yeats, especially *Wisdom of Two: The Spiritual and Literary Collaboration of George and W. B. Yeats* (Oxford: Oxford University Press, 2006), has helped shape the readings of that relationship, as has R. F. Foster's two-volume biography of Yeats, notably *W. B. Yeats: A Life*, vol. 2, *The Arch-Poet, 1915–1939* (Oxford: Oxford University Press, 2003).

4. Tom Eyers, *Lacan and the Concept of the "Real"* London: Palgrave, 2012).

5. This is the first of many moments where my use of the word "sovereignty" draws on the insights of Eric Santner's *The Royal Remains* (Chicago: University of Chicago Press, 2011).

6. Jean Laplanche, "Time and the Other," in *Essays on Otherness* (New York: Routledge, 1999), 241. I am grateful to Linda Gibson for first calling my attention to Laplanche's work and also to Tom Eyers.

7. For productive misrecognition in Yeats, see Gregory Castle's essay "'The Age-Long Memoried Self': Yeats and the Promise of Coming Times" in this volume.

8. W. B. Yeats, *A Vision* (London: Collier/Macmillan, 1937), 213–14. Hereafter cited parenthetically as *AVB*.

9. *A Vision: The Original 1925 Version* (London: Macmillan, 2008), 204. Hereafter cited parenthetically as *AVA*.

10. Laplanche, "Time and the Other," 245.

11. Ibid., 234.

12. This was surely in part Yeats's experience in undertaking the writing of his memoirs in the years when, still undergoing a kind of mourning for the loss of his ideal of Maud Gonne, he was partially, and only partially, recompensed for that loss by the actual closeness the two old friends shared during this period of Yeats's intensive literary retrospection. If the move toward Maud Gonne in knowing friendship suggests something like peacemaking, however, there was surely in reserve a further danger for Yeats, in the second decade of its realization, from that loss of her as an ideal, which may have left in its wake a keener sense of their differences, including the political difference of her activism, the violence of which had so often shocked him. A daimonic "fatedness" is how Yeats in *Per Amica Silentia Lunae* came to understand "love" and "hate," or "love" and "war," where daimon and sweetheart are indistinguishable. The work toward "peace," domestic and national, which is the work that disentangles and differentiates the lost (idealized) object from it daimonic afterlife will be henceforth in Yeats's poetry what, when it succeeds, turns "afterwardsness" into the "after words" that, for Yeats as for his central model for Romantic creation, William Blake, constitutes the shaping of not only loss but its daimonic, enigmatic signifiers into the structure of words, of images, and of rhythmic temporal lags that is

a poem. It is work that is analogous to what Yeats called the "stitching and unstitching" of words of love in the "old high way of love," even when those words have become (like the hare's nest, and now like that conventional image of romantic love, the "moon") "hollow" (*VP*, 204–6). Such work Laplanche himself compares to Penelope's work at her loom, insofar as it suggests a distinction between the work of mourning and the work of art, hers (the latter) bringing forth something new (her own art) even as it summons from the dead her lost beloved.

13. Paul Muldoon recasts Yeats's lines, bringing further to the fore the violence of the "automatism" of memory's testing of reality and of truth, in the conclusion to one of his most moving poems of the Troubles: "Now let us talk of slaughter and the slain / the helicopter gun-ship, the mighty Kalashnikov: / let's rest for a while in a place where a cow has lain" (*The Annals of Chile* [New York: Farrar, Straus, and Giroux 1994], 35). Muldoon, like Yeats, is keenly attuned to the complicity of "romance" (including a romance with republican nationalism) and those structures of authority that claim most assiduously to have freed themselves of the fantasies that have brutalized the heart.

14. Jacques Lacan, *The Four Fundamentals of Psychoanalysis: Seminar XI* (New York: Norton, 1998).

15. Slavoj Žižek, *Metastases of Enjoyment: Six Essays on Woman and Causality* (Verso, 1996); *Welcome to the Desert of the Real* (London: Verso, 2002); and *Less than Nothing* (Cambridge: Cambridge University Press, 2012).

16. In the same vein, Yeats married a young family friend of Olivia Shakespear's, one who looks remarkably like her in certain photographs.

17. Paul de Man, *The Rhetoric of Romanticism* (New York: Columbia University Press, 1984), 203–4.

18. I allude here to Carl Schmitt's *Political Theology*, a text contemporaneous with Yeats's own emerging attraction to fascism, and a text central to Santner's and Žižek's recent work.

19. Marjorie Howes's reading in "Culture and Enlightenment: W. B. Yeats" of form, "beauty," and mathematical order in this poem, offered in her far-reaching discussion of Yeats, the aesthetic, and the ethics and politics of cultural diversity in postcolonial and speech-act theory, has influenced my reading generally in this essay of these topics (*Colonial Crossings* [Cork: Field Day, 2006]).

20. Foster cites Yeats's *Autobiographies*, where he remembers being ashamed, as a young man, of being "full of thought, often very abstract thought, longing all the while to be full of images, because I had gone to the art schools instead of a university," even as he senses that what attracted him to "abstract thought" also drew him to "my Irish subject-matter" and an

"attempt to found a new tradition," precisely because he lacked "all that great erudition" that comes from university training. "I knew almost from the start that to overflow with reasons was to be not quite well-born; and when I could I hid them, as men hide a disagreeable ancestry" (Foster, *The Arch-Poet*, 178–79).

21. "Sexual difference can, indeed, be found in Kant, not in an accidental way, in his use of adjectives or examples, but, fundamentally, in his distinction between the mathematical and the dynamical antinomies" (Joan Copjec, "Sex and the Euthanasia of Reason," in *Read My Desire* [Cambridge, MA: MIT Press, 1994], 213).

22. According to the editors of the 1925 *A Vision*, Margaret Mills Harper and Catherine E. Paul, Yeats wrote in a journal in March 1926 that "I see now that section XII Book IV in 'A Vision' should have been the most important in the book & it is the slightest & worst"; the system should be "symbolized in a study of the relation of man and woman" (*AVA*, 332).

23. Recalling the particular moment of these reflections, the Troubles from 1919 to 1923 that would lead to the founding of the Free State but that would not officially end the Troubles until the Good Friday Peace Accord at the end of the century, we might consider more directly the work by Eric Santner, *The Royal Remains*. In his own reading of Lacan (which he supports through his reading of Levinas and Žižek but also after the work of Carl Schmitt and Ernst Kantorowicz), Santner explores the state of emergency in modernity, and more specifically in modernism, as a crisis of disruptive embodiment as it is felt by the individual subject whose collective "body" is the (phantasmatic) modern republic. Alluding also to Giorgio Agamben's work on the state of exception and *homo sacer*, Santner locates the reduction of the "human" to "bare life" more particularly to times of civil war when sovereign succession is thrown into question. Questioning the integrity of the nation because it is felt at the unconscious locus where two or more individuals relate to one another in imaginary "community," the body of the nation is linked to the violence, and more specifically to the *sexual* violence (or *jouissance*, what Santner calls "agitation"), of an unresolved trauma in the histories of Great Britain and France: the dethronement of sovereign monarchs (and the decapitation of the royal body) and the conditions of republican revolution, notably insofar as democritization may in turn be followed by civil war.

24. Daniel O'Hara's pathbreaking essay on Lacan and Yeats, "The Spirit Medium: Yeats, Quantum Visions, and Recent Lacanian Studies," *boundary 2* 29:2 (Summer 2002): 87–108, reaches a quite different conclusion regarding Yeats's "confusions of the bed" than I arrive at here, but it engages energetically with the importance of thinking, through Yeats, about violence, the erotic, and national states of emergency.

CHAPTER 7

"The clock has run down and must be wound up again"
A Vision in Time

MARGARET MILLS HARPER

The essay in the *Packet* will be the introduction of a new edition of the *Vision* under the name of "The Great Wheel." But this new edition will be a new book, all I hope clear and as simple as the subject permits.

—W. B. Yeats, letter to Olivia Shakespear, September 13, 1929

A Vision seems an outlier in the Yeatsian corpus, a work different from all the others. Different, that is to say, from any other except the other *Vision*—for there are two of them, editions published in 1925 and 1937 that are distinct enough from each other that they may easily be regarded as separate works.[1] Nevertheless, critical attention to Yeats's occult treatise, whether that attention is focused on issues such as the relation of *A Vision* to Yeats's poetic or dramatic works, its embeddedness in historical contexts, its genre, or any of its internal qualities, tends either to elide the two versions of the book or discuss only the later of the two.[2] Such a situation is to be expected, of course, especially if, as was true for *A Vision* for most of its shelf life, the later version is the only easily accessible one, advertised as "revised and amplified" by the publisher, and endorsed as such by the author.[3] Readers might certainly be forgiven for following Yeats's clear lead in this matter. In the dedicatory essay of the 1925 book, the author sounds half reluctant to forego a revision he knows could result in improvement:

> I could I daresay make the book richer, perhaps immeasurably so, if I were to keep it by me for another year, and I have not even dealt with the whole of my subject, perhaps not even with what is most important, writing nothing about the Beatific Vision, little of sexual love; but I am longing to put it out of reach that I may write the poetry it seems to have made possible. (*AVA*, lv)

Similarly, in the 1937 introduction, Yeats claims that he has indeed produced a new and improved version:

> The first version of this book, *A Vision*, except the section on the twenty-eight phases, and that called "Dove or Swan" which I repeat without change, fills me with shame. I had misinterpreted the geometry, and in my ignorance of philosophy failed to understand distinctions upon which the coherence of the whole depended, and as my wife was unwilling that her share should be known, and I to seem sole author, I had invented an unnatural story of an Arabian traveller which I must amend and find a place for some day because I was fool enough to write half a dozen poems that are unintelligible without it. (*AVB*, 19)

However, there are good reasons not to take Yeats at his word on the question of whether the 1937 *Vision* is primarily an upgraded version of the 1925. In the pages that follow, I will examine some of those reasons. The differences between the two editions of the book are important in themselves, as I will show, but in that they indicate an important development in Yeats's understanding of the system, which he incorporated with increasing depth and subtlety into his creative work in his last period, the differences also throw light on important distinctions in Yeats's work from the 1920s and 1930s. Yeats's sense of purpose, we should remember, occurs in arenas that are fundamentally spiritual as well as aesthetic and intellectual—his thought ran in religious currents from the start to the finish of his life—but it increasingly incorporates violence against the peaceful, or integrative, values inherent in that very spirituality into its equation. This is not to claim that a conflict between attractions to spirit and body, swan and shadow, are not one of the constants in Yeats's work. By the time the system of *A Vision* began to be developed, Yeats had for many years been sure that the irreconcilable choice between sacred devotion and secular heroism was for him an abiding theme. In this sense, his concerns are consistent from *The Wanderings of Oisin* in the 1880s, to his deep engagement with Nietzsche in the early years of the new century, to as late as the poem "Vacillation" and the figures of the theologian Friedrich von Hügel and the secular Homer. The theme extends even to "Cuchulain Comforted," which places that hero after his violent death in the position of receiving sacred instruction from shades of former cowards.

That being said, the systematizing years following 1917 add a level of specificity and complication that are worth noting. A number of poems written in the shadow of the first *A Vision* in the 1920s seem to apply its system by accepting inherent contradiction and reaching for unity (I am thinking here of a poem like "Among School Children," which, as Helen Vendler has recently pointed out, struggles for nearly all its length before rising to a closing couplet that seems to find, suddenly, a way out of the problems of disappointment and dissolution that beset it).[4] By the 1930s, however, the tone changes. As Glenn Willmott notes, by that time, Yeats's adherence to the principles in his comprehensive philosophy seem to have made the work "more incoherent and open-ended" than work that does not have the occult unified field theory of *A Vision* to buttress it.[5] Ironically, by the late 1930s, even though the version of *A Vision* published in 1937 stresses the possibility of an escape from the unceasing oppositions that fuel all life (in the form of the "Thirteenth Cone," a sort of *deus ex machina* for souls otherwise caught in endless gyres), Yeats's writing aims powerfully at effects like harsh humor, unstable tone, repellent political rhetoric, violent yoking of sexuality and spirituality, and an advocation of hatred as a means of achieving contemplative peace. It does so while insisting on transcendence, but one that is available only through destructive forces, a "terrible novelty of light," in a phrase from the violently transformative images that end the poem "High Talk."[6]

The key issue is temporality. Using the terms Yeats would have used, and the method of meta-analysis of history and art to which he did consistently turn to understand his own life and work, we note that the historical moment for the arrival of the "system" of *A Vision* was Phase 22. This lunar Phase, in which "ambition and contemplation" are balanced (*AVA*, 29, 75), is one of the cardinal directions of the wheel of 28 Phases, in which the Tinctures—that is, the Primary and Antithetical qualities that color everything—shift. At this point, the exhaustion of the Antithetical causes it to yield to the growing Primary of the last quarter of the wheel. The position of the Four Faculties is also significant: at Phase 22, Mask and Creative Genius overlap each other at the same point on the wheel, as do Will and Body of Fate. In lay terms, this means the end of something, when desire and logic yield the same result, when drive finds its motive in the lack of drive, that is, a satisfaction with what is. When Yeats uses the same system in the 1930s, the phasal character has changed. Now the historical moment is Phase 23, in which "The clock has run down and must be wound up again," the "violent, anarchic" start of the last quarter of the wheel. Yeats and the system are now both out of phase when he applies a revelation of Phase 22 to the changed conditions of Phase 23. The man of Phase 23 who is out of phase "is tyrannical, gloomy and self-absorbed" (*AVA*, 80), a description that might be applied to the 1937 *A Vision* as well as many of the late masks of the poet.

The business of winding up that clock again was a messy one, but it resulted in chillingly powerful writing. To understand how Yeats understood his project, I will begin with discussion of the published books, then move to discuss Michael Robartes, a character who appears in both books but who serves distinct purposes within them. I will conclude by looking briefly at two segments of prose that were at one stage in Yeats's process of composition intended for inclusion in each of the two versions and that underscore the distinctions I draw about both the character Robartes and his author's late work.

VISIONS

The place to begin thinking about the two versions of *A Vision* is at the covers—in other words, with the books as material objects and artifacts of the publishing trade. Placed side by side, the fact that they are different in kind and intended readership is obvious. The 1925 edition, announcing that it is "privately printed for subscribers only" in a very small print run by an independent London publisher (T. Werner Laurie), seems aimed in good part at Yeats's fellow occultists, or at least a small public who share with them an interest in arcane symbols and inexplicit prophecies.[7] Even the attribution of the book to William Butler Yeats on the antiquarian-styled title page suggests some hidden purpose, since the frontispiece is a portrait not of this author but another: a fictional personage, Giraldus, depicted in a slyly suggestive woodcut (*AVA*, 1–li). The book is dedicated in an opening essay to "Vestigia," that is, Moina Mathers, an old friend from Yeats's period of most intense involvement with the Hermetic Order of the Golden Dawn.[8] The paragraph that precedes the passage from the dedication quoted above, in which Yeats admits his sense that the new book is inadequate, mentions the readership he does expect to be pleased—and also the readers about whose disapproval he worries (rightly, as it happened, both in the short term of reviews and the longer critical consensus). "As I most fear to disappoint those that come to this book through some interest in my poetry and in that alone," he explains, "I warn them from that part of the book called 'The Great Wheel' and from the whole of Book II, and beg them to dip here and there in the verse and into my comments upon life and history."

The easier group to please, "my old fellow students," is less worrisome: they "may confine themselves to what is most technical and explanatory" but might also consider using the book as practitioners of occult arts would be likely to do anyway—begin with esoteric details and expand them into principles for living. Yeats writes, "thought is nothing without action, but if they will master what is most abstract there and make it the foundation of their visions, the curtain may ring up on a new drama" (lv). Interestingly, one of the few contemporary reviews was by Yeats's old companion Æ (George Russell), a deeply committed mystic and Theosophist who fit the profile of "my old fellow students" better than many and whose commitment to a "new drama" of Irish culture was unwavering.[9]

Beyond the introductory material, both versions of *A Vision* present abstract geometric systems in prose that sound like a blend of philosophy, psychology, history, and theology. However, differences in tone are suggestive. The first *Vision* seems designed to be read like any number of other esoteric books, that is, as a support for a reader's personal spiritual development. It employs rhetorical conventions suggesting the possibility of transcendent benefits if readers apply its principles to their personal lives. For example, the concept of the need for expiation of strong passions by souls after their deaths, and through multiple lives, is described in terms of family and loved ones, an urging to action (what "we must" do), and the rewards that accrue from success:

> Seeing that persons are born again and again in association, mother and son at first it may be, then wife and husband, brother and sister, and that our loves and friendships are many, each person is part of a community of spirits and our re-embodiments are governed and caused by passions that we must exhaust in all their forms. . . . A purgation completed brings both good fortune and happiness, a consciousness of luck. (*AVA,* 192)

The corresponding passage in *AVB* is much less emotive, eliminating all mention of intimate relationships and making sure that readers understand that personal fulfillment is not the point:

The more complete the expiation, or the less the need for it, the more fortunate the succeeding life. The more fully a life is lived, the less the need for—or the more complete is—the expiation. Neither the *Phantasmagoria*, nor the *Purification*, nor any other state between death and birth should be considered as a reward or paradise. Neither between death and birth nor between birth and death can the soul find more than momentary happiness; its object is to pass rapidly round its circle and find freedom from that circle. (*AVB*, 236)

In *AVA*, Yeats tries through his rhetoric to create a sense of a collective spiritual path, the author at the head of a community of seekers. At one point, he even speaks of "my student, if such there be" (*AVA*, 138). The pronoun use is also suggestive. In *AVA*, the tendency is toward the plural first person pronoun: in my count, the word *we* appears 227 times in the 198 pages in Yeats's own voice after the introductory material. In *AVB*, the word *we* is used a good deal less frequently, 163 times in the 235 pages of comparable material. In 1937, Yeats adds remarks that seem at first glance more confessional and less authoritative, like these comments from the exposition in book 4 on "The Great Year of the Ancients": "What was the date? I have not read his [Ptolemy's] *Almagest*, nor am I likely to"; or "Some years passed before I understood the meaning of this sign or of the other cardinal signs in the original automatic map" (*AVB*, 254). In other words, what may seem an assertion of collectivity in *AVA* is in fact evidence of a specific rhetorical exigence, as it is in the occult texts that form this strand of the generic context of the book. When Yeats, like Eliphas Lévi or Madame Blavatsky, speaks in the first person plural, he is on some level hoping to convert readers into disciples. In *AVA*, no less than in Lévi's *Dogma et Rituel de la Haute Magie* or Blavatsky's *Isis Unveiled*, the plural pronoun masks a more personal writerly situation, a need for persuasion. The concepts in *AVA* are less smoothly explained or neatly organized than in *AVB*, and the pronouns are trying to do some of the work that the presentation of ideas is left to perform in the later book. In *AVB*, *we* is often replaced by *I*, used as the strong voice of a philosophical essayist transmitting ideas rather than a religionist enjoining practical application: "When I look in history . . . I seem to discover . . .";"If I translate . . . into the language of the system I say . . ." (*AVB*, 205, 258), and so on. When Yeats uses *we* in *AVB*, he often does so impersonally or qualified by some modifier (like "We all to some extent" [*AVB*, 237]). Tags attributing pieces of information to "my instructors" dot the discursive surface of *AVB*, since Yeats now freely discusses the source of ideas in George Yeats's and his automatic script. Unmasking the spirit communicators eases a number of discursive issues in the revised book, not least the awkward business of relying on the authority generated by a group of undefined fellow seekers, that spiritual "we" of the earlier book. (Even that nebulous group may be a quiet hint at the more specific and immediate source, however: "Vestigia," after all, was the coded name for a woman engaged in a mystical marriage, and dedicating the book to her points to another occult partnership, the one that generated the automatic script and other genetic materials for *A Vision*.[10] The name "Vestigia," short for *Vestigia Nulla Retrorsum*, "no footsteps back," is itself curiously reminiscent of George Yeats's Golden Dawn Motto, *Nemo Sciat*, "let no one know," referring as both do to the notion of absence of traces.)

The collective readership suggested by *AVA* is aligned also in temporal orientation. Like any other spiritual group, the receivers of this doctrine are on a path that projects itself toward a future goal. Rhetorically speaking, *AVA* looks forward. The text as a whole might even be characterized by the future conditional tense of its final lines of prose: "That we may believe that all men possess the supernatural faculties I would restore to the philosopher his mythology" (*AVA*, 207). A sense of prophecy or destiny runs through the book, from the dedication, with its stress on the unfinished quality of the work ("I could I daresay make the book richer"; "I have not even dealt with the whole of my subject"; "Doubtless I must someday complete what I have begun" [*AVA*, lv–lvi]), to the final sections, which echo the same sense of process and immediacy: "Much of this book is abstract, because it has not yet been lived" (*AVA*, 206).

This is not to say that a personal past is irrelevant to *AVA*. On the contrary: a highly personal subtext may be felt throughout its pages. The Yeats that speaks in its pages may not call himself "I" as often as the author of *AVB*, but his personal life is close at hand. It is as near, in fact, as the other item in what was intended to be a two-volume series: *The Trembling of the Veil*, the part of Yeats's autobiography that treats the years in which he engaged in his most intense occult study.[11] Werner Laurie had published *The Trembling of the Veil* in a volume with matching design in 1922,[12] so that a discerning collector might acquire it and *AVA* as a set.[13] That imagined collector might well find these two books matching in other ways besides their physical similarities: at several points, *The Trembling of the Veil* suggests that Yeats's life and times are a case study for ideas that receive theoretical treatment in *AVA*. For example, *The Trembling of the Veil* explains currents under the events of Yeats's life using concepts such as the fragmentation of the current age as opposed to Unity of Being or of Culture, the continuation of the soul through many lives, and the subjective/objective duality that is symbolized by lunar Phases.[14] A reader could also move in the other direction, from *A Vision* to the autobiography, noting perhaps that the "Examples" listed for Phase 17 in the short essays describing each Phase of *A Vision* do not include Yeats himself, although the piece was certainly written with that bit of information in mind; nor do discussions of inherited emotions or destinies in *A Vision* discuss Yeats's young daughter, Wilde's downfall, or Shaw's politics. For details on these and other contemporary topics the essays are meant to suggest, one must turn to *The Trembling of the Veil*.

The later *Vision*, published by Macmillan of London on October 7, 1937, and Macmillan of New York on February 23, 1938, is a far cry from the Laurie publication. It is obviously intended for the wide readership that a trade press requires.[15] The British edition consisted of 1,500 copies, with a further 1,200 in the U.S., making a total of over four times as many copies as *AVA*. As a Macmillan book by one of its major authors (whose well-fed-looking portrait by Augustus John—which Yeats disliked—complemented its standard title page), *AVB* was widely distributed and reviewed, if for the most part negatively. The reviews, in the best outlets and by many of the most highly regarded reviewers and literary figures of the day (including William Rose Benét, Babette Deutsch, Edwin Muir, Geoffrey Grigson, Sean O'Faolain, Cecil Ffrench Salkeld, Michael Roberts, Stephen

Spender, Charles Williams, and Edmund Wilson), in England and the U.S. as well as Ireland, by and large emphasized aspects of the book that would be most accessible to general readers: its relationship with Yeats's poetry, its theory of history, and its striking style.[16] In preparing *AVB* for publication, Yeats had himself been thinking of it in just such terms: at least since 1930, he had worked on the rewriting with the intention of having *A Vision* stand as the seventh and final volume in the planned Macmillan Edition de Luxe.[17] Again, imagining the shelf on which the book was intended to be placed is instructive: *AVB* would be the last of Yeats's complete works as presented in an elegant, authoritative, and expensive edition. The "I" inside its covers is the powerful confessional voice of Yeats's poetic work taken as a whole, the "idea, something intended, complete" that Yeats described in the introduction written in 1937 for the (also never published) "Dublin" edition.[18] The volume would thus embody its author's final word: it would be a summation of his oeuvre rather than an explanation of formative experiences from his earlier life, rounding things to a close rather than prophesying some indefinite energy "not yet . . . lived."

The arrangement of material in *AVB* adds to this impression. For example, although the poem "All Souls' Night" is printed after the end of the main body of the text in both *AVA* and *AVB*, the poem is numbered as the third part of the fourth and final book within *AVA*, "The Gates of Pluto," which treats the theme of life after death. In 1925, then, the poem, with its evocation of spirits as well as elegiac praise for Yeats's old friends Thomas Horton (unnamed in *AVA*), Florence Farr Emery, and MacGregor Mathers, fits the theme of the last of four books into which *AVA* is divided, of which it is the third numbered part (part 1 is the poem "The Fool by the Roadside"; part 2, the prose essay). The poem is placed and dated, in Yeats's characteristic manner, but "Oxford, Autumn, 1920," is not as distant from "Syracuse, January, 1925," the tag appended to the prose section it precedes, as is "1934–1936," the date given for the section that precedes the poem when it reappears in *AVB* (*AVA*, 211, 207; *AVB*, 302). In *AVB*, the setting has in fact changed the poem: now "All Souls' Night" is not the third section of a larger unit focused on life after death but "An Epilogue." Here, it does not resonate with the "moments of exaltation" that Yeats associates with the composition of the poem in *AVA* (*AVA*, lv), with the "ecstasy" of the moment of midnight and the ghosts it raises, so that "nothing can stay my glance" in the last stanza, and the dance of the blessed seems possible for the poet who raises the dead through remaining "bound" and "Wound in mind's wandering / As mummies in the mummy-cloth are wound" (*AVA*, 211). Rather, the position of the poem in *AVB* emphasizes the pastness of the poem, its enumerating of friends long dead as well as the contingency of the situation in the last stanza, when "thought" depends upon "meditation"—but we have just read the writer's hopeless sense that meditation may no longer be effective: "it seems as if I should know all if I could but banish such memories and find everything in the symbol. . . . But nothing comes—though this moment was to reward me for all my toil. Perhaps I am too old. Surely something would have come when I meditated under the direction of the Cabalists" (*AVB*, 301). The poem's last stanza now highlights the provisionality of vision. Nor is the context around "All Souls' Night" the only new literary setting that is apposite: in Yeats's work, by 1937, another poetic "mummy-cloth" recalls this one. The refinement of blood into elements that can drink only the "fume of muscatel," as if the afterlife were a heightened dinner party, has been replaced by terror in this other vision:

> Before me floats an image, man or shade,
> Shade more than man, more image than a shade;
> For Hades' bobbin bound in mummy-cloth
> May unwind the winding path;
> A mouth that has no moisture and no breath
> Breathless mouths may summon;
> I hail the superhuman;
> I call it death-in-life and life-in-death.
>   ("Byzantium," *VP* 497)

Another example of how the ordering of material changes meaning in the two *Visions* occurs in the last prose section of *AVB*, the book "Dove or Swan." This book, containing the theory of history that was book three of four in *AVA,* has greater pride of place in 1937. It is followed in *AVB* only by a page or two of meditative prose entitled "The End of the Cycle." This End looks back, exhausted, at the philosophical system in the book in the pages that precede it—"Day after day I have sat in my chair turning a symbol over in my mind." It arrives at its conclusion after that expression of near despair: "But nothing comes. . . . Perhaps I am too old" (301). The enervation is suddenly overcome, however, in a poetic move that is typical of Yeats's mature and late periods. We might notice the strategy, for example, in the poem "The Second Coming," with its abrupt volta followed by a rhetorical question ("The Second Coming! Hardly are those words out . . ."; "What rough beast . . . ?" [*VP,* 402]). In *AVB,* the turn comes on the last page: "Then I understand. I have already said all that can be said." Then, in the last lines, Yeats asks his question:

> Shall we follow the image of Heracles that walks through the darkness bow in hand, or mount to that other Heracles, man, not image, he that has for his bride Hebe, "The daughter of Zeus, the mighty, and Hera, shod with gold"? (*AVB,* 302)

AVB ends with an image of an old man musing on the relation between his life and larger patterns, asking a question (to which he does not expect an answer) about the relationship between a timeless image and a mortal, sexualized man. The man, we might note, has as his wife the goddess of youth. The Yeats who wrote these words was preoccupied with the liminal state between life and death (a preoccupation very much in evidence in the poem "Byzantium," to which as we have seen the "All Souls' Night" of *AVB* alludes). He was nearing the point at which the philosophy of *A Vision* would be part of a finished life's work, not the latest book from a living writer. If the timeless Heracles is a nod to this posthumous Yeats, who "walks through the darkness," the bridegroom Heracles may gesture covertly to another, the man to whom the miracle of the automatic script occurred shortly after his marriage to George Hyde-Lees in 1917. The end of *AVB,* in other words, circles back to its introduction, which tells the story of the genesis of the documents upon which

A Vision is based. Their miraculous beginnings occurred when a man had for his bride a young wife, she for whom is poured the second of the "two long glasses brimmed with muscatel" that "Bubble on the table" in "All Souls' Night."[19]

MICHAELS

The character Michael Robartes, along with his counterpart Owen Aherne, is a portal into a world that resembles the comedic excess of latter episodes of *Ulysses* more than it does much of Yeats's other work. These characters, we recall, usher readers into a welter of masks, anti-selves, fractured personalities, voices, and stories-within-stories, in a number of texts that refract each other like halls of mirrors. This melee obtains to some degree where Robartes and Aherne appear for the first time, as part of the cast in the trilogy of magical stories whose first versions date from the 1890s (*Rosa Alchemica, The Tables of the Law*, and *The Adoration of the Magi*).[20] Decades later, Yeats reinterpreted the characters for new purposes, and they become intense parts of what he terms the "phantasmagoria" surrounding the system of *A Vision*.[21] This second incarnation is itself doubled, though. It is important to notice that the Robartes-Aherne team has significantly different resonances in *AVA* (and the materials surrounding the book of the 1920s) from *AVB* (and the texts of the 1930s).

When Robartes and Aherne reappear in the materials leading to the first *A Vision*, they have changed from the already complex duo of the 1890s and 1900s, in which they seem to stand for heterodoxy versus timid adherence to Christian doctrine. When they reappear in *AVA*, the dominant note is multiplicity and mediation. Robartes is the bearer of wisdom that is itself from both the West (embodied in the figure of Giraldus, the faked Renaissance philosopher whose portrait is the frontispiece) and the East (figured by the Judwalis, a mysterious Arab tribe who dance suggestive patterns on the sands of the desert). In *AVA*, Aherne, though still admitting his Christian inclinations, is allowed to comment in an introduction and notes to the main text, which Yeats has been commissioned to write, based on information given him by Robartes. Two characters, two forms of the same universal wisdom, two lives for each character: when they appear in the versions of *AVA* and related texts, Robartes and Aherne comment on their original context as well as acting in the new one, a doubled position that creates a delicious irony. In their second lives, in poems such as "The Phases of the Moon" (*VP*, 372–77) and unpublished material like the dialogues into which Yeats first cast the material from the automatic experiments,[22] Robartes and Aherne become a sort of talking team, presenting occult material and also offering two opinions on it. If they were a double act of stage performers, of the sort that was common in British music halls and American vaudeville from the latter part of the nineteenth century (a structural model that is not irrelevant to them), Aherne would play the straight man, feeding Robartes cues for the punch lines.[23] Aherne is the sidekick, whose role of baffled auditor elicits explanations from Robartes, the dominant partner. His Western orthodoxy has become what he acknowledges as his "Christian or *primary* prejudice" (*AVA*, 194), but which is now no barrier to his full participation in the elaborate fun. The second opinions of Aherne create distance from the wisdom Robartes dispenses, drawing attention to the mediated nature of the wisdom itself, which is available only to those who to some degree misunderstand it— including the mage himself, not to mention Yeats.

Part of the point of the characters in the texts from the 1920s, then, is to lighten the touch. The humor of *AVA* tends toward irony or even whimsy, featuring multiple valences and labyrinthine turns, all of which serve to add to the high seriousness of occult investigation the verbal equivalent of a nudge and a wink. In other words, Aherne and Robartes prevent the tone of the texts in which they function, whether that function is as full-blown characters or mouthpieces in dialogues, to stabilize fully. The implicit suggestion is that the reader is being played, suggesting another generic template: stage magic. Despite the efforts of occultists, be they Swedenborgians, Theosophists, Rosicrucians, members of the Society for Psychical Research, or what have you, in Yeats's time as well as now, the distinction between "high" supernormal theories and practices and "low" entertainment is seldom completely clear. Part of the entertainment provided by an illusionist, as Yeats knew well, relies on the lack of utterly reliable truth. Audience members of a performance by an artist like Harry Houdini no less than Coleridgean theatergoers are willingly suspending disbelief, to some degree at least: they must suspect they are being hoodwinked but must never be completely sure to what extent or how. All that is certain is that reality, perception, and cognition are being displayed as a complicated set of variables. Likewise, Yeats's fictions from 1917 through the mid-1920s are reworked precisely to allow their creator increasing elaborations of identity, fiction, and image-making. They are Byzantine and mysterious, ranging in mood from the serious to the ironic to the tongue-in-cheek comic.

In *AVB,* all is changed. Yeats claims now that he reinvented Robartes for the first version of *A Vision* in order not to divulge the source of the system in the automatic script: "as my wife was unwilling that her share should be known, and I to seem sole author, I had invented an unnatural story of an Arabian traveller which I must amend and find a place for some day because I was fool enough to write half a dozen poems that are unintelligible without it" (*AVB,* 19). It should go without saying that Yeats's disclaimer is not to be taken at face value—if for no other reason than recognizing that any number of Yeats's poems are "unintelligible without" explanatory contexts, from Irish prehistory to contemporary national politics. Curiously, this broad hint by Yeats that the Michael Robartes of *AVA* is connected with George Yeats has not been systematically pursued. To the extent that Robartes is awarded biographical identification, the original most often mentioned is MacGregor Mathers. Certainly Mathers went into the making of Michael Robartes, especially in the first incarnation of the arch magician of *Rosa Alchemica,* amongst other sources. Yet the character also helps to veil someone whom Yeats was strongly inclined to keep hidden, despite a poetics that required him to ground much of his poetry and drama in autobiography. George Yeats is not the only figure whose identity is concealed or half-concealed in Yeats's work, of course. Nor is Robartes her only disguise. She may be partly seen behind various other figures: as the queen of Sheba, the unnamed wife of Kusta ben Luka, Minnaloushe the cat, Emer, the wife of Cuchulain, the anonymous mother in

"Among School Children," or even a figure evoked by custom and ceremony in the poem "A Prayer for my Daughter." Nonetheless, Michael Robartes, when he reappears after the watershed period beginning in about 1916, is a figure associated in varying ways, and to varying degrees, with George Yeats. The identification is complicated by the fact that one important aspect of it involves taking Robartes down a peg. When he comes to reflect a woman of immense practicality and sense of humor about matters about which she was also perfectly serious, a change comes to her husband's presentation of occult truths. Suddenly, there is a sense of double-voicedness: the tone is so nearly humorous a reader might be tempted to laugh, if only it were a bit more clearly so. Incidentally, the title poem from the 1920 volume *Michael Robartes and the Dancer* needs to be read with this attention to doubled tone in mind, as critics such as Elizabeth Cullingford have shown.[24]

By the second edition of *A Vision,* however, the sense that something of George Yeats inheres in the character of Robartes has dissipated, just as she nearly disappears, in all her disguises, from the poetry and plays. Her disappearance helps to understand *AVB* as well as Yeats's other works from the difficult last decade of his life. Ironically, in *AVB,* the book in which George Yeats's role in the automatic script was made visible to the largest part of her husband's public, she is still unnamed (she becomes "my wife" in the introduction) and is a passive figure, without any defined personality. Meanwhile, the sense of Robartes and Aherne as double act is gone from the rest of the introductory material, leaving Robartes the sole player onstage. In the framing *Stories of Michael Robartes and His Friends: An Extract from a Record Made by His Pupils,* for example, Robartes introduces Aherne as his "messenger,"[25] and he, like "my wife," is nearly colorless. His one interjection into a conversation seems not even to have been heard by the rest of the group.[26] Aherne's written text is even displaced onto a newly invented brother, John Aherne.[27] Taking the place of Aherne as foil is a group of disciples. They play a distinctly different role than he did in *AVA,* however: he fed Robartes lines and also served as someone who talked back. The additional disciples merely increase the authority of Robartes, who understands all their very odd stories, of shoes thrown at the theatre, sexually inept lovers, adulterous affairs, and eggs of love and war. Robartes himself has changed in turn: as Walter Kelly Hood notes, although he "began in the early period as a Rosicrucian wearing Druid robes and speaking like Walter Pater," he developed "first into an occult teacher concerned with the intricacies of the new system and then into an aristocratic social commentator."[28]

Just as two talkers have been more or less replaced by one, a discursive double-voicedness has given way to a text that privileges the hieratic discourse of Robartes. The humor has hardened, becoming Bergsonian in its rigidity: characters with developed personalities have been replaced with characters who are two-dimensional gestures to unexplained principles from the system rather than developed personalities (their very names reveal their lack of roundedness: Huddon, Duddon, and O'Leary are from a doggerel rhyme and an Irish folk tale; Denise de l'Isle Adam is named for the author of the play *Axël*).[29] The high modernist moment of *AVA*, which was influenced by and matches George Yeats's temper and interests, has yielded in *AVB* to the highly idiosyncratic version of combative modernity and antimodernity that finds expression in Yeats's other work from the 1930s.

It is all very unsettled, as if readers and the comedy itself were part of some larger, hidden, and deeply unpleasant whole. As Yeats composed the stories, he wrote to his old friend Olivia Shakespear about them: "Having proved, by undescribed process, the immortality of the soul to a little group of typical followers, he [Robartes] will discuss the deductions with an energy and a dogmatism and a cruelty I am not capable of in my own person. I have a very amusing setting thought out."[30] *AVB* is the version of *A Vision* that Yeats, in one of the stranger moments in Irish history from this period, showed to the Blueshirt leader Eoin O'Duffy. Again, in a letter to Olivia Shakespear, Yeats writes,

When I wrote to you, the Fascist organiser of the blue shirts had told me that he was about to bring to see me the man he had selected for leader that I might talk my anti-democratic philosophy. I was ready, for I had just re-written for the seventh time the part of *A Vision* that deals with the future. The leader turned out to be Gen[eral] O'Duffy, head of the Irish police for twelve years, and a famous organiser. (*L*, 813)

With regard to this meeting, Foster remarks only, "What O'Duffy made of this may be imagined."[31] As with *AVA*, someone mistakenly thought that Yeats's convictions about violence and the state could have an actual role to play in politics. With regard to any actual future, as Yeats wrote in the nearly contemporary introduction to the never-completed edition of collected works, the "modern heterogeneity" of the contemporary moment brings up "a vague hatred . . . out of my own dark," and he knows that "all I can do to bring it nearer is to intensify my hatred."[32] A postscript to the letter to Olivia Shakespear sounds the same "plague on both your houses" tone: "[P.S.] We are about to exhaust our last Utopia, the State. An Irish leader once said 'The future of mankind will be much like its past, pretty mean'" (*L*, 813).

It is a mistake, however, to decide that Yeats, near the end of his life, has merely given in to despair or bitterness—or to singlemindedly authoritarian politics. This equation trades in a commitment to change and conflict for a resolution, and Yeats passionately avoided stasis, very much including the stasis of an equation that posits any ultimate truth. His work from the 1930s aims directly to present and also undercut itself, or subject itself to new pressures on older ideas and form (from the contentious *Oxford Book of Modern Verse* to *On the Boiler* to the reworkings of ballad form, sequence, meter, or refrain). The play with temporality in the two *Vision*s helps to clarify the project behind these effects. In 1925, a witnessed moment of revelation propels itself forward; in 1937, back, from the same point. This is spiraling rhythm, not linear progression; anticipated recurrence with difference, not unidirectional teleology. Yeats's preoccupation with movement, according to Calvin Bedient, culminates for the poet in *A Vision*, Yeats's "concerted contribution to a scientific knowledge of reality as a great and constant agitation of change." Bedient continues,

Here was, he thought, a book to stand beside Oswald Spengler's coeval work, *The Decline of the West*. And indeed, like Alfred North Whitehead's writings of process and event, Henri Bergson's on creative evolution, and Walter Pater's earlier *Plato and Platonism*, which Yeats had read and marked up, it constituted an enormous recapture of pre-Socratic theories of the nature of reality. Yeats was and knew he was strictly and profoundly of his time in being obsessed with the laws and accidents of change.[33]

By *A Vision*, Bedient means *AVB*. Yeats had indeed not only marked up his older copy of Pater, but his copies of Spengler, Bergson, and Whitehead are also heavily annotated from the years when he revised *A Vision*.[34] In *AVA*, the system elaborates itself in an array of images, in an inherently dialogic frame: it is oriented toward and with others. After its publication, Yeats seems to have lost the dialogue that underpins its inherent multivocality and sense of purpose, the need for mutual understanding and explanation that drives the book as a whole. In *AVB*, distance from the system wars with an unsatisfied need for involvement: the material is assessed in terms of other thinkers, but the presentation is solitary.

To illustrate this distinction more clearly than can be done by looking at the published texts, I will conclude by glancing briefly at two stray unpublished manuscripts, where the phenomenon appears in higher relief than in the finished books. The two texts, entitled respectively "Appendix by Michael Robartes" and "Michael Robartes Foretells," edited together by Walter Kelly Hood, are anything but a matched set. The first exists as an early draft in George Yeats's hand, suggesting her availability to comment on and correct her husband's attempt to formulate the philosophy at a fairly early stage in its development (Hood dates it between 1918 and 1921, before Yeats had given up on the idea of framing the book as a set of dialogues between Robartes and Aherne). The second is a late-stage typescript, with corrections in Yeats's hand; it features the cast of characters from the *Stories* and contains historical prophecy that requires a reader's familiarity with various terms of the system.[35] It was very possibly intended to be the conclusion of *AVB*, raising the question why Yeats changed his mind about how to make his exit from his ambitious treatise.

The "Appendix," written in the voice of Michael Robartes, explicates the Great Wheel in terms slightly different from the published book, placing stress on Good and Evil as they may be yoked with Ugliness and Beauty, and making distinctions between Eastern and Western versions of the philosophy in theological terms. Its final section posits Phase 27 (later named that of the Saint) as the point where the soul is "set free." The "Appendix" breaks off mid-sentence, as if unable to solve the problem of having one of the Phases be the location of any ultimate condition in which a soul might "[contemplate] the sorrow and evil of the world and contemplating it . . . in relation to God who is the Spiritual objectivity" (Walter Kelly Hood, 215). This sort of stretch toward transcendence is nowhere evident in "Michael Robartes Foretells," which begins by framing the mage's prophecies by setting the characters Hudden, Duddon, O'Leary, and Denise back together after the passage of years, at Thoor Ballylee by the now-empty Coole House. "Perhaps we are growing old," Dudden remarks, and Denise echoes him: "Yes, that is it. . . . Even I am faithful to the past" (Walter Kelly Hood, 219). They recall the prophecies of the current age and the historical Phases of the immediate future given to them by Robartes before he "disappeared into Arabia" seven years earlier. According to their inexpertly remembered testimony, Robartes said that things are moving toward a head, since "The 22nd. phase of our civilisation has just passed" and the triad of Phases at the end of the cycle has begun (itself a small wheel, so that the current Phase 23 is also a beginning, if the beginning of an end). The present moment, Phase 23, typified by "the Russian violence and the art and thought of our time," is "where even logic has compelled the isolation & exaggeration of a single element." It is represented by "young men marching in step, with the shirts and songs that give our politics an air of sport," a finish to our civilization that Robartes cannot speak of "without hatred," but which will yield in its turn to a time when a new knowledge will come. That new knowledge, "of a form of existence, of a private aim opposite to any our civilisation has pursued," will, by "affecting minorities, and organising their disgust, . . . create a turbulence, like that we see about us to-day, but moral and spiritual; the knowledge enforced upon Primary Minds of antithetical civilisation" (Walter Kelly Hood, 222–24). At this point, "Michael Robartes Fore-tells" breaks off with a long note in Yeats's own voice, which thus becomes another distancing device to the presentation of obviously disturbing material.

As "Michael Robartes Foretells" and "Appendix by Michael Robartes" make clear, the differences between *AVA* and *AVB* are far greater than is often suggested. They present material that Yeats regarded as his ultimate intellectual and spiritual work, but their dif-ferent temporal positions suggest that the system is at the same time never ultimate. Elaborated in the 1920s and understood as given in the 1930s, expressed in multivocality and desire in *AVA* or distanced hatred in *AVB,* aimed forward into transcendence or back into a moment of vision now gone, Yeats's two version of *A Vision* demon-strate their own dynamic. That energy enabled him to extend himself beyond even the stasis created by polarities, a doubled vortex of thought and inspiration that sustained him to his final, highly creative days.

NOTES

1. Scribner's *The Collected Works of W. B. Yeats* devotes two of its four-teen volumes to the two versions: *A Vision (1925),* vol. 13, published in 2008, and *A Vision (1937),* vol. 14, forthcoming. Both versions will be cited in the text, the 1925 (from the edition above) as *AVA* and the 1937 (from the Lon-don: Macmillan edition) as *AVB.* For an easily readable chart of the differ-ences between the two versions, see the invaluable web site created and maintained by Neil Mann: http://www.yeatsvision.com/Versions.html.

2. For studies representing various critical currents, see Helen Vendler, *Yeats's "Vision" and the Later Plays* (Cambridge, MA: Harvard University Press, 1963); R. F. Foster, "Protestant Magic: W. B. Yeats and the Spell of Irish History," in *Paddy and Mr. Punch: Connections in Irish and English His-tory,* 212–32 (London: Allen Lane/Penguin Press, 1993); Leon Surrette, *The Birth of Modernism: Ezra Pound, T. S. Eliot, W. B. Yeats, and the Occult* (Mon-treal: McGill–Queen's University Press, 1993); Northrop Frye, "The Rising of the Moon: A Study of *A Vision,*" in *An Honoured Guest,* ed. Denis Donoghue and J. R. Mulryne, 8–33 (London: Edward Arnold, 1965; rpt. in

Spiritus Mundi: Essays on Literature, Myth, and Society, 245–74 [Blooming-ton: Indiana University Press, 1976]); Steven Helmling, *The Esoteric Come-dies of Carlyle, Newman, and Yeats* (Cambridge: Cambridge University Press, 1988); and Hazard Adams, *The Book of Yeats's Vision: Romantic Modernism and Antithetical Tradition* (Ann Arbor: University of Michigan Press, 1995). An important exception to the general tendency to valorize or focus only on the 1937 book is Barbara Croft's *Stylistic Arrangements: A Study of William Butler Yeats's "A Vision"* (Lewisburg: Bucknell University Press, 1987).

3. The dust jacket for the *AVB* calls the new edition "a revised and am-plified version of an important book which has not hitherto been available to the general public" (Connie L. Hood, "A Search for Authority: Prolegomena to a Definitive Critical Edition of W. B. Yeats's *A Vision* (1937)," Ph.D. diss., University of Tennessee, 1983, 61).

4. Helen Vandler, *Poets Thinking: Pope, Whitman, Dickinson, Yeats* (Cambridge, MA: Harvard University Press, 2004), 93–107.

5. Glenn Willmott, *Modernist Goods: Primitivism, the Market, and the Gift* (Toronto: University of Toronto Press, 2008), 63.

6. *The Variorum Edition of the Poems of W. B. Yeats,* ed. Peter Allt and Russell K. Alspach (New York: Macmillan, 1957), 623. Hereafter cited par-enthetically as *VP*.

7. Allan Wade, *A Bibliography of the Writings of W. B. Yeats,* 3rd edi-tion, rev. and ed. Russell K. Alspach (London: Rupert Hart-Davis, 1968), 149 (citation by item number).

8. Mina (later Moina) Bergson Mathers (1865–1928) was the sister of Henri Bergson and widow of Samuel Liddell (MacGregor) Mathers, found-ing Chief of the Golden Dawn.

9. See George Russell [Æ], "A Review of 'A Vision,'" *Irish Statesman,* February 13, 1926, 714–716; rpt. in A. Norman Jeffares, ed., *W. B. Yeats: The Critical Heritage* (London: Routledge and Kegan Paul, 1977), 269–73.

10. I am indebted for this suggestion to Neil Mann, personal corre-spondence.

11. *The Collected Works of W. B. Yeats,* vol. 3, *Autobiographies,* ed. Wil-liam H. O'Donnell and Douglas N. Archibald (New York: Scribner, 1999), 109–286. Hereafter cited parenthetically as *A*.

12. Wade, *A Bibliography of the Writings of W. B. Yeats,* 133.

13. One of the few material differences in the two books as objects is that one thousand signed copies of *The Trembling of the Veil* were issued to subscribers, but the run was decreased to six hundred for *AVA*.

14. See *A*, 162–68, 207–18, and 227–30.

15. Wade, *A Bibliography of the Writings of W. B. Yeats,* 191 and 192.

16. The vast majority of these reviews have been reprinted on the web site by Neil Mann: see http://www.yeatsvision.com/Reviews.html.

17. This edition fell victim to the economic depression of the early 1930s and was never completed, although Yeats's plans for it, especially the ordering of poems, have exerted considerable influence on textual scholarship since. See R. F. Foster, *W. B. Yeats: A Life*, vol. 2, *The Arch-Poet, 1915–1939* (Oxford: Oxford University Press, 2003), 415; Connie L. Hood, "Search for Authority," 50, and "The Remaking of *A Vision*," in *Yeats: An Annual of Critical and Textual Studies*, vol. 1., ed. Richard J. Finneran, 33–67 (Ithaca and London: Cornell University Press, 1983); and, for a summary of the scholarly debates, Warwick Gould, "Appendix" in *Yeats's Poems*, ed. A. Norman Jeffares, 706–49 (London: Macmillan, 1989). See also William H. O'Donnell's "Textual Introduction" to what was called in 1961 "A General Introduction for my Work" (W. B. Yeats, *Later Essays*, ed. William H. O'Donnell, with assistance from Elizabeth Bergmann Loizeaux [New York: Scribner, 1994], 483–87).

18. Yeats, *Later Essays*, 204.

19. Elizabeth Cullingford first proposed that this poem, like "Shepherd and Goatherd," blends elegy and epithalamium: "the poet enact[ing] a summoning ritual in which he offers to bring his dead friends . . . to meet his mediumistic bride" (*Gender and History in Yeats's Love Poetry* [Cambridge: Cambridge University Press, 1993], 107).

20. These stories are presented in Warwick Gould, Phillip L. Marcus, and Michael J. Sidnell, eds., *The Secret Rose, Stories by W. B. Yeats: A Variorum Edition*, 2nd ed. (London: Macmillan, 1992), as well as in the magisterial edition, Warwick Gould and Deirdre Toomey, eds., *Mythologies* (Basingstoke: Palgrave Macmillan, 2005).

21. For the history of these characters, see Warwick Gould, "'Lionel Johnson Comes the First to Mind': Sources for Owen Aherne," in *Yeats and the Occult*, ed. George Mills Harper, 255–84 (Toronto: Macmillan of Canada, 1975); Michael J. Sidnell, "Mr. Yeats, Michael Robartes and Their Circle," in Harper, *Yeats and the Occult*, 225–54; see also Gould and Toomey, *Mythologies*, passim. It might be mentioned that my word "revived" is rather literal: part of the fun of the reappearance of Robartes in particular is that he was presumed to have been killed by a mob at the end of *Rosa Alchemica*; when he returns, he is at first miffed at Yeats for engineering his "death." Soon, however, he realizes that Yeats "had done me a service" by inadvertently engineering some privacy: "but for that rumour I could not have lived in peace even in the desert" (*AVA*, lix).

22. George Mills Harper and Margaret Mills Harper, ed., *Yeats's "Vision" Papers*, vol. 4 (London: Macmillan, 2001), 13–135.

23. Among the suggestive connections between Yeats and music halls is the near obsession with them by his old friend Arthur Symons, who "studied the music-halls as he might have studied the age of Chaucer," according to

Yeats (*A*, 236). See Barry J. Faulk for an analysis of Symons's interests (*Music Hall and Modernity: The Late-Victorian Discovery of Popular Culture* [Athens: Ohio University Press, 2004]).

24. See Cullingford, *Gender and History in Yeats's Love Poetry*, esp. 86–88, where Cullingford argues for a generic change to the love lyric when "The woman who ceases to be silent makes it impossible to impose the traditionally uninterrupted homage of the male gaze" (86).

25. W. B. Yeats, *Stories of Michael Robartes and His Friends: An Extract from a Record Made by His Pupils* (*AVB*, 37).

26. Ibid., 50.

27. John Aherne was invented originally to excuse a potentially embarrassing editing error, when Yeats mentioned Owen Aherne in print by a different Christian name. See Sidnell, "Mr. Yeats, Michael Robartes and Their Circle," 229.

28. Walter Kelly Hood, "Michael Robartes: Two Occult Manuscripts," in Harper, *Yeats and the Occult*, 204–24, at 217. Hereafter cited parenthetically as Walter Kelly Hood.

29. Huddon, Duddon, and Daniel O'Leary appear in the story "Donald and His Neighbors," included in Yeats's edition of *Fairy and Folk Tales of the Irish Peasantry* (1888). See also the poem "Tom the Lunatic" (*VP*, 528–29). Villiers de l'Isle Adam's romantic play *Axël* had long been one of Yeats's favorites.

30. *The Letters of W. B. Yeats*, ed. Allan Wade (London: Rupert Hart-Davis, 1954), 768–69. Hereafter cited parenthetically as *L*.

31. Foster, *The Arch-Poet*, 474.

32. Yeats, *Later Essays*, 215–16.

33. Calvin Bedient, *The Yeats Brothers and Modernism's Love of Motion* (Notre Dame, IN: University of Notre Dame Press, 2009), 2.

34. Yeats's library is now housed in the National Library of Ireland; annotations are also noted in Edward O'Shea, *A Descriptive Catalog of W. B. Yeats's Library* (New York: Garland, 1985). See Nicholas Allen, *George Russell (Æ) and the New Ireland, 1905–30* (Dublin: Four Courts Press, 2003), for a recent analysis of Yeats's annotations in *Time and Western Man*.

35. I do not know whether or not George Yeats was the typist. Hazard Adams, who published the typescript as an appendix to his *Blake and Yeats: The Contrary Vision* (Ithaca: Cornell University Press, 1955), suggests that it may have been she who typed it (Hazard Adams, *Academic Child: A Memoir* [Jefferson, NC: McFarland, 2008], 100).

CHAPTER 8

Yeats's Graves

Death and Encryption in *Last Poems*

MARJORIE HOWES

W. B. Yeats spent more time thinking about death, both his own and in the abstract, its relation to writing, and the various possible forms that afterlives might take, than most writers. When he was a child he thought he would "like to die fighting the Fenians."[1] As a young man he was moved by Villiers de l'Isle Adam's pretentiously decadent line, "As for living, our servants will do that for us." As he aged, he confronted his mortality over and over again; such confrontations became a major wellspring for his work.[2] Not surprisingly, *Last Poems* has long been understood as their culmination, and this essay seeks to examine Yeats's meditations on death in that volume by focusing on his obsession with representations of graves. Through them, I will argue, *Last Poems* asserts, and then systematically dismantles, Yeats's project to shape and manage his own death and afterwords, both public and private. Read as a carefully organized whole, the volume explores death and what lies beyond it by submitting to the keenly felt failure of that project. I will also argue that the conclusions *Last*

Poems comes to are presented in indirect and coded form, in a narrative that we can track, not through discursive statements, but in its changing images of graves. Yeats encrypts himself in a series of graves and, in doing so, he encrypts or encodes his meaning.

Yeats's works are full of graves, crypts, and tombs, and they have various physical features and prompt or request various responses from readers or passersby. In "The Song of the Happy Shepherd"[3] the speaker records his disenchantment with the modern world by dedicating his art to the dead fawn he imagines his songs resurrecting. "To a Shade" (*VP*, 292–93) invokes a monument to the dead Parnell to register a more specific and political critique of contemporary Ireland and concludes that his ghost is "safer in the tomb." "The Mountain Tomb" (*VP*, 311) proposes a crypt that incites the futile pursuit of its secrets in the followers of Father Rosicross. At the end of "Coole Park, 1929" (*VP*, 488–89) Augusta Gregory's grave is found in the ruins of her house, and the speaker asks the passerby to dedicate a "moment's memory" to her. The "broken sepulchre" of "The Gyres" (*VP*, 564–65) will produce a new antithetical age, and in "The Ghost of Roger Casement" (*VP*, 583–84) Casement's "family tomb" and its epitaph describing the "fame and virtue" of the dead form an ironic counterpoint to the unquiet ghost of Casement and the colonial history he embodies. Some Yeatsian graves solicit memory, some provoke art, some record the degenerate nature of the modern, and some presage historical change.

The graves in *Last Poems* are carefully arranged to illustrate the conflict between Yeats's wish to manage his own death and the forces of contingency and uncertainty that threaten to thwart that wish. This conflict also occurred in a well-known biographical story about Yeats's actual grave. In September of 1938 Yeats wrote to Dorothy Wellesley that one of his reasons for composing "Under Ben Bulben" was in order to enforce his will about how and where he would be buried. He did not want a big state funeral in Dublin, as his friend George Russell had recently had; Yeats was distressed to find so many of the dead man's enemies there. The poem, he told Wellesley, "contains also a description of my own grave & monument in a remote Irish village. It will bind my heirs thank God. I write my poems for the Irish people but I am damned if I will have them at my funeral. A Dublin funeral is something between a public demonstration & a private picnic."[4] After he died, the poem did help him make sure his wishes were followed. Various people in Ireland began calling for a state funeral and for Yeats to be buried in St. Patrick's Cathedral or Glasnevin cemetery in Dublin, so his wife George published "Under Ben Bulben" in three different newspapers, five days after his death. As she observed in a letter, "I published the poem . . . because there had been some activity in Dublin to have a burial at St. Patrick's Cathedral; I decided to use that poem to ensure that this activity should not continue. After that publication in the 3 daily newspapers no one in Ireland could decently press what was against his own written wishes."[5]

But Yeats's management of his death did not end up conforming to his wishes after all. He had told George to bury him in France, where he died, wait a year, and then move him to Sligo. World War II intervened, however, and it was 1948 before his body was brought back to Ireland. That is, *a* body was brought back to Ireland. The question of whether it was actually Yeats's body may still be open. He had been buried in a temporary grave, and when Yeats's friends and relatives began to make inquiries about moving the body, the grave could not be found, and the bones had apparently been placed in the ossuary, a communal area of the cemetery. Bodies were thrown there together, the heads were often separated from the limbs, and they were not marked. Chagrined French officials assembled a set of bones they said was Yeats, and these were conveyed to Sligo and buried. Yeats's family claimed to be satisfied about the identity of the remains, but there has been some speculation since then about whether it is actually Yeats who is buried there.[6]

While Brenda Maddox concludes that the "evidence suggests that it probably *is* Yeats who lies at the foot of Ben Bulben,"[7] neither Roy Foster nor Ann Saddlemyer offers an explicit opinion on the authenticity of the remains in Yeats's grave, and the story remains suggestive and intriguing. Several scholars have seen it as analogous to *Last Poems* in some way. In his masterful and rigorous edition of the manuscripts for that volume, for example, James Pethica finds an ironic connection between the letter to Wellesley and the difficulties that remain in establishing an authoritative text of the volume. As he wrestles with these difficulties on an editorial level, Pethica offers us a *Last Poems* preoccupied with closure of various kinds, one that stages a "carefully managed dramatic narrative which [he hoped] might condition critical responses after his death."[8] He points out just how creatively enabling Yeats found his confrontation with death, noting his "repeated tendency to make imaginative linkages between inscription and death."[9] He also emphasizes mastery, defiance, and closure as Yeats's goals in that confrontation. "Collectively," he concludes, "the poems voice an overwhelming desire to provide both a heroic closure to his life and a resonant and fitting culmination to his poetic self-figuration."[10] I agree that *Last Poems* presents a carefully managed dramatic narrative, and that Yeats's confrontation with death was immensely enabling for his poetry. But I would like to offer a somewhat different interpretation of what happens if we read the poems collectively. An alternative heroism, and an alternative but resonant and fitting culmination to Yeats's writing life, emerges.

It is certainly true that a drive towards physical and poetic closure is evident in much of Yeats's life and work. Not only was he committed to a belief in reincarnation; he was also preoccupied, on a more practical level, with how things would look to people later, with the kind of afterlife that the memory of the living bestows or enforces. In 1916 George Russell observed wryly that Yeats was "his own coffin and memorial tablet."[11] Hugh Kenner suggested that Yeats had prepared a "cunningly managed death" in his own poetry at least twice before *Last Poems:* in 1908, with *Collected Works,* and in 1928 with *The Tower.*[12] But *Last Poems* confronts mortality by recording and then systematically thwarting the desire to manage death and determine his own memorial and afterwords. This thwarting, and a reluctant embrace of the results, is what *Last Poems* dramatizes without actually articulating it explicitly. It appears in a chain of images, in a kind of code. Yeats wrote to Elizabeth Pelham in January of 1939: "I know for certain my time will not be long" and he told her, famously, that "when I try to put all into a phrase I say, 'Man can embody truth but he cannot know it.'"[13] Through its preoccupation with encryption, with both graves and coding, *Last Poems* embodies something about death without "knowing" it, that is, without stating it directly.

What it embodies is an insistence that death and other endings may provoke a desire for manageability and closure, for a reliable afterlife in memory or the spirit world, but they do not actually produce or offer such things. This manner of linking death and inscription does not figure poetry as the means of transcending death; rather, it casts the absolute loss of death as the spur that provokes poetry. Edward Said called it "late style," art produced under the sign of approaching death and defined not through "harmony and resolution" but through "intransigence, difficulty, and unresolved contradiction."[14] It is also related to Diana Fuss's distinction between an elegy and a "corpse poem." Fuss defines a corpse poem as a poem spoken by the dead from inside the grave that provides a "counter or corrective to the aging elegy."[15] Rather than offer the traditional consolations of the elegy, the corpse poem seeks to "reconstitute death, not compensate for it." Fuss summarizes: "While the traditional elegy may be an 'art of saving' and the modern elegy an 'art of losing' the corpse poem constitutes neither a simple art of saving nor of losing but a complex art of saving loss itself." Through this complex art the corpse poem seeks to "make dying 'Dying' once again."[16]

It was precisely this sense of death as irremediable loss that energized the late Yeats. He may have had Crazy Jane say "all find safety in the tomb," but *Last Poems* owes far more to the idea that, as Walter Benjamin's famous formulation has it, "even the dead will not be safe."[17] Benjamin was another twentieth-century writer whose grave was lost, mismarked, and possibly faked. In his meditation on Benjamin's grave, Michael Taussig imagines various unconventional, alternative monuments or afterwords as more adequate to the task of memorializing Benjamin's life and work than a traditional gravesite—the larger landscape on the border between France and Spain where Benjamin died, the actions of the living, even the wind. He also describes a real alternative memorial built there in 1994. The monument is a series of steps, enclosed in a metal tunnel, leading down a hill to the sea. To descend the stairs, Taussig says, is to enter a kind of common grave, one which memorializes (through an inscription at the bottom) the nameless victims of the holocaust, the kind of people Benjamin's historical method sought to remember. For Taussig, the sum of Benjamin's "life after death," which lacks "bones we can point to" and an "honest gravestone," becomes his "final essay"—a continuation of his life's work.[18]

Yeats's *Last Poems* enacts a similar engagement with alternative memorials, with graves that violate conventional ideas of what a grave should be. Read collectively, the chain of images that structures the volume enacts a process or narrative that rejects conventional graves, and the drive for authority and closure they connote, and embraces alternatives that are increasingly macabre. We might call this process or narrative "getting out from under Ben Bulben." For a while, scholars thought that Yeats had intended "Under Ben Bulben" to be the last poem in *Last Poems*. In that position it might seem to offer a magisterial and authoritative summing up, a way for Yeats to determine what kind of afterlives he would have. It turns out that this placement was probably suggested to George by Yeats's publisher after his death, and that she assented.[19] We now know that Yeats wanted "Under Ben Bulben" placed at the beginning of *Last Poems*. The day before he died he dictated a list of contents for the volume; it was probably the last piece of work he did.[20] In "Under Ben Bulben," the speaker plans a particular kind of grave. He writes his own epitaph, establishes his own burial site and monument, and gives orders to the future and his audience. But Yeats spends the rest of the volume rescuing his readers, and himself, from the oppressive closure and authority of that project. Or, to put it another way, Yeats wrote his own epitaph in the initial poem, only to spend the rest of the volume rewriting it in somewhat different terms; he buries or encrypts himself under Ben Bulben only to re-bury himself in other ways. *Last Poems* stages a sequence of corpse poems, spoken from various kinds of graves.

There has been a good deal of critical ambivalence about "Under Ben Bulben." While some critics have taken it as a definitive, authoritative statement or epitaph, many others have emphasized its arrogance, ideological unattractiveness, and hectoring tone. Jahan Ramazani argues that we are meant to be suspicious of its "bravado,"[21] and Harold Bloom insists that it is just "bad and distressing."[22] I agree, and suggest that its bad and distressing nature has a purpose within the volume. The poem presents versions of certainty, authority, and control so extreme that, particularly in the work of a poet as dialectical as Yeats, they cry out for some kind of counterpoint. As Pethica's edition indicates, the original title had been "His Convictions," and at another stage it was "His Certainties." Drafts show the poem beginning with a section called "Creed" which proceeds through a series of statements, each beginning "I believe." Yeats retitled the poem "Under Ben Bulben" just two days before his death, but much of the finished poem still records the speaker's certainties, his claim to oracular authority, and his assertion of closure and control over his legacy.

This helps to account for the downright abusive tone with which the speaker addresses the poem's audience. As critics have often observed, the speaker, who echoes Hamlet's father, is already dead. This makes the poem a corpse poem, but one that seeks to control how he will be buried and remembered. The poem is full of commands and imperatives: we are enjoined to "swear," to "know," to "do," to "make," to "bring," to "learn," to "sing," to "scorn," and to "cast"—all in obedience to the speaker's wishes. And many of these words occur at the beginning of a line, giving those commands a special emphasis. All this bullying appears to be successful within the poem; the speaker gets what he wants. The last section recounts Yeats's burial according to his orders:

Under bare Ben Bulben's head
In Drumcliff churchyard Yeats is laid.
An ancestor was rector there
Long years ago, a church stands near,
By the road an ancient cross.
No marble, no conventional phrase;
On limestone quarried near the spot
By his command these words are cut:
> *Cast a cold eye*
> *On life, on death.*
> *Horseman, pass by!*
>   (*VP,* 640)

The confident description of a knowable landscape, the commands to the reader, and the epitaph not merely wished for but achieved, at least in imagination, are all part of the regime of certainty and authority we might expect from a poem originally titled "His Convictions" or "His Certainties." Numerous other elements in the poem bolster this regime, such as the idea that "there's a purpose set / Before the secret working mind: / Profane perfection of mankind" (*VP,* 639), the invocation of fate and the Gyres, and the scorn heaped on a degenerate modern Ireland, full of "Base-born products of base beds" (*VP,* 639).

"Under Ben Bulben" constitutes the volume's first scene or image of self-encryption. As a grave, it has some significant and specific features. The first is that it is constructed to the speaker's specifications and, despite the speaker's claim to eschew conventionality, it is deeply conventional in several respects. It encompasses several traditional, lasting monuments—the old stone cross, the grave stone, and the church. The material used (limestone) and the location of the grave in Drumcliff support the speaker's claims to the territory and local history of the landscape. The site is also connected to a dignified family history for the speaker in the figure of the rector. The second significant feature is the epitaph cut into the stone. The epitaph itself participates in, and revises, the epitaphic tradition of *seste viator*—"pause, traveler"—in which the epitaph encourages the passerby to pause and contemplate his own mortality. Yeats follows Swift, whose epitaph he called "the greatest epitaph in history"[23] in changing this tradition to *abi viator*—"go traveler." In this version, the traveler is challenged, not to contemplate death, but to imitate the life of the deceased. The ghost of the dead becomes an example of heroic living rather than a reminder of inevitable dying.[24] Third, "Under Ben Bulben" imagines a particular kind of audience or public for the dead speaker: readers and travelers who will emulate the cold, passionate ideal he places before them. The cold eye, of course, is not the cold eye of indifference. It indicates the kind of passionate intensity Yeats liked to think of as cold, as in his wish to write "one / Poem maybe as cold / And passionate as the dawn" from "The Fisherman" (*VP,* 348), or the claim in "On the Boiler" that "The Irish mind has still . . . an ancient, cold, explosive, detonating impartiality."[25] The horseman is at once supernatural, like the Sidhe, and aristocratic, like the "hard-riding" Anglo-

Irish. The speaker is directing his epitaph at his own kind, whether we view that kind in class terms or as exemplars of a more metaphorical Yeatsian heroism. Moreover, the beginning of the poem invoked "those horsemen" as one in a series of iconic authorities that we are enjoined to "swear" by. In direct contrast to a poem like "To Ireland in the Coming Times" (*VP,* 137–39) there is a circularity here, in which the poem becomes its own authority, rather than having to rely on future readers or remembering minds.

We can trace what, exactly, *Last Poems* encodes about death and its afterwords by tracking the other versions of the ghost, the grave, the epitaph, and the reader or passerby that follow and revise "Under Ben Bulben." It is through the transformation of these images, rather than through explicit statement, that *Last Poems* establishes its dramatic narrative about death. Helen Vendler's *Poets Thinking* argues in compelling fashion that the late Yeats often thinks through series of images rather than through a set of discursive or philosophical statements, and that he arranges "chains of images in such a way as to make them become the structural, and revelatory, principle of much of his poetry."[26] Vendler makes this argument about individual poems; here I am extending her logic to the volume as a whole. Indeed, given the fact that it is almost impossible to overestimate the degree of self-referentiality in the late Yeats in particular, the dramatic narrative this essay traces through a chain of images is arguably just one of many such chains.

The transformations of the volume's initial masterful image of encryption are already hinted at in the exaggerated authority of "Under Ben Bulben." Bloom notes that Yeats was a "subtle self-satirist," and, in many ways, the speaker of "Under Ben Bulben" is already the same kind of raving figure that Yeats invoked at the beginning of "On the Boiler," the notorious political tract he wrote in 1938. It has often been observed that the two contemporaneous texts share many of the same ideas—an interest in violence as an agent of historical change, praise of war, a preoccupation with eugenics, a conviction that modern Ireland is degenerate, and so on. Brenda Maddox's pithy characterization is that "Under Ben Bulben" is "On the Boiler" "poeticized and detoxified."[27] Yeats took the title of "On the

Boiler" from his Sligo childhood, explaining that there was a "mad ship's carpenter" who would get up on top of an old boiler and denounce his neighbors. Yeats remembers, "I knew the old boiler, very big, very high, the top far out of reach, and all red rust. . . . Then I saw him at a Rosses Point regatta alone in a boat, sculling it in whenever he saw a crowd, then, bow to seaward, denouncing the general wickedness, then sculling it out amid a shower of stones."[28] The views expressed in "On the Boiler" are certainly expressed elsewhere in the late Yeats, but his major motivation for writing the tract was to help the ailing Cuala Press make money; Yeats was aiming for a provocative, controversial publication that would sell well. Similarly, I want to suggest that the speaker of "Under Ben Bulben" is, at least in part, up on a boiler, striking a mad, exaggerated pose that we are expected to treat with some skepticism. Yeats's subtle self-satire is already at work. Yeats was generally very good at recognizing the potential ironies, even the potential silliness, of any of the poses he liked to strike—and was perfectly capable of remaining attached to those poses nevertheless. If we do not see the self-satire upon first reading the poem, Yeats spends much of the rest of the volume encouraging us to see it.

In the table of contents he dictated just before his death, Yeats followed "Under Ben Bulben" with "Three Songs to the One Burden," in which the first speaker is "the Roaring Tinker" Mannion. He shares the previous speaker's conviction that modern Ireland is degenerate, and he shares his wish to enforce his violent, eugenically oriented will on the modern world in order to prevent further decay: he invokes Crazy Jane and says that the two of them would

> . . . out and lay our leadership
> On country and on town,
> Throw likely couples into bed
> And knock the others down.
> (*VP,* 606)

A mountain, by implication Ben Bulben, is still in evidence. The horsemen of "Under Ben Bulben" have been transformed into more explicitly threatening and apocalyptic figures in the refrain, figures whose activities are not as carefully controlled by the poem: "*From mountain to mountain ride the fierce horsemen.*" The second speaker is Henry Middleton, a cousin of Yeats's, and he rewrites the dignified local history and connections represented by the (presumably less eccentric) rector of Drumcliff. Like the speaker of "Under Ben Bulben," Middleton has rejected modern Ireland and locked his gate against it, encrypting himself in his own property. But, unlike the speaker of "Under Ben Bulben," Middleton's alienation from the present is as much a function of his own eccentricity, which is evident in the poem, as it is a function of the degeneracy of the present.[29] "Under Ben Bulben's" proud assertion of local ancestry and unconventionality looks somewhat different here. The third section's speaker tries to gather a crowd around him like the old man on the boiler—"Come gather round me players all"—praises the dead rebels of 1916, and invokes Pearse's praise of bloodshed. But he also acknowledges the limits to his oracular authority, remarking that "no one knows what's yet to come" (*VP,* 608).

"Under Ben Bulben" and "Three Songs to the One Burden" strike poses that are cognates, and the relationship between them is meant to pursue the process of tearing down the version of the grave and monument "Under Ben Bulben" sets up. What "Under Ben Bulben" figures in terms of nobility and oracular pronouncement, "Three Songs" figures as something more eccentric, more ranting, verging on farce. The resistance to the authority of "Under Ben Bulben" has already begun, in a poem that rewrites parts of it and makes its speaker look more like a mad ship's carpenter haranguing his neighbors than a great poet engaged in the serious business of writing his epitaph. Subsequent poems in the first half of *Last Poems* also pursue this project. They present versions of heroism, authority, and closure that are undercut, vulnerable, or mocked in some way. If, as critics have repeatedly observed, "Under Ben Bulben" allows Yeats to speak from beyond the grave for the rest of the volume,[30] it has been less often observed that he is trying out a wide range of ideas about what kind of space "beyond the grave" is, and about what kind of afterlife and afterwords it might offer. He returns again and again to changing images of physical graves, the speakers or ghosts who inhabit them, and their audiences or passersby.

The volume's next poem, "The Black Tower" (*VP*, 635–36), follows this pattern and continues Yeats's thinking about encryption. It was the last poem Yeats wrote before he died, but he placed it here in the sequence of the volume. Its most direct origins probably lie in a story in Standish O'Grady's book *Finn and His Companions* about the loyal remnants of a Fenian force. It begins with the kind of injunction that opened "Under Ben Bulben":

> Say that the men of the old black tower,
> Though they but feed as the goatherd feeds,
> Their money spent, their wine gone sour,
> Lack nothing that a soldier needs,
> That all are oath-bound men:
> Those banners come not in.

These men have sworn an oath related to the one Yeats's letter to Wellesley and "Under Ben Bulben" asked for; they have allowed the dead to bind them to something. The opening word of "The Black Tower," "Say," is weaker than that of "Under Ben Bulben," "Swear," but still functions as a claim to authority. Within the poem, it is an instruction to a messenger sent out to refuse whoever is carrying the banners. Simultaneously, of course, it is also an instruction to the reader about how the men should be remembered. The men in the black tower have, in effect, written their own epitaph, encrypted themselves in their tower, and entered a kind of living death or a space beyond the grave.

The refrain offers yet another image of encryption in an unquiet grave, invoking O'Grady's description of ancient Irish heroes buried upright:

> *There in the tomb stand the dead upright,*
> *But winds come up from the shore:*
> *They shake when the winds roar,*
> *Old bones upon the mountain shake.*

This image, however, is ambiguous. Do the bones shake because they are being reanimated, or because the wind threatens to scatter them?

Interestingly, one of Yeats's complaints about the generation of modern poets writing in the 1930s in his introduction to the *Oxford Book of Modern Verse* was that they were all obsessed with images of bones, images that he found contradictory, expressing both horror of life and horror of death.[31] This ambiguity illustrates the central question the poem raises about the men in the black tower. Is their loyalty a noble cleaving to a more heroic tradition in the face of the modern degeneracy represented by the banners, which commentators, going on the authority of George Yeats, often associate with political propaganda? Are they, as Hazard Adams claims, "the poet's most extreme example of the heroic" because theirs is "a heroism that holds to its loyalties even after loss of all hope that the absent object of loyalty will return?"[32] Or is their loyalty a foolish obstinacy, a misguided clinging to the idea of their own heroic defeat and alienation, as other scholars, such as Jon Stallworthy, have suggested?[33]

The presence of the cook suggests that the latter reading is, at least in part, more plausible. The cook, occupying the crypt of the living dead with the warriors, is the figure whose labor sustains their ability to maintain their vigil:

> The tower's old cook that must climb and clamber
> Catching small birds in the dew of the morn
> When we hale men lie stretched in slumber
> Swears that he hears the king's great horn.
> But he's a lying hound:
> Stand we on guard oath-bound!

The cook "swears" something very different from the oaths of the men in the black tower or "Under Ben Bulben." He swears that he hears what they have been waiting for: the king's horn, which has mythological meanings in both the Irish and Arthurian traditions. They conclude that he is lying, but I am not so sure. A phrase like "we hale men" can, it seems to me, only convey irony in Yeats. It echoes the critique in "On the Boiler" of the fascist countries for accelerating degeneration by encouraging everyone, even the eugenically unfit, to have more children: "any hale man can dig or march."[34] The poem offers a contrast between the onerous and undignified work of the cook on the one hand, and the soldiers who claim to be perpetually on guard, even while asleep in bed, on the other. In the last refrain, "*There in the tomb the dark grows blacker,*" perhaps an indication of the increasing obstacles they face, and therefore of their heroism, but also an acknowledgment of just how dark their self-delusion is. There may, for Yeats, be something admirable about the men in the black tower, but there is surely a subtle mockery at work here too.

Not all poems in *Last Poems* feature speakers who immolate themselves in crypts, but these images keep recurring, and they keep offering less controlled, more disturbing graves than "Under Ben Bulben." When the volume arrives at "Three Marching Songs" a few pages later, the men in "The Black Tower" have become "those renowned generations" who "Fled to far countries, or sheltered them-selves /In cavern, crevice or hole, /Defending Ireland's soul" (*VP*, 613). Their oath to defend ancient values has again led to self-burial, but in less overtly heroic terms. Also, this poem's refrain dismisses the impulse to memorialize those renowned generations for their loyalty to an original purpose or grievance: "*But time amends old wrong, /All that is finished, let it fade.*" And the speaker asks "*What marches through the mountain pass?*" (*VP*, 614), retreating further from the specificity and nobility of the initial horsemen in "Under Ben Bulben." In the third section the grandfather, who represents the superior heroic vitality of an earlier generation, utters his praise of violence "standing on the cart" (*VP*, 616)—another version of the boiler—and then is hung in the middle of a sentence. The dignified grave gives way to cavern, crevice, and hole; the commanding *abi viator* modulates into acknowledgments of the ghost's irrelevance to the present. And the character of the reader or traveler has become increasingly uncertain.

We could read the dialogical character of *Last Poems* as being structured around a contrast between the degenerate modern world and the heroism that no longer has a place in that world and that must struggle on in the face of all the obstacles the corrupt present throws up. This is a common reading, and it is plausible enough for individual poems. But instead I argue that it is heroic poses, the authority of ghostly utterance, and the regime of certainty and closure *themselves* that are being questioned, rather than their ability to survive in modern Ireland. This is what we can see if we examine the chain of images, or the code, of the volume, in which images first introduced as masterful subsequently begin to disintegrate. The impulses that animate "Under Ben Bulben" do not disappear; they continue to make themselves felt as *Last Poems* proceeds. "In Tara's Halls" (*VP*, 609) praises an ancient king who plans and manages his own death with more success than Yeats did:

> He bade, his hundred and first year at end,
> Diggers and carpenters make grave and coffin;
> Saw that the grave was deep, the coffin sound,
> Summoned the generations of his house,
> Lay in the coffin, stopped his breath and died.

He achieves his purpose unmolested by other impulses in the poem. And yet this fantasy of complete control and self-encryption also has something faintly ridiculous about it. The king has determined to die before he violates his self-effacing code of conduct. But his preparations for death are not the self-examination and making of his soul that much of Yeats's other work (like "The Tower," for example) would lead us to expect. Instead they are material and mundane— digging, building—and we are left at the end with the somewhat comic image of the king lying in his coffin, holding his breath.

As figure after figure in *Last Poems* contemplates death and pursues projects of self-burial and self-memorialization, the hectoring voice of "Under Ben Bulben" becomes one ghostly voice among others, trying, and often failing, to occupy a controlled space beyond the grave. As *Last Poems* proceeds, it rewrites "Under Ben Bulben" more and more insistently. Terry Eagleton has argued perceptively that "Under Ben Bulben's" "hair-raisingly triumphalist epitaph" serves to "repress the reality of death."[35] In contrast, "The Man and the Echo" (*VP*, 632–33), the volume's most direct counterpoint to "Under Ben Bulben," seeks to reconstitute death as loss, to make dying "Dying" again. Yeats returns to the rhyming tetrameter couplets of "Under Ben Bulben," and turns to a different mountain, Knocknarea, and to the "cleft that's christened Alt." This self-encrypting speaker speaks from a different kind of grave:

Under broken stone I halt
At the bottom of a pit
That broad noon has never lit,
And shout a secret to the stone.

This crypt is more ossuary than proper tomb, the speaker is Hamlet rather than Hamlet's father (he says "There is no release / In a bodkin or disease"), and "Under Ben Bulben's" arrogant self-assertions have become painful self-questioning. The darkness of this broken grave offers no safety or rest to a speaker who must "lie awake night after night / And never get the answers right." No memorials or afterwords that he can supply will be adequate. To "lie down and die" like the king in "In Tara's Halls" is not the answer either: that would be "to shirk / The spiritual intellect's great work, / And shirk it in vain."

The need to judge, sum up, and achieve closure is still felt, but the speaker cannot assert his authority, determine how he will be remembered, or write his own epitaph. He imagines a time when the work of self-examination is done and the Man "sinks at last into the night," but this does not happen in the poem, and stating it as a goal merely provokes more questions:

O Rocky Voice,
Shall we in that great night rejoice?
What do we know but that we face
One another in this place?

We cannot know the nature of the space beyond the grave. And "this place" has become alien and haunting, no longer part of a locality the speaker has a comfortable set of ties and claims to. The only audience this speaker has is the inhuman and unsympathetic Echo whose imitation of the speaker is meaningless. As a reader or traveler, it passes him by completely; as an oracle, it will not answer. The speaker cannot even follow his uncertain meditations out to the end. Instead, in the poem's last lines, he is distracted by the cry of a stricken rabbit, the sign of a life, and a death, not his own. Not only is the speaker forced to cede control over his death and afterlife to the forces of confusion and contingency, he is also forced to share the poem with another story altogether.

The chain of images through which Yeats is thinking death and afterwords extends further; Yeats's graves keep decaying. But as they do, as I hope is clear by now, something else happens too. The more physically decrepit the graves are, the more imaginatively rich they become, and the more appropriately they memorialize, and extend, Yeats's thought and work. Accordingly, the speaker of "The Circus Animals' Desertion" (*VP*, 629–30), who is grappling with an apparent loss of poetic power, encrypts himself in an alternative grave that looks like a cross between an ossuary and a garbage heap. Rather than give abusive advice to future poets and readers, he examines his own poetic history, and does not necessarily like what he sees. The speaker does not command; he is not up on a boiler or a cart. Rather, he himself is compelled: "I must lie down." And he must lie down, not in a coffin, but in the "foul rag and bone shop of the heart," where the bones of the dead are thrown in among the other garbage:

> A mound of refuse or the sweepings of a street,
> Old kettles, old bottles, and a broken can,
> Old iron, old bones, old rags, that raving slut
> Who keeps the till. . . .

Rather than celebrating the heart, he makes it as grotesque as possible. He would rather not submit to it, but he has no choice. If "Under Ben Bulben" is the kind of corpse poem one writes from one kind of grave, a magisterial, self-willed poem, full of authority, the closing poems in *Last Poems* are the kind of corpse poem one writes from another kind of grave, the ossuary: a fragmented, uncertain state that was not what one chose.

Last Poems does indeed entertain the drive for closure and a cunningly managed death over and over again. But as the volume proceeds, the images that encode this desire change and degrade: from the grave to the ossuary to the garbage, from the stately commanding ghost to the ranting lunatic to the tortured questioner, from a managed Sligo landscape to "this place," from the horseman to the echo. The volume as a whole embodies a struggle between Yeats's impulses to write his own epitaph and make himself one kind of grave and the forces that make this impossible and force him to accept another kind.

The version of encryption in "Under Ben Bulben," an authoritative, successful exercise in monument building, gives way to other, less controlled versions of encryption. These are more effective corpse poems in Fuss's sense, in that they deliver us death precisely *as* loss rather than compensating for it.

Citing Giorgio Agamben, Fuss observes that "the corpse poem as a specific poetic type tells us something important about literature as a whole: poetry can ventriloquize the dead because literature, as a medium, already incorporates death." Every poetic utterance is "a disembodied voice detached from a living, breathing body," so that every poem, in a sense, is a corpse poem.[36] And Yeats is not just acknowledging his ultimate inability to manage death and its particular afterwords; he is also relinquishing his desire to master language itself, the meanings of which perpetually slip beyond his control. Death is central to the literary. Thus it makes sense that, in the end, Yeats decided that these less controlled versions of self-encryption, the anti-tomb and anti-epitaph, made for better poetry and allowed him to keep producing a different kind of afterwords. The volume's penultimate poem, "The Circus Animals' Desertion," turns the dearth of inspiration into a vehicle for the production of new images. As in Taussig's meditation on Benjamin, we can see a continuation of his work in the way the end of *Last Poems* represents Yeats's end. The very last poem in the volume, "Politics," which has an epigram rather than an epitaph, features a speaker whose quarrel with the kind of modernity embodied in the epigram recapitulates the structure of the volume as a whole: an initial authoritative statement is followed by a counterpoint that rejects that statement and proceeds more through images than through discursive argumentation. Read individually, each poem can appear to champion a heroic drive to manage and defy death in the face of an inhospitable modern world. But read collectively for the coded dramatic narrative embedded in the transformation of the images that were central to Yeats's graves—the crypt, the ghost, the epitaph, and the audience or passerby—the poems in *Last Poems* embody a realization that this impulse is less vital, and less fitting, than a heroic submission to the uncertain afterlife and afterwords offered by the ossuary.

NOTES

1. W. B. Yeats, *The Autobiography of William Butler Yeats* (New York: Macmillan, 1965), 7.

2. The most sustained and accomplished exploration of Yeats's engagement with death remains Jahan Ramazani's *Yeats and the Poetry of Death: Elegy, Self-Elegy, and the Sublime* (New Haven: Yale University Press, 1990), in which Ramazani observes that, over and over again, "Yeats contemplates his dependence on the muse of death for the aesthetic life of his poetry" (3).

3. *The Variorum Edition of the Poems of W. B. Yeats*, ed. Peter Allt and Russell K. Alspach (New York: Macmillan, 1957), 64–67. Hereafter cited parenthetically as *VP*.

4. Quoted in R. F. Foster, *W. B. Yeats: A Life*, vol. 2, *The Arch-Poet, 1915–1939* (Oxford: Oxford University Press, 2003), 635.

5. Quoted in Ann Saddlemyer, *Becoming George: The Life of Mrs. W. B. Yeats* (Oxford: Oxford University Press, 2002), 570.

6. See Foster, *The Arch-Poet*, 653–59.

7. Brenda Maddox, *George's Ghosts: A New Life of W. B. Yeats* (London: Picador, 1999), 611.

8. James Pethica, ed., *Last Poems: Manuscript Materials* (Ithaca: Cornell University Press, 1997), xxiii.

9. Pethica, *Last Poems*, xxiv–xxv. Pethica also observes that "the poems repeatedly figure death as a starting point for potential new discovery and as something to be deliberately and defiantly embraced" (xxiv).

10. Ibid., xxiii.

11. *The Letters of George Russell*, ed. Alan Denson (London: Abelard-Schuman, 1961), 110. Quoted in Pethica, *Last Poems*, xxv.

12. Hugh Kenner, "The Three Deaths of Yeats," *Yeats: An Annual of Critical and Textual Studies* 5 (1987): 87–92.

13. *The Letters of W. B. Yeats*, ed. Alan Wade (New York: Macmillan, 1955), 922.

14. Edward Said, *Late Style: Music and Literature Against the Grain* (New York: Pantheon, 2006), 7.

15. Diana Fuss, "Corpse Poem," *Critical Inquiry* 30:1 (Autumn 2003): 1–30, at 2, 22.

16. Ibid., 25.

17. Walter Benjamin, *Illuminations* (New York: Schocken Books, 1968), 255.

18. Michael Taussig, *Walter Benjamin's Grave* (Chicago: University of Chicago Press, 2006), 25.

19. Richard J. Finneran, *Editing Yeats's Poems: A Reconsideration* (New York: St. Martin's Press, 1983, 1990), 79; Pethica, *Last Poems*, xxvii.

20. Roy Foster calls this Yeats's "final act of self-canonization" (*The Arch-Poet*, 651).

21. Ramazani, *Yeats and the Poetry of Death*, 146.

22. Harold Bloom, *Yeats* (New York: Oxford University Press, 1970), 467.

23. Quoted in James Lovic Allen, *Yeats's Epitaph: A Key to Symbolic Unity in His Life and Work* (Washington DC: University Press of America, 1982), 25.

24. In this, too, however, Yeats is revising the tradition he invokes. Helen Vendler points out that, by dropping the original fourth line of the stanza, Yeats "repudiates ... Christian communion ... and substitutes for it a modernist and skeptical haughtiness" (*Our Secret Discipline: Yeats and Lyric Form* [Cambridge, MA: Harvard University Press, 2007], 97).

25. W. B. Yeats, *Later Essays*, ed. William H. O'Donnell (New York: Charles Scribner's Sons, 1994), 243.

26. Helen Vendler, *Poets Thinking* (Cambridge, MA: Harvard University Press, 2004), 118. For another recent and accomplished effort to track the repetition of individual words and images in Yeats's works, see Nicholas Grene, *Yeats's Poetic Codes* (Oxford: Oxford University Press, 2008).

27. Maddox, *George's Ghosts*, 355.

28. Yeats, *Later Essays*, 220.

29. Joseph Hone recorded a story about Yeats and George visiting Middleton in 1919. The gate was indeed locked, but Yeats climbed the wall and found Middleton, dressed in a white suit in a room that was littered with cheap novels and had a butter churn in the middle of it. And he said to Yeats, "You see that I am too busy to see anyone" (A. Norman Jeffares, *A Commentary on the Collected Poems of W. B. Yeats* [Stanford: Stanford University Press, 1968], 489).

30. See, for example, Curtis Bradford, "On Yeats's *Last Poems*," in *Yeats, "Last Poems": A Casebook*, ed. Jon Stallworthy (London: Macmillan, 1968), 77.

31. Yeats, *Later Essays*, 189–90.

32. Hazard Adams, *The Book of Yeats's Poems* (Tallahassee: Florida State University Press, 1990), 241.

33. Jon Stallworthy, "The Black Tower," in Stallworthy, *Yeats, "Last Poems,"* 214.

34. Yeats, *Later Essays*, 230.

35. Terry Eagleton, "Yeats and Poetic Form," in *Crazy John and the Bishop* (Cork: Cork University Press, 1998), 291, 292.

36. Fuss, "Corpse Poem," 30.

Part III

YEATS'S AFTERTIMES

———

CHAPTER 9

"Echo's Bones"
Samuel Beckett After Yeats

SEÁN KENNEDY

Samuel Beckett's need for Yeats was complicated and altered over time, but he was oddly evasive about it. The early writings are full of wry references to Yeats's work, as with the parody of "The Tower" in *Dream of Fair to middling Women* (1932), yet he told Aidan Higgins flatly in 1952 that he had "never read much Yeats."[1] In 1957, by contrast, he told H. M. Oliver of Trinity College, Dublin, that he was rereading Yeats, while insisting to Mary Hutchinson, a year later, that Yeats's symbolism was something he wished to forget.[2] Beckett had always been ambivalent about the theatre of the literary revival, and, as late as 1954, told Hans Naumann that he "loathe[d] that romanticism."[3] Yet, in 1956, he suggested Yeats's *Plays for Dancers* or *The Hawk's Well* as alternatives to the work of Eugène Ionesco on a bill with his *Acte sans paroles*.[4] Later again, in 1961, he admitted to Thomas MacGreevy that he was reading Yeats with "intense absorption."[5]

In seeking to make some sense of this, we might want to distinguish between Yeats the revivalist and Yeats the mature poet and experimental playwright.[6] Yeats's verse plays, in particular, had a lasting impact on Beckett's conception of the theatre, containing, in his estimation, "much great poetry."[7] *At the Hawk's Well* (1917) was a personal favorite, and numerous commentators have identified *Purgatory* (1939) as an important influence.[8] Anthony Roche suggests that Yeats became important to Beckett after he took the decision to write plays in 1947,[9] though it is more that the tone of the relationship began to change at this time—becoming more considered—as there is ample evidence of interest in Yeats from much earlier.[10] Until recently the tenor of their relationship has been judged largely on evidence furnished by "Recent Irish Poetry" (1934), but critics since have shown how this essay oversimplifies matters by setting up a number of binaries, such as the "antiquarians" and the moderns, that have since been applied too neatly to the Irish scene, and to Beckett and Yeats.[11] According to Sinéad Mooney, for example, "Recent Irish Poetry" provides a reductive reading of Yeats's significance that "deforms" his relationship to modernism,[12] while Alex Davis has characterized Beckett's account of the revival as a "burlesque."[13] Overall, the dismissive tone of the essay belies the complexity of Yeats's achievement and provides an inadequate sense of Beckett's interest in Yeats at this time.

That said, there were significant obstacles to be overcome on the way to admiration, and this essay will seek to offer an account of Beckett's critical dialogue with Yeats during the 1930s, reading his unpublished short story "Echo's Bones" (1933) against Yeats's contemporaneous writings on the Big House. Beckett came after Yeats in an obvious chronological sense, and went after him in the sense that he wrote in the wake of Yeats's extraordinary achievements, but he also went after him in the very different sense that he followed Yeats's career closely and was critical of his growing authoritarianism, especially during the 1920s and 1930s. Indeed, it will be argued here that Beckett's prose of the 1930s offers a proleptic critique of Yeats's late politics before many of the definitive texts—*Purgatory* (1939) for example—had even been written. For the purposes of the present essay, then, what is most interesting about "Recent Irish Poetry" is not what it says about Yeats but rather what it *does not* say, in that it excoriates an "antiquarian" writer who had long since moved on from peddling what Beckett terms the "Irish Romantic Arnim-Brentano combination [of] Sir Samuel Ferguson and Standish O'Grady."[14] In the eyes of Yeats's contemporaries, the appearance of *Collected Poems* (1933) placed him at the "cutting-edge of modernity,"[15] yet you would be forgiven, in reading Beckett's piece, for thinking he was reviewing *The Wind Among the Reeds* (1899). By the 1930s, even Yeats was lecturing America on Ireland's "now obsolete romantic movement,"[16] yet Beckett's essay provides a very different impression.

One reason for this is that "Recent Irish Poetry" was a commissioned piece in which Beckett was concerned less with Yeats per se and more with his influence on subsequent generations of Irish poets. Beckett borrows the language of "Coole Park and Ballylee, 1931" to deride the postrevivalist pantheon as "segment after segment of cut-and-dried sanctity and loveliness," and the essay exhibits a pervasive impatience with the stock-in-trade of revivalist tropes.[17] Beckett is scornful of Yeats's tendency to act as arbiter of his own legacy, and he is explicitly criticized for the promulgation of self-regarding genealogies of Irish writing, as when he casts Oliver St. John Gogarty as a specimen of Anglo-Irish solitude in his preface to *Wild Apples* (1930), "as though he were to derive in direct descent that very latest prize canary from that fabulous bird, the Mesozoic pelican."[18] This tendency gained notoriety in 1935 with the publication of Yeats's *Oxford Book of Modern Verse,* but Beckett had noted the tendency earlier, and his impatience with these "historicizing" gestures forms an important link to his growing displeasure with Yeats's authoritarianism, what Roy Foster terms Yeats's "new fanaticism,"[19] in the sense that Yeats was increasingly given over to idiosyncratic accounts of Irish history and culture that served deeper purposes.

Adrian Frazier has shown how the ideology of the Abbey was always conservative on the issue of property and popular politics and,[20] as is well known, in the 1920s and 1930s Yeats grew increasingly disposed to an authoritarian vision of Irish history. This view privileged the Anglo-Irish at the expense of their Catholic counterparts, whilst bemoaning the minorities' inability to shoulder the burden of responsibility entailed by their position: Anglo-Irish solitude; the tyranny of the mob; the preeminence of the eighteenth century in

Irish history; the need for a new government of the elite; these were the great motifs around which Yeats organized his growing attraction to authoritarian government. Politically, the backdrop to all of this was the eclipse of the landed classes; the rise and fall of Cumann na nGaedheal with the birth of the Irish Free State; the surprise election of Eamon De Valera in 1932; and the brief rise to prominence in Irish politics of the Blueshirts. As events in Ireland played out, Yeats was increasingly convinced of the need for a return to violent elitism: "I find myself constantly urging the despotic rule of the educated classes as the only end to our troubles," he told Olivia Shakespear at this time.[21] It was an attraction largely mediated by the decline of ascendancy influence in Ireland and, relatedly, by Yeats's growing interest in the great families of the Irish Big House as the preeminent site for transmission of power and influence: what he termed "complete culture."[22]

All of this is hardly registered in "Recent Irish Poetry," which caricatures Yeats as a revivalist cheerleader. Between mid-1931 and mid-1933, however, Beckett wrote the ten short stories that would become *More Pricks than Kicks* (1934),[23] where he takes more direct aim at Yeats's contemporary interests. *More Pricks than Kicks* documents the misadventures of an upper-middle class Protestant, Belacqua Shuah, and his solipsistic rebellion against the strictures of his family background. Relatively little of contemporary political events is discernible, but Beckett does take aim at the authoritarian Yeats. In "Walking Out," a story in which Belacqua plays Peeping Tom in the Dublin mountains, the narrator refers to Belacqua's fiancée, the "lovely Lucy," as, in fact, "better than lovely, with its suggestion of the Nobel Yeats."[24] Yeats had been awarded the Nobel Prize for literature in 1923 and, at the ceremony in Sweden, had regretted that no institution like the Swedish Court could "show its work of discipline and taste" in democratic Ireland.[25] Beckett was impatient of this kind of posturing, seeing it as another act of self-aggrandizement on behalf of Ireland's now obsolete ruling class, and he deftly critiques Yeats's vision of a resurgent aristocracy when Belacqua's fiancée is paralyzed in a hit-and-run by a "drunken Lord" driving a "Daimler." In this incident, as James McNaughton suggests, "Yeats's high-horse aristocratic fantasies and embarrassing fascist sympathies . . . meet the futuristic violence of German technology—a grim warning of the irresponsibility fascism entails."[26] By the 1930s, Yeats saw the protection of a leisured aristocratic class as "a crucial necessity for Ireland."[27] In Beckett's very different reading, the aristocrats were not ready— indeed, never had been ready—to take on such responsibility. By now, although *On the Boiler* (1939) was still some five years away, Beckett recognized the dangers in Yeats's revisionist impulse and saw how his growing interest in fascism and eugenics dovetailed uncomfortably with his calls for a new Irish ascendancy.

Another story written for *More Pricks than Kicks* provides far more compelling evidence for such a claim. On October 9, 1933, Beckett wrote to MacGreevy that his book had been accepted for publication at Chatto and Windus on provision that he write another story to bulk out the manuscript. This presented no small difficulty as he had killed off his main character in the penultimate story, "Yellow," but he responded by bringing the deceased hero back to life, "Belacqua revididus," and restoring him to "the jungle" in a story called "Echo's Bones."[28] John Pilling describes it as "Beckett's version of the Gothic or ghost story mode," and it is a bizarre tale in which Belacqua Shuah returns from the dead to fecundate the lady of a Big House.[29] Beckett claimed it was a story into which he "put all I knew and plenty that I was better still aware of,"[30] but it horrified Chatto's editor, Charles Prentice, who said it gave him "the jim-jams," and it was not published.[31] Pilling concludes Prentice was right to reject the story, describing it as a "brilliant but very conflicted mish-mash,"[32] which might even be an overgenerous assessment of what is, in many ways, an aesthetic failure.

However, Pilling is right to read "Echo's Bones" as a caricature of the Anglo-Irish Gothic tradition, in particular in what Vera Kreilkamp identifies as its "single-minded preoccupation with family lineage."[33] An overriding concern with genealogy and inheritance were features of Big House literature beginning with Maria Edgeworth, and the genre offers a recurring critique of the ascendancy classes as incapable of producing a legitimate and responsible heir. In a landmark study, Marjorie Howes shows how Yeats was similarly conflicted in his view of the Anglo-Irish, seeing them both as "a noble and worthwhile tradition" and also as "a tradition founded on crime, perpetually in crisis and inherently subject to degeneration and decay."[34] His response, Howes suggests, was to promulgate a theory of ascendancy as "a repeated crisis of foundations," and "Echo's Bones" constitutes a parody of this ongoing crisis-in-continuity of Anglo-Irish culture, especially as it was being reformulated by Yeats. Beckett's story contains many direct references to Yeats's work, including the appearance of Seanchan from *The King's Threshold*, a dying swan, and the repeated phrase "a vision."[35] However it is at the thematic level that his presence is most keenly felt. At its heart, "Echo's Bones" recounts the terminal decline of an Irish Big House, Wormwood, "one of the few terrestrial Paradises outstanding in this country" (EB, 12). In an obvious twist on the Yeatsian theme of resurrection,[36] and in a remarkable anticipation of *Purgatory* (1939), Belacqua Shuah is dragged back from the dead for the purposes of "atonement." He has, we are told, failed to pay his "debt to nature" (EB, 1), and, while the precise character of the debt is not specified, the story's themes and imagery suggest that it is the passing on of property (including the property of life) by way of viable and legitimate offspring.

Yeats's sense of crisis in the 1920s and '30s was being fed by growing concerns about the demography of Irish Protestantism, because Irish Catholics were exhibiting the highest levels of fertility in Europe, while the Protestant minorities struggled to replace their numbers.[37] In the circumstances, he became increasingly convinced of the validity of a eugenic analysis of modernity, which posited a dysgenic fertility differential between the well-off and healthy, who limited their births, and the masses of the poor, who bred with scant regard for social welfare.[38] To Yeats, this appeared to make sense of the Irish situation in particular and compounded his sense of Anglo-Irishness as "a nationality in crisis."[39] Mixed marriages further complicated the issue for Yeats, since improper marriages "coarsened" the blood,[40] and, in poems like "A Prayer for my Daughter," Yeats's child comes to embody the possibility of an Anglo-Irish future predicated on "custom and ceremony," while the Big House becomes the preeminent site of conflict where that future might either be jeopardized or secured. It was at Coole Park that Yeats had hoped his children might learn "what deep roots are," and its passing signified a crisis, if not a terminal point, in his account of Anglo-Ireland's history.[41] As early as 1919, Yeats was claiming that "the family is the unit of social life," and he was increasingly given over to counterfactual fantasies of "the culture of Coole as an Ireland that might have been."[42]

In this, Yeats sounds oddly like mainstream Irish nationalists of the time, who also viewed the family as the basic reproductive unit of society. Among nationalists, a Roman Catholic politics of fertility was being used to bolster the claims of the emergent Irish nation so that for both groups, church and state, sexual reproduction was a moral duty. In Foucault's analysis of biopolitics, during the nineteenth century population gradually ceased to be viewed as a good in itself—the basis of the vitality of the state—and became, rather, a force to be managed in the state's interest.[43] In the Irish Free State, however, the emphasis was still very much on repopulation as inevitable good, as a young nation sought to overturn losses occasioned by the Irish Famine and subsequent waves of emigration. The result was a coercive coupling of religion and politics as exemplified by the Censorship of Publications Bill of 1928. One of the less controversial measures of the bill was a ban on literature advocating the sale of contraception, since nationalist politicians viewed birth control as an assault, by stealth, on the future of the nation. In 1942, the chief of the censors reiterated the purpose of censorship: "The very foundations of this higher community called the State is the family. . . . That is the cause the censorship is maintaining."[44] This was merely a different iteration of Yeats's own views, of course, and his pronatalism needs to be read against that of his nationalist antagonists. Whilst they differed markedly in their emphases, both parties were invoking what Lee Edelman has termed "reproductive futurism."[45] Even if we might see the later Yeats as utterly opposed to the pronatalism of the Irish Free State, his own position exhibits the same identitarian logic regarding reproductive resources, albeit mustered to opposing ends.

Needless to say, Yeats did not support the Censorship Bill. Rather, he expressed delight that the issue had brought "men and women of intellect" together and, in an article published in the *Spectator*, painted a grim picture of rising illegitimacy and infanticide in the Irish Free State.[46] Samuel Beckett followed all of this closely and, in an unpublished essay, "Censorship in the Saorstat" (1934), was also critical of the measure. As a creative writer, one might have expected him to focus chiefly on the government's banning of great books, but Beckett was also concerned with the biopolitical function of the bill and considered the issue of birth control to be the "essence of the bill and its exciting cause."[47] Sexuality, as Foucault makes clear, offers a privileged point for the operation of biopower because it operates at the point where the body and population meet,[48] but as Marjorie Howes points out of this period in Ireland, sexuality also offered a way of distinguishing a morally upright Irish Free State from a degenerate England, and so the state of the Irish family became a touchstone for assessments of the progress of Irish decolonization. The resulting quest, for purity as well as repopulation, exerted considerable demands on Irish women in a society that "praised and valued married women for their fecundity."[49] Beckett observes:

> For the Irish are a characteristic agricultural community in this, that they have something better to do than read and that they produce a finished type of natural fraudeur having nothing to learn from the nice discriminations of Margaret Sanger and Marie Carmichael Stopes, D. Sc., Ph. D, F.R.S. Litt., etc.[50]

Picking up on the tenor of the discourse around the bill, Beckett employs the rhetoric of degeneration, outlining the bill's appeal to what he terms "amateurs of morbid sociology."[51] Eugenicists often portrayed degeneration as a moral condition, and Beckett's "natural fraudeur" is drawn from the terms of that analysis.[52] He suggests the Irish are too busy reproducing to take cognizance of the case for birth control, or, indeed, read anything at all, and he intimates that this inherent ignorance has only been exacerbated by the censorship of books. Five years after the passing of the bill, Beckett suggests, the results have been devastating: "Sterilization of the mind and apotheosis of the litter."[53] Beckett's remarks ratify, if only for the purposes of comedy, the eugenicist coupling of intellect and reproductive responsibility, and resonate with Yeats's reading of the feckless fecundity of the native Irish. Beckett's work reiterates certain prejudicial views of Irish Catholic fertility (as depicted with some hilarity in *Watt* and *All that Fall*), and we can imagine him taking grim satisfaction in this account. Having read the Dáil and Seanad debates on the Censorship Bill, Beckett is responding here to the pronatalist rhetoric of the bill's supporters, but he is also expressing something of the "indignant marginality" of Ireland's minorities.[54] He is suitably scathing of the coercive nature of the Irish Free State's audacious exercise in bio-power: "to waive the off chance of a reasonable creature is no longer a mere mortal sin," he notes, "but a slapup social malfeasance, with corollary in the civic obligation to throttle reason itself whenever it happens to be 'flung' into a form obnoxious to the cephalopods of state."[55]

To say this is not to suggest that Beckett and Yeats's views on the future of the Protestant minorities coincided. "Echo's Bones" suggests otherwise, providing further evidence of the usefulness of a histori-cally inflected reading of Beckett's antinatalism. One important way in which we might read the antinatalism of Beckett's work is as a rejection of the pronatalism of both Yeats and Irish nationalists: an antinatalism that is also an antinationalism, be it Irish or Anglo-Irish.[56] If Yeats's ruminations on an Anglo-Irish future focus on the future of the Big House, Beckett's account of the decline of Worm-wood renders any hopes for the regeneration of the landed classes absurd, in a depraved account of congenital deformity and residual alcoholism. Beckett makes a nonsense of any hopes of resurgence, as an onomastic analysis makes clear: Wormwood (the apocalyptic star of Revelations 8:10) is owned by Lord Haemo Gall (blood/foreigner) and Lady Moll Gall (prostitute/foreigner), who are preyed upon by Baron Extravas (to ejaculate "outside the vessel"),[57] and seek redemp-tion in Belacqua Shuah (an "indolent masturbator").[58] If the Anglo-Irish predicament is a crisis-in-reproduction, as Yeats believed, then in the person of Belacqua they have surely resurrected the wrong per-son to amend the situation.

Yeats's model for the transmission of Big House culture "focused on reproductive heterosexuality and femininity as the central guaran-tors of traditional continuity and national integrity."[59] Beckett, too, focuses on the reproductive travails of Wormwood's inhabitants, but with a different emphasis: Lord Gall, who is congenitally impotent, cannot fecundate his wife, Moll Gall, who is a syphilitic adulterer of childbearing age. One of the more egregious failures of the Anglo-Irish in their government of Ireland was their inability to naturalize or legitimate their status, which had been achieved by way of violent imposition and was maintained by a complex blend of conciliation and coercion.[60] Beckett figures their dubious status, rather as Somerville and Ross had done, by focusing on the use and abuse of certain laws of inheritance that were exploited to protect their social standing.[61] Concerns about the legitimacy of the Big House were a recurring feature of the novel going back to its origins with Edgeworth,[62] and "Echo's Bones" figures this crisis by way of a sustained interest in property law.

Given Lord Gall's predicament, Beckett focuses in particular on the legal complexities that threaten inheritance where there is a failure of issue. Lord Gall's problem is that his estate is entailed—entailment being the common mechanism used to keep the land of any given family intact in the main line of succession—and so the heir "in tail" cannot sell the land nor bequeath it to an illegitimate child.[63] Rather, under entailment law, where there is no legitimate heir, the estate reverts to the grantor or to the grantor's successor, an individual known as a "remainder-man" or "reversioner," in this case the syphilitic Baron Extravas. In Beckett's telling, it is the very laws that were used to ensure the persistence of the Anglo-Irish that now threaten its future, as a function of the degeneration of the landed classes generally. In a private letter, Yeats had declared the perambulator "the conqueror of all idealists,"[64] and Beckett resorts to rather heavy-handed symbolism when both Lord Gall and Belacqua are reduced to tears by the sight of an empty "Drumm pram"—a rather obvious moniker of the ascendancy's predicament—and of a "tiny tot on her own" (EB, 15), representing the futility of sexual reproduction in the absence of strong familial institutions and apposite socialization (the theme of "A Prayer for my Daughter").

Gradually it becomes clear that Belacqua, who is described as a "dense tissue of corporeal hereditaments" (EB, 1), reiterating his responsibility to his heirs and decedents, has been brought back in "cruel reversion" to see off Baron Extravas by producing an heir (EB, 1). He tries to avoid the sexual encounter by recommending disentailment of the property, which would defeat the restrictions on inheritance, but this, we are told, would only play into the hands of the estate's "protector under the instrument," also Baron Extravas, whose permission would be required. This complex double-bind is further complicated by the fact that the estate is held in "tail male special" (EB, 7), meaning that Wormwood can only be inherited by a male heir begotten of Gall's present wife.[65] Where Lennox Robinson's *The Big House* (1926), for example, describes a reinvigorated Big House under the care of the emboldened daughter, Kate Alcock, only the birth of a son to Moll Gall can secure Lord Gall's estate. Desperate for continuance, he pleads with Belacqua to impregnate his wife threatening to "take to the drink and die in the rats intestate" (EB, 17). The deal is eventually sealed by way of a drunken German toast, "Ach Kinder!" (EB, 17), and there is no surprise when a girl is born and Wormwood is lost (EB, 19).[66]

Of course, a male heir begotten of Belacqua would only have rescued Wormwood by way of miscegenation, and this, in the Yeatsian schema, is the greatest crime of all: "a capital offence."[67] For Yeats, choice of love object was critical since a "single wrong choice" could "destroy a family, dissipating its tradition or its biological force,"[68] and the principle danger came from women, who prefigured both the "continuity" and "disintegration" of Big House culture.[69] With "Echo's Bones," Beckett complicates these gendered assumptions. Certainly, Lady Gall inherits the Yeatsian burden of expectation as "a fruitful earth," and Beckett's portrait of her is amongst the least fortunate of his many misogynistic portraits in this period (EB, 19). Also, in another eerie anticipation of *Purgatory* (1939), Moll has committed adultery and is a clear threat to the line of succession. However, Beckett makes just as much of the congenital impotence of the "aspermatic colossus" Lord Gall (EB, 12), and of his willingness to father an illegitimate line by way of Belacqua. Neither Lord Gall nor Belacqua offers hope of a particularly auspicious future for Wormwood, since Gall was the "backmarker in every form of athletic contest open to the peerage," while Belacqua declares himself a "post-war degenerate"

(EB, 12, 13). In the bedroom of the Beckettian Big House, degeneration is ubiquitous, and Beckett presents the Anglo-Irish as an illegitimate and abortive social formation from the outset.[70] All persons relating to the redemption of Wormwood are impotent, diseased, or some combination of both, so that where Yeats oscillates between elegy and trenchant critiques of aristocratic degeneracy, "Echo's Bones" opts firmly for the latter emphasis. As with *All that Fall* (1956), written some twenty years later about a different class of Protestant Irish, the overriding theme is of impotence leading to demise, or rather "lingering dissolution."[71]

"Echo's Bones" represents a considerable thematic departure from the rest of the stories in *More Pricks than Kicks*, most of which are urban in focus, but there are some important continuities. One of the central themes of the collection is Belacqua's flouting of the social mores of his background, what I have termed elsewhere "the performance of ascendancy."[72] The performance of ascendancy describes the manner in which the Protestant minorities responded to the whittling away of their privileges under British rule and to their determination to keep up appearances in the Irish Free State. Since economic privilege and political clout no longer served to differentiate them from their Catholic neighbors,[73] ascendancy meant being seen to do certain things, in certain ways, and at certain times, in an ongoing assertion of genealogical preeminence and social superiority. As Elizabeth Bowen puts it, "Ascendancy cannot be merely inherited or arrived at; ... only by character is it to be maintained."[74] In this vein, Belacqua is full of trite advice for Lord Gall: "It is not enough to be continent. ... You must be sustenant also" (EB, 13). Of course, this performance offered no way back to power for the Anglo-Irish, and Beckett parodies the entire impulse in an extended reprise of the advice scene in *Hamlet*. As Elizabeth Bowen's *The Last September* (1928) had revealed, the performance of ascendancy grew more ludicrous the longer it went on, and, in the absence of offspring and some counter-revolution in Irish politics, mere performance of ascendancy offered scant consolation. Keeping up appearances could only function as a nostalgic throwback to the days, "a million years ago, in the nineties," when the ascendancy had been in charge, but it changed nothing. In this sense, Beckett figures any elegiac refiguring of Irish history as pompous farce.

What is remarkable in all of this is how Beckett came after Yeats but managed to critique some of his governing preoccupations before they had found their most fulsome expression in *Purgatory* (1939): the fate of a house decided by a misalliance; the adulteress Lady; the theme of purgatorial return for purposes of atonement; the Gothic tropes—all of these central strands of Yeats's great play are rehearsed in Beckett's odd story. Overall, "Echo's Bones" offers an extremely prescient and proleptic critique of Yeats's "flirtation" with fascism by way of his interest in the fate of great houses, which Beckett takes more seriously than many of Yeats's subsequent critics. Beckett's odd inclusion in the story of "a Nazi with his head in a clamp" (EB, 15), together with the German toast shared by Lord Gall and Belacqua, "Ach Kinder!" implicate the politics of the Yeatsian Big House in the broader European currents to which Yeats's attention was increasingly drawn. Beckett, it seems, followed events in Germany very closely, where, as he was writing "Echo's Bones," the Nazi party was enacting an inheritance law that allowed for the compulsory sterilization of persons deemed unfit to inherit property, a measure Yeats later supported. W. J. McCormack has suggested that Beckett negotiated his relationship to Yeats after World War II by way of "betrayal,"[75] and that the Nazi purges added particular urgency to this impulse given that Yeats died on the eve of war and did not witness the event he had longed for in *On the Boiler* (1939). However, "Echo's Bones" (1933) provides remarkable evidence of an impulse to betray Yeats years before the war, and lest we consider the younger Beckett an impatient reader of Yeats, given to reductive reading of Yeats as revivalist cheerleader, "Echo's Bones" reveals that he had already discerned the more unsavory affiliations of Yeats's late politics, anticipated the dubious company Yeats would be keeping in posterity, and discerned important continuities between Yeats's early interest in eugenics and his enduring conviction that nations needed to be led by elite minorities, a conviction that shaped both the early, mandarin revivalism of Yeats and Lady Gregory and Yeats's later racialist views on Anglo-Irish natalism. All of which suggests that one main reason for Beckett's reticence about the significance of Yeats into the 1950s was the legacy of his unseemly investment in authoritarian patterns of ethnonationalist governmentality (spoofed by Beckett in the toast "Ach Kinder!") as a function of his nostalgia for the old "patriotic" Protestant Ascendancy (enshrined for Yeats in Berkeley's magisterial use of the phrase "We Irish"). This, it seems, was something it took Beckett many years to work through on the way to a deeper appreciation of Yeats's achievements. Far longer, indeed, than it took him to overcome any reservations he may have had about Yeats's influence on recent Irish poetry.

NOTES

1. "It is time I learnt, he thought. I will study in the Nassau Street School, I will frequent the Railway Street Academies" (Samuel Beckett, *Dream of Fair to middling Women* [New York: Arcade Press, 1992], 137). See C. J. Ackerley and S. E. Gontarski, *The Grove Companion to Samuel Beckett* (New York: Grove Press, 2004), 657–58.

2. In a letter to Oliver dated April 15, 1957 (Trinity College Dublin MS 3777). In a letter to Hutchinson dated January 21, 1958 (Harry Ransom Humanities Research Center, University of Texas at Austin).

3. In a letter to Thomas MacGreevy, dated August 7, 1936, in *The Letters of Samuel Beckett Volume*, vol. 1, *1929–1940*, ed. Martha Fehsenfeld and Lois Overbeck (Cambridge: Cambridge University Press, 2010), 366; in a letter dated February 17, 1954, in *The Letters of Samuel Beckett*, vol. 2, *1941–1956*, ed. Daniel Craig et al. (Cambridge: Cambridge University Press, 2011), 465.

4. In a letter to George Devine dated December 5, 1956, in Craig, *The Letters of Samuel Beckett*, 2:683.

5. In a letter to Thomas MacGreevy, dated January 9, 1961. Quoted in John Pilling, *A Samuel Beckett Chronology* (London: Palgrave Macmillan, 2006), 153.

6. Katherine Worth's *The Irish Drama of Europe from Yeats to Beckett* (Athlone: Continuum, 1986) has argued that Yeats was the source for a lineage in European drama that culminates in Beckett. See also Bernard O'Donoghue, "Yeats and the Drama," in *The Cambridge Companion to W. B. Yeats*, ed. Marjorie Howes and John Kelly (Cambridge: Cambridge University Press, 2006), 103. On the issue of modernism and the revival, see Emer Nolan, "Modernism and the Irish Revival," in *The Cambridge Companion to Modern Irish Culture*, ed. Claire Connolly and Joe Cleary, 157–72 (Cambridge: Cambridge University Press, 2005).

7. Samuel Beckett, "Recent Irish Poetry," in *Disjecta: Miscellaneous Writings and a Dramatic Fragment*, ed. Ruby Cohn (London: Calder, 1983), 76. See also a comment made in the same letter to George Devine dated December 5, 1956, in Craig, *The Letters of Samuel Beckett*, 2:683.

8. See Joep Leerssen, "The Theatre of William Butler Yeats," in *The Cambridge Companion to Twentieth-Century Irish Drama*, ed. Shaun Richards (Cambridge: Cambridge University Press, 2004), 59. See also Ronán MacDonald, *Tragedy and Irish Literature: Synge, O'Casey, Beckett* (Houndsmills: Palgrave, 2002), 35.

9. Anthony Roche, *Contemporary Irish Drama from Beckett to McGuinness* (Dublin: Gill and Macmillan, 1994), 15.

10. Beckett was in the habit of reciting from the plays and poems as late as the 1980s. See Anne Atik, *How It Was* (London: Faber & Faber, 2001).

11. On the issue of Yeats and modernism in an Irish context, see Anne Fogarty, "Yeats, Ireland and Modernism," in *The Cambridge Companion to Modernist Poetry*, ed. Alex Davis and Lee Jenkins, 126–46 (Cambridge: Cambridge University Press, 2007).

12. See Sinéad Mooney, "'Kicking against the Thermolaters': Beckett's 'Recent Irish Poetry,'" in "Historicising Beckett/Issues of Performance," *Samuel Beckett Today/Aujourd'hui* 15, ed. Marius Buning et al. (Amsterdam: Rodopi, 2005), 36.

13. Alex Davis, "Reactions from Their Burg: Irish Modernists of the 1930s," in *Locations of Literary Modernism: Region and Nation in British and American Modernist Poetry*, ed. Alex Davis and Lee M. Jenkins (Cambridge: Cambridge University Press, 2000), 143.

14. Beckett, "Recent Irish Poetry," 76.

15. See R. F. Foster, *W. B. Yeats: A Life*, vol. 2, *The Arch-Poet* (Oxford: Oxford University Press, 2003), 494.

16. Quoted in Foster, *The Arch-Poet*, 436.

17. Beckett, "Recent Irish Poetry," 71.

18. Ibid, 72. Yeats subsequently embarrassed Gogarty, of course, by making him the preeminent modern poet in his *Oxford Book of Modern Verse*. See Foster, *The Arch-Poet*, 555.

19. Foster, *The Arch-Poet*, 466–95.

20. Adrian Frazier, "The Ideology of the Abbey Theatre," in Richards, *The Cambridge Companion to Twentieth-Century Irish Drama*, 33–46.

21. Quoted in Foster, *The Arch-Poet*, 473. For an historical account of the period, see John Regan, *The Irish Counter-Revolution, 1921–36: Treaty Politics and Settlement in Independent Ireland* (Dublin: Gill and Macmillan, 2001).

22. Quoted in Foster, *The Arch-Poet*, 475.

23. See John Pilling, *Samuel Beckett's "More Pricks than Kicks": In a Strait of Two Wills* (London: Continuum, 2011), 6.

24. Samuel Beckett, *More Pricks than Kicks* (London: Calder, 1993), 114.

25. The December 15, 1923, speech can be found online through the Nobel Prize web site: www.nobelprize.org/nobel_prizes/literature/laureates/1923/yeats-lecture.html.

26. Beckett, *More Pricks than Kicks*, 118. James McNaughton, "'The Futility of Protest': Beckett, German Fascism and History," in Buning et al., "Historicising Beckett/Issues of Performance," 101–16. The Daimler was an icon of German modernity and the preferred mode of transport for Hitler's administration. For a history of Daimler during the Nazi period, in which it is suggested that the corporation even claimed that it was responsible for "helping to motorize the movement," see Bernard P. Bellon, *Mercedes in Peace and War: German Automobile Workers, 1903–1945* (New York: Columbia University Press, 1990).

27. Marjorie Howes, *Yeats's Nations: Gender, Class, and Irishness* (Cambridge: Cambridge University Press, 1997), 169.

28. Beckett in a letter to MacGreevy, quoted in Fehsenfeld and Overbeck, *The Letters of Samuel Beckett*, 1:167. Samuel Beckett, "Echo's Bones," 1. I consulted "Echo's Bones" via a photocopy at Harry Ransom Humanities Research Center, University of Texas at Austin, Leventhal Collection; hereafter cited parenthetically as EB.

29. Pilling, *Samuel Beckett's "More Pricks than Kicks,"* 67.

30. In a letter to Thomas MacGreevy, dated December 6, 1933. See Fehsenfeld and Overbeck, *The Letters of Samuel Beckett*, 1:171.

31. See Mark Nixon, "Belacque Revididus: Beckett's Short Story 'Echo's Bones,'" *Limit(e) Beckett* 1 (2010): 92–101. This journal is available online: http://www.limitebeckett.paris-sorbonne.fr/.

32. Pilling, *Samuel Beckett's "More Pricks than Kicks,"* 101–2.

33. Vera Kreilkamp, *The Anglo-Irish Novel and the Big House* (Syracuse: Syracuse University Press, 1998), 102.

34. Howes, *Yeats's Nations*, 103.

35. The word "vision" is repeatedly used, recalling Yeats's psychical credulity as well as his privately published historical and philosophical system, *A Vision* (1925). "It's a prime story," said Lord Gall, "told me in a dream, or rather a vision." Belacqua repeats: "Very nice. . . . In a vision, did you say?" (EB, 8, 9).

36. Beckett later told Thomas MacGreevy in August 1934 that he had seen a revival of Yeats's *The Resurrection* alongside the new play, *The King of the Great Clock Tower,* at the Abbey. See Pilling, *A Samuel Beckett Chronology,* 48.

37. See Kurt Bowen, *Protestants in a Catholic State: Ireland's Privileged Minority* (Montreal: McGill University Press, 1983).

38. Robert A. Nye, "Sociology and Degeneration: The Irony of Progress," in *Degeneration: The Dark Side of Progress*, ed. J. Edward Chamberlain and Sander L. Gilman (New York: Columbia University Press, 1985), 65. On Catholic fertility, see Bowen, *Protestants in a Catholic State*, 28.

39. Howes, *Yeats's Nations*, 105, 102.

40. Quoted in Foster, *The Arch-Poet*, 487. See also Seán Kennedy, "'First Love': Abortion and Infanticide in Beckett and Yeats," in "Samuel Beckett: Debts and Legacies," *Samuel Beckett Today/Aujourd'hui* 22, ed. Matthew Feldman and Erik Tonning (Amsterdam: Rodopi, 2010), 79–91.

41. See Foster, *The Arch-Poet*, 482–87.

42. Ibid, 485.

43. See Michel Foucault, *Security, Territory, Population: Lectures at the Collège de France, 1977–1978*, ed. Michel Seneelart (London: Palgrave Macmillan, 2009), 323–27.

44. Quoted in William Atkinson, "Samuel Beckett and Censorship in the Saorstat," *South Carolina Review* 33:2 (Fall 2001): 128.

45. Lee Edelman, *No Future: Queer Theory and the Death Drive* (Durham: Duke University Press, 2004).

46. W. B. Yeats. "The Irish Censorship," in *The Senate Speeches of W.B. Yeats*, ed. Donald R. Pearce, 175–80 (Bloomington: Indiana University Press, 1960).

47. Samuel Beckett, "Censorship in the Saorstat," in Cohn, *Disjecta*, 86.

48. Michel Foucault, *Society Must Be Defended*, trans. David Macey (London: Penguin, 2003), 252.

49. See Marjorie Howes, "Introduction: Public Discourse, Private Reflection, 1916–70," in *The Field Day Anthology of Irish Writing*, vol. 4, *Irish Women's Writing and Traditions*, ed. Angela Bourke et al. (Cork: Cork University Press, 2002), 924.

50. Beckett, "Censorship in the Saorstat," 86.

51. On "morbid" as a key term in degeneration theory, see William Greenslade, *Degeneration, Culture and the Novel, 1880–1940* (Cambridge: Cambridge University Press, 1994), 215.

52. Greenslade, *Degeneration, Culture and the Novel*, 244. Beckett had noted the term "fraudeur" in Pierre Garnier's *Onanisme*, where it signified a fraud. See John Pilling, *Beckett's Dream Notebook* (Reading: Beckett International Foundation, 1999), 60.

53. Beckett, "Censorship in the Saorstat," 87.

54. Bowen, *Protestants in a Catholic State*, 56.

55. Beckett, "Censorship in the Saorstat," 87.

56. Kennedy, "First Love," 87.

57. The phrase was taken by Beckett from Pierre Garnier's nineteenth-century treatise on masturbation and social hygiene, *Onanisme*, where it

means to ejaculate outside the female genitals. See Pilling, *Beckett's Dream Notebook*, 62.

58. On masturbation as a degenerationist obsession, see Sander L. Gilman, "Sexology, Psychoanalysis, and Degeneration: From a Theory of Race to a Race to Theory," in Chamberlain and Gilman, *Degeneration*, 72.

59. Howes, *Yeats's Nations*, 161.

60. See Terry Eagleton, "Ascendancy and Hegemony," in *Heathcliff and the Great Hunger*, 27–103 (London: Verso, 1995).

61. Kreilkamp, *The Anglo-Irish Novel and the Big House*, 119. Somerville and Ross's work "politicizes the gothic in a society preoccupied—after centuries of dispossessions—with the dubiousness of seemingly lawful transmissions of property."

62. See Kreilkamp, *The Anglo-Irish Novel and the Big House*.

63. On issues of law, see Richard Burn and John Burn, *A New Law Dictionary* (Strahan, 1792): "Estates, either in *general* or *special* tail, may be further divided into *tail male* and *tail female:* as if lands be given to a man, and his *male heirs of his body begotten*, this is an estate given in *tail male general;* but if to a man and *the heirs female on his present wife begotten*, this is an estate in *tail female special*. And in case of an in tail *male*, the heirs *female* shall never inherit, nor any derived from them; nor, on the other hand, the *males* in the case of gift in tail female." Accessed online via Google Books.

64. Quoted in Donald Childs, *Modernism and Eugenics: Woolf, Eliot, Yeats and the Culture of Degeneration* (Cambridge: Cambridge University Press, 2001), 184.

65. Special tail asserts that the male can only succeed by male progeny borne of his present wife. See William Blackstone et al., *Commentary on the Law of England in Four Books* (Philadelphia: 602 Arch Street, 1860), 1:90: "as where lands and tenements are given to a man and *the heirs of his body, on Mary his now wife to be begotten:* here no issue can inherit but such special issue as is engendered between them two, not such as the husband may have by another wife; and therefore it is called special tail." Accessed via the Online Library of Liberty at http://oll.libertyfund.org/index.php?option=com _staticxt&staticfile=show.php%3Ftitle=2140&Itemid=27.

66. Lord Gall makes a bizarre reappearance in *Murphy* (1938), seeking a future for the Anglo-Irish in communion with his spiritual medium Rosie Dew: "he is in a painful position, spado of long standing in tail male special he seeks testamentary pentimenti from the *au-delà*, . . . the protector is a man of iron and will not bar." Yeats's spiritualism is the obvious target here (Samuel Beckett, *Murphy* [London: Calder, 1993], 58).

67. W. B. Yeats, *Purgatory*, in *Collected Plays* (London: Papermac, 1982), 683.

68. Quoted in Howes, *Yeats's Nations*, 15.

69. Howes, *Yeats's Nations*, 114–15, 119.

70. Beckett resorts to more heavy-handed symbolism when a cow—traditionally a symbol of Ireland—appears "seriously ill with . . . contagious abortion" and slips calf (i.e., aborts). Beckett took a number of pages of notes on the subject of the Irish cow, perhaps in preparation for a work to be called "The Trueborn Jackeen." He notes the phrase to slip calf as a euphemism for abortion (Trinity College Dublin MS 10971/2), as well as many instances of the cow's social and symbolic significance.

71. Seán Kennedy, "'A lingering dissolution': *All that Fall* and Protestant Fear of Engulfment in the Irish Free State," *Assaph: Studies in the Theatre* 17/18, ed. Linda Ben-Zvi (2003): 247–62.

72. Seán Kennedy, "'Yellow': Beckett and the Performance of Ascendancy," in *New Voices in Irish Criticism, 5*, ed. Ruth Connolly and Ann Coughlan, 177–86 (Dublin: Four Courts Press, 2005).

73. Bowen, *Protestants in a Catholic State*, 27–28.

74. Elizabeth Bowen, "The Anglo-Irish" in *The Mulberry Tree*, ed. Hermione Lee (London: Virago, 1986), 175.

75. W. J. McCormack, *From Burke to Beckett: Ascendancy, Tradition and Betrayal in Irish Literary History* (Cork: Cork University Press, 1994), 17.

CHAPTER 10

Yeats and Bowen
Posthumous Poetics

VICKI MAHAFFEY

Throughout his career, Yeats, like Keats, was "half in love with easeful Death," at least as an imaginative construct or idea, which he typically depicts in its most alluring guises.[1] Death was not for him the Grim Reaper, but Niamh, "A pearl-pale, high-born lady" on horseback, her lips "A stormy sunset on doomed ships."[2] Death was the domain of Niamh's father, Aengus, God of Youth and Beauty and Poetry; it was the world of dream, of Tir-na-nOg itself, with its isles of Dancing, Victories, and Forgetfulness, which Yeats entered by donning the mask of Oisin in his first published volume of poems. For Yeats as a young man, Death was a seductive, erotic, and even (ultimately) restful fantasy. Death as an idea offered him an escape that was also, at the same time, strategic: it served as a vantage point from which to view the productions and ravages of time. At the outset of his career, Yeats identified death with a world of imaginative, mythic, and erotic creation that resembled not only dream but also the more consciously crafted visions of the artist.

I want to explore here what happens when a man in the habit of using Death to gain aesthetic distance on contemporary life confronts the finality of actual death as something imminent and inescapable. After a long poetic war against time, in which he dared the shadows to whom he wrote to bid him "strike a match / And strike another till time catch" (*VP,* 476), Yeats reached a point at which he could see his own time running out. He had relished the prospect of the end of the world, willing the "Boar without bristles" to "come from the West" and root "the sun and moon and stars out of the sky / And [lay] in the darkness, grunting, and turning to his rest" (*VP,* 153). How then does he respond when eternity no longer beckons to him as an appealing "artifice," a Byzantium bedecked with golden birds untormented by the "dying generations" (*VP,* 407–8) of mortal life, but as an inescapable material reality?

If we read *Last Poems* as the "afterword" to Yeats's life and corpus, the countersignature to his lifelong love affair with a dream of Death, it becomes apparent that the pressure of impending physical death prompts Yeats to fracture and thereby complicate, or darken, the old idealized image of Death he once cherished. As his own death approached, he depicted Death as less erotic and seductive, more sexual and even violent, eventuating in a painful birth into the unknown. He revisits the myth of Tir-na-nOg, the Country of the Young, as a wild old wicked man, bringing to its languid beauty a concrete awareness of the pain as well as the fruit of long labor. Nostalgia for the idleness of youth and the simplicity of a bodily embrace punctuates his depictions of the climactic transformation he anticipates through bodily extinction. Most importantly, he presents death not in contrast to life but in intimate relation to it at every moment, as the other side of the carpet. What is death in one realm is birth in the other; the world beyond death mirrors ours, although that world, like the world of art, is eternal. Because time does not pass there, everything is "remembered" or retained, and its perspective on life's strange, dynamic mingling of generation and decay never changes. Art becomes a form of impassioned memory, a mode of imaginative time travel affording access to the realities of other times and places. The voices of the dead speak through art; their lineaments become visible to the mind's eye. Yeats's late poems do not locate beauty *in* death; instead, they use death as a lens that brings both beauty and human absurdity into sharp focus, as does the speaker in his earlier poem "The Collarbone of a Hare" (who stares "At the bitter old world" through "the thin white bone of a hare"). To put it another way, Yeats uses art to defy the limitations of time by imaginatively projecting himself into other times, offering unexpected perspectives on mortality and its transience.

For the late Yeats, birth and death are complementary; both are radical changes that mark the beginning and end, respectively, of physical growth and decline. What then is posthumous "life"? Part of what makes Yeats's late work confusing is that there are two answers to this question. One is that the afterlife is the unseen shadow to the mortal one, a kind of collective "unconscious" that completes every mortal thought and action by furnishing it with its unseen opposite. But there is also a Platonic or Neoplatonic afterlife, a kind of Ur-reality that dreams the mortal world of change into an apparent and fleeting existence. Artists mimic this creation in reverse by dreaming up and crafting changeless works of art for the human world. Yeats imagines that these human creations are in conversation with the ideal forms that create the world: art allows humans to converse with—even to instruct—the eternal. Art helps to teach the creator "how to fill the cradles right." The "gods" are continually making the art that human beings call life, but the art produced by mortals in turn inspires the creator to produce future improvements. Human art offers God a better understanding of human passion—both love and suffering.

When death becomes an imminent possibility, the thinker is freed from the relentless march of chronology, facilitating a wandering through time. This imaginative temporal dislocation is often emotional (as is hardly surprising given that "motion" is lodged inside "emotion"). Sex and death seem to inform each other, mirror one another, as twin ruptures that bring the individual into sudden imaginative contact with the eternal. Yeats's account of how this works is informed by Platonism, the Neoplatonism of Plotinus, theosophy, and the teachings of spirit-guides. These varied contexts can sometimes obscure the drama of how and why sex and death evoke one another as complementary engines of change with the capacity to propel the imagination into other lives and times. If we turn to another, slightly later Anglo-Irish writer, we can see the drama represented without Yeats's esoteric machinery. I would like to use Elizabeth Bowen's stories to illustrate Yeats's earlier poetic depictions of the psychic interdependence of eros and thanatos, dream and physical reality. It is illuminating to see how compatible their representations of life under threat of death actually are, especially in view of their reputations: Yeats is viewed as credulous, open, changeable, and interested in "spooks," whereas Bowen is depicted as worldly, sophisticated, stylish, and urbane. Yeats wasn't told about the Easter Rising due to fears that he would be indiscreet; Bowen, in sharp contrast, performed undercover work during World War II. Her reputation, unlike that of her older Anglo-Irish countryman, is for exquisite, strategic self-control.

During World War II, the place where Bowen was living was bombed, which presumably inspired the composition of one of her most powerful and haunting stories, "The Happy Autumn Fields."[3] This tale, written under the threat of sudden death for the author, presents dream and reality in a relation to one another that is surprisingly Yeatsian, but without Yeats's mystical machinery: dream acts not only as an escape but also as a powerfully inverted reflection of the main character's alarmingly unstable circumstances. In Bowen's story, Mary's dream constitutes a truth about sex and death in a form that is saturated with both meaning and feeling, unlike her present despair in her bomb-shattered house. The dream works as a story-within-a-story: Mary experiences her dream not as an unreality but as a revelation of a truth from the historical past, a message from people and a time that are dead and gone. By dreaming as the bombs fall, Mary is able to experience her own anticipated death not only as a radical rupture from her present life but also as a union with other lives, those of people now dead. Interestingly, what her dream tells her (and the reader) is that love, like death, is simultaneously a union and a rupture, although it is usually depicted only as a union (like death, which is typically treated solely as a rupture).[4] That which joins and divides the lovers in Mary's dream is the symbolic horse of love-death. It is useful to have a narrative in order to illustrate the more violent, paradoxical, and powerful view of love and death that informed Yeats's poems from *The Tower* through *Last Poems,* and I would like to propose Bowen's story as a model for such a narrative. It serves as a template for Yeats's late view of death.

The title of Bowen's story alludes to a well-known poem by Tennyson, "Tears, Idle Tears," which pays tribute to the power of nostalgia evoked by "looking at the happy Autumn-fields, /And thinking of the days that are no more." Those "fresh," "sad," and "strange" days awaken a feeling "Deep as first love, and wild with all regret," causing "useless" tears to well up from a "divine despair." Tennyson's poem provides an affective frame for Bowen's story, which initially seems to be a nostalgic account of a young Victorian girl named Sarah on the brink of womanhood. Sarah is torn between two loves, her love for her sister Henrietta, friend and bedfellow since childhood, and a new, mesmerizing feeling that she feels for her brother's friend Eugene. They walk through the stubble of autumn fields, and all Sarah's emotions and sensations are rendered in vivid detail. Eugene appears and leads himself and his horse between the two sisters in an allegorically significant moment, and Sarah feels pierced by her sister's pain at Eugene's literal and symbolic separation of them, a pain Henrietta expresses through sudden "heartbreaking singing." Only at this point does the reader learn that this vivid story is a dream, a dream far more vibrant than anything available in the dreamer's present experience of phenomenal reality. The dreamer is a woman named Mary, lying on a bare mattress in her terrace (or row) house that has been bombed. She is covered with plaster dust from the ceiling; the glassless window is covered with calico; there is no lock on the door. Mary's lover, Travis, begs her to leave before another explosion comes, but Mary bargains to stay for two more hours in a desperate effort to return to the "dream" that is her preferred reality: the "days that are no more." Her dream was inspired by the contents of a box she was sorting through in the process of deciding what she wanted to save from her wrecked house; that box contained a picture and some letters about the now-dead family who became the subject of her dream.

In contrast to her dream, in which valediction had a "colour" that could be recognized, and sadness had a "sweet" taste (*CS,* 672), in

which "light went on ripening" even after they had scythed the corn
(*CS*, 673), Mary's wrecked present seems unreal—like "figments of a
dream that one knows to be dreams" (*CS*, 677). She feels "trapped" in
"the irrelevant body of Mary" (*CS*, 677). Mary returns to the world of
her dream where Sarah, too, has a "feeling of dislocation" and "form-
less dread" that inspires her "to attach her being to each second, . . .
because she apprehended that the seconds were numbered" (*CS*, 681).
Another explosion catapults Mary out of her dream, and those whom
she loved are "lost in time" to "the woman weeping there on the bed"
who has lost her sense of identity (*CS*, 683). She tells her real-life
lover, when he returns, that life now is desiccated; their emotions are
mere imitations. She has "remembered"—through a dream inspired
by pictures of real, now-dead people—a life that felt "eventful," "strung
like a harp." She asks, "how am I to help laying that like a pattern
against the poor stuff of everything else?" (*CS*, 684).

Bowen prompts readers to realize that the experiences of Mary
and Sarah are somehow connected; in Mary's dreaming mind, they
are experientially simultaneous (although chronologically separated
by fifty years). Facing death, Mary dreams of Sarah's budding love,
with its promises of "rapture" (ecstasy and traumatic separation from
the familiar, including her sister). The dream is almost allegorical in
its depiction of love as a form of death, and Eugene's horse unites
those two extremes. It is his horse that literally separates Sarah from
Henrietta, connecting her with Eugene instead, and the horse that
kills Eugene later that same evening. At the conclusion of Bowen's
story, we learn from Travis that none of the three main protagonists
of Mary's dream lived long after that day. Eugene was thrown from
his horse after a visit to their home; Sarah and Henrietta both died
young, unmarried.

In a symbolic sense, love—as radical change—could be said to
have "killed" all three, who never existed in the same way again. Bowen
juxtaposes this symbolic death with the threat of actual death faced by
Mary in London: the "reverberation" in Ireland that "filled the land,
the silence and Sarah's being" to signal the approach of her lover—
Eugene cantering towards her on horseback—is also the sound of
explosions in wartime London. Via art or dream, the present affects

the past: an explosion in London seems to spook Eugene's horse in the "happy autumn fields" of Ireland fifty years earlier, killing him—Sarah's brother says he will always wonder "what made Eugene's horse shy in those empty fields" (CS, 685). Mary unconsciously identifies her dread of leaving her (ruined) home with the traumatic excitement of Sarah's anticipated departure from home, leaving behind a much-loved sister in the "happy autumn fields" of childhood. Both realities are true, although painted in such different hues; and both are devastating in different ways. Bowen depicts the intensity of love (charged with the capacity for change) as an emotionally rich version of the events of the blitz that covered Mary and her life in plaster-dust, also changing everything. The prospect of death and destruction has produced a vision of intense attachment that is no longer available in the present. Art is here represented through Mary's dream not only as compensation for instability and devastation, but also as a retelling that resurrects lost sensuality and feeling. Both "dreams" recount an "eternal loss" (CS, 679), but one loss is experienced as mere waste (the loss of a home in London; the loss of feeling), whereas the loss of childhood companionship, of "play that was full of fear, fear that was full of play," throbs deep and full.

The prospect of death, then, retrospectively endows both past and present with the fullness imparted by a sharp awareness of time's transience. Anticipation of death makes imperfection not only bearable, but poignant and vibrant, whereas actual destruction (such as what Mary is experiencing in London) is only deadening. The simultaneity of Eugene's death and Sarah's traumatic but desirable anticipation of union—with the rupture from Henrietta it necessitates—helps to underscore the similarity between sexual initiation (sometimes productive of new life) and death.

Yeats, too, responds to the desiccation of the present by pumping his imagination full of the beauty, feeling, and color that has, will, and must be lost. To put it another way, Yeats stopped thinking of death as antithetical to life, viewing it instead as endemic to both growth and loss. In 1938, only months before he died, Yeats described the "private philosophy" that guided his writing in a letter to novelist Ethel Mannin as a vision in which life and death are not only conjoined, but constantly in motion, gyrating together in antithetical relation at all times:

> To me all things are made of the conflict of two states of consciousness, beings or persons which die each other's life, live each other's death. That is true of life and death themselves. Two cones (or whirls), the apex of each in the other's base.[5]

I have suggested that Bowen's story concretely illustrates this abstract assertion of the dynamic interdependence of life (or sex) and death: the prospect of sexual union allowed Sarah—now dead—to join forces with Mary, who only felt dead under the onslaught of the blitz. Sex and death created a wrinkle in time that brought the two women together in Mary's dreaming mind. Mary became *aware* that her life was shadowed by that of a dead woman, that her emotional deadness was complemented by the emotional intensity of Sarah's awakening. But if we attend more closely to Yeats's famous metaphor of intersecting gyres, it raises the question of how this interdependence of life and death differs when the apex of one coincides with the base of the other—what happens then? What we discover is that there are moments of comparative stasis in which the flux of life makes contact with the eternal.

As Yeats solidified his understanding of the "life-death" dynamic by repeatedly revising and expanding *A Vision*, he intensified his poetic representations of aging and death as the complement and mirror of generative life. His growing curiosity about eternity fueled the production of poems (beginning with *The Tower*) in which mortal beings gain brief access to divinity and eternity in a sharp explosion of knowledge and feeling. "Leda and the Swan" (*VP*, 441) dramatizes one such moment, when a human girl is raped by a god in the form of a bird and the swan's orgasm engenders life and death in a single fearful shudder, conceiving Helen and Clytemnestra (according to the poem). Yeats portrays the anticipated births of these two *femmes fatales* through the climactic destruction caused by both, "the burning roof and tower" (of Troy, at the conclusion of the war over Helen) "And Agamemnon dead" (at the hands of Clytemnestra and her lover

Aegisthus). Yeats's final question about Leda wonders whether this violent union with a god-brute gave her special knowledge of eternity: "Did she put on his knowledge with his power / Before the indifferent beak could let her drop?" In essence, he is wondering whether this forced, traumatic conception extended to her mind as well as her womb: was she afforded any insight into the afterlife?

Yeats underscores the apocalyptic, generative power of the moment when divinity penetrates a human body in a way that is simultaneously sexual and deadly in the companion poem to "Leda and the Swan," "The Mother of God" (*VP*, 499), in which the Virgin Mary tells of the terror with which she conceived the Christian god. Mary, too, is raped by a bird ("Wings beating about the room"), which enters her, not vaginally, but through the "hollow" of her ear. Her physical conception of love, death, and eternity is a consequence of listening to a communication that is not human but divine (as well as avian). She describes the overwhelming intensity of bearing the Heavens in her womb, of nursing a "fallen star" with her milk, of feeling a love so strong that—like death—it makes her "heart's blood stop" and "strikes a sudden chill into [her] bones / And bids [her] hair stand up." Here, again, the moment of generation is almost indistinguishable from the destruction it anticipates and mirrors, as the human is penetrated and then transfigured by an "animal-god" who is also a Word. When the ear becomes the sexual organ and the bird-god is also a Word, what is conceived affects the mind (her thought) and the heart (through love) as well as the body. Mary's terror (and her ability to speak her own experience) suggests that she did indeed partake of the knowledge as well as the power of divinity.

Yeats attributed a "terrible beauty" to death throughout his career; it was not only attractive and terrifying, it was also useful, even indispensable for the appreciation of life. But as Yeats continued to explore the difference between the dynamism of "life-death" and the intense power and omniscience of eternity, he increasingly viewed death and life as products of an impassioned human imagination. In the poem "Death" (*VP*, 476), he asserts, "Man has created death." "He knows death to the bone" because he has invented it. This idea was adumbrated in the third section of "The Tower," when the speaker declares his faith:

I mock Plotinus' thought
And cry in Plato's teeth,
Death and life were not
Till man made up the whole,
Made lock, stock and barrel
Out of his bitter soul.
                    (*VP,* 415)

Yeats here claims to reject the popular understanding of the Platonic (and Neoplatonic) idea that the world of appearances is a mere reflection of the world of ideal forms. Instead, he argues that it is human beings who actively create the world of appearances (life and death), and the death-life they manufacture is a potentially destructive weapon derived from the soul's own bitterness. Yeats compares it to a gun, with its "lock, stock, and barrel." He clarifies the meaning of these lines in the note for *The Tower* that he included in the 1933 edition of his *Collected Poems.* He retracts his criticism of Plotinus in his poem, citing a passage in which Plotinus anticipates his claim that the human soul has created the living world:

> When I wrote the lines about Plato and Plotinus I forgot that it is something in our own eyes that makes us see them as all transcendence. Has not Plotinus written: "Let every soul recall, then, at the outset the truth that the soul is the author of all living things, that it has breathed the life into them all, whatever is nourished by earth and sea, all the creatures of the air, the divine stars in the sky; it is the maker of the sun; itself formed and ordered this vast heaven and conducts all that rhythmic motion—and it is a principle distinct from all these to which it gives law and life, and it must of necessity be more honourable than they, for they gather or dissolve as soul brings them life or abandons them, but soul, since it never can abandon itself, is of eternal being"? (*VP,* 826)

Not only is the soul both creative and eternal, it also undergoes successive incarnations (or revisions). References to reincarnation saturate the late poems, from the image of Attis hung between the

flaming and the green halves of the tree of existence in the second
section of "Vacillation," to the vampires in the earth, full of blood,
with bloody shrouds and wet lips (in "Oil and Blood"). Yeats declares
himself "content to live it all again," despite the fact that to be alive is
to be a "blind man battering blind men" (*VP*, 479). In "Vacillation,"
Yeats's "Soul" urges his heart to "Seek out reality, leave things that
seem" (*VP*, 502), but his heart remains in love with the imperfec-
tions of life-death, with "original sin" and the magnanimity of strong
human desire. The agon of his late poems is always the struggle be-
tween the soul and the heart or self, between eternity and appear-
ances, between the oil in the undecayed bodies of dead saints and the
blood on the lips of dead vampires, between the fragrant embalming
oils of those who no longer change and the determination of the un-
dead to rise again, with their magnificent and disgusting thirst for
more human blood.

ART AND ETERNITY

Yeats, then, often viewed art as an attempt to approximate the ideal
forms of eternal reality, as the Platonists saw it. Even in his early
poems, fairyland—the world of the *sidhe*, where history and myth in-
termingle with nature—is not only a representation of the posthu-
mous alter-life of the ancient Tuatha de Danaan, a magic mirror that
reverses and corrects the fever of the world, but a kingdom of art,
where "the earth and the sky and the water" are "remade, like a casket
of gold" (*VP*, 143). Art and eternity are almost interchangeable, a
fact that is especially prominent in Yeats's two Byzantium poems. In
"Sailing to Byzantium," the speaker longs for eternity, which is spe-
cifically characterized as an "artifice" and represented as the epony-
mous city of art. In "Byzantium" (*VP*, 497–98) the "starlit or ... moon-
lit dome" can be read as either the dome of the heavens or the dome
of the cathedral, perhaps Hagia Sophia.[6] Constructed or heavenly,
both domes disdain the complexity associated with human existence,
"the fury and the mire of human veins"; both are, in different ways,
super-natural. Byzantium at night is the abode of spirits and artistic

images, and both are generative, producing "images that yet / Fresh images beget." Not only is art comparable to the eternal, the artist is akin to a ghost. As Yeats wrote in an appendix to *Words Upon the Window-Pane*, "we poets and artists may be called, so small our share in life, 'separated spirits,' words applied by the old philosophers to the dead."[7] Both artists and spirits share an aesthetic distance from life, and that distance allows them to real-ize (both create and apprehend) other dimensions of being.

"Sailing to Byzantium" seems to have been designed not only as a rejection of the constant dying and generation of the mortal world, but as a vigorous defense of the eternal, represented by both the afterlife and human art (both of which partake of the miraculous). It can be seen as a kind of riposte to Hans Christian Andersen's story of "The Nightingale," which was illustrated by Yeats's friend and associate Edmund Dulac in 1911 (*The Winding Stair* was dedicated to Dulac). Andersen's story concerns the relationship between a Chinese emperor (not a Byzantine one) and two nightingales, one natural and the other golden. At first the emperor and the court marvel over the living nightingale, until the emperor of Japan gives him a golden one perched on a golden bough, which becomes the new favorite. But the mechanism in the golden one breaks, just as the emperor falls seriously ill, and the real nightingale returns outside his window to sing him to sleep and to health. The story celebrates the superiority of the natural to the mechanical and artistic, but Yeats's poem aims to reverse that judgment. In a 1930 letter to T. Sturge Moore, Yeats implies that the poem was indeed intended to champion art over nature: "You objected to the last verse of 'Sailing to Byzantium' because a bird made by a goldsmith was just as natural as anything else. That showed me that the idea needed exposition."[8] Yeats's golden bird does sing of temporal existence—"Of what is past, or passing, or to come"—but he is still doing so from the perspective of eternity. Yeats's bird, like eternity in one of William Blake's Proverbs of Hell, is "in love with the productions of time."

Yeats's afterlife, like human art, also restages the physical climaxes associated with both death and sex, as we can see from his late vision of the next world, "News for the Delphic Oracle" (1938; *VP,*

611–12), which paints an uneasy and erotic view of the Isles of the Blest. Here, according to Plato, souls are sent to be reincarnated, a process that Yeats depicts by having them weary of the "choir of Love." Bored with eternity, they begin to feel the stirrings of sexual desire that will bring them back to the seas of material existence. In this poem, Celtic figures mingle with the Greek,[9] all of whom are sighing (along with the water and wind)—with boredom? fatigue? desire? The poem's three sections intertwine art, desire, and death: the first rewrites the second stanza of Yeats's earlier Delphic poem ("The Delphic Oracle upon Plotinus"); the second is in poetic dialogue with a statue of a dolphin carrying one of the Holy Innocents to heaven;[10] and the third is indebted to Poussin's painting that was formerly thought to depict the marriage of Peleus and Thetis (recently reidentified as Acis and Galatea), a painting that was part of Hugh Lane's bequest to the National Gallery in Dublin.

The vision of the afterlife offered by "News of the Delphic Oracle" is saturated with evocations of death, sex, and art. It turns the Byzantine vision of eternal artifice, free of dying and generation, on its head; here, art, sex, and death intermingle, as surely as do animals, humans, and gods. Although Helen Vendler has argued otherwise, this vision is not a parody, a satire, or a mockery, as we can see if we look at an actual satire on the Isles of the Blest, such as Lucian's account in the second book of his *A True History*.[11] Instead, it represents a serious attempt to imagine the process of reincarnation as the eternal spirit yearning again for the seductions of the changing flesh. The poem's meaning hinges on the etymology of the word "Delphic," which comes from the Greek word for dolphin, "delphis," and its related homonym "delphys," or womb. The dolphins that bring the Holy Innocents to the Fortunate Isles are the agents of reincarnation. The "fin" of the dolphins suggests the "end" or death of the Innocents who are riding them, an end they are ecstatically reliving, but their relation to the womb and their status as infants look forward to the sex described in the next stanza, when Peleus looks at Thetis's delicate limbs and her belly listens in response, presumably in anticipation of their imminent conception of Achilles, and nymphs and satyrs "copulate in the foam." Yeats pictures Elysium as the antithesis of Byzantium; in this winterless island, death is an ecstatic prelude to birth, and nature and art intermingle. Sculptures and paintings have informed its images of death and sex, which unfold to the accompaniment of the ocean's laughter.

The doctrine of incarnation depends upon a reciprocal relation between this world and the next; it is a kind of dialogue between worlds, and the language of that dialogue is passion. Sex and death are united by passion, the root of which means "suffering." One example of how passion becomes and affects the immortal may be found in a poem that Yeats mentions in his notes to *The Tower*, a poem that he often quoted in his American lectures, Sturge Moore's "The Dying Swan." In Moore's poem, a dying swan, struck through the breast by a golden dart, expresses through his song an undying love that has the power to pierce the heart of the sun god in order to teach him that love (*VP*, 826). Yeats dramatizes a similar idea about the power of human passion in such plays as *The Dreaming of the Bones, Calvary, The Words Upon the Window-Pane,* and *Purgatory,* when characters see ghosts who are eternally alive because of some moment of great passion: Swift, Vanessa, and Stella eternally express their frustrated desires; Diarmuid and Dervorgilla still wander through Ireland, hoping to be forgiven for their love that brought the English to Ireland; and the mother of the Old Man in *Purgatory* still waits for her husband's return on the night when their first child will be conceived (who will be the Old Man himself). Christ's passion, which Yeats reenacts in *Calvary,* epitomizes the union between the mortal and the divine, death and eternal life. In these "passion plays," sex and death emerge as comparable and comparably brief moments of wholeness, when the self meets the anti-self.[12] This is the bizarre meaning of "Cuchulain Comforted," which, along with "The Black Tower," is one of the last poems Yeats wrote before he died.[13] It is partly because of the connection between death and completeness that Yeats can treat death with such gaiety, even as he is contemplating his own. Passionate fullness or comprehensiveness, which we know most intensely through sexual union or the rupture of death, gives intimations of immortality, and it serves as a prototype of the powerful union of opposites that Yeats tried to recapture in his poems.

Yeats's late poems, then, are all about the intercourse between life and art, which he understands also as a passionate interchange between life and death. Interestingly, Bowen, too, wrote a story in the 1920s about how human passion creates a reality that does not die but can be apprehended as if it were still happening. "The Back Drawing-Room" is concerned with the nature of reality and, specifically, whether and under what conditions people and works of art become "real" in ways that are not destroyed with the death or physical removal of those who felt them. In "The Back Drawing-Room," a small group meets in Mrs. Henneker's salon to discuss "the larger abstractions," and on the evening in question they begin talking about the soul, and what happens to it after death. Defining the soul as the "finer internal fabric of the senses" (*CS*, 200), Mrs. Henneker proposes that a living person can become almost telepathically aware of those not present when they are "knit together, emotionally, or by unity of interest." She goes further, asserting that the one being known emerges as having a "second distinct vitality." One of her guests explains her theory more clearly: "You contend that imagination, memory, cognizance, have the power of carrying themselves over from the *sub*jective into the *ob*jective?" (*CS*, 201), and another guest adds, "Because you remember a thing, . . . or even imagine it, or from loving it very much really know it, it *exists* apart from itself and from you, even though you don't remember it, imagine it, or know it any more?" (*CS*, 201–2). "What it all comes down to ultimately is: a question of the visibility or—er—perceptibility of thought-forms." The illustration of how this operates comes in the form of a ghost story about Ireland told by an unknown man that the narrator compares to a forgotten umbrella. He describes coming into an Irish house and seeing a not very young lady sobbing on the sofa, only to learn later that the house (owned by a Protestant family) had been burned down two years earlier. The woman he saw wasn't dead, but had moved with her family to Dublin or England. The intensity of her emotion had created an alternate temporal "reality" that the man visiting Ireland had been able to perceive as if it were currently present. Bowen's treatment of this alternate reality is fascinating, because unlike Mrs. Henneker's hangers-on who want the tale to be full of gothic "atmosphere," Bowen has the fair-haired, umbrella-like man who tells the tale treat it as if it were utterly ordinary. Art, in fact, operates like these "ordinary" ghosts; it offers readers a passionately realized conception that is somehow "alive" and "real," but its reality exists apart from chronological time.

Yeats's friend Frank Sturm tells a remarkably similar story about Yeats's capacity to "realize" (or make real) thought-forms in a journal entry from June 4, 1936:

> Yeats must be mediumistic for he has told me of blossoms which materialize when he is abstracted by writing. Sometimes he finds the pockets of his jacket full of flowers, in the depth of winter, and sometimes his room is suddenly flooded with the scent of jasmin or heliotrope. During my stay with him in Oxford he found a spray of flowering hawthorn in his pocket, though it was February. He laid it on his writing table so that I might see it & be convinced, & went on correcting his proofs, but when I returned from my walk the blossom had disappeared as mysteriously as it had come. I do not doubt the reality of these apports, for I believe him to live in another state of consciousness, in which they are actually objective, and I know, although I have never had similar experiences, of states of consciousness in which more extraordinary happenings are not only possible but commonplace.[14]

Like Bowen's "little fair, plump man" who entered a back-drawing room that had not been there for two years, Yeats claimed to experience, with his senses, the material presence of things that for others were not there, and they are beautiful or intriguing, not "spooky" or frightening. For him, the process of creative, disciplined "realization"—achieved through the composition of his "passionate rhymes"—can produce an alter-reality briefly apprehensible through the senses.

A SYMBOL PERFECTED IN DEATH

We should now be better prepared to appreciate Yeats's frame of mind when he was composing his poetic epitaph in "Under Ben Bulben" (*VP,* 636–40). This is the poem that begins *Last Poems,* Yeats's strange volume of posthumously published verse, rearranged for the last time a few hours before he fell into the coma from which he died.[15] As Curtis Bradford argued, this placement makes the poems that follow it seem to come "from the tomb."[16] The poem is a strange, indirect dialogue between the immortals (the *sidhe* who gallop at dawn between the mountains of Knocknarea and Ben Bulben, as they did in "The Hosting of the Sidhe") and the dead poet, who speaks to them via the epitaph carved in limestone that marks his grave in Drumcliff churchyard (also under Ben Bulben). In a series of so-called "deathbed revisions" Yeats drafted a table of contents for his last volume and changed the name of the gateway poem from "His Convictions" to "Under Ben Bulben." The new title makes it clearer that the poem does not present a monologue about "his beliefs" but dramatizes the difference between a mortal being and artist, when dead, and the immortal gods and goddesses of ancient Ireland who still agitate the landscape.

"Under Ben Bulben" stages an encounter between a dying man and the undying spirits, echoing the first act of Shakespeare's *Hamlet,* which also dramatizes a conversation between the living and the dead. Each of the first two stanzas of Yeats's poem begins with the word "Swear," recalling Hamlet's repeated imprecation to Horatio and Marcellus, echoed by the ghost of Hamlet's father, to "Swear" upon his sword never to "make known what you have seen to-night" (Hamlet's encounter with the ghost of his dead father).[17] It is in this scene that Hamlet speaks "wild and whirling words" and swears by the ghost of Saint Patrick when he is offended by Horatio's skeptical response to his riddling account of what the ghost told him, that every villain is an arrant knave: "There needs no ghost, come from the grave, / To tell us this." Hamlet will not tell them what the ghost said, only that "There are more things in heaven and earth, Horatio, / Than are dreamt of in your philosophy" (*Hamlet,* Act 1, Scene 5).

The poem tells the reader—who is implicitly in the position of both Marcellus and Horatio, witness to a dialogue between a dead artist and the god-spirits—to swear by what the fourth-century monastic Christian Sages spoke "Round the Mareotic Lake" in Egypt (now Lake Maryut)[18] and by the *sidhe* themselves ("Swear by those horsemen, by those women, / Complexion and form prove super-human"). Whatever the Sages spoke was known by the Witch of Atlas (who also travels to the Mareotic Lake in Shelley's poem). What did they respectively speak, know, and embody? That death is not to be feared, because it (like love) holds out the promise of completion. In death, the spirit takes the form of life without its limitations: all understand death as the condition of extended dreaming, an extension of what in life is art, or dream, freed from the hellish constrictions of time.

In his essay on Shelley, Yeats interprets the Witch of Atlas as a metaphor for the soul. George Bornstein has analyzed the indebtedness of Yeats's reading to Platonic (and Neoplatonic) symbols of the cave (as the world and also the human mind), the fountain (the intellect), and the river (life; also the world).[19] But Shelley's Witch is also an artist-creator, and what she creates is a winged "Image," Hermaphroditus, which is compounded of sexual contraries (it is a hermaphrodite) made from the opposites of fire and snow, which the Witch kneads together in her cave. The art she creates is something whole and alive, something that, having the best characteristics of both sexes, is "sexless" by virtue of its completeness. The Witch, too, like her creature, is sexless:

> 'Tis said in after times her spirit free
> Knew what love was, and felt itself alone—
> But holy Dian could not chaster be
> Before she stooped to kiss Endymion
> Than now this lady—like a sexless bee
> Tasting all blossoms and confined to none—
> (ll. 585–90)

What the Witch of Atlas knows is that death is not an end, but a dream, not unlike Mary's dream in Bowen's "The Happy Autumn Fields."[20] When Bowen's Mary sleeps through the explosions that rock her house around her, dreaming of the "days that are no more," she approximates the image of death that Shelley depicts in his poem. To "those [living beings] she saw most beautiful" the witch gives a "strange panacea" that allows them to live "thenceforward as if some control, / Mightier than life, were in them" (ll. 596–97). When such a beautiful person dies, she throws away the coffin, takes the body and rejuvenates it by removing the "swaddling bands" of age, and lets it sleep, and live in its dreams.

> And there the body lay, age after age.
> Mute, breathing, beating, warm, and undecaying,
> Like one asleep in a green hermitage,
> With gentle smiles about its eyelids playing,
> And living in its dreams beyond the rage
> Of death or life; while they were still arraying
> In liveries ever new, the rapid, blind
> And fleeting generations of mankind.
>
> (ll. 609–16)[21]

Shelley portrays the blessed as undergoing bodily resurrection in order to sleep and dream eternally, "beyond the rage / Of death or life." Yeats's *sidhe*, while awake and galloping on horses through the dawn, are also beyond life and death, as his epitaph confirms when it enjoins them to "Cast a cold eye / on life, on death" and to "pass by." The "great night" of eternity is an unending dream, an unconscious artistic creation that unites life and death (much as Hermaphroditus unites male and female) and yet exists beyond them (as the Witch's creature is "sexless"). Both life and death are the fleeing, fragmented dreams of the immortal dead, collaboratively produced with the help of the living (immortal) soul.[22]

When Yeats turns his attention to the *sidhe* in the second stanza of "Under Ben Bulben," he makes it apparent that they, too, are immortal *because* they are complete: "That pale, long visaged company / . . . airs an immortality" that was won by the "Completeness of their passions." The rest of the poem is an attempt to convey "the gist of what they mean." What they seem to mean, based on the balance of the poem, is that the soul is eternal and repeatedly reincarnated (part 2).[23] This helps to provide a context for Yeats's disturbing celebration of war in part 3: "Send war in our time, O Lord!" The implications of such a sentiment at such a time (1938–39) are chilling, but the question that Yeats is investigating, if we can detach it momentarily from its historical context and its implications for human societies, is once again what emotions effectively make individuals complete and give them peace. Love is one of those states, and here Yeats asserts, rather paradoxically, that anger is another: when "a man is fighting mad, / Something drops from eyes long blind / He completes his partial mind, / For an instant stands at ease, / Laughs aloud, his heart at peace." The drafts make it even clearer that Yeats is primarily interested in the peace that comes from a feeling of completion. First, there is the line that was dropped from the final version: "The souls [*sic*] perfection is from peace."[24] In addition, two couplets not included in the final version show how both sex and war bring a certain psychic completion to the individuals who engage in them: "[?The] passing moment makes it sweet / When male and female organ meet // Or enemy looks at ["on" is crossed out and "at" is substituted for it] enemy, / Time less man's their honey bee."[25] These lines bear the trace of a rereading of "The Witch of Atlas," whom Shelley compares to "a sexless bee / Tasting all blossoms, and confined to none" (ll. 589–90) when she is passing among mortal forms with "an eye serene and heart unladen"; she is complete. Both the witch and "Time less man" are types of the complete person, the immortal, perfect "work of art" gathering honey from the imperfect world of mortals.

Section 4 of "Under Ben Bulben" advances a remarkable view of the purpose of art, especially visual art, which is to "Bring the soul of man to God, / Make him fill the cradles right." Yeats's injunction to poet, sculptor, and painter to represent the human soul, and use that representation to convey concrete ideas to God about how to revise natural creation, depends upon the Neoplatonic notion that nature, too, is an imitation—of "the Ideas from which Nature itself derives."[26] Since nature is an imperfect interpretation of these Ideas, the artist can also—like God—attempt to represent the Ideas (not nature) through material creation, thereby contributing the human perspective. Art represents a communication with the divine designed to further the "Profane perfection of mankind." Yeats's friend Frank

Sturm provides a useful gloss on Yeats's view when he writes that "Poets and artists are the powerful servants of the Most High," and their artistic "emblems give the reality of passion to abstract truths."[27] God, according to such a reading, is the master artist, revising his creations as they are repeatedly reincarnated. For Yeats, the relation between God and the artist is reciprocal, since the works of the painters inspire God, "Make him fill the cradles right." The "secret working mind" can either be that of God or artist; both are attempting to find ways of turning Ideal, eternal truths into impassioned forms, whether those forms are natural or artistic.

In the last section of "Under Ben Bulben" we encounter Yeats's epitaph, to be carved, or quite literally "engraved," on a stone in Drumcliff churchyard. These enigmatic lines have long puzzled readers and critics: "Cast a cold eye / On life, on death. / Horseman, pass by!" Who is the Horseman being addressed, presumably by the dead poet? Is it, as Jon Stallworthy once opined, a rider that could be either alive (one of the "Hard-riding country gentlemen") or dead (one of the fierce, mounted members of the Tuatha de Danaan from section 1)?[28] It seems clear to me that the horseman has to be one of the *sidhe*, not only because of the way the poem circles back to where it began, but because it seems to represent two parts of a dialogue. The poem tells us what the *sidhe* mean, and then the dead poet tells them not to pause and removes any suggestion that they have breath to draw (this must be why Yeats had to cut what was once the first line of a quatrain, "Draw rein, draw breath," leaving "death" without a rhyme and disrupting the formal symmetry of the epitaph). In his last volume of poems, written the year before his own death, Yeats dreams of being complete, like the *sidhe*, and he celebrates their capacity to be both "passionate" (their passions are described as "complete") and cold towards the limitations of both life and death, secure in their artistically complete afterlife. Here, Yeats has finally written the fisherman a poem as "cold and passionate as the dawn."[29]

Overall, what makes *Last Poems* powerful is its drive towards this kind of completion, defined as fullness or comprehensiveness, that manifests itself in the many different attitudes—several far from heroic[30]—adopted by various speakers faced with death. As Yeats contemplates his assignation with the "increasing Night" of death and his anticipation of being terror-stricken in the face of divinity, like a woman impregnated with a god ("A Nativity"), as he repeatedly reviews and interrogates, in successive sleepless nights, the effect of words he has spoken or failed to speak ("The Man and the Echo"), he also reckons up his "joy." That joy "Grows more deep day after day" (*VP*, 624) and he asks the "rocky voice" of the echo if they shall "in that great night rejoice" (*VP*, 633). Then night and joy lose their reality as he hears the cry of a "stricken rabbit" being seized by some hawk or owl, and he is distracted by the terror and violence of life's end. At times, Yeats depicts "We Irish" as climbing "to our proper dark," having been "wrecked" by the "formless, spawning" fury of "this filthy modern tide," in order to "trace / The lineaments of a plummet-measured face" (*VP*, 611). He depicts himself as comically high, too, a man on stilts, "Malachi Stilt-Jack," making a good show for children and women, a wild man stalking on through the loose-breaking dawn with its "terrible novelty of light" (*VP*, 623). His poems and plays are sometimes presented as similarly elevated and playful, part of an imaginative circus complete with "stilted boys," "burnished chariot, / Lion and woman and the Lord know what" (*VP*, 629). At other moments he inclines towards humility, noting the loss of his old ladders and stilts, and resolves to "lie down where all the ladders start / In the foul rag and bone shop of the heart" (*VP*, 630). Completeness, then, is not something that just happens. It is an achievement born of discipline, an artistic determination to embrace one's antithesis, to remake or revise one's self and one's art, and it emerges as a sign of immortality, whether spiritual or artistic.

The kind of art Yeats tried to produce in his later years was art imbued with posthumous life, art that was impassioned with the erotic and destructive intensity of mortals, but also spiritual and complete. His statues—whether the bronze head of Maud Gonne or the eponymous statues of "The Statues"—symbolize his artistic aims, in that they are incarnations of human bodies and spirits that inspire passion in viewers. Once again, we can see an analogue for such an aesthetic in another of Elizabeth Bowen's stories, "Dead Mabelle." Bowen, like Yeats, depicts one person's art—art that is fully realized, embodied, etherealized, and vividly experienced by another—as comprising a kind of alternate reality, a reality that is more erotic than frightening.

Dead Mabelle, a silent film star of the twenties who dies tragically in the course of the story, is an incarnation of the Image who helps to illuminate—with a certain ironic distance—a view of art much like the one that Yeats seems to have entertained at the end of his life. She is a ghost, love object, artistic effect, self, and divinity rolled into one. A caption in one of her films, *The White Rider* (1923), asks, "Can't you believe me?" (*CS*, 278). And the main character, a self-taught dabbler in philosophy who works in a bank and struggles with the nature of reality, haunted by the fear that he himself is not real, is utterly seduced by her image. In the light that projects her face upon the screen in a dark, voluminous "world of plush" (*CS*, 282) filled with orchestra music and tobacco fumes, he finds a life and reality that has eluded him in his own daily existence. He is struck by "her intense aliveness" (*CS*, 282), and he thinks, "She was too real, standing there, while more and more of her came travelling down the air. She seemed perpetual, untouchable. . . . You might destroy the film, destroy the screen, destroy her body; this endured. She was beyond the compass of one's mind; one's being seemed a fragment and a shadow" (*CS*, 283). Months after her death, he begins to see her near him, in a doorway and later in the darkness, and he tells her, "You're more here than I": "She was there, left, right, everywhere, printed on darkness" (*CS*, 284). His life becomes reflexively imitative of the greater reality he has experienced in the cinema. He experiences his life as simply being "enclosed in a body, in the needs of the body; tethered to functions," and he thinks that "it looked rather shabby, this business of living" (*CS*, 285). "This was how one impressed oneself on the material": via the "Greasy stains on the tablecloth where he'd slopped his dinner over the edge of his plate, greasy rim round the inside of his hat where he'd sweated." But he realizes that in the "business of living" he had not impressed himself on the *im*material at all: "He had no power of being" (*CS*, 285).

Bowen's story helps to illustrate what preoccupied Yeats as he was nearing death: the reciprocal relation between the material and the immaterial, between life and art/ghosts, between time and death/ eternity. An artist is someone who produces material, impassioned shapes or forms that commemorate an experience of life that seems eternal, a life that surpasses the material, so that great art can be, in a sense, supernatural. In that respect, the artist performs the role of creator on the limited stage of mortal life. Other mortal beings, such as Yeats's Dancers, do the opposite: through the beautiful materiality of their physical form or actions, they give a recognizable shape to the divine—they become a divine Image. This is what Dead Mabelle achieves, and this is what Maud Gonne was to Yeats. If he was the *mage,* she was his *i*mage, simultaneously inspiring him and making him aware of his relative insignificance. The intensity of this love between eternity and the productions of time—as mage and image mirror one another and then polarize once more in an ongoing dance—is nowhere more apparent than in "A Bronze Head," Yeats's final meditation on the image(s) of Gonne (*VP,* 618–19). As he looks at the bronze-painted plaster cast of Gonne by Lawrence Campbell in the Municipal Gallery, a work of art, that head comes to life as a bird of prey, a "tomb-haunter" that is the only living thing sweeping the sky when "everything else [is] withered and mummy-dead," terrified at "its own emptiness." That image prompts the speaker to remember her in an opposite guise: he recalls her when she was not dark, empty, and terrified, but with a "form all full /As though with magnanimity of light," "a most gentle woman," and wonders which image best captures her substance. This allows him to posit that her substance is "composite," and "in a breath /A mouthful hold the extreme of life and death." This is the real "mystic marriage" that Yeats was always trying to achieve in his poems: a wild composite of life and death that drives the observer wild as well, bringing "Imagination to that pitch where it casts out /All that is not itself." He confesses "I thought her supernatural, /As though a sterner eye looked through her eye /On this foul world in its decline and fall." The poem ends in a disturbing paroxysm of contempt and despair, as the poet pictures that "sterner eye" gazing at "Ancestral pearls all pitched into a sty, / Heroic reverie mocked by clown and knave," and wonders "what was left for massacre to save." The sense that massacre could possibly be redemptive is disturbing, but it is of a piece with Yeats's determination to value violent death over empty life, not unlike the main ghost-lover in "Dead Mabelle," who is denied the means to make "the only fit gesture that he could have offered" his idol: a theatrical (and derivative) pistol shot to the head (*CS*, 285).

In the end, massacre and nativity, with all their wildness and terror, recede in importance before the galloping, eternal *sidhe*, coldly detached from the turmoil of both life and death. Yeats's epitaph bears the faint echo of his much earlier poem, "The Hosting of the Sidhe" (*VP*, 140–41), with its call to empty one's heart of "its mortal dream." At the end of his life, Yeats reduces both life and death to the insignificance that is a consequence of their brevity: to a dream that, like the dream of Mary in "The Happy Autumn-Fields," produces only "tears, idle tears." What matters are the poems themselves, those seductive, powerful, unthreatening "ghosts" that realize the perfection and intensity of the alter-life.

NOTES

1. Much has been written about Yeats's treatment of death in his poetry and plays. See, for example, Jahan Ramazani, *Yeats and the Poetry of Death: Elegy, Self-Elegy, and the Sublime* (New Haven: Yale University Press, 1990); James Pethica, "Introduction," in *Last Poems: Manuscript Materials*, ed. James Pethica, xxiii–liii (Ithaca: Cornell University Press, 1997); Hugh Kenner, "The Three Deaths of Yeats," *Yeats* 5 (1987): 87–94; Kathleen Raine, *Death-in-Life and Life-in-Death: "Cuchulain Comforted" and "News for the Delphic Oracle"* (Dublin: Dolmen Press, 1974); Virginia D. Pruitt and Raymond D. Pruitt, "W. B. Yeats on Old Age, Death and Immortality," *Colby Quarterly* 24:1 (March 1988): 36–49.

2. *The Variorum Edition of the Poems of W. B. Yeats*, ed. Peter Allt and Russell K. Alspach (New York: Macmillan, 1957), 3. Hereafter cited parenthetically as *VP*.

3. "The Happy Autumn Fields," in *The Collected Stories of Elizabeth Bowen* (New York: Anchor-Random, 1981), 671–85. This volume is hereafter cited parenthetically as *CS*.

4. Yeats portrays death as a union with a larger physical and spiritual world in such poems as "He Wishes his Beloved Were Dead" (*The Wind Among the Reeds*). The speaker imagines his beloved "lying cold and dead" in

order to show her how closely she is connected to the heavens. If she could project herself into her postmortem future, she would know that her "hair was bound and wound/About the stars and moon and sun." Imagined death, then, would allow her to understand her intimate connection to the supernatural, those heavenly bodies that seem eternal.

5. *The Letters of W. B. Yeats*, ed. Allan Wade (New York: Macmillan, 1955), 917–18; cited in explanatory notes in *The Collected Works of W. B. Yeats*, vol. 2, *The Plays*, ed. David R. Clark and Rosalind E. Clark (New York: Scribner, 2001), 920.

6. See Helen Vendler's chapter on these two poems in *Our Secret Discipline: Yeats and Lyric Form* (Cambridge, MA: Harvard University Press, 2007), 49–61. Vendler's readings are often illuminating, but she very reasonably treats art as something different from eternity, whereas I think Yeats saw them as closely related. For example, in a footnote she recounts Curtis Bradford's reading that Yeats is asking the sages in "Sailing to Byzantium" to help him enter the artifice of eternity, to become a golden bird. She opines, "This is a frequent mistake. Why would holy sages want a human being to turn into a golden bird?" She goes on to emphasize the distinction between God's holy fire and the emperor's palace, whereas Yeats connects those two places when he refers to the sages standing in that fire "as in the gold mosaic of a wall." See 385n14.

7. Clark and Clark, *The Plays*, 715.

8. Cited by Vendler, *Our Secret Discipline*, 384n7.

9. Vendler views this mingling as an indiscriminate "hodgepodge" of mythological personages, but in fact the Fortunate Isles (otherwise known as the Isles of the Blest) figure in Celtic mythology as well as Greek, which is why it makes sense that Yeats added them to the assemblage described by the oracle. See Vendler, *Our Secret Discipline*, 52.

10. The statue is in the Hermitage in Leningrad. See Yeats's letter to T. Sturge Moore, in Ursula Bridge, ed., *W. B. Yeats and T. Sturge Moore: Their Correspondence, 1901–1917* (London: Routledge & Kegan Paul, 1953), 165. Cited in *Collected Works*, vol. 1, *The Poems*, ed. Richard J. Finneran (New York: Macmillan, 1983, 1989), note 363.15, p. 682. Yeats attributes the statue to Raphael, but it is actually attributed to Raphael's disciple Lorenzo Lorenzetti, and it is called *Dead Boy on a Dolphin*.

11. See Vendler, *Our Secret Discipline*, 51–52, and *Lucian*, trans. A. M. Harmon (New York: Macmillan, 1913), 309–31. Lucian's satiric tone is unmistakable, as when he recounts that the tall and handsome lad Cinryas, who has been enamored of Helen, decides to rape her and she agrees (329). Plato is described as absent from the Isles, living instead in the imaginary city he had himself devised (321), and Pythagoras is described as having undergone seven transformations, and having ended his soul migrations, his

entire right side has become gold (325). Delightful, unbroken music whispers through the branches "like the fluting of Pandean pipes in desert places" (311), and Rhadamanthus rules.

12. Elizabeth Cullingford also emphasized the kinship between death and love for Yeats in *Gender and History in Yeats's Love Poetry* (Cambridge: Cambridge University Press, 1993), 43–54, but she puts a different spin on the connection, arguing that Yeats's love poetry is almost always elegiac. I am more interested in exploring a view of sex and death as inversely related moments of completion with one's opposite.

13. See the reading of "Cuchulain Comforted" in Pruitt and Pruitt, "W. B. Yeats on Old Age." Raine also offers a reading on the poem (*Death-in-Life*, 22–46). The most recent treatment is that of Helen Vendler in *Our Secret Discipline.* Vendler concedes that Cuchulain encounters his anti-self in the poem, but she sees it as the important "counter-truth" of the poem that precedes it, "The Black Tower": "If 'Cuchulain Comforted' is the poem of the hero Cuchulain's anti-self as it assents to quiet, even feminized, group life, then 'The Black Tower' is the poem of the heroic creative will—the poem of self-assertion, force, and tenacity" (142). Near the end of the book, Vendler reads the poem as using Dante's *terza rima* "because it unfolds a Dantesque encounter" between the dead Cuchulain and a group of "Shrouds" (370–75).

14. Richard Taylor, ed., *Frank Pearce Sturm: His Life, Letters, and Collected Works* (Urbana: University of Illinois Press, 1969), 119–20.

15. Pethica, *Last Poems,* xxvi; Yeats's draft of the contents is transcribed on 466. For many years, readers encountered "Under Ben Bulben" as the last poem in Yeats's *Collected Poems,* a move that provoked considerable scholarly controversy. Eventually, when Finneran reedited the poems for the first volume of *The Collected Works of William Butler Yeats,* he restored the order that Yeats had sketched out shortly before his death.

16. Curtis Bradford, "Yeats's *Last Poems* Again," Number VIII of the Dolmen Press Yeats Centenary Papers (Dublin: Dolmen Press, 1966), 261.

17. Ramazani argues, wrongly in my view, that the word "Swear" "grants the voice of the dead father to the speaker, specifically the dead father who berates Hamlet from beyond the grave" (*Yeats and the Poetry of Death,* 145). In context, it seems to be Hamlet's voice, not that of his father, that Yeats is channeling; the father is simply the ghostly echo.

18. It seems likely that Yeats would have drawn his knowledge of the ascetic philosophers who lived near Lake Mareotis in Egypt in the fourth century from the Neoplatonic writings of Pseudo-Dionysius the Areopagite, who in turn was indebted to Philo's *De vita contemplativa.* The Therapeutae associated with the "Mareotic lake" were desert-dwellers who regarded literal meanings as symbols of an inner and hidden nature that expressed itself

only obliquely. Saint Anthony lived in the same area at roughly the same time as the Therapeutae.

19. George Bornstein, *Yeats and Shelley* (Chicago: University of Chicago Press, 1970), 83–86.

20. Ramazani reads the relevance of Yeats's allusion to the Witch of Atlas differently; he sees her as anticipating Yeats's own "indifference to the misery, strife and death that plague humankind" (*Yeats and the Poetry of Death,* 145). Although Yeats is indeed distancing himself from suffering in this poem, not only his own but also the suffering of others, this does not seem to be "what the Witch of Atlas knew."

21. Compare Yeats's depictions of the bodies of saints in "Oil and Blood": "In tombs of gold and lapis lazuli / Bodies of holy men and women exude / Miraculous oil, odour of violet" (*VP,* 483).

22. The first notes for "Under Ben Bulben" (then simply titled "Creed") in the National Library of Ireland, transcribed by James Pethica, reinforce this view of death as a release that is not to be feared. He writes that he gives his life to that eternal "joy & that laughter," confessing "I am old & ill / my flesh is heavy it weighs upon my / heart but I shall soon cast it off / be ["as light as" cross through] if god wills I shall / be as light as a tred [thread?] of cotton" (Pethica, *Last Poems,* 5). He also writes, more disturbingly given contemporaneous developments in Europe: "Death nothing—if the sky full of / falling bombs—children hands & dance— / The soul out lives all things & / makes it self bodies as it pleases" and "let the bombs fall—let them destroy the / hateful cities" (Pethica, *Last Poems,* 11). Interestingly, Ramazani urges us not to take Yeats's views about reincarnation "at face value," agreeing with Richard Ellmann's suggestion in *The Identity of Yeats,* 2nd ed. (Oxford: Oxford University Press, 1964), that although Yeats defended reincarnation, his defense "is scarcely that of a believer" (Ramazani, *Yeats and the Poetry of Death,* 2–3, 207n1).

23. The view of reincarnation that Yeats offers here is remarkably close to that of his lifelong friend and correspondent Frank Pearce Sturm, who wrote in his 1918 essay "Umbrae Silentes" that "Metempsychosis rightly apprehended is something more than the continuous rebirth of the soul into body after material body. . . . The need and hunger for a habitation, a material body here or a spiritual one hereafter, is not a vice of the soul, but of the essence of it; it has, in the words of St. Thomas Aquinas, a natural aptitude or exigency for existing in the body; for which very reason the imaginations of the poets are more truly spiritual than the chilly speculations of the Platonists" (Taylor, *Frank Pearce Sturm,* 300, as well as 310–12). See also Sturm's diary entry for September 27, 1936, pp. 154–55.

24. Pethica, *Last Poems,* 33; see also xxxviii–xl for Pethica's argument about the line's importance.

25. Ibid., 31.

26. See Plotinus' fifth *Ennead,* quoted in Finneran, *Collected Works,* vol. 1, note 356.43, p. 679.

27. Taylor, *Frank Pearce Sturm,* 300.

28. Jon Stallworthy, *Vision and Revision in Yeats's "Last Poems"* (Oxford: Clarendon Press, 1969), 170. The *sidhe* are identified as "Tuatha de Dananan of Erin" [*sic*] in an early draft; see Pethica, *Last Poems,* 27.

29. A. Norman Jeffares links the epitaph with "The Fisherman" in its affirmation of both coldness and passion in *The Circus Animals: Essays on W. B. Yeats* (Stanford: Stanford University Press, 1970), 142.

30. The cast of repulsive characters and sentiments is swelled when we recall that Yeats intended to finish the volume with his play *Purgatory,* in which a bitter man returns to the place where he killed his father in order to murder his own son, and with it the future, and with *On the Boiler,* which Roy Foster aptly calls a "splenetic manifesto" (*W. B. Yeats: A Life,* vol. 2, *The Arch-Poet, 1915–1939* [Oxford: Oxford University Press, 2003], 586).

CHAPTER 11

The Legacy of Yeats in Contemporary Irish Poetry

RONALD SCHUCHARD

Derek Mahon and Peter Fallon opened their Penguin anthology of *Contemporary Irish Poetry* by declaring unequivocally that "Among the contours of modern Irish poetry the work of Yeats is Everest. His poems and his other activities in the pursuit of a new national identity represent a monument which, more often than not, obscured the achievement of younger writers."[1] The editors imply that most contemporary Irish poets have of necessity sought to get out from under the cold shadow or the blinding glare of Yeats's imperious presence, scaling instead the more accessible peaks of Louis MacNeice or Patrick Kavanagh. As Desmond O'Grady wrote to Mahon in a verse-letter,

> The statuary that Yeats erected
> left his generation knackered.

We were luckier in our day
with Beckett, MacNeice, Kavanagh
who wrote for us an exit visa. . . .
Yeats may lead our poets' procession
MacNeice and Kavanagh show direction.

But then he warned Mahon: "Joyce and Beckett are *cul de sac* / from which the only out's turn back."[2] Mahon and Michael Longley certainly pay homage and debts to MacNeice; John Montague, Seamus Heaney, and Eavan Boland to Kavanagh; but other poet-critics would add Joyce, Beckett, and Austin Clarke to a list of alternative precursors and insist on the admission of Auden, at least, among non-Irish influences. Many prefer the strong grounds of Yeats filtered through Mac-Neice, who wrote the first major book on Yeats, and Auden, whose famous elegy reveals his deep comprehension of Yeats's vision on the eve of another world war—"With your unconstraining voice / Still persuade us to rejoice"—and whose 1948 essay "Yeats as an Example" would eventually reverberate in the poetry of Northern Ireland.[3]

In a succeeding generation, Paul Muldoon declares that initially he found his inspiration in Eliot and the metaphysicals, and in Joyce rather than Yeats, whom he was temporarily forced to ignore. Where Yeats, and Heaney after him, profess Coventry Patmore's belief that "The end of art is peace," Muldoon demurs: "I believe in the exact opposite," he declares, "the end of art is disquiet and discomfort and rearranging the furniture in your head."[4] And in "7, Middagh Street" he is quick to dissociate himself from Yeats's "crass, rhetorical posturing" when Yeats asks in "The Man and the Echo" a famous question of history, whether his Irish play of 1902 led to the English executions of 1916. "Certainly not," answers Muldoon. "For history's a twisted root / with art its small translucent fruit / and never the other way round."[5] However, in his Clarendon Lectures in 1998 he prefaced his brief discussion of Yeats by saying that "The work of W. B. Yeats . . . is a massive subject in itself, one to which I hope to return."[6] Moreover, when he was elected Professor of Poetry at Oxford in 1999 his inaugural lecture was on Yeats's "All Souls' Night," the first chapter, we expect, of many to come.[7] In Belfast, Medbh McGuckian prefaced her poetic career by immersing herself in Yeats, writing a masterful paper for instructor Heaney on the poet and the Anglo-Irish poetic tradition, a paper that Heaney judged "One of the best things I've read on the subject."[8] "I feel I exist somewhere on the Tree of Poetry on the same limb as Blake and Yeats," she said earlier in her career, "but many phone calls below them." And yet she could use Yeats as an example in dealing with the relation of her poetry to the Troubles: "Yeats set an absurdly rhetorical example which I don't feel able to follow. Also it got him too involved with reality—being a senator marred his vocation."[9] In McGuckian's generation there has been no lack of resistance to Yeats. An American critic seeking an interview with Ciaran Carson on Yeats and contemporary Irish poets in 1994 let it be known that he knew the word was out on Carson and Yeats: "Tess [Gallagher] says you're no admirer of Yeats. Okay."[10] Carson had also begun with Eliot in conceiving of Belfast as wasteland. "At the end of the day," he says, "I don't think that the impulse behind what I write comes from other Irish poets."[11] Yet he too still takes his parodic fun with Yeats, as in his allusion to the golden birds of Byzantium in "Sierra": "Squawk-box parrots flitted in and out like cunningly- / constructed gold machines."[12] There is no doubt that these and other contemporary poets draw much nourishment from precursors other than Yeats, but in spite of disclaimers and distancing techniques, eventually they all must negotiate their art with or play it against some of Yeats's several legacies. The most persistent and pressing legacy received by contemporary Irish poets, North and South, is doubtless the pressure to engage and transcend their historical predicaments in their art, to work out the quarrel between the free creative imagination and political-religious constraints, between artistic consciousness and historical conscience.

Yeats knew well how the emerging poetic consciousness in Ireland is torn by the aims of art on the one hand and the claims of history on the other, and in his early poems we see the young visionary and nationalist finding mythic ways of reenacting the ancient drama between artistic imagination and national allegiance. But on April 24, 1916, the reality of violence and the nightmare of history suddenly became too great and too personal for myth to bear the strain. It was the horror of the Easter Rising and the subsequent executions, which would haunt his imagination from "Easter, 1916" through his last poems and plays, that made imperative the vision of history that he began to construct through his spirit masters in 1917, in the midst of a world war.[13] That tragic vision of two-thousand-year cycles of civilizations rising from a bestial floor to great heights of intellectual, aesthetic, and spiritual achievement before turning like a tragic wheel down to apocalyptic anarchy enabled him to deal with the home-bred violence and destruction in his art. It helped him, he said, "to hold in a single thought reality and justice"[14] and to become confident of the superiority of art to history. In the three decades following Yeats's death, his intimidating construct of *A Vision* remained as unapproachable as a Chapel Perilous, and no Irish poet dared draw too closely on his overbearing achievement.

In 1969, however, with the onset of the Troubles, a group of writers in their late twenties were coming to poetic maturity—Eavan Boland, Michael Longley, Seamus Heaney, and Derek Mahon, brought closely together in their college days as they moved between Belfast and Dublin, Queen's and Trinity. The successive shock waves that had shaken Yeats's poetic sensibility—the Easter Rising, the atrocities of the Black and Tans, and the Civil War—were felt anew in these poets by the Bogside Rising, Bloody Sunday, and the Dublin bomb blasts. Torn by the conflict of private imagination and civil violence, they suddenly found themselves conscripts of Yeats's poetic dialogue with history, a dialogue entered into with an urgency and necessity much greater than that felt by the succeeding generation of Muldoon, McGuckian, Carson, and others. For the entirety of their careers these four poets have struggled in their separate ways to work through what they have intuited, embraced, and resisted in Yeats. Numerous misperceptions about their continuous engagements with him have accrued, but the accessibility of previously unexamined archival materials now makes it possible to bring new perspective and detail to their phenomenal historical turn to Yeats.

When Eavan Boland was an undergraduate at Trinity College in the mid-sixties, she befriended and wrote poems for Michael Longley, Derek Mahon, Brendan Kennelly, and others in that Dublin-

Belfast coterie.[15] In 1966 she wrote to Longley about her exciting discovery of Yeats's note to "The Stare's Nest by my Window," part six of "Meditations in Time of Civil War." She described to Longley "how, during the Civil War in Galway, Yeats became desperate not to lose his understanding of beauty and not to become embittered," and she quotes from his note to the poem: "Presently a strange thing happened. I began to smell honey in places where honey could not be." "Out of this hallucination," she continues, "he wrote that exquisite poem, 'O honey-bees, / Come build in the empty house of the stare.' That sentence of his in the note is the most perfect expression I've found for the way in which a poet rescues his imagination from violence and sorrow—in fact, I can't put it in words but its meanings seem infinite."[16] What she also reveals in the letter is that she is flush with the excitement of a new poem, "the best I've ever written." Entitled "Yeats in Civil War," the poem borrows the quotation from Yeats's note for epigraph and concludes in direct address to the master, "Whatever I may learn / You are its sum, struggling to survive— / A fantasy of honey your reprieve."[17]

Yeats's "Meditations in Time of Civil War" was already a poem deep in the consciousness of Longley, and she wanted to know his response. The previous year Longley had published his *Ten Poems* in a Queen's University pamphlet series that included Mahon and Heaney, and he was now writing out his critical opinion of Yeats for a BBC Northern Ireland film biography of the poet. He declared unequivocally at the outset, "I regard Yeats as the greatest poet in English since Shakespeare," though he modestly admitted that "Attempting a professional critical account of Yeats would be for me like climbing Mount Everest in my carpet slippers."[18] But he went on, both as an apologist for Yeats and as a passionate student of his poetic technique, to declare Yeats's importance to himself and to Ireland:

> As an Ulster Protestant, a West Briton, an Anglo-Irishman, I personally have a vested interest in Yeats, who was virtually the first artist to bring the Anglo-Irish tradition into line with a positive nationalism. He was proud of coming from Anglo-Irish stock, and yet took as an inspiration, especially in his earlier work, the Celtic

legends of the west, rifling translations in English for raw material. In his later years he claimed his place in the line of Swift, Goldsmith, Berkeley and Burke, but saw himself always as an Irish poet, a successor of the Irish Bards. He reconciled in his life and work the purely Gaelic tradition with the younger Anglo-Irish tradition. When I was talking about Yeats some years ago with an ultra-patriotic Ulster folk singer, he shouted, "But Yeats wasn't an Irishman." I often wish that I had said then, quietly but firmly, "Yeats extends our notions of what an Irishman may be." Yeats turns upside down the prejudice that the heritage of Irish genius is the monopoly of any single class or type.

In his commentary, Longley describes Yeats's reaction to the Easter Rising as "what his poetry . . . had been waiting for," the poem as "one of the greatest war poems ever." Regarding "Easter, 1916," wrote Longley,

> Yeats is doing a lot more than commenting on a single political event. In the ensuing creative period the eruption of violence in Ireland joins in his mind both with the anarchy of the 1st World War and a philosophical conviction that a new destructive era of human history was beginning. . . . He was now facing as a poet universal disorder.

In making this assertion, the young Longley affirms that for him poetry constitutes "man's biggest and gravest endeavour to make sense out of all that is chaotic in his life." He thus turns to "Meditations in Time of Civil War" as Yeats's exemplary attempt, in his lonely tower, to "exalt a lonely mind" with "Befitting emblems of adversity." "To clear a devastated site and build on it, as Yeats did," Longley declares, "is the most responsible, the indispensible, achievement of a great poet." Boland could not have wished for a richer response.

In 1969 Longley published his first volume, *No Continuing City*, taking his title directly from Saint Paul's Epistle to the Hebrews, but more immediately perhaps from Eliot's *Murder in the Cathedral*, where the Chorus describes Canterbury as he would describe Belfast:

"Here is no continuing city, here is no abiding stay. / Ill the wind, ill the time, uncertain the profit, certain the danger."[19] But where he may have found his title in Eliot, he certainly found his form in Yeats. Just after the volume appeared, Longley was invited to lecture at the Yeats Summer School in Sligo. On the morning of August 12, 1969, as he addressed the audience on "Yeats's Effect on Young Contemporary Poets," declaring in no uncertain terms that "anyone writing poetry today cannot have the interests of poetry at heart if he is not at least challenged by the way in which the great stanzaic and metrical tradi- tion of English poetry grows organically out of Yeats's struggles with himself and his material."[20] In his characterization of "the vastness and the *humanity* of Yeats's formal achievement," and in his assertion that "our artistic decisions will be arbitrary . . . if we deny or ignore such a presence and such an example," he affirmed the presence and example of Yeats in *No Continuing City:*

> For myself, of the 38 poems in my first collection, all but two are rhymed. I know that I would certainly feel self-conscious about such "traditionalism" were it not for the endorsement of Yeats's example. And I know that I speak for those Irish poets who are my contemporaries and friends. Kennelly, Heaney, Mahon, Eavan Boland all rhyme in an unforced and unselfconscious fashion in their poetry. . . . Like so much else it was preserved by Yeats . . . for succeeding generations of poets.

On that fateful day, as he spoke on the inheritance of Yeats's formal qualities, the Battle of the Bogside broke out in Derry.

In the year after Bogside, Longley's passionate interest in Yeats shifted from the formal to the tragic qualities of his writing. On the anniversary of his first lecture, Longley returned to Sligo with a re- markable script entitled "Yeats as Tragedian," focusing not on the dramatist but on the lyric poet. Describing his conscious awareness of how in the past year "Yeats was helping me to clarify my own re- sponses to almost daily violences," Longley had become preoccupied with the idea that the complex lyric was "a mode capable of encom- passing and solving extreme experience."[21] At the back of his mind was "the shamelessly hypothetical notion that if Shakespeare were writing in the 20th century, he would judge the Yeatsian lyric a more than adequate vehicle." Contemplating the first anniversary of the Bogside Rising, which he described as possessing its own kind of "terrible beauty," Longley discussed Yeats's "Easter, 1916," "Nineteen Hundred and Nineteen," "Meditations in Time of Civil War," and "The Tower" as poems of truly tragic dimensions, poems in which Yeats achieves what Longley calls "Shakespearean altitude." In drawing the Yeats-Shakespeare parallels, he sees "Nineteen Hundred and Nineteen" as Yeats's *Macbeth*, "Meditations in Time of Civil War" as his *Hamlet*. It is evident that Longley is using the lecture to define his own poetic and his own poetic response to Bogside, and what he discovers in the Shakespearean altitude of Yeats's tragic lyrics is an unflinching exploration of the poetic imagination in the face of a tide of anarchy. What Yeats is telling us, says Longley, is that "the poet's only line of action is to be a poet; he is saying that such a line of action can endure and encompass the worst possibilities of man and of man's situation; . . . he is saying that whatever the circumstances and however grim the backcloth a poet's first and last loyalties must be to his own imagination." Longley's debt to Yeats is immeasurable, but what he reveals so early is that "Meditations in Time of Civil War" and other tragic lyrics embody the legacy that the poets of the Bogside generation have carried for over forty years.

In the early 1970s Boland turned to her first political poem, "War Horse," still working within a Yeatsian system of values, but not without increasing discomfort. Then the 1974 bomb blasts in Dublin shattered her belief in Yeats's vision of cultural unity. She wrote in the *Irish Times* an article entitled "The Weasel's Tooth," a title taken from section 4 of Yeats's "Nineteen Hundred and Nineteen." Writing with a sense of personal guilt for the violence, for the "flying limbs, lost lives, broken hearts," she accuses herself of, and as a poet sets out to answer for, sharing and spreading "the damaging fantasies of the writer I have admired and loved most of my life: William Yeats."[22] She specifically rejects the fantasy of his statement, "in a fine and empty phrase," that Irish culture is "a community bound together by imaginative possessions." "I believed that once," she writes in self-bitterness,

Now I know it to be arid rhetoric. . . . Yet his fantasy of cultural co-
herence has not—more's the pity—been thrown out intellectually
by writers with the force and decision with which his final, single
achievement has been kept and rightly cherished. In fact it has
tipped the pen of many an Irish writer since and, of course, I in-
clude myself, with the poison of confusion. . . . Once and for all I
feel we should rid ourselves of Yeats's delusion; let us be rid at last
of any longing for cultural unity in a country whose most precious
contribution may be precisely its insight into the anguish of dis-
unity; let us be rid of any longing for imaginative collective dignity
in a land whose final and only dignity is individuality.

Our "one strength" as writers, she declared, is to use our individual
voices "in speaking in tones of outcry, vengeance, bitterness even,
against our disunity, but speaking, for all that, with a cool, tough ac-
ceptance of it." If in her outrage as a twenty-nine-year-old poet it was
a strong and daring moment publicly to renounce the alleged delu-
sion of her master, it was perhaps an impulsive and incautious mo-
ment for her art, placing it in the servitude of politics and violence,
surrendering it to the conscription of history. As she gained distance
from the article and the anger, she would correct it, but, importantly,
it had moved her beyond her former adulation into a continuous love-
hate dialogue with Yeats.

"I was to learn how hard it would be," she wrote of that dialogue,
"to set different values."[23] In the early Yeats, and in Irish male poets
generally, she had found repeatedly the traditional image of Ireland
as Cathleen ni Houlihan, the Poor Old Woman, and she had come to
resent not only a simplification but a violation of reality in the image,
an image that was being "handed on from poet to poet, from genera-
tion to generation [as] orthodox poetic practice" (*OL,* 152). "So many
male Irish poets—" she wrote with a qualification, "the later Yeats
seems to me a rare exception—have [so] feminized the national and
nationalized the feminine that . . . it has seemed there is no other
option" (*OL,* 144). Thus, Boland began to subvert the traditional Irish
political poem, and to do so she returned to Yeats's "Meditations in
Time of Civil War" as her model. "Yeats had proposed a private world

in a political poem," she declared. "To me this was the Irish political poem as it should be. . . . It made an encouraging sign about the real ability to suffer the outer world so powerfully that history itself faltered before that gaze" (*OL,* 189).

Armed once again with this Yeatsian model, Boland used it to journey first into "the noise of myth," and then "Out of myth into history" to sound the voices of those women silenced by history, turned away from by history—determined as a poet "to be / part of that ordeal / whose darkness is / only now reaching me from those fields."[24] This has been movingly achieved in her poetry without denying or discrediting Yeats, as others have done, but by incorporating his legacy into her own poetic world. Indeed, in a recent interview, she replied, when asked what poets had most nurtured her, "Kavanagh and of course Yeats, who is still the poet I love most."[25]

In 2001, when she looked back with perspective upon what she had termed thirty years earlier the "crisis of conscience" of Longley, Heaney, and Mahon,[26] implicitly including herself in their company, she described how

> the Troubles put a huge shadow in the space between the page and the pen. Inevitably, a lot of play and the chance of some private directions went out of the poems. By the start of the 1970s their work was being pulled into something bigger. It was being drawn in by this back-and-forth rhythm of conscription which Irish poetry goes through. A zigzag between a chosen subject matter and one imposed from Irish history. It's what Yeats is getting at in "The Grey Rock." . . . What is surprising is how independent they stayed. They kept their own lyric identities and they progressed.[27]

In 1966 Seamus Heaney was writing "Requiem for the Croppies" for the fiftieth anniversary of the Easter Rising, positing rightly or not "that the seeds of violent resistance sowed in [1798] had flowered in what Yeats called 'the right rose tree' of 1916."[28] Heaney did not realize then, any more than did Boland or Longley, that the murderous encounter between Protestants and Catholics would be initiated again in the summer of 1969. From that time forward the problems of poetry changed, and Heaney too felt it imperative "to discover a field of force" in which poetry could maintain its integrity "and at the same time grant the religious intensity of the violence its deplorable authenticity and complexity" (*FK*, 26). The poet finds himself caught between the "territorial piety" of Irish Catholics and the "imperial power" of Ulster Protestants: "The question," he asks "as ever, is, 'How with this rage shall beauty hold a plea?' And my answer is," he says, calling upon Yeats in "Meditations in Time of Civil War," "by offering 'befitting emblems of adversity'" (*FK*, 26).

In taking Yeats as his example in the art-violence conflict, Heaney had to confront, with Boland and Longley, those who resisted him. What all three came to assert vociferously as Yeatsians was, in Heaney's words, "that poetry is its own reality and no matter how much a poet may concede to the pressures . . . of historical reality, the ultimate fidelity must be to the demands . . . of the artistic event."[29] There are many places in Heaney's poetry where this continuous conflict is dramatized: in "Casualty," that elegy in *Field Work* for a Derry bomb-blast victim whose harsh questioning makes Heaney's art a "tentative art"; in "Station Island," where he meets the accusing ghost of his murdered cousin, where the shade of James Joyce tells him that his guilt over "That subject people stuff is a cod's game" and that as poet "You lose more of yourself than you redeem / doing the decent thing"; and in *The Spirit Level*, in a poem entitled "The Flight Path," where he recounts a train journey to Belfast in 1979. An angry, grimfaced man sits down opposite him, "and goes for me head on": "'When, for fuck's sake, are you going to write / Something for us?' 'If I do write something, / Whatever it is, I'll be writing for myself.' / And that was that. Or words to that effect."[30] Yet at its greatest moments, Heaney declares, poetry "would attempt, in Yeats's phrase, to hold in a single thought reality and justice" (*GT*, 108).

In January 1989, on the fiftieth anniversary of Yeats's death, Heaney paid tribute to Yeats in various venues in Ireland, England, and America. He was sharply aware of the revisionist academic criticism that was interrogating and assailing Yeats for "all that intercourse between politics and literature that his cultural nationalism set out to sponsor."[31] It was an important transitional time in Heaney's own poetry, when a skylight cut in the Glanmore Cottage roof began to let the marvelous and the miraculous lighten the murderous, and Yeats played a prominent role in that process. So, in obliquely addressing Yeats's critics, he said deliberately, "Yeats's overall intent was to clear a space in the mind for the miraculous, for all kinds of rebellion against the tyranny of physical and temporal law. Indeed, it is time we redirected our attention to this visionary courage in his oeuvre and laid off pressing him too trimly into our own cultural arguments, and even blaming him for our predicaments." Heaney precipitated the various versions of his talks into an uncollected essay, "Yeats's Nobility," in which he turns us back to 1915, to the poem "Ego Dominus Tuus," written in the midst of a world war and on the eve of the Easter Rising, a poem in which he declares that "art / Is but a vision of reality," a poem in which Heaney sees Yeats "foresuffering his predicament as visionary poet in a time of violence and catastrophe."[32] When he follows that predicament to Yeats's civil war poems, he distinguishes the tragic lyrics not for their Shakespearean altitude but for "the high pitch of sacred rite" that they have about them. "In them," says Heaney, "Yeats divests himself of his domestic identity to become the voice of dramatically encompassing imagination, he dons the mantle of the wisdom-speaker and the memory-keeper, becomes the shaman figure who confronts menace with ritual song." It is as though Heaney too is revising or expanding his own poetics through his reengagement with Yeats and his tragic lyrics. In the sequences of "Nineteen Hundred and Nineteen" and "Meditations in Time of Civil War," says Heaney admiringly, "the fortitude and composure of Yeats's *gaze* is equal to the violence and danger of the historical disintegration which it witnesses. His 'vision of reality' is in line with and adequate to the historical reality which cruelly imposes itself; and, in achieving such a combination of tough-mindedness and plangency, Yeats brings into modern poetry a quality which is rare indeed and which we may call 'nobility.'"[33] In terms of Yeats's noble gaze, his Sophoclean ability to see life steadily and to see it whole, it took two decades for Heaney to turn Auden's borrowed title "Yeats as an Example" from a personal question back to a declaration.

For the three-volume edition of *The Field Day Anthology of Irish Writing*, Heaney undertook the editing, selecting, and introducing of the section devoted to Yeats. In his introductory essay he sets himself the delicate task of examining Yeats's career in the context of Irish tradition, nationalism, violence, and Yeats's unorthodox spirituality. Fully aware of and sensitive to the present political, cultural, and academic criticism of Yeats, and not uncritical of his unexemplary excesses, Heaney aims to define and measure Yeats's achievements in balance with both personal extremes and historical changes: "If Yeats's greatness as a writer has grown indisputable, the virtue of his example has not. Much opposition has been engendered by his ultimate embrace of the high aesthetic mode as the basis not only of a poetic but of an ethic as well."[34] As he traces the course of Yeats's career, it is clear that for Heaney the main tension underlying the poet's various conflicts is between imagination and reality, the poet's determination to create and launch an imaginative vision in a climate of convulsive changes, changes which he catalogues: "Britain and Europe moved out of the pomp and confidence of the high imperial epoch into the devastation of World War I and its aftermath, on through the effects of the Russian Revolution, the rise of fascism in Italy, the Nazi takeover in Germany, the Spanish Civil War, and, finally, the months of haunted apprehension before the outbreak of World War II. In Ireland also he witnessed drastic changes" (*FD*, 787). Heaney can now assert in an impersonal introductory commentary what has meant so much to him personally as a poet: "And to all of these crises Yeats responded with his own idiom, at his own pace" (*FD*, 787). To Heaney, Yeats's poems absorb the shock of history, but they do not arise from the immediacy of events or from the necessity of recording them; they arise, rather, "from the resonance that the happenings produced within his consciousness and from the mediated meaning they engendered there.... Indeed the whole force of his thought worked against those philosophies which regarded the mind's activity as something determined by circumstance and which consequently limited its possibilities to empirical discovery" (*FD*, 787). That observation and declaration form the dramatic center of the introduction and constitute the primary drama of Heaney's continuous engagement with Yeats.

In his Oxford lectures on "The Redress of Poetry," and again in his Nobel address, "Crediting Poetry," he reaffirms that Yeats's poetry consistently fortifies the spirit against assaults from a violent reality. He turns to Yeats's late poem "The Man and the Echo," praising the poet for trying to make sense of a world where suffering and violence prevail over the virtue of being kind, and praising the poem for showing *how* the spirit must endure "by pitting the positive effort of mind against the desolations of natural violence, by making 'rejoice' answer back to the voice from the rock, whatever it says."[35] In his Nobel address of 1995, Heaney was finally able to take a step beyond his commemorative address of 1989; he now saw clearly at last, through yet another return to "Meditations in Time of Civil War," that in Yeats's poem was provision and proof that "poetry can be equal to *and* true at the same time," equal to the historical crisis *and* true to the poetic imagination (*OG*, 428). With that long-sought understanding, Heaney expressed his admiration for Yeats's own Nobel speech in 1923, in which the poet chose not to allude to the Civil War just ended but to focus solely on the achievement of his great fellow-writers of the Irish Dramatic movement—art outfacing history again—and Heaney thus asked his audience "to do what Yeats asked his audience to do and think of the achievement of Irish poets and dramatists and novelists over the past forty years, among whom I am proud to count great friends" (*OG*, 427).

We turn now to Derek Mahon's early, studied resistance to Yeats—not unmindful that he was schooled to an early appreciation of his work by a teacher (John "Basher" Doyle) who "taught Yeats as if Yeats were an historian of the time: Yeats as documentary."[36] Mahon has said that the first poem that excited his imagination as a poet was Yeats's "The Stolen Child,"[37] and he once confessed to Dillon Johnston that "only a lobotomy could remove from his mind the Yeatsian line."[38] Even though he has found poetic techniques to suppress the rhythm, he cannot keep himself from bringing Yeats's phrases and lines into his poems, either in a serious or parodic manner. (Neither can Muldoon, the master parodist of Yeats, as in the elegy to the Gore-Booth sisters, "Both beautiful, one a gazebo").[39] But it is Yeats's vision of history that Mahon most determinedly resists in his early poetry, for among contemporary Irish poets at that time Mahon held the darkest, most deterministic view of history, which constantly invaded his art with its murderous barbarity and crushing materialism. For Mahon, like Stephen Dedalus in *Ulysses*, history is the nightmare from which he is trying to awake, and like Beckett he does not flinch from the bleakest absurdity or reality. At a snow party in Nagoya, in a room off a courtyard in Delft, in any of his constructed havens of the imagination, he cannot shut out the screams of history's violent acts: "Elsewhere they are burning / Witches and heretics / In the boiling squares, / Thousands have died since dawn / In the service of barbarous kings."[40] The tension between art and history and the demands of a violent culture on the artist are overwhelming for a poet who would slough it all off. Not unlike Yeats's King Goll or Fergus, the poet who deems himself the "last of the fire kings" longs to perfect his "cold dream / Of a place out of time," and thus he declares that he is "Through with history," that he shall "Break with tradition and / Die by my own hand / Rather than perpetuate / The barbarous cycle" (*CP*, 64–65).

But of course Mahon cannot perfect his cold dream of art outside the heat of history, and as he ransacks historical places he can only find precedents for his predicament in Ulster. In "A Postcard from Berlin," addressed to Paul Durcan, he hears as he writes in a quaint quarter of Berlin "echoes of Weimar tunes" and the beer-garden laughter of "a razed Reich" and knows that "the first / Of abstract rage, exhausted there, / Blaze out of control elsewhere—." At once he imagines Durcan in battle-torn Ulster reading "of another hunger-strike, / A postman blasted off his bike."[41] Thinking of the women in Rathlin, of Brecht in Svendborg, of Knut Hamsun in old age, or observing Edvard Munch's "Girls on the Bridge," he hears unremittingly the screams that have become "The serenade / Of an insane / And monstrous age" (*SP*, 172).[42] Mahon's "The Sea in Winter," a verse-letter addressed to his friend Desmond O'Grady and surely one of his most disaffected laments about the cruelties of history, evoked a sympathetic response in verse from O'Grady, who prescribes his own cure—in Yeats:

What I may say in this reply
may sometimes seem to give the lie
to where my head and heart now bend;
but as my friend you'll understand.

Tragedy's *penchant* is live laughter
loud in the face of all disaster.
A lesson I've grievously learnt at last.
I've sworn now to renege my past,
but watch out for what comedy,
casual or otherwise, could destroy
values for which I'm willing to die.[43]

But for Mahon at this time every historical instance militates against any Yeatsian consolation or laughter, and in an ironic poem entitled "Everything Is Going To Be All Right," he obliquely mocks Yeats on the matter: "There will be dying, there will be dying, / But there is no need to go into that." We find the ironic context for this poem and its title in Mahon's review of an edition of Baudelaire:

> There are certain figures in the history of literature before whom one falls silent. Shakespeare, of course; Yeats maybe; certainly Baudelaire. In the cases of Shakespeare and Yeats, the silence is not a disagreeable one; we know that, despite the storms and rages, everything will be all right in the end, and so it is.[44]

At this time, however, Mahon aligns his sensibility not with English and Irish literature but with the European:

> Anglophone literature is . . . ultimately consolatory. European literatures are different. No masterful heaven intervenes to save us. We live there with the consequences of our thoughts and actions, however deranged.

Back in his poem, Mahon declares that in his deranged state "the poems flow from the hand unbidden / and the hidden source is the watchful heart," ever alert to the reality of historical terror and dying.

Mahon does not fall silent before Yeats. Indeed, in the succeeding poem, "Heraclitus On Rivers," he breaks his silence and goes face to face with Yeats and his gyres and astrological phases, confronting Yeats's belief in the power of art and language over history. In the poem, which takes off from the image of the "living stream" in "Easter, 1916," Mahon evokes the image of Maud Gonne, who finally told Yeats she loved him and may have surrendered to him sexually one summer night in Paris in the summer of 1908:

> the precise
> Configuration of the heavenly bodies
> When she told you she loved you
> Will not come again in this lifetime.
>
> You will tell me that you have executed
> A monument more lasting than bronze;
> But even bronze is perishable.
> Your best poem, you know the one I mean,
> The very language in which the poem
> Was written, and the idea of language,
> All these things will pass away in time.
>
> <div align="right">(<i>CP,</i> 114)</div>

If Mahon here dissociates himself from one of Yeats's legacies, in his more recent poems he begins to surrender to another, later one—turning down the volume of history to sound the hidden source of that watchful heart; turning away, like Yeats, from themes of the embittered heart to the heart mysteries that suffuse "the foul rag and bone shop." In a poem entitled "After Pasternak," Mahon had ended with a semi-prayer "that the river of suffering may release the heart-constraining ice" (*CP,* 140).

We first begin to see the thaw of Mahon's icy attitude toward Yeats in 1989, when he too agreed to make a statement on the fiftieth anniversary of Yeats's death. Recounting how he had been taught to think of Yeats as a monument whose heights were unscalable, Mahon describes how to him Yeats the man and the poet gradually began to disappear from his mind: "Such was the force and ingenuity of his self-creation that he seemed to have spirited himself away until only the work remained, 'a monument of its own magnificence.'"[45] But Mahon, like Heaney, also attributed part of Yeats's disappearance to what he called the mountainous "scholarly snow" that had occluded the heart of his work in many poetic minds: "the scholarly snow precipitated by his own coldly passionate dreams disfigured his dream-status in our minds, he became his admirers, as Auden predicted he would. The myths took shape, the critical books piled up, the deconstructionists visited Sligo; and somehow the man himself ceased to exist." In recounting the absence and distance of Yeats in his work, Mahon clearly seizes the moment to signal a reengagement, and even though such anniversary occasions tend to be hyperbolic, his homage here seems reliably sincere as he brings the ghostly man back into human visage: "No doubt he could be affected and insufferable, and remained for too long an earnest boy," Mahon concluded,

> yet how come such a man had so many friends? His admirers increase daily and I would find it hard to believe that anyone coming upon his work for the first time could fail to realize that they were in the presence of an almost super-natural genius. More exciting still is the thought that it is the work of one man, who died only 50 years ago. His example shames and ennobles us all.

This was a striking testimonial, the memorial occasion notwithstanding, and it was followed by Mahon's characterization of Yeats's distant, monumental presence in the Penguin anthology: "Yeats is Everest." The generous public endorsements, however, were still accompanied by a personal uncertainty about the nature of Yeats's presence in his own work, as evident in a subsequent interview with William Scammell in the *Poetry Review*, where Scammell seeks Mahon's confirmation of a widespread view: "Yeats doesn't seem to have been a useable influence for your generation. Heaney went to Kavanagh and Hughes. You went to . . . MacNeice? And Beckett?"[46] But Mahon would not oblige him: "The shadow of Yeats has to be there somewhere," he replied, as yet unable to bring this dark figure into the light of mind; "it's like being influenced by Shakespeare." It was during the composition of *The Hudson Letter* (1995) that Yeats began to step out of the shadows of Mahon's imagination, and in his warming presence we begin to feel the trickling thaw of Mahon's own "heart-constraining ice."

In *The Hudson Letter*, where the poet seeks to "kick-start" his poetic powers, "to draw some voltage one more time" after life-threatening illness, he declares in a Yeatsian prayer to his daughter that "even the *being* is an art / we learn for ourselves, in solitude, on our very own, / listening to the innermost silence of the heart . . . and dreaming at all times our uninterruptible dream of redemptive form" (*CP*, 201). Now, in listening to the slowly warming heart, Mahon's cold dream of redemptive form, like Yeats's "cold heaven," is no longer interruptible by unaccommodated history. We sense it again in lines that he worked and reworked beyond last proofs and finally got right only in press, that in the midst of New York or any city "rife with confrontation" and conflict,

> Never mind the hidden agenda, the sub-text;
> it's not really about male arrogance, "rough sex"
> or vengeful sisterhood, but about art
> and the encoded mysteries of the human heart.
>   (*CP*, 199)

There had been a significant transformation of head and heart in *The Hudson Letter*, but the explicit time and nature of the change were not evident until the spring of 2000, when an interview with Mahon, conducted by Eamon Grennan on the appearance of *Selected Poems* in 1991, four years before *The Hudson Letter*, finally appeared in the *Paris Review* (*PR*). When Grennan asked Mahon if the Dionysian/Apollonian combination made sense to him, he replied, "Yes, that's the combination that has the greatest potency, I think. The hissing chemicals inside the well-wrought urn; an urnful of explosives. That's what's so great about Yeats, after all: the Dionysian contained with the Apollonian form, and bursting at the seams—shaking at the bars, but the bars have to be there to be shaken" (*PR*, 169–70). Mahon went on to define the poem as a "secular act of faith," a "faith in meaningfulness, a defiance of nihilism—to which one is rather prone of course. I mean, we do know it's all a lot of nonsense, really, just as Mr. Camus knew, but it doesn't do to say so, even to oneself" (*PR*, 173). Sensing this startling change in his former nihilistic view, Grennan went to the heart of the matter: "Although, if you're a poet," he posited, "you *have* to say it to yourself, I guess, but you also have to say the other thing—what Yeats would call holding reality and justice in a single thought. You're after that, too?" he asked. "Yes, of course," Mahon replied. "'Derry Morning' has something of what we're talking about. . . . I like the idea of a defiance of nihilism, that's certainly true in my own case. It's very easy to have said at some point, even to say still, 'It's all a lot of nonsense, it's not to be taken seriously.' But that attitude never produces anything" (*PR*, 173). When Grennan followed up by asking if he thought that the poem itself was a Yeatsian journey toward going on, Mahon replied, "Yes, Heaney quotes Coventry Patmore's phrase, 'the end of art is peace.' *Peace* in the sense of contributing to the world, to life, which is finally all we have, I suppose. Though perhaps we shouldn't be talking about peace, but only about faith—the poem as an act of faith. So let's forget peace; let's stick with the faith" (*PR*, 174). As Desmond O'Grady had prescribed, Mahon had slowly begun to recover from a nihilistic solitude to a new Yeatsian defiance and a new faith in community that we see at work in *The Hudson Letter*. When Grennan asked him how solitude and community were connected in the kinds of poems he was writing then, Mahon replied, "It's practically my subject, my theme: solitude and community; the weirdness and terrors of solitude; the stifling and the consolations of community. Also, the consolations of solitude. But it is important for me to be on the edge looking in. I've been inside. . . . Now again, I appear to be outside" (*PR*, 177).

Mahon's definition of his new angle of vision, on the edge looking in (not unlike a Chinaman on the mountain looking on), is further reflected in his filmed interview with Michael Silverblatt at the Lannan Foundation in March 1994. Silverblatt brought up the "despairing and pessimistic" nature of Mahon's poetry, asserting that of the poets in his generation he was regarded as "the darkest." When Silverblatt asked, "Why do you choose to present your work in this way?" Mahon adamantly resisted him. "I don't agree that I'm in any sense the darkest," he replied. "I was always very fond of something Edmund Wilson once said of Scott Fitzgerald: 'His message is despair but his style sings of hope.' You know. Something like that."[47] Such a Yeatsian attitude is inherent in the poem with which he concluded his Lannan reading, "Kinsale": "The kind of rain we knew is a thing of the past— / deep-delving, dark, deliberate you would say. . . . We contemplate at last / shining windows, a future forbidden to no one" (*CP*, 167).[48]

Two years later, in August 1996, with *The Hudson Letter* a year in print, Mahon arrived in Sligo to address the Yeats Summer School on "The King and I."[49] As he moved toward the heart of his lecture, he delineated some of the familiar objections to Yeats's verse—his magical system, his archaism, the excess "fury" and "bitterness," his too relentless heroism, and his standards of beauty and performance that "are too elevated to be humanly interesting." One criticism seemed to come out of the evolved poetic of *The Hudson Letter*—Yeats's "studious refusal" to make room in his poetry for the mechanism and the raucous machinery of the early century: "Perhaps in the long run, he will be proved right, and post-industrial society will turn for endorsement to his ecological purism; but even so he misses out on an exciting and challenging feature of his period. Readers of the future will turn in vain to Yeats for a sense of the texture of twentieth century life." With these reservations noted, he went on to say that "it seems indisputable that Yeats's influence survives among contemporary practitioners."

On the strength of that affirmation, he proceeded to bring Yeats onto the well-lit stage of his own craft of verse. "I know my *own* work is full of Yeatsian echoes," he admitted; "and, aside from incidental allusions scattered throughout as freely as one might make allusions to Shakespeare or Sophocles, I for one have perpetrated passages that owe, I realize, their whole pitch and tone to Yeatsian precedent." He pointed out specific passages in such poems as "Beyond Howth Head," "A Disused Shed in Co. Wexford," "Going Home," "Derry Morning," "The Sea in Winter," and "Imbolc" from *The Hudson Letter*.[50] Seeking to place the Yeatsian precedent in perspective, he observed on behalf of his own generation that "We've inherited Yeats as an example, to use Seamus's word; what we haven't inherited . . . is his deep structure; for we were born at a later time, into changed conditions, and have often felt it necessary to resist the Yeatsian charm and the Yeatsian authority. We've lost or abandoned the Yeatsian deep structure (his view of Ireland is no longer ours); yet his influence is everywhere, and the argument . . . continues."

Mahon's long argument with himself about the Yeatsian inheritance, however, was no longer an argument of insidious intent. "To the poets who come after him," affirms Mahon, "he has left phrases like talismans, consolatory and inspiring," inhabiting phrases like "a lonely impulse of delight"[51] and "our proper dark," but more than that he has left

> an ideal of audacity and empowerment; and a paradigm of transmutation, personal and historical. Adept of a severe code, he resists the liberal hospitalization of the world; even so, his very violence is therapeutic, cathartic. Above all, he tells us everything is possible, that personal defeat is incidental to the larger picture.

In the personal moment of that declaration of faith, Mahon quoted those great lines in those great poems that ring with tragic joy, "The Gyres" and "Lapis Lazuli." In Yeats's Sligo, *rapprochement*.

It was not only the New York experience and the subsequent return to Dublin that brought the mind-and-heart change we see in the later poems, but the cumulative effect of his periodic pilgrimages to Kinsale, the locale of several meditative poems. In "The Yaddo Letter," a prelude to *The Hudson Letter*, he reminds his children of the days when

> I'd wander round the hills above Kinsale
> where British forces clobbered Hugh O'Neill
> in Tudor times, wrecking the Gaelic order
> (result, plantations and the present Border).
>   (*CP*, 183)

He doesn't elaborate that wandering, but he concludes *The Yellow Book* in 1998 with a section entitled "Christmas in Kinsale," in which he observes facetiously that under the Advent sky "the isles are free of intolerable noises / and the young are slouching into Bethlehem" (*CP*, 264). But he is moved to question in a more serious Yeatsian mode, "Does history, exhausted, come full cycle? / It ended here at a previous *fin de siècle*, / though leaving vestiges of a distant past / before Elizabeth and the Tudor conquest—." Meditating on the exhaustion of history, and cognizant of "the garbage and trash" and mounds of refuse littering the harbor, here, he says suddenly and deliberately, "The harsh will dies . . . its grave an iridescence in the sea-breeze." Astonishingly, the poem then closes with a dream-vision of a Yeatsian figure standing before him:

> A cock crows good-morning from an oil drum
> like a peacock on a rain-barrel in Byzantium,
> soap-bubbles foam in a drainpipe and life begins.
> I dreamed last night of a blue Cycladic dawn,
> a lone figure pointing to the horizon,
> again the white islands shouting, "Come on; come on!"
>
> (*CP*, 265)[52]

With the death of the harsh will, which Yeats had insisted must not usurp the work of imagination, the poet seems on the threshold of a new vision. Certainly his old nihilistic quarrel with Yeats has gone.

The figure of Yeats stalks *The Yellow Book*, his trail blazed with those talismanic phrases. Indeed, his presence is dominant there: "safe home from New York," writes Mahon, "I climb as directed to our proper dark," echoing Yeats's "The Statues" and identifying himself among those "thrown upon this filthy modern tide." Under Yeats's direction, Mahon climbs to his new poetic haven, his "attic next the sky," his own equivalent of the tower in Fitzwilliam Square, Dublin, and there from his new angle of vision begins a metastasis, a rewriting of his old vision of the world. In his long poem *Roman Script*, written in Yeats's familiar *ottava rima*, he declares with the Italian poet Pasolini, amidst the rubbish of modern Rome, "*in the refuse of the world a new world is born*"—as close as he can get to the Yeatsian view of tragic joy. Mahon appends to the final octet a separate sestet, thereby turning the final section into a remarkable sonnet entitled "(*A Rewrite: Metastasio*)." In echoing and letting reverberate the belief of Coventry Patmore, Yeats, and Heaney that "the end of art is peace," and on the verge of awakening from the nightmare of history, he confesses that the designs of his art have long deceived his heart, which now lies soft and open before us. In his extraordinary "rewrite" of the relation of art and history and the source of the true, the concluding stanzas reveal the ennobling force and the transformative power in time of Yeats's great legacy on another poet:

> I invent dreams and stories, and even as I outline
> dreams and romances on the unwritten page
> I enter into them with so soft a heart
> I weep at evils of my own design.
> I've more sense when not deceived by art;
> The creative spirit is quiet then and rage,
> love, genuine emotions, spring for once
> from real life and from felt experience.
>
> Ah, but words on the page aren't the whole story
> for all my hopes and fears are fictions too
> and I live in a virtual fever of creation—
> the whole course of my life has been imagination,
> my days a dream; when we wake from history
> may we find peace in the substance of the true.
> (*CP,* 276–77)

Though it seems that Mahon kept the greatest distance for the longest time from Yeats, his return journey was perhaps evident to others at the beginning. When Longley wrote his lecture "Yeats the Tragedian" in 1970, he believed that the one Belfast poet with Yeats's tragic sense was Mahon. "No one has written better about Belfast than Derek Mahon," he wrote. "His vision of that city is profounder, more critical and more generous than MacNeice's I think. MacNeice never really journeyed beyond a kind of fascinated distaste for the 'city built upon mud, the culture built upon profit.'"[53] Longley believed that, for anyone who wants to understand the North of Ireland, Mahon's "In Belfast" should be required reading. "I think that these lines," he said as he prepared to quote the poem (which Mahon has since banished from his canon),[54] "for all their surface cheekiness, demonstrate a Yeatsian sweep and generosity." Now, forty-three years later, the gyres and the antinomies of art and history, imagination and anarchy having run yet another generational course, what Longley, Boland, Heaney, and Mahon have achieved in their finest poems is precisely that hardest won of legacies, that Yeatsian sweep and generosity, that altitude and nobility of the unconstrained imagination.[55]

NOTES

1. Peter Fallon and Derek Mahon, eds., *The Penguin Book of Contemporary Irish Poetry* (London: Penguin Books, 1990), xvi.

2. Desmond O'Grady, *My Fields This Springtime* (Belfast: Lapwing Publications, 1993), 10.

3. In paying tribute to Yeats's influence on both himself and his entire generation, Auden stated that "there is scarcely a lyric written today in which the influence of his style and rhythm is not detectable." See *The Complete Works of W. H. Auden: Prose*, vol. 2, *1939–1948*, ed. Edward Mendelson (Princeton: Princeton University Press, 2002), 384–90.

4. Quoted in an interview with Lucy Hodges, "Poetry in Motion," *Times Higher Education Supplement*, November 17, 1995, 18.

5. Paul Muldoon, "7, Middagh Street," in *Meeting the British* (1987), in *Poems 1968–1998* (New York: Farrar, Straus, and Giroux, 2001), 178. For earlier studies of Yeats and Muldoon, see Jonathan Allison, "Questioning Yeats: Paul Muldoon's '7, Middagh Street,'" and William A. Wilson, "Yeats, Muldoon, and Heroic History," in *Learning the Trade: Essays on W. B. Yeats and Contemporary Poetry*, ed. Deborah Fleming, 3–38 (West Cornwall, CT: Locus Hill Press, 1993).

6. Paul Muldoon, *To Ireland, I* (Oxford: Oxford University Press, 2000), 130.

7. The lecture was published in Paul Muldoon, *The End of the Poem* (Oxford: Oxford University Press, 2000), chap. 1, "'All Souls's Night' by W. B. Yeats." Muldoon more recently wrote the introduction to the Modern

Library reissuing (2003) of Yeats's *Irish Fairy and Folk Tales*, and in an online interview from December 9, 2002, he says that Yeats is "head and shoulders above all of us . . . so much so that he is ignored rather than addressed" (the interview can be found through the WBUR Boston Radio web site: http://theconnection.wbur.org). He goes on to describe the intricate ways in which he used Yeats's "A Prayer for my Daughter" for his poem "At the Sign of the Black Horse, September 1999" in *Moy Sand and Gravel* (2002).

8. McGuckian's holograph "Hons III" paper at Queen's University, Belfast, "The Idea of an Anglo-Irish Poetic Tradition," with Heaney's commentary, is in the McGuckian papers, Special Collections, Robert W. Woodruff Library, Emory University.

9. "An Attitude of Compassions," interview with Kathleen McCracken, *Irish Literary Studies* (Fall 1990), 20. In a later interview McGuckian describes how she finds Yeats (along with Beckett) terribly overpowering: "Even to *say* the word *Yeats* or *Beckett*. I say those words and it's like a fly talking to a horse. It's like two different species." See Deirdre Murphy, "Interview with Medbh McGuckian," *Irish Literary Supplement* 16 (Spring 1997), 22. And yet, she seems to have subtly rewritten "Leda and the Swan" as "Sky-Writing," where the poet as Leda, relishing her after-love, impregnated inwardness, wonders if she shall "ever again be caught up gently / As the rustle of a written address by the sky?" See Medbh McGuckian, *Marconi's Cottage* (Winston-Salem, NC: Wake Forest University Press, 1992), 79.

10. Unpublished letter of 1994 from Calvin Bedient to Ciaran Carson, writing of a meeting to be arranged with Carson in Belfast regarding Bedient's work on Yeats and contemporary Irish poets. Carson papers, Special Collections, Emory University.

11. "Ciaran Carson: Interviewed by Rand Brandes," *The Irish Review* (Fall 1990), 89. Carson continued: "I've mentioned other genres like SF and crime writing . . . then I read a lot of American poetry, European poetry. I've recently been re-reading Yannis Ritsos, the Greek poet, and I feel some kindred spirit there . . . images of imprisonment, mutilation, the bizarre and surreal things which happen in a police state . . . and W. S. Merwin's translations of Mandelstam are always hanging around in the back of my mind."

12. Ciaran Carson, *Opera Et Cetera* (Winston-Salem, NC: Wake Forest University Press, 1996), 85. In an undated letter to Peter Fallon, Carson wrote: "I enclose Opera Et Cetera. . . . I also thought of dedicating each poem in Opera as follows: . . . B: W. B. Yeats." Carson papers (Box 6, fol. 13), Emory University.

13. Yeats himself dates the change from "Nineteen Hundred and Nineteen," as evident in his 1938 inscription in James Healey's copy of *Seven Poems and a Fragment:* "I think the poem called 'Thoughts upon the present state of the world' ['Nineteen Hundred and Nineteen'] was the first poem in

what critics call my 'later manner.' It was written when the Black & Tans were busy, and their actions more than anything at the time had plunged me into gloom. Before this I had written of old myths & personal passion" (James A. Healy Collection, Stanford University Archive, printed in *W. B. Yeats and the Irish Renaissance: An Exhibition of Books and Manuscripts from the James Healey Collection* [Stanford: Stanford University Libraries, 1990], 46). See Conrad A. Balliet, *W. B. Yeats: A Census of the Manuscripts* (New York: Garland Publishing, 1990), 51, 292; and Michael B. Yeats, *"Something to Perfection Brought"* (Stanford: Stanford University Libraries, 1976), n.p.

14. W. B. Yeats, *A Vision* (New York: Collier Books, 1972), 25.

15. In "The Young Eavan and Early Boland" (1993), Mahon recalls the influences on the poems that made up *New Territory* (1967): "First there is Yeats—with whom, as I *do* remember, Eavan was obsessed when I first knew her" (Derek Mahon, *Journalism* [Loughcrew: Gallery Press, 1996], 107). He later recalled that in her "Belfast vs. Dublin," written for Mahon, "The Belfast spirit she sees as Whiggish, rancorously egalitarian and democratic; while the Dublin spirit, best described as 'republican royalist,' she derived in large measure from Yeats." See Mahon's typescript, "The King and I" (27), a lecture delivered at the Yeats International Summer School, Sligo, in August 1996. Mahon papers, Special Collections, Emory University.

16. Unpublished letter of March 25, 1966, Longley papers, Special Collections, Emory University.

17. Eavan Boland, *New Territory* (Dublin: Allen Figgis, 1967), 22. The poem first appeared in the *Dublin Magazine* 5 (Summer 1966): 26. The volume was dedicated to her mother with a line from Yeats's *Sophocles' Oedipus at Colonus* (1934), "A word, a solitary word tells all, and that word is love" (*The Variorum Edition of the Plays of W. B. Yeats*, ed. Russell K. Alspach [New York: Macmillan, 1969], 896).

18. Longley's holograph scripts and typescripts for the film program are in the Longley papers (Box 30), Emory University.

19. T. S. Eliot, *Complete Poems and Plays* (New York: Harcourt Brace, 1952), 180.

20. See Longley's holograph manuscript, "Yeats's Effect on Young Contemporary Poets" (7), delivered August 12, 1969. Longley papers (Box 37), Emory University.

21. Longley papers (Box 37), Emory University.

22. Eavan Boland, "The Weasel's Tooth," *Irish Times*, June 7, 1974, 12. On this episode in Boland's career, see Terence Brown's essay, "Heart Mysteries There: *The War Horse*," *Irish University Review* 23 (Spring/Summer 1993): 34–39.

23. Eavan Boland, *Object Lessons* (New York and London: W. W. Norton, 1995), 25; hereafter cited parenthetically as *OL*.

24. Eavan Boland, "Outside History," in *Outside History: Selected Poems 1980–1990* (New York: W. W. Norton, 1990), 50.

25. René E. Olander, "An Interview with Eavan Boland," *AWP Chronicle* 29 (May/Summer 1997), 6.

26. Eavan Boland, "The Northern Writers' Crisis of Conscience," *Irish Times,* August 13, 1970, 12.

27. Jody Allen Randolph, "A Backward Look: An Interview with Eavan Boland," *PN Review* 26 (May–June 2000), 43.

28. Seamus Heaney, "Feeling into Words," in *Finders Keepers* (New York: Farrar, Straus, and Giroux, 2001), 25. This volume is hereafter cited parenthetically as *FK*.

29. Seamus Heaney, *The Government of the Tongue* (New York: Farrar, Straus, and Giroux, 1989), 101; hereafter cited parenthetically as *GT.*

30. Quotations from Heaney's poems are from *Opened Ground: Selected Poems 1966–1996* (New York: Farrar, Straus, and Giroux, 1998), 148, 245, 385; hereafter cited parenthetically as *OG.*

31. "The Visionary Daring of Yeats Undiminished," *Boston Globe,* March 12, 1989, B17. A revised version of Heaney's untitled poem for the occasion, "Where does spirit live? Inside or Outside" (Derry: Field Day Theatre Company, 1989), appeared in *Seeing Things* (*OG,* 346).

32. Originally delivered in the Guildhall, Derry, on January 28, 1989, the fiftieth anniversary of Yeats's death; subsequently published in *Fortnight* (Belfast), March 1989, and in America in *Four Quarters* 3 (Fall 1989): 11–14, here 11.

33. Heaney continued to reflect on the nature of Yeats's nobility in his review of R. F. Foster's biography. To Heaney, Yeats "created an enduring profile of himself as a noble poet working toward high national (and supranational) purposes," and he concludes that "the real attraction of Yeats lies in the essential nobility of his mind, the way he combined ardor with rigor, the ideal of service behind and beneath the self-centeredness and the attitudinizing." See Seamus Heaney, "All Ireland's Bard," *Atlantic Monthly* 280 (November 1997), 158, 160.

34. Seamus Heaney, "William Butler Yeats," in *The Field Day Anthology of Irish Writing,* vol. 2, ed. Seamus Deane (Derry: Field Day Publications, 1991), 783. Hereafter cited parenthetically as *FD*.

35. Seamus Heaney, *The Redress of Poetry* (New York: Farrar, Straus and Giroux, 1995), 163.

36. Interview with Eamon Grennan, "Derek Mahon: The Art of Poetry LXXXII," *The Paris Review* 154 (Spring 2000): 150–78, here 159. Hereafter cited parenthetically as *PR*.

37. See James J. Murphy, Lucy McDiarmid, and Michael J. Durkan, "Q. and A. with Derek Mahon," *Irish Literary Supplement* 10 (Fall 1991), 27.

38. See Dillon Johnston, *Irish Poetry after Joyce*, 2nd ed. (Syracuse: Syracuse University Press, 1997), 24.

39. Muldoon, *Poems 1968–1998*, 189.

40. Derek Mahon, *Collected Poems* (Oldcastle: Gallery Books, 1999), 63. Hereafter cited parenthetically as *CP*.

41. See Mahon's *Selected Poems* (London: Viking/Gallery, 1991), 49. Hereafter cited parenthetically as *SP*. The poem was not included in *Collected Poems*. Mahon's distance from Yeats is evident in the final stanza of another poem dedicated to Durcan, "Hunger":

One fortunate in both would have us choose
"Perfection of the life or of the work".
Nonsense, you work best on a full stomach
As everybody over thirty knows—
For who, unbreakfasted, will love the lark?
Prepare your protein-fed epiphanies,
Your heavenly mansions blazing in the dark.

(*CP*, 119)

42. The stanzas in which these lines appear were among the four stanzas deleted from "Girls on the Bridge" when it was republished in *CP*, 152–53.

43. O'Grady, *My Fields This Springtime*, 3. O'Grady clearly alludes to the "casual comedy" that precedes the "terrible beauty" of Yeats's "Easter, 1916."

44. Mahon, *Journalism*, 129.

45. "A Yeats Symposium," *The Guardian*, Books, January 27, 1989, 26.

46. William Scammell, "Derek Mahon Interviewed," *Poetry Review* 81 (Summer 1991), 5.

47. Lannan Literary Videos, No. 38 (Los Angeles: Lannan Foundation, 1994). Mahon read from his poems and gave the interview on March 8, 1994.

48. It was about this time that Mahon proposed and signed on with the Lilliput Press in Dublin to bring out a new anthology of Yeats's poems, under the title *This Craft of Verse: A Yeats Reader*, selected and introduced by Derek Mahon, but the project was abandoned. In his earlier anthology, *Modern Irish Poetry* (London: Sphere Books, 1972), Mahon duly recognized Yeats's genius and the permanence of his poems but qualified the nature of his heritage in maintaining a personal and editorial distance from him: "It has become fashionable in recent years to denigrate Yeats's virtues and achievements. . . . It's when we come to his extrapoetical activities that the

problems begin. . . . The rejection of plays by the Abbey Theatre and the exclusion of poets from anthologies, no less than his generous (if often misguided) encouragement to those writers of whom he approved, determined the course and character of the Revival and delineated a received version of the Irish literary imagination from which it took many years to recover. At least three writers of international stature (Joyce, George Moore, O'Casey) refused to recognise the Yeatsian court; but the poets themselves, for whom expatriation was not an attractive prospect, stayed at home and toed the line. Which is an unkind way of saying that they wrote the verse they wrote and it met with the Master's approval" (11–12).

49. Mahon papers (Box 24), Emory University. A revised version of this lecture appears as "Yeats and the Lights of Dublin" in the *Dublin Review* 8 (Autumn 2002): 68–81.

50. Mahon identifies passages with page numbers in his *Selected Poems;* from "Beyond Howth Head," 44, the stanza beginning "lost townlands on the crumbling shores"; 46, stanza beginning "I woke this morning (March) to hear"; 49, stanza beginning "the light that left you streaks the walls"; from "A Disused Shed in Co. Wexford," 62, stanza beginning "Deep in the grounds of a burnt-out hotel"; from "Going Home," 97, stanza beginning "Crone, crow, scarecrow"; from "Derry Morning," 123, stanza beginning "Here it began, and here at last"; from "The Sea in Winter," 117, stanza beginning "One day, the day each one conceives—"; and from *The Hudson Letter*, "Imbolc." When "Beyond Howth Head" appeared in *Lives* (London: Oxford University Press, 1972), Mahon provided notes to the poem that identify additional Yeatsian sources: "*Embroidered cloths*. Yeats: 'Aedh Wishes for the Cloths of Heaven'. . . *Still break stone*. Yeats: "Parnell came down the road, he said to a cheering man: Ireland shall get her freedom and you still break stone'" (39).

51. When Mahon was asked about the "business" of poetry readings in an interview, "Is there any point in all this literary business beside the 'business'?" he replied, "My answer is a quotation from Yeats, which is quite simply, 'A lonely impulse of delight.' To tell the honest truth, I try to fend off thoughts of those things . . . I believe in the lonely impulse of delight. I hate the 'business.'" See Murphy, McDiarmid, and Durkan, "Q. and A. with Derek Mahon," 28.

52. Derek Mahon, *The Yellow Book* (Winston Salem, NC: Wake Forest University Press, 1998), 57. Mahon deleted the line "a lone figure pointing to the horizon" when he revised the poem for inclusion in *Collected Poems* (265).

53. See MacNeice's "Autumn Journal," section 16, "A city built upon mud; / A culture built upon profit; / Free speech nipped in the bud, / The minority always guilty. / Why should I want to go back / To you, Ireland, my Ireland?"

54. "In Belfast" first appeared in *Icarus* 42 (March 1964) and was subsequently published as "Poem in Belfast (for Michael Longley)" in Derek Mahon, *Twelve Poems* (Queen's University Belfast: Festival Publications, 1965), [8]. It then appeared without the dedication in Derek Mahon, *Night-Crossing* (London: Oxford University Press, 1968), 6. It last appeared under a new title, "The Spring Vacation," with the dedication restored, in Derek Mahon, *Poems 1962–1978* (Oxford: Oxford University Press, 1971), 4.

55. The original version of this essay was delivered as a plenary lecture at a conference entitled "'The Resilient Voice': Northern Irish Poetry 1960 to the Present," held at the Institute of English Studies, University of London, March 2003. This essay was first published in the *Irish University Review* 34:2 (Autumn–Winter, 2004): 291–314, and is reprinted here with permission.

CHAPTER 12

"All that Consequence"
Yeats and Eliot at the End of the End of History

JED ESTY

T. S. Eliot admired the late Yeats precisely because it was this Yeats—
not the Celtic Revivalist of the 1890s—who had become fully Irish,
just as he himself had become fully English only during the compo-
sition of a late, unconventionally Anglocentric poem, *Four Quartets*
(in which Yeats makes a spectral cameo appearance). Several ques-
tions are raised by the casting of Yeats and Eliot as fellow national
poets who meditate during the 1930s on the fallen houses of the
state's patrimony (Coole Park, Burnt Norton). Does their late work
invest in the nation as an organic entity subject to cycles of life,
death, and resurrection within the broader, more linear metanarrative
of civilizational decline? Do the personae adopted by Yeats and Eliot
in their later works represent a shift away from the belated "end of
history" viewpoint so often featured in their earlier work? What are
the temporal and historical models implied, in each case, by the at-
tempts Yeats and Eliot made to allegorize their own aging in terms of
national or civilizational decline?

What makes these questions intriguing is the fact that both Yeats and Eliot were prematurely old poets who in their early careers frequently struck poses of satiric distance and assumed masks of cold irony amidst the passions and attachments of heady youth. No reader of the early poetry of Yeats or of Eliot can fail to notice how curiously aged so many of their speakers and personae seem to be; the progeria runs from Prufrockian inhibition to Yeats's stifled rage, from the world-weary, meaning-starved spirit of Eliot's "Gerontion" to the word-weary, passion-starved speakers of *The Green Helmet.* The more we look back on anti-Romantic Eliot, the more he seems never to have been young; a poem like "La Figlia che Piange" offers a master class in poetic distantiation from adolescent lust and sensation, introducing an agitated speaker who conjures a beautiful girl, but quickly wraps her in Italianate conventions, derealizes her with abstraction, then settles on his own sighing neuralgia as the true subject of the poem; it is the equal of any of Yeats's Maud-Gonne-driven lyrics of thwarted passion.[1] Of course it is a minor paradox of modernist impersonality, a concept overlapping early Eliot and mid-period Yeats, that only a poet susceptible to great sweeps and dark depths of feeling need invent, and so rigorously continue to reinvent, such means of distantiation—those masks and poses, those baffled or etiolated desires.

In Yeats's case, the reticence and antiquarianism of the 1890s gave way to zesty, lusty experimentation in middle age. Few of the stories we tell about Yeats cling as tenaciously as the myth of a man and poet growing in reverse, moving toward greater immediacy and forceful sexuality, begetting new styles, late-fathered children, and a dazzling Chinese box of artistic selves opening up even in the shadow of a great, and thus potentially stultifying, reputation. Whether midwifed by Pound at Stone Cottage, sparked by late marriage, triggered via the discovery of automatic writing as Parnassian mediumship, inspired by the example of the newly hatched Irish nation-state, or self-begotten in a remarkable series of critical and aesthetic renovations, Yeats's youth seems to be happening not just belatedly but, after a certain point, almost continuously.

What is striking and interpretively challenging about the rhetoric of youthful progeria and late juvenescence in Yeats is that he (like

Eliot) continually tries to conceptualize the problem of history in relation to the running drama of youth, maturity, senescence, mortality, and death. The aged personae of the early poetry tend to allegorize history from the point of view of detached witnesses, desensualized bystanders. By contrast, the mature poems of both Yeats and Eliot come far closer to assimilating historical time and civilizational crisis into the life story or lifespan, the organismic being, of the speakers so that they are no longer simply observing but somehow embodying the creative destruction of modernity. Just as this assimilative historicism occurs, though, it appears to trigger a counterhistorical panic of sorts, resulting in the most famous and most famously modernist achievements of the two poets, the great myth-making and system-building works of the 1920s. It is almost as if time's bullet, once threaded through the barrel of the mortal poet, must be comprehensively retarded or diverted into some other kind of cosmological time-scheme projected beyond or beneath the secular-historicist crust of modernity. Vulnerable to history as they were, Yeats and Eliot seem nevertheless to become antihistorical writers in the period of *The Tower* and *The Waste Land*.

In this essay, I compare the poetic responses of Yeats and Eliot to the predicament of their failed antihistoricism, with special attention to the intersecting problems of creeping mortality and civilizational crisis in the later 1930s work, a period of significant aesthetic reinvention (and ideological strain) in the careers of both poets. Rather than return to the question of how Yeats and Eliot attempted to dehistoricize time in general, to convert *chronos* to *kairos* in the model of Frank Kermode, my line of inquiry turns on a more specific question about the relation of national time to civilizational time. Instead of reading Yeats and Eliot according to a familiar narrative of older poets who subside into conservative forms of religion and national politics, we might come to view their later stages and last works in terms of a fatal grappling with history qua existential time, untethered at the last from all those mythopoetic thresholds and minor apocalypses, from the booms and busts of modernism's moralized historical imagination.

In their early and middle phases, both Yeats and Eliot wrote a number of poems using what we might call the "Gerontion" perspective of belatedness, a vantage point from which the poetic persona looks back on the wastes of history. In those poems, the speaker or poet witnesses a long trajectory of historical or civilizational decay but does not himself embody the decadence. In their later works, however, both Yeats and Eliot present speakers who assimilate rather than merely witness the ruin of history. Before taking that consideration all the way into one of the last acts of Yeats's career in the form of his blasted, stunted play, *Purgatory,* let us briefly consider the broader modernist problematic of afterwords—of aging personae and late style. The prose and poetry of Anglophone modernism, for all that it has been characterized as a bluff or vanguardist youth movement turning tables on a sclerotic and senescent Victorian world, contains a surprising preponderance of symbolically central old men and women. Aging bodies and old souls proliferate across the pages of modernist texts, with wise widows and toothy crones, old scarecrows and grizzly prophets appearing to embody any number of millennial or valedictory projects in the modernist canon. Consider, for example, the dignified older women of Forster and Woolf: Mrs. Wilcox and Mrs. Moore, Mrs. Dalloway and Mrs. Ramsay (in *Howards End, A Passage to India, Mrs. Dalloway,* and *To the Lighthouse*)—all living centers of humane values as well as emblems of a frail and faltering humanism.

Indeed as twenty-first-century readers watch modernism recede into the background of a century now well past, the movement's unrepentant adolescent self-regard and rebellious energy are slowly losing their art-historical salience. Edward Said notes in *On Late Style:*

Modernism has come to seem paradoxically not so much a movement of the new as a movement of aging and ending, a sort of "Age masquerading as Juvenility," to quote Hardy in *Jude the Obscure.* For indeed the figure in that novel of Jude's son, Father Time, does seem like an allegory of modernism with its sense of accelerated decline and its compensating gestures of recapitulation and inclusiveness.[2]

Gestures of recapitulation and inclusiveness make it tempting, and often productive, to read Yeats and Eliot together and to think about how each addressed his own sense of civilizational decline even amidst discourses of national renewal. As late as Yeats's 1914 volume *Responsibilities*, and, in Eliot's case, "Gerontion," many of their poems appear to face the broad problem of decline from perspectives that put the lyric speaker himself outside the stream of history and generation, outside the laws of time and biology (the Teiresias of *The Waste Land* being only the most conspicuous example). To some extent, though, both poets begin in the 1920s to gain ironic distance on the ironically distanced personae who populate their earlier work and who can neither compose history's fragments nor countenance its drift.

Moving schematically through the most celebrated phases of the two careers in question, we might say that Eliot and Yeats developed strong forms for confronting the depredations of modernity and the nightmare of history after World War I. Both began to build antihistorical concepts into their poems and into the defensive ramparts of their critical prose, using these forms to manage and contain the raw drip of historical time. Such an aesthetically heroic project (not entirely a term of praise) encompasses Eliot's mythic method and endlessly self-collating Tradition as well as Yeats's perning gyres and exorbitantly collated *Vision*. Critics have offered many different and differently compelling ways to periodize the careers of Yeats and Eliot; many of those ways overlap and intersect on this fulcrum point: that the works of the 1920s mark the acme of modernist myth-making and system-building power, where poetic texts seem somehow to overcome or transcode a fragmented historical memory, turning the pure linear or mechanical time of *chronos* into the harmonic or redemptive time that Kermode calls *kairos*.

For Yeats as for Eliot, the early motifs of thwarted libido, of masking and posing, marked off occasions on which the poetic subject could lyricize its own separation from history. Speakers in those early Yeats/Eliot poems stay attuned to the social reverberations of large events and to a historical context pregnant with eschatological meaning, but they are unable to round *chronos* into *kairos*. Later, in the high-modernist phase of the 1920s, the Yeats/Eliot lyric speaker moves beyond disaffected witnessing and antimodern plaint by staging the fate of a self or soul whose crises are fully bound up with—not just moodily refracting—the major historical problems of the day, such as war, revolution, economic crisis, and spiritual collapse. In this rough two-phase framing of their careers, the first features an overweening crisis mentality about the decline of the west matched to a series of personal crises of sexual nerve animating a mannered neo-Symbolist aesthetic. The second features a set of projects designed to force the mannered observer into more full-throated and hot-blooded participation in social life, or to force a simultaneous interpenetration of soul and collective, of poetic form and historical meaning.

After the myths-and-systems of the 1920s, we might then propose a third phase in which both Yeats and Eliot struggled to admit the devastating force of history back into poetry without exerting the same degree of eschatological control over its temporalization. With this possibility in mind, we might say that history's corrosive power is (a) witnessed in phase one by detached individuated subjects; (b) contained in phase two by mature and magisterial poetic forms signaling communal modes of reference; and (c) suffered in phase three as both an individual and collective predicament. Vulnerability to time returns in this third moment, this rigorously historicist late-career burst, and the concept of a graphed or bounded *kairos* gives way to a *chronos* more radical than ever. In the final, compacted phase of the late 1930s, the effective end of the two poetic careers (though not of Eliot's career as a writer), both the early aesthetic of witnessing and the mature aesthetic of embodiment seem co-present, partially transcended and recombined into a language of metahistorical reflection.

At this point, though, it becomes less critically productive to co-narrate the two careers, for Eliot's concept of a Christian England provides a temporal backstop that Yeats, one might say, cannot conceive from his more secular (pagan) vantage point within an Irish nation rapidly forfeiting what he sees as its high destiny.[3] Eliot, wrestling afresh with the force of *chronos*, comes to a new way of assimilating raw historical and existential time into a more stable temporal order, but it requires more than the high style of the poetic magus—it requires the language and indeed the ground conditions of cultural revival on a broad scale. Meanwhile, Yeats, working now at a safer distance from the blandishments of cultural revivalism, finds a new way to objectify his own longstanding impulses to bury *chronos* in *kairos,* a new way to cast doubt on his own recuperative and order-making, time-tempering devices, whether composed in the key of Celtic myth or tragic joy.

In view of this split, and bearing Eliot in mind as an important point of aesthetic and analytical reference, we might attempt to insert a third term into the fairly well-established dialectical or dyadic shape of historical thinking in Yeats. Such thinking was laid out systematically years ago in Thomas Whitaker's *Swan and Shadow,* which argues that two basic positions jockey for command across the length of Yeats's long career:

> The first, that of the creative vision, affords a God's-eye view of the panorama of history. . . . The second perspective is, in a sense, the daimon's retort to the potential or actual hubris of the first. It is the perspective of dramatic experience, of existential immersion in history, where the anti-self may be, as in "Ego Dominus Tuus," more disturbingly and dangerously confronted.[4]

Whitaker's second or "shadow" position still has an implied eschatology, an end of history that the self or poetic subject comes to embody. I want to explore the end of that end in the very last stages of Yeats's writing.

When the mature Yeats looks back on his ability to intertwine the import of a single life (his own) with the matter of historical time, he remains generally willing to assume the allegorical burden of the representative soul. Consider these lines from "Private Thoughts" (1938), where Yeats meditates on his own forebears:

> Now that I am old and live in the past . . . I discover all these men in my single mind, think that I myself have gone through the same vicissitudes . . . then I go beyond those minds and my single mind and discover that I have been describing everybody's struggle, and the gyres turn in my thoughts. Vico was the first modern philosopher to discover in his own mind, and in the European past, all human destiny.[5]

James Longenbach cites this passage in his authoritative account of Yeats's thinking about history, in which he canvasses the congruities between "Yeatsian mysticism" and the existential historicism of Dilthey. The latter was a strand of thinking that the young Eliot, scenting romantic individualism, already sensed was too subjectivist for his taste.[6] This germ of a difference, evident in Eliot's 1919 review of *The Cutting of an Agate,* resurfaces, I would suggest, on the far side of their careers.

For both Yeats and Eliot, but also for novelists like Lawrence, Ford, Woolf, and Joyce, the *kairos/chronos* problem—or, one might say, the problem that Hegel described in the memorable phrase *schlecht Unendlichkeit* ("bad infinity")—was the besetting crisis of aesthetic form. It required heroic methods to address it. Like so many modernist intellectuals inheriting the bitter entailments of nineteenth-century secular historicism, Yeats and Eliot tended to doubt that modernity's temporal regime represented rational progress; instead modernity seemed to be unfolding as a painful succession of one valueless moment by another, the time of *chronos* or "mere successiveness."[7] As an artistic counterdiscourse, high modernism seeks to give narrative form, aesthetic meaning, or spiritual value to time—to (re) endow it with *kairos*. As Kermode defines it, *kairos* refers to meaningfully shaped or end-directed time, time that integrates past, present, and future. Some of anglophone modernism's most ambitious projects were motivated by the ideal of *kairos* and its opposition to linear history: Joyce's Viconian cycles and Lawrence's apocalyptic endings, not to mention the system-building works of Yeats and Eliot described earlier. These counternarratives to secular, linear time were self-consciously marginal positions taken against the mainstream bourgeois view of history.[8]

The time of "mere successiveness" plagued Eliot in his high modernist phase. The historical horizon of *The Waste Land* requires that it acknowledge the regnant conditions of empty time, of time demoralized and drained of its meaning, and thus of space spattered into the fractured albeit stimulating life of the European capitals. Eliot's later work, however, moves away from this high modernist formation precisely insofar as it assumes not the continued dominance but the potential and imminent failure of the linear, homogenous time guaranteed by modern progress and expansion. If World War I was the cataclysm that ended European visions of endless progress, the subsequent economic and political crises of the interwar period only offered more ill omens pointing to a dark cyclical spin of history. From this basis, however, Eliot begins in the 1930s to think of his own non-linear temporal models (based on Christian eternity) as something more than a vexed wish expressed in art. Modernism's fierce investment in the principle of *kairos*—its cultural Bergsonism—seemed suddenly to be confirmed and reinforced by the external machinations of history, even if the way up to redemption, for Eliot's reintegrated English culture, entailed the way down for an entropic European civilization. With imperial decline and fascist rebarbarization working to discredit the progressive narratives of secular modernity, *kairos* migrates from its confinement within the aesthetic sphere to become the principle of what Eliot will imagine as an Anglocentric revival. Under this new dispensation, his writing no longer needs to rage at shapeless time, nor to retail aesthetic wholeness to an unwhole and untimely metropolis. Instead, it begins to posit and elaborate a distinctive (and eschatological) shape for English culture, and it does so precisely at the moment that Yeats begins finally to despair of Ireland ever achieving its high national destiny, of saving itself from the cursed fate of Western modernity at large.

In Eliot's *Four Quartets*, we see the concept of national revival return to England itself and provide temporal limits to what would otherwise be the infinities of open-jawed secular historicism. History is here and now in the *Quartets*, a slogan that refers not just to England as a place or source of history, but as something in which the fusion of historical time and historicist logic into a more absolute, eternal concept allows Eliot to think through and beyond crisis, that is, to imagine not just apocalypse but redemption for the individual (the poet) and the culture (the nation). Consider a typical temporal conundrum in "Burnt Norton":

> To be conscious is not to be in time
> But only in time can the moment in the rose-garden,
> The moment in the arbour where the rain beat,

The moment in the draughty church at smokefall
Be remembered; involved with past and future.
Only through time time is conquered.[9]

In personal terms, the passage seems to suggest that an achievement of a spiritually meritorious kind of consciousness, an awareness of permanence, depends on living through moments defined by an ordinary and painful knowledge of loss. The poem's allegorical extension of this same principle to the collective or cultural level means that we might think of history (experience) as the necessary precondition to collective spiritual readiness. A collective ability to conceive of timelessness requires having suffered and lived through a certain accumulation of experience—something that the Yeats of the late 1930s could not have conceived similarly for Ireland, which still seemed so raw and fresh and dangerously uncertain as a national project. To put it another way: there is a necessary quantity of moments, of accumulated cultural tradition, that lays the groundwork for a national culture's ability to project itself beyond history. English Christianity, with its historical depth and stability as idealized by Eliot, has accreted a sufficient amount of continuous experience for it to get beyond mere historical time. Thus Eliot's provisional "conquest of time" depends on a cultural formation whose specific history allows it to store—and to symbolize—transhistorical values.[10]

If *Four Quartets* aligns the fate of suffering soul and contracting nation, it also—by dint of that allegorical logic—revises the Symbolist aesthetic so crucial to Eliot's early experiments (up to and including *The Waste Land*). Where Symbolism lends itself to the authority of aesthetic forms (and of distant Platonic ideals), allegory aims for completion through, and reference to, collective tradition. To invoke the symbol/allegory divide in this general way is to propose that *Four Quartets* operates with an assumption of a shared cultural situation, a cultural circuit between text, artist, and audience.[11] As an historically embedded form, allegory tends both to assume and to project cultural order. Here once again one must pause to note how much Yeats reacts to this same phase of late-thirties crisis-mongering by lamenting the actual cultural disorder rather than the potential cultural order of

Ireland. Given the failure of the national ideal in Yeats and its rebirth in Eliot, it is not surprising that Yeats broke more bitterly with Symbolist aesthetics than did Eliot. By the time of *Four Quartets,* Eliot had replaced his high modernist sense of the "futility and anarchy of contemporary history" with the idea that reality already contains a pattern.[12] Such a shift depends on the restoration of a meaningful, manageable English (that is, classical) culture, one that vitiates the bad effects of historical time in ways not previously available to poets working in the long Romantic era from Milton to Modernism. Marking the transition to a new era, *Four Quartets* binds together and authorizes its elements—lines, images, vignettes—according to their relation to *a* culture, not, as in *The Waste Land,* in relation to "culture" per se, after the fashion of cosmopolitan aesthetics.

The meaning of Eliot's late-career religiosity best reveals itself within the context of English revivalism, a context thrown into relief by contrast with Yeats's growing sense of the failure of Irish revivalism. Eliot saw himself as the poet of an old country being reborn just when Yeats saw himself as the poet of a new country dying. What makes the pathos of this Eliot-Yeats comparison all the stronger is that Yeats felt that he had had a major hand in the forging of his nation, Ireland, and that this Frankenstein's creature of a new state had so appalled his conscience that he could no longer even muster for it the vocabulary of tragic dignity, let alone the glory notes of redemptive beginnings.[13] Ireland was a made thing to Yeats; England an inherited one to Eliot, and necessarily so. For only when a national culture predates and undergirds the poet's own attempt to make meaning can a poet like Eliot feel permanence under the phenomenal surfaces of modernity and modernization. Here we begin to see why Yeats's late writings— scoured so fully by time and left unredeemed—have gained potency in the long denouement of our own secular culture while Eliot's have (alas) come more and more to seem like liturgically heavy postscripts to a once-vital poetic career. Yeats's final works suggest that the modernist project that Leo Bersani aptly identified as the culture of redemption was, and had to be, in a strong sense, abandoned to history.[14] Eliot's Dantesque invocations of the way down and the way up were words still aiming to bend the wood of history to the curved frame of eternity, but Yeats's afterwords encode a late, last attempt to do the opposite, to peel away and to purge all the vanities and vestiges of lifelong poetic achievement, to forget the fine art of giving shape to time, to chip and blast away at the high modernist language of crisis and redemption.

Of course, even with this Eliot comparison in view—a comparison that tends to throw Yeats's relative distance from religion into relief, it is very hard to argue that the Yeats of the 1930s manages to let go of the will to tame secular historicism, to shape *chronos* into *kairos*. Through all the various phases and stages and mythoi and topoi recapitulated in his late style, Yeats seems to stay loyal to the project of finding systemic shape or *kairos* for historical time. In that sense one might read the late Yeats as still "radically anti-historical," still dedicated to mitigating what David Lloyd calls the "irreversible temporality of history" at the level of the collective and with what Paul de Man calls "authentically temporal destiny" at the level of the individual.[15] Certainly the poems of Yeats's old age, such as "Lapis Lazuli"[16] with its gaiety "transforming all that dread," continue to try to blunt the brute force of history and mortality through the mechanisms of tragic joy.

Yet in the very final stage of his life and career, and indeed on the stage rather than in the lyric form, Yeats finds a way to imagine an authentic afterwards to his life and works—that is, an afterwards that is not in any sense *his:* a concept of death sufficiently existentialized and secularized as to scrub away the residues of apocalyptic thinking left from the monumental forms of the 1920s. This final decathexis, or withdrawn investment, defines the crucial separation of Yeats from Eliot. It is the decathexis that marks *the end* of the end of history in Yeats, the moment when soul-death and cultural apocalypse no longer seem so fully coextensive and intertwined, and in which historical time can become open-ended and infinite rather than magically or tragically round. In the case of Yeats, we can follow a meaningful career arc implied by the deep shift from "responsibility" (as in "Pardon Old Fathers") to "consequence" (as in *Purgatory*), from an ethical implication in the tragic cycle of historical violence to a kind of impersonal philosophy of history. Drawing together the besetting

modernist problematics of historical viewpoint (belatedness, aliena-
tion) and the historicity of the subject (aging, mortality), Yeats man-
ages, in the end, to outstrip the limits of those themes and thus
to convert the ostensibly humanizing projection of history-as-
autobiography (shortened but shaped by the organismic concept of
lifespan) into an austere and tragic account of historical consequenti-
ality without pathos—an end to the "end of history" and therefore a
valediction to modernism itself.

In *Purgatory*, the ruined house, burned like the holy houses of *Four
Quartets*, stands not just as a foretoken of the coming conflagrations
across Europe, but as an immediate and vivid (vivid in its bare stage-
craft) echo of the Big Houses already destroyed in Ireland, echoing
out along the same past glories as Eliot's valedictory poems:

> Great people lived and died in this house;
> Magistrates, colonels, members of Parliament,
> Captains and Governors, and long ago
> Men that had fought at Aughrim and the Boyne.[17]

The Old Man who takes center stage in *Purgatory* announces that
the leering, whoring jockey who is his own father is also a house-
murderer:

> But he killed the house: to kill a house
> Where great men grew up, married, died,
> I here declare a capital offence.
>   (*VPl*, 1044)

The Old Man stalking and purging a criminal of history cannot win
over the audience (though neither can the Boy, who seems to repre-
sent a casual and ahistorical amorality). It is the Old Man's mistake to
imagine that he can end the consequentiality of history, of humanity,
of error. He states his belief as if the nightmare of history could ever
be biologized, lodged in the blood of a race, restricted to a masculine

line of descent, or even funneled to a single body: "For when the consequence is at an end / The dream must end" (*VPl*, 1042). And this is the central flawed premise not of the play but of its protagonist, the Learlike persona who still believes in tragic action, in the myth of eternal recurrence, in a story of corruption and cycles implicating him, an Oedipus of the will pointing his jack-knife in two directions, both patricidal and filicidal.[18]

After stabbing his son in the face of the burned house and ruined line, the Old Man declares to the spirit of his dead mother:

> I finished all that consequence.
> I killed the lad for he was growing up,
> He would soon take some woman's fancy,
> Beget and pass pollution on.
> (*VPl*, 1049)

But the failure of a merely biological, mythically antipatrilineal solution to the devolutionary spirit of modernity quickly becomes palpable to the Old Man and to the audience:

> Hoof beats! Dear God
> How quickly it returns—beat—beat—
> Her mind cannot hold up that dream
> Twice a murderer and all for nothing.
> (*VPl*, 1049)

The plaguing of the Old Man by historical recurrence in the hoofbeats is not a sensory event for the audience—the stage directions do not indicate that hoofbeats should be produced (though apparently they were, using the percussive verisimilitude of dry coconuts, on the opening run in Dublin in 1938).[19] Absent hoofbeats seal the "eternal recurrence" motif into the limited and failing consciousness of the Old Man—along with the shopworn gender-myth of an Irish maternal soul condemned to suffer its corruption at the hands of a greasy, venal, and tainted modernity (embodied in the antichivalric jockey, that ersatz horseman of the national apocalypse).

But even before the reenacted murder fails the Old Man, there is a problem for his fantasy of finishing "all that consequence": the reenacted coitus of his parents also fails, and for a curious reason. As the Old Man metadramaturgically conjures the scene of his own begetting, the marriage bed of his ruined mother and his profligate father, he is forced to realize that tragic or willful reenactment cannot repair history:

> But there's a problem: she must live
> Through everything in exact detail,
> Driven to it by remorse, and yet
> Can she renew the sexual act
> And find no pleasure in it, and if not,
> If pleasure and remorse must both be there
> Which is the greater?
>
> *(VPl,* 1046)

Marjorie Howes notes that the basic tension in Yeats at large between individual desire on the one hand and racial/national rectitude on the other plays out precisely here in *Purgatory*, at the point where the Old Man realizes the problem of his mother's incorrigible desire.[20] This realization belongs to the perspective of the character, not to Yeats himself; it is in fact the Old Man's impulse to view history through the conception of original sin and violent counter-sin that is incorrigible. Once that impulse has been dramatized as such, Yeats can finally cast the defeat of tragic ends by endlessness not as an aesthetic flaw or social failure, but as a bedrock existential fact.

In *Purgatory*, the long repressed dimension of running history itself comes back on those imaginary hoofbeats. Desire outlasts the moral and tragic dramas of the scene, outlasts the eschatological visions and oedipal compulsions of the Old Man with his wild urge to cancel corruption—the urge that so many readers have seen as an echo of the sinister social hygiene evident in "On the Boiler." But the play does not so much repeat as objectify that moralized reading of a fallen modernity. The scene foretells the play's ending: no ritual act of repetition or destruction stops the machinery of history, the long drama of humanity's regeneration. This Yeats is not just caught up in the possibility of his own death paralleled by the Spenglerian death-spiral of Western civilization, or by the apparent end-days of an Irish Protestant class of worthies, but is also caught up, as the reference to Tertullian in this same passage of *Purgatory* suggests, in the drama of the persistence of history beyond its supposed ends, the persistence of all the life forces—desire, violence, remorse, pleasure—after the death of the individual soul. What David Lloyd properly identifies as the play's "irreducible remainder"[21]—what can no longer be aestheticized, mythologized, or stabilized in the colloidal suspension of poetic language, nor absorbed into myths-and-symbols modernism, is that elemental quantum of pagan time.

Because the play's rhetoric appears to echo the eugenicist screed in "On the Boiler," critical commentary on *Purgatory* has often centered on the problematic figure of miscegenation, but its valence in the two texts is quite different. The miscegenated subject in the play is not simply one more of those "base-born products of base beds" infamously scorned in "Under Ben Bulben." While it is true that the Old Man sees himself and his son (conceived with a tinker's daughter in a ditch) as base-born, the dramatic logic of miscegenation widens to include humanity itself, the species at large. As "Leda and the Swan" reminds us, for Yeats, humanity was always misbegotten and miscegenated—part divine, part bestial—and therefore subjected to history. Even against the deepest arts of *kairos, chronos* wins out. For this reason, and despite the many prevailing readings of *Purgatory* inflected by the specter of fascism and the legacy of Irish national politics, it is, I think, the existentialist frame rather than the eugenicist one that most crucially shapes the meaning of the play.[22]

The Old Man is not a direct spokesman for Yeats to set on stage to vivify the rhetoric of "On the Boiler" in dramatic form; he is, rather, a device used to revisit and test the mettle of eugenicist fantasy. As Howes notes, Yeats appears to have taken some pains in revision to expose the Old Man's failed sensibility, making him "an increasingly unreliable commentator on events." The Old Man's understanding of history and lineage is neither credible nor compelling but an occasion for Yeats to try to exorcise what had become in the end a "degenerate symptom."[23] Yeats's distance from that persona is what *Purgatory* stages for its audience; in the process, the play also takes its distance from the gendered myth of the female Irish body or "mother's soul" as the ever-central symbolic arena for visions of national redemption, cultural reproduction, and tainted transmission.

What draws the bright line between the denunciatory rhetoric of taint and abasement in Yeats's late prose and the late literary act of *Purgatory* is precisely the cessation of inimical thinking. Antinomial concepts had fueled Yeats his whole poetic life, but in these last words the violent, troubling vision of civilization as corrupted and crumbling and dogged by dark auguries gives way to a more fundamental comprehension that one need not drum up meaning out of the long linear blankness of historical time but can, indeed must, accede to its blankness. This is Yeats's mortality dirge rung out in the tones not of tragic or apocalyptic crescendo, but in minor-chord diminuendos, filling the stage with proto-existentialist thrums as the modernist mage exits the scene. Helen Vendler notes that in "The Gyres," written just a few years before *Purgatory*, Yeats had already cleared the way for a relaxation of his charged antinomial dualism by removing the notion of the culture-enemy from the scene.[24] All the vapid and greasy destroyers of ancestral beauty, all the philistine challengers to high lofty conception begin to fall away along with their more famous counterparts, the emblems and images of "The Circus Animals' Desertion." And in "The Gyres," the seeping of meaning, its leaching of itself by the offices of pure time is the story to be told: "Things thought too long can be no longer thought / For beauty dies of beauty, worth of worth" (*VP*, 565). Yeats may still be masking at the end with his projection of eugenicist rage into the symbolic marionette of the Old Man, but he seems bent on deflating the value of masks and their signature affects on the tragic stage (anger, lust, grief, joy). The Old Man's "rage to end all things" is the precise type of anger that one might mistakenly take as the engine of Yeats's own late style, but *Purgatory* gives Yeats an opportunity to externalize, and thus gain aesthetic distance from, the finalizing fury. In the play, the fury, rhetorically amplified and dramatically concentrated, dies of itself.

Reading the Old Man as an ironic figure (rather than as the spokesman of Yeats's age and rage) means pushing the play outside the norms of Aristotelian catharsis: what is purged here is tragic purgation itself, especially to the extent that tragic emotions tend to dignify existential time by embedding it into some deeper, stronger concept of destiny.[25] Even the most desperate and self-negating acts of the human will, as in the Old Man's filicide-patricide, are not capable of rounding time into tragedy, forcing history into apocalypse or rapture. History animates this dramatic piece not in the guise of fate, myth, or gyre, but in its emptiest form, as *chronos*. Late Eliot seems to absorb historical time into religious meaning, and late Yeats to absorb it into myth, but neither of them ever underestimated the social or symbolic power of time-as-*chronos;* both stage the confrontation with linear time as a kind of epic battle for poetic language, forcing it into ever-adapting swoops of paradox, ever-more austere and gnostic positions and negations.

Despite their shared respect for the challenge of secular or existential historicism to the innate dignity of art, however, late Eliot and late Yeats part company at this turning point in literary history.[26] Yeats manages to execute a final swerve away from *kairos*, a swerve that has had long-lasting consequences for his afterlife as a poet and dramatist. By objectifying the antihistorical, indeed history-killing, impulses of the Old Man in *Purgatory*, Yeats opens up his last public script to the existential plenitude of pure time—time not used up by history, time not sacrificed to timelessness, time neither hardened nor frozen by the tectonic shifts of western empire and eastern church, neither exhausted nor emptied by the fact of death, nor by the abolition of the poet's ego, nor even by art's rage for order. At the end of *Purgatory*, the state of things does not merely decline, nor do events simply repeat; no apocalyptic or dialectical transformations are triggered. Moments tick on after the last words are uttered, after the curtain falls, and those grand, gyroscopic Yeatsian motifs of recurrence and repetition, those long-legged themes of ancestral and national declension, are themselves and at last relativized by the unending sweep of time.[27]

Purgatory purges the temptation to use poetry to deprive death and history of their sting. It is surprising to many readers of Yeats to find in the end a concept of time that is no longer heroically, tragically, or mythically charged with meaning, but lies out in the open, on stage, quite fully decathected and existentialized. But if it is true that Eliot's

Christian homiletics finally subordinate the historical bottom line to an allegory of eternity, it is equally true that Yeats marks out his own course by showcasing the Old Man's inability to end history. Yeats's afterwords—his valediction to modernism—unlike Eliot's, point the way forward to the postwar age of anxiety and to the existential, absurdist motifs associated with Auden and Beckett, Camus and Sartre. The blasted tree on the stage in *Purgatory* may, on the one hand, refer back to the standing laurel of high culture featured in "A Prayer for my Daughter," but it also looks forward to the bare existential stagecraft of Beckett.[28]

The long career of Yeats reaches into the 1940s, nearly overlapping with that of the postwar Existentialists, and it certainly plays an underappreciated role in describing the cultural turn by which existentialism aimed to outmaneuver the mythic and eschatological temporalities of interwar modernism and surrealism. Yeats of course had long held interests in the philosophical roots of existentialism (back to Kierkegaard and Nietzsche), but this late-developing existential turn in his work was the product of a lifetime of struggle, of systematic yet passionate experiments designed to test literature's capacities in the face of historical nightmares and mortal wounds.[29] So the existentialism of the 1940s and 1950s, which we often associate with a certain modish or *poseur* intellectualism, was no mere fad or pose for the late Yeats. It was not an occasion for theatricalized or stylized bleakness for its own sake, or for some cheap grab at soulful depth; it was a way to make a late style in which the aging body shed rather than claimed the mantle of mythic return and in which the hard-earned poetic signifiers of *kairos* could be traded for the self-marginalizing signs of *chronos*. After the desertion of the circus animals and the glowing emblems, Yeats's aging came to the end even of endings. One can sense the problem in the moment when the Old Man, having attempted to finish consequence itself—the one-damn-thing-after-another of history—hears those coconut hooves arriving to refuse his ending of his own line. As the Yeatsian concept of ruined lineage comes, at the last, to interfuse the Yeatsian poetics of failed lineation, one can appreciate the courage it took to abandon the Old Man of *Purgatory* so completely to his folly. After all, for Yeats, the whole game had been to herd the metrical feet of time properly into the poetic line and so to redeem self and nation with beauty and meaning in the here and now. But here, now, in the last moments of *Purgatory,* those phantom hoofsteps sound across the stage not as harbingers of the myth of eternal return, but as the footbeats of time—and indeed perhaps the footbeats of rhyme—running on outside the lines, running on after life, after death, after the will and after words, just as time spills forward even after the supposed end of history.[30]

NOTES

1. This is the Yeats who writes, in a well-known and desperately poignant letter of 1888, "I have buried my youth and raised over it a cairn of clouds" (qtd. in Terence Brown, *The Life of W. B. Yeats* [Oxford: Blackwell, 1999], 39).

2. Edward W. Said, *On Late Style: Music and Literature Against the Grain* (New York: Pantheon, 2006), 135.

3. The comparison of English and Irish revivalism as lodestar concepts for Eliot and Yeats turns, of course, on the further ironic chiasmus of their religious backgrounds, with one gravitating to the Anglo-Catholic high-church fringes of a highly anticlerical society and the other to the pagan occult edges of licentious Protestantism within an increasingly (in the era of the Saorstat) rigid Catholic-identified society.

4. Thomas R. Whitaker, *Swan and Shadow: Yeats's Dialogue with History* (Chapel Hill: University of North Carolina Press, 1964), 8–9.

5. Quoted in James Longenbach, *Modernist Poetics of History: Pound, Eliot, and the Sense of the Past* (Princeton: Princeton University Press, 1987), 41–42.

6. Ibid., 43–44.

7. Frank Kermode, *The Sense of an Ending* (London: Oxford University Press, 1966), 47.

8. Longenbach offers a nuanced reading of the modernist reaction to nineteenth-century linear and positivist models of history associated with Hegel and Comte (Longenbach, *Modernist Poetics of History,* 5–16).

9. T. S. Eliot, *Collected Poems 1909–1962* (New York: Harcourt, 1970), 178. Hereafter cited parenthetically as *CP.*

10. Michael North's analysis of the process is apt: "The historicist principle of cultural specificity and unity has become an ahistorical, normative value" (Michael North, *The Political Aesthetic of Yeats, Eliot, and Pound* [Cambridge: Cambridge University Press, 1991], 88).

11. To put that another way, whereas symbols tend to arrogate aesthetic totality to themselves in a kind of perfection of form per se, allegory tends to seek completion extratextually, by reference backward to a cultural endowment that presupposes a shared tradition. As Benjamin puts it: "it is as something incomplete and imperfect that objects stare out from the allegorical structure" (Walter Benjamin, *The Origin of German Tragic Drama,* trans. John Osborne [London: NLB, 1977], 186).

12. As Terry Eagleton rightly notes, the Eliot of the *Four Quartets* period no longer emphasizes poetry's ability to impose order on reality but, rather, focuses on what Eliot himself called "perception of order *in* reality" (Terry Eagleton, *Exiles and Emigres* [New York: Schocken, 1970], 169).

13. Across many different poetic phases in Yeats's career, Ireland's destiny—first embryonic, then flourishing, then corrupted and threatened—gave shape to time and allowed him to imagine historical time as charged with rising and falling significance. When that brand of national ethos and mythos begins to lose its charge altogether, so too does Yeats's own mortality become a mere existential fact rather than a mythical or mystified event.

14. See Leo Bersani, *The Culture of Redemption* (Cambridge, MA: Harvard University Press, 1990).

15. David Lloyd, *Anomalous States: Irish Writing and the Post-Colonial Moment* (Durham: Duke University Press, 1993), 75; Paul de Man, *Blindness and Insight: Essays in the Rhetoric of Contemporary Criticism* (Minneapolis: University of Minnesota Press, 1983), 206.

16. *The Variorum Edition of the Poems of W. B. Yeats,* ed. Peter Allt and Russell K. Alspach (New York: Macmillan, 1957), 565–67. Hereafter cited parenthetically as *VP*.

17. *The Variorum Edition of the Plays of W. B. Yeats,* ed. Russell K. Alspach (New York: Macmillan, 1969), 1043. Hereafter cited parenthetically as *VPl*. Compare these lines to an excerpt from "East Coker," where the purifying darkness surfaces in the trope of "death the mighty leveler":

> The captains, merchant bankers, eminent men of letters.
> The generous patrons of art, the statesmen and the rulers,
> Distinguished civil servants, chairmen of many committees,
> Industrial lords and petty contractors, all go into the dark.
> (CP, 185–86)

But material decay prefigures spiritual redemption. This passage records Eliot's unsentimental response to the historical crises of the 1930s in the form of a national allegory, offering a vision of remote salvation to a nation in immediate decline. Faced with war—and with the wider failures of cosmopolitanism—these poems propose a kind of national ascesis. Ascetic themes also cinch the poem's basic allegory: for both an old master poet and an old European nation, the same dark night of the soul becomes a station on the long stony path to redemption. In this time and place, for both poet and nation, the way down becomes the way up.

18. The father-son murder chain is perhaps less stark or shocking when one considers just how prevalent the themes of patricide and filicide were across Irish modernism in general. From Synge's *Playboy* and Yeats's Cuchulain figures through to Joyce and Beckett, these oedipal struggles of violent patrilineal disruption are legion.

19. *Purgatory* debuted in August 1938, just four months before Yeats died. Austin Clarke's letter giving his response is cited in Brown, *The Life of W. B. Yeats*, 372: "Coconut horse hoofs indicated haunted house. Not impressed."

20. Marjorie Howes, *Yeats's Nations: Gender, Class, and Irishness* (Cambridge: Cambridge University Press, 1996), 183–84.

21. Lloyd, *Anomalous States*, 81.

22. The existential reading contrasts, at least in emphasis, with recent and influential readings that focus on the play's relation to Yeats's disappointment in national politics and his bitter valediction to what Seamus Deane calls the "dignity and coherence" of the "Irish Protestant Ascendancy tradition" (Seamus Deane, *Celtic Revivals* [Winston-Salem, NC: Wake Forest University Press, 1985], 28). Cullingford reads *Purgatory* as a dark meditation on dynastic decline and "class miscegenation" in Ireland (Elizabeth Cullingford, *Gender and History in Yeats's Love Poetry* [Syracuse: Syracuse University Press, 1981], 149); for the most detailed account of *Purgatory* within the framework of national politics, see Howes, *Yeats's Nations*, 176–85. David Lloyd, too, establishes a political context for the rhetorical violence and extremity of Yeats's late writings, noting that those works "discover death at the heart of the culture and at the base of the state"; for Lloyd, though these works point toward a fascist turn, they ultimately refuse the "consolatory myths of belonging on which fascism relies for its legitimation" (Lloyd, *Anomalous States*, 79). *Purgatory* stands out even in this field of late Yeats, I think, for its refusal not just of fascist organicism, but of the eschatological dignification of death itself as a load-bearing motif for poetic subjectivity.

23. Howes, *Yeats's Nations*, 183–84.

24. Helen Vendler, "The Later Poetry" in *The Cambridge Companion to Yeats*, ed. Marjorie Howes and John Kelly (Cambridge: Cambridge University Press, 2006), 94.

25. Brown notes, rightly of course, that "On the Boiler" too features a kind of rhetorical persona, and insists that one cannot save Yeats simply because of the latter's penchant for "exculpatory masking" (Brown, *The Life of*

W. B. Yeats, 367). But *Purgatory*'s dramatic devices establish a greater sense of distance from the main character than "On the Boiler" does from its main speaker.

26. Eliot's 1940 commentary on the play makes this clear: "the play *Purgatory* is not very pleasant either. There are aspects of it which I do not like myself. I wish he had not given it this title, because I cannot accept a purgatory in which there is no hint, or at least no emphasis upon Purgation" (*Selected Prose of T. S. Eliot,* ed. Frank Kermode [New York: Harcourt, 1975], 253).

27. McAteer holds that *Purgatory* stands out even among Yeats's most austere and wrenching tragic plays because of its "refusal to accord any transformative power to the intensity of the single moment" (Michael McAteer, *Yeats and European Drama* [Cambridge: Cambridge University Press, 2010], 190). Paul de Man pushes the autocritical dimension of Yeats's poems past the existentialist post and into nihilism: "The failure of the emblem amounts to a total nihilism. Yeats has burned his bridges and there is no return out of his exploded paradise of emblems back to a wasted earth" (Paul de Man, *The Rhetoric of Romanticism* [New York: Columbia University Press, 1984], 238).

28. As McAteer notes, Beckett was among those who saw *Purgatory* in its original 1938 run, and its stripped elemental staging appears to have influenced him in the conception of *Godot* and several other plays after that (McAteer, *Yeats and European Drama,* 176).

29. For more on the Nietzschean dimensions of Yeats's thinking, see Vereen Bell, "Yeats's Nietzschean Idealism," *The Southern Review* 29:3 (1993): 491–513; Denis Donoghue, *William Butler Yeats* (New York: Ecco Press, 1988); Richard Ellmann, *Yeats: The Man and the Masks* (New York: Norton, 1999); Frances Oppel, *Mask and Tragedy: Yeats and Nietzsche, 1902–1910* (Charlottesville: University of Virginia Press, 1987); and Otto Bohlman, *Yeats and Nietzsche* (London: Macmillan, 1982). As Donoghue notes, it was the Nietzschean strain that gave Yeats a modernized concept of tragic joy, and of historical patterns—recurrence and return—that run athwart the mere successiveness of linear time (Donoghue, *William Butler Yeats,* 87–89). In the end, Yeats's existential turn may come closest to Kierkegaardian uncertainty about time; he evinces real skepticism about the splenetic Nietzsche-Spengler investment in crisis-rhetoric and about attendant projections of the end of history via secular or religious apotheosis.

30. I would like to thank Joe Valente and Marjorie Howes for their editorial vision on this collection and for valuable critical insights along the way.

CONTRIBUTORS

GUINN BATTEN, associate professor of English at Washington University in St. Louis, is the author of *The Orphaned Imagination: Melancholy and Commodity Culture in British Romanticism* (Duke University Press, 1998). Co-author of "Irish Poetry in English, 1940–2000" for *The Cambridge History of Irish Literature,* she has published more than a dozen essays on Irish poetry of the Troubles, Romanticism, and literary theory and is completing a book-length manuscript, *The Bodies of the Nation: Romanticism and Irish Poetry of the Troubles,* that brings together those concerns.

GREGORY CASTLE is professor of British and Irish literature at Arizona State University. He has published *Modernism and the Celtic Revival* (Cambridge University Press, 2001), *Reading the Modernist Bildungsroman* (University Press of Florida, 2006), and *A Guide to Literary Theory* (Blackwell, 2007). He also edited *Postcolonial Discourses* (Blackwell, 2000) and the *Encyclopedia of Literary and Cultural Theory,* vol. 1 (Wiley-Blackwell, 2011). A second edition of the *Guide,* with the new title *The Literary Theory Handbook* (Wiley-Blackwell), is due out in 2015. He has published numerous essays on Irish authors, including W. B. Yeats, J. M. Synge, Oscar Wilde, and Bram Stoker. Current projects include an edited *History of the Modernist Novel* (for Cambridge University Press) and a monograph, *Modernism and the Temporalities of Irish Revival, 1878–1939.*

ELIZABETH CULLINGFORD is Jane Weinert Blumberg Chair in English Literature, University Distinguished Teaching Professor, and chair of the English Department at the University of Texas at Austin. She is the author of *Ireland's Others: Ethnicity and Gender in Irish Literature and Popular Culture* (Field Day, 2001); *Gender and History in Yeats's Love Poetry* (Cambridge, 1993); and *Yeats, Ireland and Fascism* (1981). Her latest article is *"Evil, Sin, or Doubt:* The Dramas of Clerical Abuse," published in *Theatre Journal* 62 (2010), and she is currently writing a book entitled *The Only Child in a Crowded World: Literature, Culture, and Ecology.*

JED ESTY is professor of English at the University of Pennsylvania. He is the author of *Unseasonable Youth: Modernism, Colonialism, and the Fiction of Development* (Oxford, 2012) and *A Shrinking Island: Modernism and National Culture in England* (Princeton, 2004). With Joe Cleary and Colleen Lye, he co-edited a 2012 special issue of *Modern Language Quarterly* entitled *Peripheral Realisms;* with Ania Loomba, Suvir Kaul, Antoinette Burton, and Matti Bunzl, he co-edited *Postcolonial Studies and Beyond* (Duke University Press, 2005). He has published essays in *Modern Fiction Studies, Victorian Studies, Modernism/Modernity, ELH, American Literary History, Contemporary Literature, Narrative, Novel,* and the *Yale Journal of Criticism.* Esty is currently at work on a new project entitled *Ages of Innocence: Culture and Literature from Pax Britannica to the American Century.*

RENÉE FOX received her Ph.D. from Princeton University and is assistant professor of English at the University of Miami. She has published essays on Robert Browning, Joseph Sheridan Le Fanu, and Michael Longley, and co-edited *The Cracked Lookingglass: Essays in Honor of the Leonard L. Milberg Collection of Irish Prose Writers* (2011), and a collection of original essays by Paul Muldoon, Colm Tóibín, Michael Wood, and others that traces the history of Irish prose from 1800 to the present. She has received fellowships from the Giles M. Whiting Foundation, the Josephine de Kármán Fellowship Trust, and UCLA's William Andrews Clark Memorial Library, and is currently at work on a book entitled *Necromantic Victorians: Reanimation and Historical Aesthetics in British and Irish Literature.*

MARGARET MILLS HARPER is Glucksman Professor of Contemporary Writing in English at the University of Limerick. She specializes in

Irish literature, literary modernisms, and poetry of the long twentieth century. Works include *Wisdom of Two* (Oxford, 2006), on the occult collaboration between W. B. Yeats and his wife George Hyde-Lees, and *The Aristocracy of Art* (Lousiana State University Press, 1990), an examination of the autobiographical fictions of James Joyce and Thomas Wolfe. She is the co-editor of two volumes in the four-volume series *Yeats's "Vision" Papers* (Macmillan, 1992 and 2001). With Catherine Paul of Clemson University, she has edited *A Vision* (1925) as volume 13 of *The Collected Works of W. B. Yeats* (Scribner, 2008) and is now preparing the 1937 version of *A Vision* for the same series.

MARJORIE HOWES is associate professor of English at Boston College. She is the author of *Yeats's Nations: Gender, Class, and Irishness* (Cambridge, 1996), *Colonial Crossings: Figures in Irish Literary History* (Field Day, 2001). She is the co-editor of *Semicolonial Joyce* (Cambridge, 2001), *The Cambridge Companion to W. B. Yeats* (Cambridge, 2006), and a contributor to *The Field Day Anthology of Irish Writing*, volume 4.

SEÁN KENNEDY is associate professor of English and coordinator of Irish Studies at Saint Mary's University, Halifax, where he also coordinates the Irish Studies Program. He is the editor of "Historicising Beckett" (2005), *Samuel Beckett: History, Memory, Archive* (Palgrave Macmillan, 2009, with Katherine Weiss), *Beckett and Ireland* (Cambridge, 2010) and *Queering Ireland* (2010), as well as *Queering the Issue* (2013, with Mulhall et al.). He is also founder of the Queering Ireland Conference Association.

VICKI MAHAFFEY is the Thelma and Clayton Kirkpatrick Professor of English and Gender and Women's Studies at the University of Illinois, Urbana-Champaign. She is the author of *Reauthorizing Joyce* (Cambridge, 1989), *States of Desire: Wilde, Yeats, Joyce and the Irish Experiment* (Oxford, 1998), and *Modernist Literature: Challenging Fictions* (Blackwell, 2007). She is also the editor of the volume *Collaborative Dubliners: Joyce in Dialogue* (Syracuse University Press, 2011). She is currently completing a book entitled *The Joyce of Everyday Life*.

JAMES H. MURPHY, Ph.D., D.Litt., FRHistS, is professor of English at De Paul University, Chicago. He was previously head of the English Department at All Hallows College, Dublin City University, and has twice been president of the Society for the Study of Nineteenth-Century Ireland. He is a scholar of the long nineteenth century in Ireland, with two principal interests, political history and the history of fiction. His most recent books are, as author, *Irish Novelists and the Victorian Age* (Oxford, 2011) and, as editor, *The Oxford History of the Irish Book*, volume 4, *The Irish Book in English, 1800–91* (Oxford, 2011). He has recently completed a book called *Ireland's Czar: Gladstonian Government and the Lord Lieutenancies of the Red Earl Spencer, 1868–74, 1882–85* that carries forward the work of his 2001 book, *Abject Loyalty: Nationalism and Monarchy in Ireland during the Reign of Queen Victoria* (Catholic University of America Press). He is presently at work on a history of Dublin. Earlier books, as author, include *Catholic Fiction and Social Reality in Ireland, 1873–1922* (Greenwood Press, 1997) and *Ireland: A Social, Cultural and Literary History, 1791–1891* (Four Courts, 2003), and, as (co-) editor, *Gender Perspectives in Nineteenth-Century Ireland* (Irish Academic Press, 1997), *The Irish Revival Reappraised* (Four Courts, 2004), and *Evangelicals and Catholics in Nineteenth-Century Ireland* (Four Courts, 2005).

RONALD SCHUCHARD, Goodrich C. White Professor of English, emeritus, Emory University, is the author of numerous studies of modern authors, particularly W. B. Yeats and T. S. Eliot. His *The Last Minstrels: Yeats and the Revival of the Bardic Arts* (Oxford, 2008) won the ACIS Robert Rhodes Prize and was co-winner of the Modernist Studies Association Book Award. He is co-editor, with John Kelly, of *The Collected Letters of W. B. Yeats*, vol. 3 (Oxford, 1994); vol. 4 (Oxford, 2005), which won the MLA's Morton N. Cohen Award for a Distinguished Edition of Letters; and vol. 5 (2014). A former director of the Yeats International Summer School, he founded the Richard Ellmann Lectures in Modern Literature and received the M. L. Rosenthal Award for distinguished contributions to Yeats studies. A former Guggenheim Fellow, he is a member of the American

Academy of Arts and Sciences and an honorary member of the T. S. Eliot Society and the South Atlantic Modern Language Association. He is currently general editor of the multivolume *The Online Complete Prose of T. S. Eliot*, to be published by the Johns Hopkins University Press and Faber and Faber.

JOSEPH VALENTE is UB Distinguished Professor of English and Disability Studies at SUNY-Buffalo. He is the author of *James Joyce and the Problem of Justice: Negotiating Sexual and Colonial Difference* (Cambridge, 1995), *Dracula's Crypt: Bram Stoker, Irishness and the Question of Blood* (University of Illinois Press, 2002), and most recently *The Myth of Manliness in Irish National Culture, 1880–1922* (University of Illinois Press, 2011). He is also the editor of *Quare Joyce* (University of Michigan Press, 1998), *Urban Ireland* (2010), and, with Amanda Anderson, *Disciplinarity at the Fin de Siecle* (Princeton, 2002). He has published widely in such journals as *Critical Inquiry, ELH, Novel, Modern Fiction Studies, Diacritics, Narrative, Irish University Review, Eire-Ireland*, and the *James Joyce Quarterly*. His latest projects are entitled *The Crux of the X: Literary Dispatches from Ireland's War on Children* (with Margot Backus) and *Autism and Moral Authority in Modern Literature*.

INDEX OF NAMES